PARADIGMS LOST

The Life and Deaths
of the Printed Word

WILLIAM SONN

THE SCARECROW PRESS, INC.
Lanham, Maryland • Toronto • Oxford
2006

For Edie, Alexa, and Eliza
Where most warmth seems to begin

SCARECROW PRESS, INC.

Published in the United States of America
by Scarecrow Press, Inc.
A wholly owned subsidary of
The Rowman & Littlefield Publishing Group, Inc.
4501 Forbes Boulevard, Suite 200, Lanham, Maryland 20706
www.scarecrowpress.com

PO Box 317
Oxford
OX2 9RU, UK

British Library Cataloguing in Publication Information Available

Library of Congress Cataloging-in-Publication Data

Sonn, William, 1948–
  Paradigms lost : the life and deaths of the printed word / William J. Sonn.
      p. cm.
  Includes bibliographical references and index.
  ISBN-13: 978-0-8108-5262-4 (pbk. : alk. paper)
  ISBN-10: 0-8108-5262-4 (pbk. : alk. paper)
   1. Printing—History. 2. Written communication—History. 3. Printing—Social
aspects—History. I. Title.

Z124.S673 2006
686.2'09—dc22
                                                        2005023073

CONTENTS

1

PETER PRINTING PANTS IN
LINOTYPE HELL, 1993

It is 8:00 A.M., but sixty-seven-year-old Louis Felicio ignores a table laden with breakfast rolls. He is nervous and a little excited. It's been a long time since he's been in a situation like this. Uncertain about what he is supposed to do, he navigates purposefully through small knots of businesspeople making casual conversation in this suburban Denver hotel ballroom. He makes his way toward a far wall.

Lou has dressed carefully for the event, a corporate open house staged by a company located far away. He worried for days that he might not have the proper professional clothes left in his closet. He has, after all, been retired for quite a while. Ultimately he and his wife, Anne, found an ensemble of dress pants, shirt, string tie, and brown vest for the occasion.

He is a quick and lively man, lean and perhaps five feet three inches tall. Ever alert behind large, black-framed glasses, he stays frantically busy at home, taking his none too friendly bowlegged little dog for brisk walks every morning, trimming his lawn, painting, and practicing on a piano keyboard in his basement until late at night. Whatever chore he does, he tends to do directly, determinedly, single-mindedly.

This morning, at one of four product demonstration areas set up around the ballroom, he settles politely and a little reverently into a chair in front of a cream-colored device, perhaps eight feet long, four feet high, three feet wide. A television, or at least something that looks like a television, sits on one end of the thing. Making sure the crease on his dress pants stays straight, he frowns and cranes his neck to look at other sleek machines along the other walls of the ballroom.

"Does any of this mean anything to you?" Lou is asked.

"The word is 'threatening,'" he grumbles.

1

Twenty years before, primitive versions of these machines had put him out of business. Once a union man at various New York newspapers and printing companies, Felicio made a good living, got married, helped raise a daughter, and played vibes at weddings and bar mitzvahs on weekends around the region. A second-generation Italian American, Felicio knows enough Yiddish to lead many of the bourgeois immigrants he now lives among in Denver into thinking he is Jewish. "They don't know better," he laughs indulgently. "But, hey, the Jews and the Italians, you know, we're the same anyway."

His profession was fixing clanking machines called hot-metal typesetters. They were once the crucial, largely invisible tools that made modern printing—best-selling books and high-speed newspapers, invoices, posters, claim tickets, packaging—possible. At the places Lou worked, operators typed on the great contraptions to cast letters and images in heated metal. The images were then used to print phone directories, boxes, manuals, invoices, anything. Called Linotype or Intertype or Monotype machines, the typesetters were bigger, darker, and smellier than the bright device now in front of Lou. His machines sometimes stood eight feet tall and five feet wide. From back to front, they could span six feet. At their top and inside them was a busy web of belts and pulleys. On one side hung a pot in which a careful blend of molten minerals brewed. Their huge, broad keyboards had their own language, with special "em" and "en" and burly "quad" characters that caused gears to shift, shafts to move, liquids to spill into channels and down into small reservoirs, all placed with metric precision in an open maze beyond the keyboard. Felt met rubber met metal, which met more felt. There was clanking. Air hissed or a motor briefly growled, and, right then and there inside the machine, liquid was miraculously cooled into solid. Groups of letters were forced upward through the maze and left to fall gently, with an ironically soft tinkling sound, into a shelf in a tray. In the end, the letters and words and paragraphs in the tray formed mirror images of the printed page that, one step down the production line, appeared on paper. Another craftsman bolted and locked the images securely into the tray and then carted it to the pressroom to be printed while the compositor, as the Lino operator was called, worked on creating the next page. All the casting and hissing and roaring, clacking and tinkling, locking of forms and shouting might be happening at once around a single machine as the compositor worked. He or she usually labored, moreover, in large rooms crowded with similar machines. The racket on deadline was constant and, in its own way, exciting. Lou's job was to make sure the machines, alive and complex and finicky, never stayed broken for long. When one of them broke down, the operator would switch on a light, and Lou would hustle through the cacophony to the scene.

"But there were only four things that went wrong most of the time." With mock gravity, he counts them on his thick, gnarled fingers. "One, [the Lino operator] didn't sleep well. Two, he had a fight with his wife. Three, he had an accident coming to work, or, four, he had a tooth pulled." Lou would listen, first to the operator and then, after eliminating human causes for the malfunctions, to the machine to find out what needed to be done.

He raises his eyebrows. "You know, I was pretty good." It took six years of apprenticing for Lou to learn how to fix the things. He was a craftsman and an artist, somehow able to communicate with gears, pins, and levers. "Aw," he adds with a modest wave of his hand, "you probably hear that from everyone."

Today he is among fifty-some guests of Linotype-Hell, as the company that used to make his hot-metal patients is now called. In the twenty years since Lou last fixed one of its printing machines, the firm repeatedly changed its name from Mergenthaler Linotype to Eltra to Linotype, from Linotype to Allied, back to Linotype and, after a merger with a European firm that had a long history with electronics, to Linotype-Hell. Since its founding during the Grover Cleveland administration in 1886, it had, like Lou, assumed many adaptive forms. Sometimes they were aggressive postures and, depending on business conditions, sometimes protective: private corporation, aggressive litigator and predatory public company, diversified conglomerate, spin-off, downsized subsidiary, freestanding "hollow" corporation, and merger partner. The company had stopped making Lou's machines in 1971, back when it was called Eltra. Now it produced cream-colored mysteries and showed them off at open houses like this one. The gathering's theme is "Surviving the '90s," which is puzzling to Felicio, who did not survive the '70s. Told the devices around him are graphic workstations and proofing mechanisms and drum scanners, he smiles without parting his lips and raises his eyebrows again.

He turns to listen to a pleasant young woman showing off a nearby machine. During the next hour he endures with tolerant good humor other product demonstrations, slide shows, and alien gibberish about "dot gain" and "integrated films." In a darkened auditorium, he hears about "RGB colors." One presenter talks of "pre-media." Printers, Lou finds out, are no longer compositors. The only printers in the slide show he watches are mute computer accessories, filled with toner and run by electricity, and lacking teeth that might occasionally need to be pulled. Reporters, editors, and designers now worked in cool, hushed rooms, and casually did for themselves what Lou and squads of other tough guys once scrambled to do amid barely contained chaos. Their devices and the cables that connected them were maintained by "system administrators," a fresh, well-compensated lot fully and often immodestly aware that the species could barely communicate without them anymore. Lou and his fellow Lino operators used to carry themselves in the same way.

"A lot of people died" in the computer revolution, he recounted later that day in the parking lot, one hand shielding his eyes from the sun.

For Lou, the carnage started one day in the mid-1960s. Working in the composing room at a newspaper in New York, he had been frustrated by a mechanical problem and finally called in an expert from Linotype to look at it. "This guy pulled out this little thing and, *whoop*, he hooks it up and, just like that, he knows what the problem is." Lou's hands shoot upward in memory. "He made the adjustments and was gone. I saw that thing [it was an oscilloscope] and I knew it was almost over. I went home to my wife that night and said, 'It won't be long now.'"

He was right. In 1971, Felicio was working at a business, huddled in a New York City colony of five other printers, that specialized in pharmaceutical printing. "One day I go out and see somebody's just thrown their (hot metal) machines in the dumpsters." He puts a hand to his cheek to suggest his shock and his eyes widen. "I thought 'wow,' and I ran across the alley and took the machines to use for, you know, spare parts and things. Little did I know that, three months from that very day, we'd throw out all our Linotype machines too."

His employer brought in new devices called phototype machines and then laid off most of the staff, including Felicio.

Lou caught on with a couple of more firms but he was losing his grip. In the past, whenever Linotype would improve its machine in some way, his union, the International Typographical Union (ITU), would dispatch a member to learn about it. Then he would return to the shop and train his colleagues. But now the ITU was sending members to learn to use equipment with space age names like VAX, Photon, and Autologic. What had been mechanical and electromechanical now was mathematical, dependent on the propulsion of invisible light particles, tripped by alphabets measured in binary ones and twos. The members tried to describe what they learned to Lou, but it didn't work well. This stuff was just too different.

Lou worked here and there on Linotypes and Monotypes still in operation and even fixed a few phototypesetters, essentially faking it. "I felt uneasy because my knowledge was minimal. The industry was moving so fast electronically. We were encountering machines we were unsure about how to repair."

After many of the New York type houses went to phototype in the 1970s, certain laid-off union members could draw a partial salary from the International Typographical Union for a while. Lou was one of them. The only catch was that "you had to sit around the union rooms."

The craftsmen would mope around the union offices, reading or playing cards while they awaited rare calls to go out on jobs. One day, Lou recalls, a union official emerged from his private office, looking rushed and harried, holding a manila envelope. Lou happened to be the first person the official saw. "'Excuse me,' he says, 'do you want to take this downtown for me?' You know, like a messenger. I said 'okay' and I took it."

The next day, the same official had a parcel to go downtown. Not wanting to impose on Lou two days in a row, he asked the man sitting next to Lou if he'd make the trip.

"The guy says, 'no way! I'm a Lino operator. I'm no messenger.'" So Lou took the parcel. And the next day, the official asked yet a third union member to take another message. "And the guy says, 'no way I'd do that. I'm a compositor!' Like it was an insult."

On Friday, the union official asked Lou to come into his office. To a man who'd gotten little but bad news recently, the invitation was ominous. "I figure, uh-oh, I messed up somehow." The official instead offered Lou a job as a maintenance man around the union hall.

He jumped at the opportunity. "I figure I gotta put bread on the table. That's how I got myself a job. Why?" He leans forward, whispering emphatically and patting his chest. "Because I put my pride in my pocket.

"A lot of guys couldn't do that. The compositor I told you about? Well, he died a year or so after that. I think it was because of his pride. You can't just go from being a [professional] to sitting around without something to do."

"Those were something," he says politely of the strange new machines as he moves with the crowd at the Linotype-Hell open house into the lobby for refreshments.

Most of the other guests in the lobby are younger than Lou, perhaps in their thirties or forties—salespeople, company owners, and "technical people," a company sales rep explains as she stops by to say hello. Many know finance and computers and marketing. They are not, she adds, "you know, Peter Printing Pants types."

The sales rep grimaces in her next breath, realizing she may have offended Lou.

"You know," Lou's companion urgently whispers to him, trying to make him feel better as the embarrassed saleswoman moved into the crowd, "these people are threatened, too."

He smiles politely again, mostly because he always smiles politely when he is unsure what else to do.

But the prosperous attendees around him truly are threatened. The printed word did not stop tilting when Felicio left it. In fact, it mutated wildly at ever faster rates as new machines appeared. Then those machines changed and were replaced. By the time Lou walked into what he soon joked was Linotype hell, the business was rudderless amid frenetic technological upheaval. Something called digital printing, for example, was rising. Phenomenal new $600,000 devices as revolutionary as Gutenberg's created brilliantly colored pages one at a time, economically, without film and without ink. Clerks and finally customers themselves ran them. Many of the guests at the open house probably knew of once-successful businesses that had bought a new tool and then died for want of laborers who could operate it efficiently or of capital to match the daunting investments of their competitors. Amortization tables for their expensive, short-lived equipment didn't work anymore. Business school didn't describe the commercial carnage they were experiencing; there wasn't time to depreciate the equipment—pay for it—before it was outgunned by a newer technology. Just a few years earlier an obscurantist "postscript language" reached the market and in twenty-four months had obliterated the value of all their investments in all previous generations of type machines. Then more tools came: scanners that made their big darkroom cameras obsolete and computerized controls that made multi-million-dollar presses uncompetitive. Each month, manufacturers unveiled new machines at coming-out parties in overcooled hotel ballrooms like this one, amid bagels and croissants and vacuum-sealed plastic containers of juice. Linotype-Hell alone, the saleswoman told Lou that morning, introduced at least twenty new products a year. Nevertheless, there were rumors around the open house that Linotype-Hell itself was also in trouble.

Lou uneasily said "wow" when told of the pace of change, but the industry's captains as well as its soldiers were unmoored by it. A short while earlier the head of one of the world's biggest printing firms had portentously—and none too logically—resolved that half his corporation's earnings by the year 2000 would have to come from services it had not yet invented. His quote was widely repeated in trade magazines and at conferences as proof that all bets were off. Most of the almost 50,000 firms that identified themselves as part of the printing industry at the time were small. Many of their owners now confessed without much prodding that they were confused and worried. They feared electronic bulletin boards, broadband television, compact discs, and multicolor laser printers. Something called the Internet was supposed to be threatening them soon, though few at the time could say exactly how. However, they were pretty sure that paper, disparagingly called "treeware" in the same computer journals that dismissed the difficult art of writing and preparing knowledge as "premedia," was dying out.

The printed word would go with it. BY 1993, words on paper were only one among many vivid, instantaneous communications media. Big and mature, the business that produced them no longer grew quickly. Where revenues in the New Age cable TV business, headquartered on that day just a few miles from the open house, grew at 15–20 percent a year, printing sales grew at 2–3 percent. Its prestige and the content it produced were faded. In the prior five years, the industry's ranks had thinned dramatically. Almost 10 percent of the printing firms in the United States had died suddenly. Most were phototypesetting companies that replaced the hot-metal companies at which Lou worked just a dozen years earlier.

Worse was on the horizon. Just a few weeks before the open house, another study—released in Dallas in yet another powerfully air-conditioned hotel ballroom—predicted an additional 20 percent of the nation's printers would be out of business by the turn of the century. With them would go perhaps a third of the employees in this particular industry that was, in the sum of all its big and small plants across the land, at that moment still the nation's fourth-largest employer.[1]

If history's lessons remained true, something more important than an industry might be ending.

For every time the *way* media were produced changed in the past, politics shifted. So did economics. Migrations and emigrations followed; even mating habits changed sometimes. It is hard to trace how one particular tool—the telegraph, the radio, a device that made printing cheaper—directly led to one particular change; but all hell seemed to break loose when a new communications device superseded an old one, or even when the nitty-gritty manufacture and distribution of old media changed.

Lou looks away, then down. He wets his lips, considering the notion that something more than unemployment resulted when the unglamorous manufacturing of glamorous communications changed. Ultimately the idea seems immodest to modest Lou. He shrugs as if to suggest his companion might be, well, overstating the case.

"I lost my job," he explains. Happens all the time. "That's the price of progress."

A little later, his companion thought up a better rejoinder than the pre-verbal sputtering he actually offered. As in physics, energy is released when a new tool adds speed or mass to human interaction. Each time we learn to create information faster, new facts and impressions pile onto old ones. The sheer weight and mass of our knowledge grows. Just as the physicists predicted, heavier objects move faster. And with the accelerating physical speed and heft of information comes momentum: images and ideas and data crashing into, propelling, stopping, and altering each other's paths, usually in unpredictable ways. Old elites lose their monopoly over certain kinds of information. New groups join or supplant them. Their new governments reallocate land and water, and cede privilege. Then a German patent clerk might happen to read about Asian timekeeping devices. Still more energy is released. "When information from previously unrelated sources is structured in a meaningful way," former patent clerk Albert Einstein once noted, "human beings are capable of thinking thoughts that were previously unthinkable."

When looked at from a certain angle, it was possible to glimpse something even broader in these new thoughts: a changing of the species. In 1962, at about the time certain new tools—the television, the phototypesetter—were ascending, media philosopher Marshall McLuhan described an evolutionary version of *Homo sapiens* called Typographic Man. The beast was in its own way a successor to Neanderthal and Cro-Magnon. With his new tool—printing—Typographic Man had learned to think linearly, from letter to letter, word to word, line to line in a certain order. His predecessors learned by listening and memorizing, receiving knowledge. Typographic Man was on to something new: *conceiving* knowledge, learning by reading, sometimes without a mentor, and applying his own imagination to the written words of book culture.[2] This newly outfitted creature extended Euclid's logic to everything. He fashioned logical tools, logical theologies, notions that life moved in logical, ordered patterns. Everything Typographic Man conceived and understood was conceived and understood in the same way we read: methodically, from letter to letter, word to word, until a thought emerges. Thesis, antithesis, synthesis. All that, McLuhan figured, would change as we watched more television. TV wasn't linear.

Others saw it coming too, although not necessarily through television. For example, a wonderfully curious, driven engineer named Vannevar Bush had headed the U.S. government's military science effort during World War II. One contemporary writer felicitously described his funding of research with seemingly unknowable results as similar to a golfer "aiming at faraway greens he cannot see." After the war even Bush was daunted by the remarkable changes he and his far-flung army of scientists had wrought. There were atomic bombs and incredible weapons, to be sure, but also the accelerated production of penicillin (we routinely lost more men to infection in previous wars than to bullets), radar, and, among the 3,000-some patented products and processes he helped create, electrical computing machines. Knowledge itself had accelerated. So the real problem hobbling the evolution of postwar civilization, he wrote in a now legendary *Atlantic Monthly* article in 1945, was that we suddenly knew so much that we could not remember or use it all.

His solution, then on some faraway green he could not see, was a sort of knowledge machine that would do away with type itself. He dubbed the faint vision memex, which in his description sounded much like the search engines we have fifty years later. But in 1945 he foresaw someone sitting at a keyboard and a screen scrolling through information—probably, he guessed, stored on microfilm—to meet the moment's need. The raw information would amount to "wholly new forms of encyclopedias" that would be printed on paper only when we needed it. "The lawyer has at his touch the associated opinions and decisions of his whole experience . . . The physician, puzzled by a patient's reactions, strikes the trail established in studying an earlier similar case, and runs rapidly through the pertinent anatomy and histology. The chemist, struggling with the synthesis of an organic compound, has all the chemical literature before him." You could fit whole libraries of data in a few drawers of microfilm, Bush noted. He went on to suggest that this ability to blaze "associative trails through ever-expanding forests of all accumulated human knowledge," choosing our own ways according to our individual needs, able to organize information in new and unprecedented and, as a result, fantastically creative ways was the key to our evolution as a species.[3]

By the time of the Linotype open house, it was coming true. We continue to learn by reading the printed word and applying whatever inductive or deductive reasoning we need to accomplish a goal. But we also learn by sampling thousands of brief sounds, sights, and signals. Many of them are electronic impressions, gathered each day through radio or TV or Internet flashes, half-ignored exposures, or by darting through digital memories, following whims.

We have at our disposal Bush's permanently expanding forests of accumulated human knowledge, and we can change our direction through its scholarly and even its distasteful inventories according to the moment's mood as easily as we can by a predictable, logical pattern. We do it at ever increasing speeds. Where in the past one person communicated to many via expensive, hard to operate printing presses or even expensive, difficult to secure radio or TV station licenses, multitudes of commoners communicate easily with other multitudes.[4] Better yet, we need no special expertise to do it.

As the manufacturers of the printed word gathered at the Linotype-Hell open house sensed the approach of a new digital age, it was not unreasonable to fear that soon the foundations of Typographic Man's world—his economic life, his political life, his emotional life—would pass away with the older, slower ways of communicating. Already Newton's patient, mechanical physical laws were inadequate to explain the new kinds of things people could see and imagine. Hegel's inevitable historical marches, Toynbee's clockwork cycles of history, or Keynes's patterned adjustments to the state's economic machine could not guide the politics we needed to allocate energy, knowledge, donated cells, bandwidth, vaccines, and the other half ethereal raw materials of the twenty-first century. Old notions of everlasting love and duty are increasingly inaccurate descriptions of how we actually live our lives. Instead of mating for life, we often move through a series of monogamous relationships. Instead of working one plot of land or job for decades, we migrate as independent agents from one employer to another as the moment requires or associations suggest. Emotionally, we often think of life itself as an open-ended journey of meeting speedily evolving, private needs. Much like the way we learn, we blaze associative trails through easily accessible physical and social intimacies. Amid our distractions and resources, we assemble hybrid "sampled" music and create ever larger hybrid species of our own to serve us, our health, our nutrition. Looking for more plausible descriptions of what we were seeing and doing in the kaleidoscopic maze of knowledge, we imagine random universes, game theories, and consciously impermanent, strategic alliances. We try continental currencies and global town meetings to regulate them. Our notions of authority and even our places in our families, in short, have become fluid.[5] Our attention span withers. With pocket-size devices and tiny phones, we develop addictions to not only games but data and the very act of communicating. The result could be a different kind of human, intellectually and emotionally, from Typographic Man, Peter Printing Pants, and his predecessors.

No one at the open house could be sure how this half-sensed unraveling began or who pulled the first thread. Lou guessed it was whoever invented the phototypesetter. Other veterans blamed the government for taxing small businesses too much and environmentalists for regulating them too closely. Some printers saw the copier as the root of this evil. Phototypesetters blamed laser printers. The desktop publishers who used laser printers blamed manufacturers like Linotype-Hell and Xerox and computer companies, who placed cheaper, easier to use, and more amazing machines in the hands of everyday people. Everyday people, in turn, would not buy typesetting or printing or, with the advent of faxes and e-mail, mailing services anymore. Everyday people could do it all themselves. With a connection to an invisible network, they could concoct, design, and distribute writing to nearby offices and distant relatives, to Mongolia and Africa and the now looted swamps where life began, without physically moving. The means of production, long the defining property of the boss, cost about two weeks' worth of an average worker's pay on the day of the Linotype-Hell coming-out party.

For all those reasons and more, four generations of graphics businesses appeared in the last half of the twentieth century. Three immediately passed into obsolescence. As the century ended, the fourth chatted politely near the lobby refreshment cart between presentations, pretty much ignoring the polite, nervous, still animated fossil in its midst.

The event itself was of no special importance. More significant was the ominous sense of epoch-ending chaos in its hallways, walked by displaced and soon to be displaced professionals. This time the forces that produced the printed word and linear thinking and scientific method and representative government and the industrial revolution and postindustrialism finally might be crowded out by bigger, faster, stronger predators. Something, in any case, seemed about to change again.

NOTES

1. The study was unveiled in Dallas. See Printing Industries of America, Union Camp Paper Co., Kodak Graphic Arts, *Print 2000* (Arlington, Va.: Printing Industries of America, 1993).

2. James A. Dewer, *The Information Age and the Printing Press: Looking Backward to See Ahead* (RAND Corporation, 1998), www.rand.org/publications (accessed August 5, 2000).

3. Vannevar Bush, "As We May Think," *Atlantic Monthly*, April 1945, www.theatlantic.com/unbound/flasshbks/computer/hushf.htm (accessed June 17, 2004).

4. This theme is thoroughly explained and explored in Dewer, *Information Age.*

5. On social organizations as products of communications tools, see David Ronfeldt, *Tribes, Institutions, Markets, and Network*, P-7967 (RAND Corporation, 1996), www.rand.org/publications (accessed August 5, 2000).

I

THE BIRTH OF TYPE: FROM HAND TO LEVER

2

PRIMORDIAL SCRATCHES

The Linotype-Hell open house arguably could be traced back about 160,000 years, when the attendees' grunting ancestors started etching lines and images in dirt and stone. Anthropologists don't yet know why they did it. Historians have even less of a clue. One of the best guesses is that our strange impulse to write, draw, stamp, and duplicate is somehow related to our strange impulse to make pies out of mud.[1]

At some point, we started using tools to do it. Someone fashioned colored paste to paint on cave walls about 37,000 years ago. After about 29,000 years—after we accumulated our first sets of standardized stone and bone tools, plus multipart weapons that allowed us to kill dangerous animals from a safe distance, and added nutrients to our diets—some tribes started to control land and trade property.[2] Then they found they needed to keep records. In the embryonic cities of Mesopotamia, in what is now southern Iraq, administrators began using seal stamps to identify people, track taxes, and record services performed by individuals around 4000 B.C.E. By 3100 B.C.E., the Sumerians were regularly etching records on clay slabs. If nothing else, the slabs were more portable than cave walls and more permanent than pictures scratched in dirt. On them were coded pictures of abstract signs. It took thirty-four pictograms on weighty tablets to portray a sheep in Sumeria. Thousands were needed to tell a story, much less express an abstract thought, first by writing curved images and then by using a small, triangular stylus to make standardized wedge-shaped impressions, eventually called cuneiform, into the wet clay. As much of an improvement as the method was, the Sumerians, who produced the most literate culture of their time, produced only fifty-six tablets a year, each amounting to a page of a document, during the next three centuries.[3]

Still, something new—recorded knowledge—had appeared. There were math tables for trade, lists of birds and mammals for hunting, pictures of the heavens for navigating.

But writing remained barely detectable in other groups in the areas where people had tried it. It moved across the map at a grudging, miserable pace. A few centuries passed before the experiment made it the 1,500 miles from Iraq eastward to northwest India, where a still undecipherable alphabet was picked up and bastardized by the locals. (It died out in about 2000 B.C.E., when the area was conquered and the old culture of the Indus Valley was obliterated.) In nearby Turkmenistan, a strange prewriting, akin to the kind of characters that later emerged in China, arose, died, and remained unnoticed until archaeologists found evidence of it in 2000 C.E.[4]

Writing may have moved so slowly because the content was boring. In the Indus Valley, archaeologists characterized the written records as full of "dreariness." One historian, speculating why the text was less than engaging, suspected "the dead hand of the civil servant was in operation."[5]

A few hundred more years went by before knowledge got a little easier and a little faster. That's when the Egyptians, who had been communicating on stone and stone pots, began using a plant that grew wild in the shallow marshes of the Nile River to make papyrus. Obviously lighter and easier to write on, it was a more practical way to store and transport writing. The Egyptians eventually produced eight different grades of papyrus and could make scrolls of up to twenty sheets. Not coincidentally, longer kinds of thought emerged. On papyrus, bodies of medical, religious, astronomical, and commercial knowledge appeared, capable for the first time in history of being shared in a wider circle. They were written in hieratic script, a shorthand version of the hieroglyphics the Egyptians used on their monuments. Written with a brush or pen, hieratic also was a faster medium. Both versions of the alphabet were our most complex and expressive means of communicating yet. The thousands of pictures were formalized cave images. Some stood for sounds. Some were symbols of animals or other physical objects. Some were meant to be assembled like a rebus (combining a picture for bee and a picture for leaf, for example, to come up with "belief"), and some stood on their own.[6]

But hieroglyphics and hieratics, while easier to write than incising figures in wet clay, chipping letters into stone, or fashioning seals out of stone, were not easy to understand. Only elite scribes, trained for years, were capable of it. There is little evidence that Egyptians outside certain royal and priestly circles could read any of it.

Written knowledge therefore remained invisible not only from one culture to another, but to the great masses of humans even in the tiny corners of the world where it existed. A few exalted cliques traded impressions and images among themselves, but their slowly etched ideas, kept close, often died quickly. For example, a Sumerian clay tablet from about 2400 B.C.E. "describes how a new ruler of the city of Lugash had 'established the freedom' of its citizenry, a reform achieved by restraining the bureaucratic scribes, who had invented taxes on just about everything that was in sight, and on some things, such as divorce, that were not. . . . The reform went further, for 'men of power' were also restrained from exploiting the poor."[7] There was no way for most people to read such heady ideas, no way to distribute them, and no real way to sustain them.

Even the idea of one God was tested out, written down, and, for want of distribution, left to gather dust for a long time. Almost 1,400 years before Jesus and 150 years before Moses, the Egyptian Pharaoh Amenhotep IV claimed a formless, omnipotent god controlled all the forces on Earth. His idea, however, lasted only about four years after his death. Its failure probably had more to do with media than with heaven. Amenhotep gave his hieroglyphic icon for one God—an image of the sun—to his priests, the only people who could read about it or promote it. The priests, of course, were also the people most threatened by this new monotheism. They killed it as soon as they got the chance, perhaps by poisoning Amenhotep's successor, the otherwise undistinguished but now famous Tutankhamen, in about 1350 B.C.E. With Tut went the whole movement.

It was "one of the most important demonstrations in all of history of the power of media to make or break the ideas they carry," media philosopher Paul Levinson points out.[8]

But communicating, once again, seems to be something of a biological urge, and, as would become evident again and again during the next four thousand years, even the stooped and poor have it. Some time between 1900 B.C.E. and 1800 B.C.E., commoners deep in the Egyptian desert had began using about thirty crude symbols among themselves. Each symbol represented not an idea or object, but a sound. The invention, a sort of slang hieroglyphics, amounted to the first popular alphabet, easy to learn and easy to use.

Lower classes were, in effect, improvising a way to formalize their writing and store knowledge then held, if at all, by the wealthy and the elite. "These people," a linguist explained many millennia later, "adopted a crude system of writing within the Egyptian system, something they could learn in hours, instead of a lifetime. It was a utilitarian invention for soldiers, traders, merchants."[9] That phenomenon too would occur more than once.

By the time Moses was working with the desert God around 1200 B.C.E., he had an alphabet of many sounds. Within a few years of his flock's flight from Egypt, the Hebrews had five "books" of written legend and law. It was this stored, accessible knowledge that, readily reworked by generations of thinkers and dreamers, grew into the monotheism of Judaism, Christianity, and Islam. All of Western and not a little Eastern thought grew from it. The same notion, promoted by a powerful pharaoh in abstract symbols and distributed only to a priesthood whose code no one else could crack, had died, unread, fifteen decades before.

Similar writing inventions then appeared in distant spots, probably all traceable to the appearance of the small cities and tax-collecting governments that evolved in certain areas. Halfway around the globe in China, a man named Ts-ang Chieh, mimicking animal footprints and bird claw marks, developed calligraphy at about the same time as the Egyptian commoners were shaping their characters. (Because calligraphy is so graphic, most writing scholars see it more as a signing system than as an alphabet; it initially was used for soothsaying more than record keeping.)[10] Even before the Hebrews got there, the Canaanites in the Palestine-Syria area were refining the Egyptian alphabet between 1600 and 1400 B.C.E. Their letters, in turn, were adopted by the seagoing Phoenicians, who lived by trade and presumably needed to keep accounts. By 950 B.C.E., the Greeks had adopted the Phoenician alphabet. They added vowels, tweaked shapes, and created the first really beautiful, graceful, widely useful sets of letters. They, apparently for the first time, occasionally wrote on leather. From their colonies along the coast of what is now Turkey, they learned to use seals to mark documents. And, within a few years, a tribe of Etruscans transported these innovations across the Aegean Sea to the Italian peninsula. Mixing some local idiosyncrasies with a few misunderstandings, the Etruscans shaped what became the Latin alphabet. Where a user of hieroglyphics had to master the meanings and mind-boggling combinations of as many as 20,000 characters to scratch out a thought or a list of grains, an Etruscan had to memorize only a couple dozen letters.

The letters were a boon. History's first intellectual explosion followed, especially in Greece. A phenomenal flow of written works poured from the relatively tiny population that had mastered the new tool. The Greeks produced something like 400,000 manuscripts, written on and read from parchment, in about three hundred years. There were legends, of course.

And there were Plato, Euclid, Aristotle, Herodotus, "legal codes, political discourses, [and] plays by writers major and minor."[11] There were treatises on military organization, on maritime conventions, on deciding how to divide up civic resources, on self-government. All were recorded and, thanks to Ptolemy, many were stored in the library of Alexandria beginning in the third century B.C.E.

Few copies were made of the works at the library of Alexandria. When anyone wanted to reproduce the words in the West or the signs in use in the East, they redrew them. We were not yet up to engineering a tool to manufacture copies of writing, to print.

Someone, however, was tinkering with the idea. In what is still a terrific archaeological mystery, a printed plate was unearthed in Crete in 1908. The stone, now called the Phaistos disk, dated from about 1700 B.C.E., at a time when the nearest known writing cultures were in faraway Mexico, China, Egypt, and Mesopotamia. It is the oldest printed object yet found, featuring an alphabet that never showed up before or after the era, on Crete or anywhere else. It remains undeciphered. Its level of workmanship, moreover, was centuries ahead of the time. Letters were imprinted on both sides of the piece with metallic stamps. "Making these stamps," one anthropologist speculated, "must have entailed a great deal of work, and they surely weren't manufactured just to print this single document."[12]

During the two thousand years after the alphabet reached Greece and Turkey, the things we wrote on improved too. Most new writing surfaces came from China, where quality paper first appeared around 300 B.C.E. Another Chinese, Ts'ai Lun, refined the process two centuries later. The practice spread with a slow, eight-hundred-year migration of Chinese westward across the Eurasian land mass. At least two Chinese papermakers happened to be in Samarkand in Central Asia when, during the eighth century, robust new Arab armies roared into it. Taken prisoner, they apparently taught their captors their art. As Arab power spread, so did papermaking. A parchment industry eventually arose in the Turkish city of Pergamum.[13] But parchment, made from mashed plant fibers, still was not really paper, at least as it came to be known by the celebrants at the Linotype-Hell reception.

Despite the new inventions, the written word barely changed in the three thousand years after someone made the Phaistos disk. By the fifteenth century C.E., many of the planet's cultures still lived in more or less separate, mutually ignorant pockets. One society did not usually know what another was doing if, in fact, it guessed other people might even exist. In Australia,

North America, and much of Africa, people still functioned as hunter-gatherers. Central America was tightly ruled by complex Inca, Mayan, and Aztec political organizations, theologies, and priesthoods, all built with stone tools. Farther south, ducking in and behind the impassable Andes, locals were just then producing standardized bronze tools. Through Asia, North Africa, and Europe, some cultures and tribes—unimpeded by significant geographical obstacles—fitfully came to share or steal from each other metal tools, immunities to certain diseases, and finally writing.[14]

By 1400 writing remained time-consuming and difficult to manufacture. In Europe, North Africa, China, and Central America, it was reproduced by copyists, usually employed by courts and temples, the richest institutions of the time. Stroke by stroke, copyists mostly produced maps of their sponsors' properties, commercial papers, and correspondence. The political ones, in any case, tended to have short lives. (In 238 B.C.E., China's emperor ordered a burning of "books"—written by stylus on wood—that were critical of him; it apparently encompassed "all but a few" of the political documents in the capital.) Books as we know them, with flat bound pages, replaced scrolls in the fourth century and made reading infinitely easier, but copying a book was an ambitious, expensive act, performed and reproduced line by line. Tomes appeared in small numbers. The Arab empire had 9,620 titles by the year 988, a collection that served a huge population stretching from the Indian subcontinent across North Africa and into Spain. Muslim politicians and chieftains were the primary buyers of books. A library in northwest China had about a thousand titles in it in the year 1000; at least one of them (now called the Diamond Sutra) included duplicated block prints of an illustration. In all the monasteries of Europe in the early 1300s, there were only about 1,400 copied book titles.[15]

For actually scrawling out lines was thankless, physically demanding work. "It crooks your back, it dims your sight, it twists your stomach and your sides," a malcontent copyist scribbled into the margin of a book he worked on in a medieval European monastery. He moaned about the "excessive drudgery." Labor relations were not good; on some days, supervisors put him to work "under compulsion, bound by fetters, just as a runaway and fugitive has to be bound."[16] Since the year 1200, ecclesiastical law allowed scriptorium bosses to punish unwilling scribes by withholding their daily wine.

The wretches also were drains on monastery budgets. Many monasteries produced their own food well into the Middle Ages, with monks planting and harvesting the fields. Devoting a monk's time to the indoor task of redrawing texts was, in effect, taking a worker out of the field and cutting the amount of food on the table. His manuscript, moreover, was usually a devotional commodity, much like a rosary or cross, needed for daily ritual. (Monks had been required to read Scripture every day since about the year 300, when the first rules of monastery life were formed. The reading usually consisted of one brother reading out loud to the others.) Nor was his book for sale. "Making money" was a sinful concept in much of Europe at the time. In addition, it would be difficult for anyone in any age to make a profit on a product that took so many months, so much labor, and such expensive parchment to produce. Costs were high. The market was thin.

Consequently almost no one was recopying the few ancient works that had survived the waves of insensitive louts through the centuries. In 390, a Christian general named Theophilus burned down a large part of the library of Alexandria, the great warehouse of Greek culture. Arab armies conquered the area in 690 and destroyed the rest of the building. With it went most of the copies—never numerous—of works by and about Plato, Aristotle, Hippocrates, Herodotus, Socrates, democracy, medicine, theater, military strategy, philosophy, navigation, poetry, and mathematics. The Crusaders, on their brutal way to Palestine, burned and scoured the continent of any Jewish, Arab, and other non-Christian scrolls and books they saw. When they got to Byzantium, they did the same to Eastern Church literature and knowledge. If a scribe of the Middle Ages managed to get hold of a surviving document to copy, it had to have been momentous. The painfully wrought copies of both modern and ancient writers consequently were immensely valuable things to be safeguarded under lock and key, away from those who might touch, soil, or steal them.

"It is," one historian eventually reflected, "sometimes difficult to realize how much effort was needed to reconstitute the bodies of Knowledge such as those of astronomy and arithmetic as they had been known in the ancient world. It was not a question of going beyond the ancients—the impulse to 'research' in the sense of extending the boundaries of scientific knowledge was only faintly stirring even in the twelfth century—but simply to learn what had been known and what the world had since lost was a stupendous task, demanding the labors of many scholars."[17]

Scholars often were questionable translators and inspired misinterpreters. Aristotle's *Metaphysics*, for example, had been recopied over the centuries from Greek to Syriac, Arabic, and Hebrew before a European found a copy of a commentary to put into Latin. Both the commentator, named Averroes, and the translator thus passed on a "last"—and forged—work of Aristotle to the world. In the end, their Aristotle was a homespun philosopher who believed in a personal God and immortality (which, of course, the real Aristotle did not) and advised people not to sail southwest from Spain, lest a terrible heat cause their brains to boil.

Similarly, a translator named Gerardus de Cremora bungled a Latin translation of Avicenna's *Canon of Medicine*. His flawed description of certain symptoms was dutifully copied and laboriously recopied for use in the Continent's new medical schools. Its advice ultimately caused "many untimely deaths" among the misled students' unfortunate patients.[18]

Yet a nifty little trade in those and other handwritten materials, however inaccurate or fanciful, had begun to bubble during the 1300s and 1400s. Short devotional works, poems, and the compromised works of medicine, law, theology, and grammar for the strange new universities of Europe appeared, and sold. Knowledge of medicine and law, even more so than today, amounted to professional achievement. Glimpses at those expensive, rare bodies of thought were carefully apportioned. In the universities, a few lucky students rented or shared texts while the rest just listened to the teacher who, like the monks, read out loud to them. By the 1400s, the Sorbonne had painstakingly accumulated thirty copies of one book to lend to poor students.[19] Most used the library, where the precious manuscripts were chained for safekeeping to the tables.

To reproduce that grudging trickle of knowledge, as many as 10,000 copyists were at work in France's monasteries, courts, and universities at the beginning of the fifteenth century. England's chancery, turning out administrative documents, employed sixty scribes. Its Court of Common Pleas had one hundred employees, although not all were copyists. Italy probably produced a greater quantity of written documents, and at least a handful of its copyists toiled in what may have been history's first privately owned printing business. The Italian ventures were more like art reproduction studios than what later would be called print shops. The most famous "printer," Frederick of Montefiltro, had about forty copyists on staff. His best were called *scrittori*, well-paid artisans who could understand and translate the Greek writers who Frederick's customers—a few fabulously wealthy families—demanded. The rest of the scribes were mere *copisti*, or clerks. Usually "school masters or needy men of learning," a great many were German. Frederick and his cohorts, apparently with memories long enough to recall the sacking of Rome a mere millennium before, did not hesitate to call them "barbarians" to their faces.[20]

Frederick's clients belonged to a historically overachieving class of Italian merchants, at a time when fashion and romance began to turn toward learning. Of all mankind's fads during its long journeys, this surely was its most fortuitous. In addition to trinkets and castles, the newly rich families of Italy's booming city-states commissioned the copying of books and built grand private libraries. They had Frederick craft two or three copies—typically on vellum, an expensive leather-like paper made from goat or sheep skin—of the works of Thomas Aquinas, Sophocles, and other lost Greek scholars and, increasingly, of scandalous moderns like Dante and Boccaccio. Why these people abruptly started spending their disposable income on thought instead of, say, more castles is hotly debated among scholars of this burst of the Renaissance. One particularly overwrought writer from Victorian England saw it as an "age of passionate desire." He imagined "Petrarch poring over a Homer he could not understand, and Boccaccio in his maturity learning Greek in order that he might drink from the well-head of poetic inspiration."[21] According to that theory, there was a great unslaked thirst for stimulation after centuries of stern, dark deprivation. Other Italians instinctually turned to literature, science, and stored wisdom to try to understand their sudden new world of commerce, frightening foreign influences, and startling private wealth. As we'll see in the next chapter, something more profound—a rediscovery of the value of the flesh, an appreciation of knowledge for its own sake—also was stirring. But, then too, the Italian aristocracy's ferocious taste for knowledge probably also was related to the eternal taste for impractical baubles and useless beauty. So saintly works about abstinence and poverty were copied into extravagant tomes of gilt and—a particular favorite of the time—exotic velvet. Scholars these days still describe the hand-scripted and illuminated volumes of the era as "magnificent" paragons of "costly beauty." The suppliers of these works were scholar-merchants like Frederick, who also produced a handwrought index of the documents in the Vatican's growing library, as well as catalogs of the libraries of St. Mark in Florence, at Oxford, and at Pavia. One of Frederick's patrons spent a mind-boggling 30,000 ducats to stock his library over several decades.[22]

(Hundreds of years later, love of learning in the ruling classes took a similar turn. Enriched by another technological earthquake in communications, twentieth-century newspaper baron William Randolph Hearst tore up fifteenth-century vellum prayer books—perhaps made by Frederick of Montefiltro's *scrittori*—to make into lampshades for his new castle in California.)

But the book lovers of the Italian city-states were a tiny cult. About 50 million people were spread between the Urals and the Atlantic coast in the early 1400s, and only a minuscule few had the money, time, ability, or inclination to dig into the wisdom of the past. Fewer still had access to the spare copies of the modern works that might, in turn, have stirred a desire for knowledge, for method and logic, for possibility.

On the eve of the great change, in sum, knowledge in the dimly literate human colonies scattered around the globe remained hard to duplicate and distribute, rare and expensive. Awareness of life beyond one's immediate vision and even of myth generally remained special, secret, almost exclusively the property of the wealthy and blessed. When the great mass of people got close to knowledge, it was interpreted for them by those who knew better, who could read the mysterious words and might at times present them in primitive, easily understood forms. Books, it was said, were to be heard, not seen. News of gods, wars, illness, and kings usually was communicated orally, in stained glass, by music, by whip, and in frightful carved portals. Artisans might also carve an image onto a slab of wood, paint ink over the wood, and then press paper or material onto it. Europe's "block printers," however, were mostly engaged in making textiles or, more profitably still, playing cards. Their methods too were painstaking and expensive, usually a service for the privileged. Those with thoughts—ecclesiastical, civic, or unofficial— could not communicate to more than a very few people.

Yet some inventive souls long had been trying to mechanize the laborious process of hand carving or hand writing images over and over again. Asians had the most success. Someone in China used carved blocks of type to stamp a multipage document onto a thinner, cheaper type of paper in about 838. In the 900s, the Chinese court started using ornately carved blocks to impress single-sheet promissory notes—the first real paper money—to raise cash. In 1041, an inventor named Pi-Sheng fashioned some semipermanent letters from hardened clay and pressed them, one by one, onto paper to make words. Two years later, someone in Korea used type characters to produce a collection of Buddhist scriptures. In 1147, monks at the Benedictine monastery at Engelberg, Switzerland, shortened their labors by carving woodcut capital letters to use in their otherwise handwritten documents. Some one hundred years later, according to a diary entry by an admiring son, a book using metal letters was produced in China. Still later, in 1313, a fellow named Weng Chen made some 60,000 characters out of hardwood. He used them to create a treatise on agriculture. And in 1403, Korean King Yung-lo offered "money in great abundance" to develop cast-metal characters—letters that could be used over again—to be used for printing. His court produced a book about the subsidy in 1410. It used, apparently for the first time ever, portable metal characters.

To produce the thing, the artisan set the letters, one at a time, into a thick layer of adhesive (probably made of resin and wax) and let it dry so that the letters couldn't be easily bumped out of position. He'd then brush the type with ink and carefully lay a sheet of paper or cloth lightly on the form. Last, he'd brush or pat the paper onto the type with a felt pad and carefully lift it off. Some of the most gifted printers in Korea and China were, according to legend, able to make 1,500 impressions per day.[23]

Then, in about 1450 in central Europe, a dour tinkerer named Johannes Gutenberg invented a tool for casting metal letters, keeping as many as forty-two lines of them straight, and mechanically stamping onto sheets of paper whole paragraphs at a time, as often as you wanted.

NOTES

1. Warren Chappell, *A Short History of the Printed Word* (New York: Knopf, 1970), 3.

2. Jared Diamond, *Guns, Germs, and Steel: The Fates of Human Societies* (New York: Norton, 1997), 16–19.

3. Henry Hodges, *Technology in the Ancient World* (New York: Barnes & Noble Books, 1992), 77–79; Frederick G. Kilgour, *The Evolution of the Book* (New York: Oxford University Press, 1998), 12–13, 18. All told, the Sumerians produced about 17,000 clay tablets from 3100 to 2800 B.C.E. Hodges, *Technology*, 82.

4. Hodges, *Technology*, 252–54; John Noble Wilford, "Prewriting Discovered in Central Asia," *New York Times*, May 13, 2001, 1. The scholar who thought the writing resembled the Chinese characters that later emerged was Fredrik T. Hiebert of the University of Pennsylvania, a member of a joint American–Russian team of archaeologists excavating remains of the still unidentified ancient Central Asian culture.

5. On "dead hand," see Hodges, *Technology*, 254.

6. Paul Levinson, *The Soft Edge: A Natural History and Future of the Information Revolution* (London: Routledge, 1997), 13.

7. Kilgore, *Evolution*, 19.

8. On Amenhotep, monotheism, and Moses' relative success, see Levinson, *Soft Edge*, 11–14.

9. P. Kyle McCarter Jr., a professor of Near Eastern languages at Harvard University, quoted in John Noble Wilford, "Egypt Carvings Set Earlier Date for Alphabet," *New York Times*, November 19, 1999, 1, 10. On the difference between pictographs, alphabets, ideograms, and sonograms, see Chappell, *Short History*, 20.

10. The first Chinese writings from about 1500 B.C.E. were characters etched into bone. Citizens seeking advice would have a character signifying an idea scratched into a bone. If it cracked one way, it was a good omen. If it cracked differently, it was a bad omen. Some 5,000 characters eventually evolved before administrators overhauled and shortened the alphabet in 100 B.C.E. Hodges, *Technology*, 263.

11. Levinson, *Soft Edge*, 18–19.

12. Diamond, *Guns*, 241.

13. After papyrus, the biggest advance in writing surfaces took place in about 100 B.C.E., when Chinese craftsmen began mashing plant fiber, spreading it in a thin layer over a sieve, and then sticking it to dry in the sun against a wall. Some speculate they stole the idea from nomadic tribes who perfected making felt. "In essence," one author noted, "paper is merely a felt made of vegetable matter rather than of animal hair." Hodges, *Technology*, 270. By the Middle Ages, the best and— short of stone—most durable writing material was vellum—calf, sheep, or most often goat skin, stretched and pounded and treated so that ink adhered to it. Elites came to love it. By the mid-twelfth century, the stuff had reached the influential monastery at Cluny, France, which controlled monasteries and landholdings throughout Europe. There church copyists tested it. Like a popular new dance, the new material was adopted by the nobility (whose sons composed most Catholic clergy and monks at the time). One hundred years later, the Holy Roman Emperor forbade the use of all paper, usually flimsy stuff cross-pollinated to Italy by travelers from Arab lands, for official use. Vellum was expensive, however. Only the rare war-lord or Church leader could afford to produce whole documents on it. Writing on it was difficult; the tacky, oil-based inks that had been around for two hundred years before the technological earthquake after 1450 smeared on vellum. The egg-based inks that worked on vellum were pricey and hard to make. Using them to inscribe multiple copies of books on sheets of vellum was beyond most medieval Europeans' imagination. Their books, which replaced scrolls around the fifth century, were instead written on brittle, impermanent stock until the Turks set up their Chinese papermaking operation near the end of the first millennium. "The History of Typography," in *Pocket Pal: A Graphic Arts Handbooks* (International Paper, 1934–1970), www.dmgi.com (accessed September 11, 1999). On the westward spread of paper and papermaking, see Willam Hendrick van Loon, *Observations on the Mystery of Print* (New York: Book Manufacturers Institute, 1937), 30–31.

14. On the state of cultures at about 1450, see Diamond, *Guns*, 241.

15. On the number of titles in Europe and the Arab empire, see Kilgour, *Evolution*, 70, 62. On China, see British Library Board, *The Diamond Sutra: The World's Earliest Dated Book*, British Library, Or. 8210/P.2, diamond-sutra-closeup.gif (accessed November 10, 1999). Svend Dahl, *History of the Book* (Metuchen, N.J.: Scarecrow, 1968), 13.

16. Leila Avrin, *Scribes, Script, and Books* (Oxford: Phaedon, 1991), 224, cited in Kilgour, *Evolution*, 71.

17. R. W. Southern, *The Making of the Middle Ages* (New Haven: Yale University Press. 1953), 188. Joseph Dahmous, *A History of the Middle Ages* (Barnes & Noble Books, 1995), 69.

18. George Faludy, *Erasmus* (New York: Stein & Day, 1970), 19, 59.

19. Kilgour, *Evolution*, 76; Peter Ackroyd, *The Life of Thomas More* (New York: Nan A. Talese, 1998).

20. Frederick W. Hamilton, *A Brief History of Printing, Part II* (Chicago: United

Typothetae of America, 1918), 10; Ronald J. Diebert, *Parchment, Printing, and Hypermedia* (New York: Columbia University Press, 1997), 89; Jakob Burckhardt, *The Civilization of the Renaissance in Italy*, as cited in Chappell, *Short History*, 35–37.

21. John Addington Symonds, *The Renaissance in Italy*, 7 vols. (London, 1875–1886). Cited in Chappell, *A Short History*, 16.

22. Henri Bouchet, *The Book: Its Printers, Illustrators, and Binders from Gutenberg to the Present Time*, ed. H. Grevel (New York: Scribner & Wilford, 1890), 308; Chappell, *Short History*, 36–38.

23. *Pocket Pal*; "Koreans Were Ahead of Gutenberg," *Natural History*, October 1951, 376–78; Thomas Francis Carter, *The Invention of Printing in China*, as cited in "Koreans," 171; Cor Knops, *Book History Chronology*, November 1998, www.xs4all.nl/-knops/index3.htm; Moo-Young Han, correspondence to T. Matthew Ciolek, January 7, 1996, Global Networking Timeline Project of Australian National University, Canberra, cited in Global Networking Timeline, www.ciolek.com (accessed November 3, 1999).

3

THE MACHINE IN THE MANGER

Johannes Gutenberg had a lifelong, almost uncanny streak of bad luck. He was unappreciated and underpaid during his lifetime, bankrupted at least twice. His ill fortune lasted even longer than he did. It wasn't until 1889, for example, that the discovery of a notarized paper from 1438 finally proved he had something to do with the invention of movable type and the printed word. Even attempts to honor him were a little botched. In 1900 German officials preparing to celebrate his five hundredth birthday discovered, on the eve of the festivities, that the inventor had been born in 1397 or maybe 1394. His five hundredth birthday, in any case, was years past. Since then, evidence that his ideas were borrowed from a Dutchman named Laurens Coster has surfaced. One historian refers to a Coster assistant named Johann who stole secrets and fled to nearby Mainz.[1]

Gutenberg lived in Mainz, born to a patrician family just at the moment of history when patricians in Mainz lost their power. He grew up in an exhausted, depressed, spiritually bankrupt, and politically tumultuous Europe. In a ten-year period in the mid-1300s, plague had killed off from 25 to 40 percent of the population. Sweden had lost 60 percent of its people. The scourge had returned at ten-year intervals ever since. So did witch hunts for the devils responsible for it. During most of Gutenberg's life, Moorish invasions, the Hundred Years War, and a vicious civil war in England ran over and into each other as classes and interest groups fought over the spoils of decaying kingdoms and fiefdoms. To the southeast, the armies of the Ottoman Turks were approaching Constantinople, still the seat of empire and the Orthodox Church. Thanks in no small part to the unceasing warfare and epidemics, economic activity on Gutenberg's continent had been moribund since 1370. The amount of land under cultivation in England and Germany had decreased. Lords' rental incomes were in constant

decline. Trade between towns and certainly with foreign lands, some economists contend, was probably lower in 1400 than it had been in 1300.[2]

Military power was in flux. In 1346, an English army had brought a
new weapon, the crossbow, to a battlefield at Crecy, France, where it destroyed an army of French knights. In 1387, a Swiss general added a new
wrinkle. When German knights in Sempach tried to blunt his thrust by attacking his crossbowmen, the general surrounded his archers with men carrying large, sharpened pikes. It worked. Their horses wounded on the pikes,
the knights could not get to the bowmen, who continued to pick them off
with their long-range missiles. In 1415, the English learned to hold and
thrust cavalry—musketeers—to sweep away French knights attacking their
crossbowmen and pikemen at Agincourt.[3]

The new tools and tactics pretty much compromised the knights' sway
over the region. Their fearsome horseback speed on the battlefield was
largely negated by the antihorse pikes and the rapidly fired, high-powered
longbows. The untrained serf foot soldiers who accompanied them into
battle were no match for the coordinated onslaughts of their opponents' disciplined professional soldiers. And soon, as gunpowder and siege cannons
began to show up around the Continent, even their impregnable castles became vulnerable.

In the disarray that followed, Europe grew "pessimistic, self-doubting,
and obsessed with magic." What had been effective institutions for hundreds
of years—kingdoms, churches—no longer could reliably distribute food,
provide security, or even offer spiritual sustenance. The Catholic Church
was divided, scrambling to contain internal heresy. Bishops made war on
one another. Inquisitors kidnapped and killed Jews, Cathars, Arabs. Sex was
demonized. A panel of careful, learned people solemnly convicted sixty-
five-year-old Angele, Lady of Labarathe, of having sex with the devil and
giving birth to a baby-eating monster "with a wolf's head and a serpent's
tail." In a convent near the precious private libraries of the Italian merchant
princes, a woman awakened each morning with bruises inflicted, she swore,
by evil spirits who whipped her in her sleep with dead snakes and dunked
her into the gooey remains of corpses alive with thousands of worms. After
a formal investigation into her horror, Francesca Romana was elevated to
sainthood.[4] Today, a therapist might gently help her figure out why all her
nightmares featured wet, slimy things. Then, however, hell had nothing to
do with fifty-minute hours, Linotype, or bright suburban hotel ballrooms.
Hell was a real place, populated by demons who visited frequently and had
a lot to do with most Europeans' real, otherwise unexplainable woes.

In Mainz, for example, upstart shopkeepers, organized into secret and troublesome guilds, were blamed for the woes of besieged patricians like Friele Gensfleisch zur Laden zum Gutenberg. Not much is known about Friele Gutenberg. We know he had money; he controlled several houses and perhaps some outlying farmland. We also know he had enough status to marry one of his daughters to the town mayor and that he had a series of bitter disputes with the newly emboldened shopkeepers and guildsmen of western Germany.[5]

This strange new class of merchants, traders, and middlemen evolved in the eleventh century in what is now Belgium. According to the writings of a shocked English monk who "discovered" these landless, none too popular tribesmen on a historic journey to Rome back in 1010, they were much disliked. In the day's rigid caste system of peasant, vassal, and master, they were none of the above. Where everyone else in the area dependably worked near or around their castles, these folks usually didn't. Where everyone else paid the estate's sovereign in crops and by serving in armies, these scurrying expediters often didn't have crops. For most of the Middle Ages, they were barely covered in French, English, or German laws, operating as something short of free merchants but as something different from obligated serfs.[6]

Yet they had an important civic role. Eighty to ninety percent of the Continent's residents still produced their own food, and it was a struggle. Weather, crop failures, and plagues regularly wrecked their meager harvests. Hunger, malnutrition, and even starvation were real recurring problems in many areas. And so "outcasts and aliens such as Jews and Arabs" who were prohibited even from being serfs, began to trade, probably first to buy wheat in bulk. They then baked or paid others to bake bread, which made up most of Europe's diet in those days, and sold it to their hungry neighbors. Their investments inspired the spread and improvement of agriculture in some parts of the Continent, and regularized the food supply in lean times.[7]

But most people found the practice, if not the bread, distasteful. Many blushed at the notion of paying a "price" for something. Medieval buyers— usually lords—simply announced what they would give in return for goods or services. Their offers reflected what was "fair," not how much they might value the product or how much it cost the supplier to make. It was an age of duty, not commerce. Everyone—peasant, smith, miller, artisan, and vassal lord alike—"labored under an obligation to furnish their services to those who offered to pay," to obey whatever family member, knight, clergyman, lord, bishop, king, or pope happened to be above them. The notion of personal gain was derided as something foreign, filthy. Those who supplied others with necessities in return for personal gain were thus openly hated through-out most of medieval Europe. Sacred law and popes explicitly denounced their practices as sinful, prideful, and selfish.[8]

So secular authorities felt free to bully the miserable bourgeoisie. In many locales, they restricted or simply prohibited the merchants' "faires," markets where suppliers and consumers, instead of bartering, occasionally exchanged goods for money. They fitfully expropriated their belongings. They set the prices the merchants could get, punished those who charged too much, and exiled traders who cut portions in times when raw materi-als were scarce. More often the nobility levied heavy taxes on them and, when necessary, kidnapped them into their armies, despite how drastically such actions might disrupt the flow of goods to the fiefdom.

By the 1200s, as they came to create and distribute larger and larger portions of Europe's goods, the bourgeoisie's guilds gained influence and then some control over wider swaths of the Continent's commerce. By the 1300s, often acting in the name of local lords and clergymen, they gained in many places the power to set prices and dictate the sizes certain products could be.

By 1400, the time of Gutenberg's father, the burghers' ascent was quicken-ing. One reason was that the lords and knights who had overseen them had become weaker, less able to impose their will. The burghers, by compari-son, had begun to grow as rich as their faltering masters. Many of the manor lords in France and England, in fact, were leaving their estates for seemingly safer royal courts. Thanks to their widening tax bases, those royal lairs—alone among the era's institutions—could afford to raise and maintain the expensive new professional armies. But the country aristocrats then arriving at the courts immediately needed money. The in-kind goods and services they used to live on at their estates could not purchase positions and favors in a throne room. Thus, by the early 1400s, many were paying more atten-tion to the cash value of their estates. They tried to improve crop produc-tion and squeezed costs and even laborers from their operations, all for "profit," in fact if not in name. Slowly but surely, first in Holland and then in England and France, cash-starved noblemen allowed peasants to buy their way out of their feudal obligations. The ex-serfs either stayed on the land as tenant farmers or moved to the towns and cities.[9] There they also learned to use money to make and buy goods.

In the fading feudal system's least-regulated cracks—in what is now Italy, Belgium, Holland, eastern France, and the towns of western Germany, where military authorities were weakest—traders already had branched out to other regions and, finally, other lands. Some were trading with the North Sea and Baltic states, the Black Sea states to the southeast, and the Mediterranean states to the south.[10]

It proved to be lucrative. Around Friele Gutenberg's German towns, where no king or central authority held much sway, the burghers thus grew richer and stronger.[11] Their regulation of commerce, once done for the lords, was now often done for themselves. They became, in essence, gatekeepers. They handed out licenses to practice crafts, and, like the noblemen still living among them used to do, thus decided who in this mortal incarnation could eat well and who would not. Officially their guilds admitted only colleagues who did honorable, high-quality work. Perhaps more importantly, they also kept competitors at bay, denying licenses to traders or artisans with similar goods and thus preserving the fortunes of existing guild members. The step from conducting commerce to needing civic resources—land, water, labor, security—to conduct business better was, as happened repeatedly during the next half millennium, a short one. The guildsmen took it.

In 1411, yet another dispute between Mainz guilds and the patricians erupted, and Friele Gutenberg decided he'd had enough. He left town, announcing he was going into "voluntary exile" with his wife and his three youngest children. The youngest, Johannes, was in tow.

The Gutenbergs fled neither far nor completely. They landed in the warm bosom of Strasbourg, where patricians still had a toehold in city government and where the family had some property. Family members—probably Friele and certainly Johannes among them—kept returning for long periods to their native Mainz, where they still owned at least one house. One sister married a Mainz city official, another wed a nobleman there.

So, from Mainz to Strasbourg to Mainz again, the Gutenbergs in effect tacked against the era's shifting political winds, looking for a way to protect their property as the family fortune apparently leaked away. The generally loathed Friele died in 1420, leaving Johannes and his siblings to claim their Mainz holdings in the first of what would be many court appearances. They lost. The burghers expropriated at least some of the property, and the battered Johannes retreated once again to Strasbourg. There he and an unemployed knight tried money lending, co-guaranteeing a loan to another nobleman.[12]

No one, however, knows for sure. Details of the fellow's early years are even sketchier than those of his latter years. Gutenberg left no papers, and his name appears on no works of the time. (Authors and printers did not start putting their names in books until 1457, and some resisted doing so for years after that.) Records are so thin and so contradictory that Gutenberg and his work remain, as even one of his most careful biographers puts it, "shadowy."[13]

Others called him "crotchety." He grew, it seems, into a contentious, disagreeable, litigious man. Conflict, fallings-out, and bitter breakups marked his life. In 1428, the guilds of Mainz spitefully exiled all its patricians, forcing Gutenberg back to Strasbourg. Six years later, Mainz called its patricians back home, promising to pay reparations for property it had seized from them. Gutenberg promptly had the city scribe arrested for failing to pay him what the town still owed him for seizing family property in the troubles of 1411. He soon was back in court, this time defending himself against a shoemaker who sued him for using "libelous language." In 1436, he again was dragged into court. This time it was by a woman named Ennele, who claimed Gutenberg had jilted her at the altar. Rather than pay the fine the magistrate imposed on him, the frugal Gutenberg agreed to marry the woman.[14]

The newlyweds landed in Strasbourg, where Gutenberg by 1438 had a new plan, and formed a partnership with three others. Just what the partners intended to do became in the future a matter of bumptious academic debate, featuring much hissing and the bibliographic equivalent of trash talking. Some historians say it was to produce mirrors to sell to pilgrims on their way to a nearby religious festival at Aachen. Still another notes that the Latin word for "mirror" is *speculum*, which was also the title of the day's most popular publication. It was "a collection of precepts addressed to the faithful, which were copied and recopied without satisfying the demand."[15] In nearby Haarlem, churchwarden Laurens Coster had block-printed and sold copies of *Speculum*. Gutenberg thus may have set out to steal Coster's bestseller, or at least to compete with him. The language of Gutenberg's contract, in any case, suggested the partners meant to go about "the casting of multiple objects in lead or a lead alloy." While mirrors could be cast in lead, so, at least theoretically, could alphabet letters. Another, more informal historian, later translated the thick contract as meaning the partners baldly intended "to print books."[16]

The document probably was deliberately vague. Gutenberg, for one thing, was elaborately secretive about his workshop's activities. An employee later described how Gutenberg directed him to disassemble parts of the weird devices they were building, lest prying eyes steal the ideas.[17]

Caution, however, would have been prudent even for a nonparanoid in the 1400s. The inventor had seen guildsmen chip away his family's properties for decades. Intellectual property was even harder to protect. There were no copyright or patent laws to legally protect a new idea. And, much like the innovative hothouses of later centuries in other parts of Germany, England, Japan, and the United States, a handful of dreamers in and around western Germany were working on strikingly similar ideas. Coster was one of them. Like the Chinese masters on the other side of the planet, Coster carved drawings, or occasionally a caption and a drawing, into a block of wood. Then, using a thick ink, he imprinted it onto paper, a sheet at a time. It was exacting work. Make a mistake on one part of the carving, and you had to recarve the whole thing. According to legend, Coster was on the floor playing with his kids one night. Eyeing one of their toy blocks, he had an epiphany: he could break his images into smaller parts. He could carve part of the image on a block of wood and, if he made a mistake, he could simply dispose of it without having to carve the whole image over again. When he was done, he could put the blocks together to form a complete drawing, ink it up, and press parchment to it. He apparently also figured he could carve single letters into small blocks and then assemble them to make words. Coster knew he was onto something. Like Gutenberg, he tried to keep it close. "It was of importance to him not to divulge it, so that he should not forego his profit," said a later historian who thought Coster the true inventor of printing. But a Coster workman, the same historian says, stole the secrets and fled. Some say it was to Mainz or Strasbourg, where Gutenberg was starting his own hooded printing partnership. Johannes Mentelin also was in Strasbourg at that time. He had solved the problem of keeping wood type stable as he pressed paper to it by threading string through the blocks and tying them together. Prokop Waldfoghel showed up in Avignon in 1444 bragging that he knew of an artisan—maybe Gutenberg—in Mainz who could do "artificial writing." (Waldfoghel offered to build a similar machine but apparently never did.) Diebold Lauber, a copyist in the nearby Alsatian town of Hagenau, also may have been exploring ways to speed up copying. Still another, the melodiously named Pamfilo Castaldi, was working on a similar tool in Italy, but a connection to his competitors to the north is hard to trace. It is not hard, however, to imagine that in their proximity Coster, Mentelin, Waldfoghel, and Gutenberg knew they were working on similar projects.[18]

Gutenberg himself had been fussing with type and letters at least since 1436. In 1438, he and his partners had a man named Konrad Saspoch build a press to Gutenberg's specifications. It was a glommed-together assemblage of parts from the wine and olive presses that had been in use for hundreds of years, fitted to hold pieces of type. Gutenberg also was buying lead at the time. The investments were not cheap. Gutenberg and his partners paid Senspoch and other subcontractors at least one hundred florins, perhaps the modern-day equivalent of about $125,000. One of the partners invested the equivalent of $375,000 in the venture.[19]

But the project ended quickly. The partnership dissolved within twelve months, after the death of one of the principals and, once again, litigation. The bitter collapse included allegations that Gutenberg had withheld information from his partners and had improperly hired someone to avoid having to make a payment to his deceased partner's widow. The lawsuit seems to have depleted what was left of the patrician's inheritance.[20]

But Gutenberg continued the work. For the next twenty-seven years, he scrounged for funds to complete his process and then, presumably, create things he could sell. His idea seems to have been to make metal letters that he could then set in a proper order, ink up, and, using his gerry-rigged screw press, squeeze a piece of paper onto the inked type. His biggest problems during the 1440s had to do with the metal letters and ink. The metal could not be so soft that it would change shape when paper was pressed onto it. (Softness was one of the troubles with wood type, which tended to be crushed or misshapen when squeezed between the jaws of a press. The other problem was that you could not readily wash ink off wood letters, which meant you could not use them more than once or twice. Recopying a document with wood type often meant recarving a whole new set of letters.) On the other hand, the metal type could not be too hard. Hard or sharp letters would rip the paper. The metal also needed to be porous enough to hold ink through a project, but solid enough to be washable. To find the right recipe for type, Gutenberg experimented with different alloys, mostly with proportions of tin, lead, and zinc. He had to keep reshaping the pieces of type, adding a long-enough shank for a printer to pick it up between his thumb and finger but making it precisely even, so that all the shanks would be the exact same length and strength when paper was pressed onto them. The ink question also proved to be difficult. The watery stuff copyists used ran off metal letters. The gummy stuff block printers used was too tacky. Paper stuck to it.[21]

In time, he added lamp black to the ink. To hold the metal block letters he'd fashioned in place when he pressed paper to them, he apparently copied Mentelin and threaded string through them.[22]

Still, he got only rickety results and continued to borrow money. In 1442, the Chapter of St. Thomas in Strasbourg loaned him £80, perhaps to produce a devotional work. Three years later, he delivered a twenty-eight-page book, its remaining parts now called the "Fragment of the Word Judgment." If it was the promised work, it apparently did not generate much revenue. While he kept up interest payments on the St. Thomas loan for more than a decade, he never repaid the principal.[23]

The world was closing in on him again. His sister Else, who may have helped support him, apparently died in 1444. At the same time, the patrician-dominated civil authority of Strasbourg broke down. "Roving hordes of Armagnacs" invaded and looted the suburb where Gutenberg lived. Gutenberg, one biographer believes, feared he was about to be drafted to fight them.[24] For whatever reason, he left Strasbourg in 1444 for Mainz again.

There he continued to get some income—perhaps the equivalent of $11,500 a year—from a property in Strasbourg, but it wasn't enough to build books to sell. So he borrowed more money. In 1448, a Mainz relative loaned him the equivalent of $75,000. He used it to produce an astronomical calendar and four editions of the *Donatus*, a popular Latin grammar tract that, as coincidence would have it, Coster was selling as a block-printed document in nearby Haarlem.[25]

Despite the troubles he was having with money and technology, Gutenberg by then had decided on a really big project: he'd produce a Bible.

It was every pioneer printer's dream hit in the ensuing centuries in every European country, in Spanish America, and ultimately in British America. Monarchs and religious societies regularly subsidized printers, transported presses across seas, hired workers, and often seeded the very heresies that blunted their power just to create Bibles in native European languages, Indian tongues, and even polyglot editions. Similarly, when the technology spread to the Muslim world and prohibitions against mechanically reproducing Arabic type were dropped, printing the Qu'ran became the single best investment bet for aspiring printers. While the holy books aimed to care for souls, their economic effect often was to fund start-up printing operations.

Gutenberg hatched the idea, several biographers speculate, sometime in the mid-1440s. In 1450 a "wealthy Mainz merchant" named Johann Fust loaned Gutenberg some eight hundred florins (perhaps $400,000) at 6 percent interest to produce it. The revolutionary type Gutenberg had engineered, the tools he had fabricated, all the papers and inks he had modified and the press he had designed to make it all work were the collateral.[26] Fust clearly was a different kind of investor, a member of the newly ascendant bourgeoisie. His activities during the next seventeen years suggested he saw sales and profit, not necessarily salvation, in Gutenberg's inventions. He was a fully evolved son of the secular, nonpatrician class that was, at that historic moment, gaining control of Europe's economic life. His loan, in turn, was to a broken-down nobleman who never figured out how to adapt to Fust's emerging new world, even as he ultimately made it possible.

To make sure Gutenberg spent the funds well, Fust befriended—and might even have required Gutenberg to hire—an assistant named Peter Schoeffer. Fust loved Schoeffer, a young scribe from Gernsheim who had already made a name for himself as a calligrapher in Paris. Schoeffer's first job apparently was to replace Gutenberg's big, blocky metal letters with smaller, more readable letters. Adapting the age-old practice of making printable seals, young Schoeffer designed a "matrix," a mold into which the inventors could pour liquid metals to harden type into consistent, letter-like shapes. He may also have designed frames in which to line up and keep each of the cooled letters straight. Whoever actually thought such things up, Gutenberg's contraptions began to work better soon after Schoeffer arrived. Fust was excited. He put more money into the venture and also married off a family member (his daughter, according to most accounts; his grand-daughter, according to another) to the younger man.

The Bible, however, was going slowly. Able to fit only forty-two lines of text on a page, it grew to more and more sheets. For each one, Guten-berg and Schoeffer and an assistant would arrange letters, put them in order in the frame, lock the frame into the press, and then turn a screw to press a piece of paper onto it. The screw had to be tightened just so in order to avoid smearing the ink onto paper. Finally they'd turn the wheel of the screw in the other direction to raise the paper, being careful to prevent the paper and ink from sticking to the type. Then they'd secure another piece of paper in the machine. Perhaps they'd check to make sure that none of the metal characters had been damaged in their last impression. If damaged, they would have to manufacture yet another piece. They might next have to ap-ply more ink to the type or chip off some that had dried. Then, at last, they could press the next sheet into the type and ink. After repeating the process more than a hundred times, they made about 150 copies of that page. They would remove the pieces of type from the frame and lay out the next small portion of sacred text to be printed on the sheet's other side. Gutenberg's Bible ended up being more than 1,270 pages long, imprinted on two sides, bound into two volumes. To manufacture them, Gutenberg probably had to tighten and unscrew and check his press as many as 240,000 times.[27] It took years.

While he was at it, the Turks conquered Constantinople in 1453. In 1454, Pope Nicholas V issued "letters of indulgence" to raise money for an army to drive them out. Like the fund-raising direct mail campaigns of later centuries, these letters promised blessings and benefits to those who forwarded money. Church officials "scattered (them) abroad by the thousands to every corner of the world," employing "numerous copyists."[28]

When they got to Mainz in December 1454, Fust saw opportunity. He could, he figured, print them by the barrel and see a faster return on his investment. Gutenberg apparently stopped work on his Bible to print an unknown number of two letters of indulgence. But they were not enough for Gutenberg to keep up his substantial payments to Fust. By 1455, he owed Fust the modern-day equivalent of $1 million.[29]

By then, about 150 copies of the Bible were off his press, but Fust, his eyes perhaps opened by the easy money of the letters of indulgence, had grown impatient. The deadbeat, difficult nobleman had become "more of a hindrance than a profit." The merchant foreclosed and gave the collateral to Schoeffer.[30]

Gutenberg was ruined when his devices fell into new hands. Happily, those hands made it possible to make many readable, economical copies of something for the first time in human history. Strange forces—political, economic, scientific, geographic, religious, and, later, even technological hell like Linotype's—soon broke loose.

NOTES

1. Equally credible evidence suggests Gutenberg was born in 1393, 1394, or 1397. "A Brief History of Early Printing," *Scientific American*, supplement, July 7, 1900, 20501. The Coster assistant probably was Johann Mentelin of Strasbourg, one of the many who at one time or another were thought to have invented the device. Mentelin apparently engraved letters and words and syllables in wood. Willam Hendrick van Loon, *Observations on the Mystery of Print* (New York: Book Manufacturers Institute, 1937), 31.

2. Nathan Rosenberg and L. E. Birdzell, *How the West Grew Rich* (New York: 1986), 40; Norman F. Cantor, *Medieval History: The Life and Death of a Civilization* (London: Macmillan, 1969), 533.

3. Paul Kennedy, *The Rise and Fall of the Great Powers* (New York: Random House, 1987), 21; Rosenberg and Birdzell, *West*, 63–64; Cantor, *Medieval History*, 542.

4. Peter Stanford, *The Devil: A Biography* (New York: Henry Holt, 1996), 145–52. The saint with terrifying nightmares was Santa Francesca Romana (1384–1440).

5. Douglas C. McMurtrie, *The Gutenberg Documents* (New York: Oxford University Press, 1941), 27–28.

6. Cantor, *Medieval History*, 253–54.

7. Fernand Braudel, *The Wheels of Commerce*, trans. Sian Reynold (New York: Harper & Row, 1982); Cantor, *Medieval History*, 253.

8. Authorities thus prohibited sellers from setting the price for their wares, and for the centuries before Gutenberg's arrival had not allowed prices even to fluctuate. They kept the price of bread, for example, the same when wheat was plentiful and when it was scarce. When it was scarce, however, they permitted the merchants to shrink the size of the loaf while charging the same as they had for larger loaves. Rosenberg and Birdzell, *West*, 91–92.

9. Rosenberg and Birdzell, *West*, 96–97, 60.

10. Rosenberg and Birdzell, *West*, 91. "Decentralized, largely unsupervised growth of commerce and merchants and ports and markets were of the greatest significance," adds Paul Kennedy (*Rise and Fall of the Great Powers*, 19). "There was no way in which such economic developments could be fully suppressed."

11. Continuing to buckle under to the noblemen no longer appeared inevitable for a number of reasons. Notions of honor and duty—potent inhibitors of the bourgeoisie's power for four centuries—had been muddied by the cynical brutality of the constant warfare and the unfairness of epidemics. The patricians' weaponry was no longer as formidable. And the "moral" case for continuing to pay the feudal lords, often promoted by the clergy, was weak. The burghers in many towns resented the clergy as much as they resented the patricians. Traders and merchants enthusiastically supported the anticlerical movements that swept through the region with regularity. (So did a number of popes; Innocent III, cracking down on dissidents, called the leading priests of France "dumb dogs who can no longer bark.") Town and even court writers regularly made fun of clergymen. In Italy, Europe's most urban and sophisticated culture, Boccaccio's writings in the 1300s characterized Church authorities as randy, lazy, and fat. A typical guildsman in Gutenberg's stern, devout, less worldly German towns "felt that every clergyman should work for a living and that the cleric should not enjoy the powers and privileges of ecclesiastical office unless he demonstrated by his personal life that he was truly a minister of Christ. The burgher should be a businessman and the priest a saint; everyone should fulfill the obligations of his calling in life." Cantor, *Medieval History*, 412–18.

12. "Brief History of Early Printing," 20501; van Loon, *Observations*, 12–18. Gutenberg in the early 1450s was receiving income (26 florins a year) from a Strasbourg property, suggesting that the family either had the property when it moved to the area or later acquired it. Douglas C. McMurtrie, *The Gutenberg Documents* (New York: Oxford University Press, 1941), 36, 28. Gutenberg's partner knight was Luthold von Ramstein. McMurtrie, *Gutenberg Documents*, 35–36.

13. Janet Ing, *Johann Gutenberg and His Bible: A Historical Study* (New York: Typophiles, 1988), 22.

14. Van Loon, *Observations*, 7; Chappell, *Short History*, 59; "Brief History of Early Printing," 20501. McMurtrie, a careful scholar and one of the few to catalog documentary slips of evidence suggesting that Gutenberg existed, was not sure that Jo-

hannes did marry the woman immediately after the lawsuit: *Gutenberg Documents*, 38; Ing, *Gutenberg*, 12.

15. Ing, *Gutenberg*, 51; James Mosley, "The Enigma of Early Lyonnaise Printing Types," *La lumitype-photon: Rene Higonnet, Louis Moyroud et l'invention de la photo-compostion moderne*, ed. Alan Marshall (Lyon: Musee de l'impermerie et de la banque, 1994), 13–28; S. H. Steinberg, *Five Hundred Years of Printing* (Baltimore: Penguin, 1955), 23–26. The partnership he formed in 1438 in Mainz with Andres Dritzehn—a goldsmith with whom Gutenberg had worked—and Andreas and Anton Heilmann is discussed in all these sources. It is van Loon who interprets a legal document from Mainz as pegging the business's purpose as printing books, not producing mirrors.

16. Van Loon, *Observations*, 34; Henri Bouchet, *The Book: Its Printers, Illustrators and Binders from Gutenberg to the Present Time*, ed. H. Grevel (New York: Scribner & Welford, 1890), 10.

17. Hans Dunne, the former employee, was hired in 1436 to help Gutenberg build "forms" and a "press." McMurtrie, *Gutenberg Documents*, 39.

18. Controversy over whether to credit Gutenberg or Coster, Castaldi or Mentelin or even Schoeffer with the invention of the printing press has had a vibrant academic life of its own. The lack of any substantive documentary evidence from the time has left a fertile field for myth—some of it entertaining—to grow over the subject. Even among those who champion Gutenberg, there's debate over whether he did the deed in Mainz or Strasbourg. A history written in 1587, more than a hundred years after the fact, credits Mentelin. Still others see Coster as the original genius. The only documentary evidence in Gutenberg's favor seems to come out of his lawsuit over the failure of his 1437 partnership. Coster's champion was historian Hadrian Junius, who originated the story of Coster coming up with the idea of small blocks of type while playing with his children. Bouchet, *The Book*, 16; Steinberg, *Five Hundred Years*, 25. Concise examinations of the allegations that Gutenberg stole the idea for his press and that Coster or later the Italian Castaldi were the true European inventors of movable type are from Ing, *Gutenberg*, 40–48; and van Loon, *Observations*, 28–30. On Waldfoghel, see H. L. Johnson, *Gutenberg and the Book of Books* (New York: Rudge, 1932).

19. Chappell, *Short History*, 59–60; "Brief History of Early Printing," 20502.

20. Gutenberg's partnership with Andrew Dritzehen and Andrew Heilmann included a provision that if one of the partners died, the survivors would repay the investment to dead partner's heirs. The heirs, however, had no rights in the venture. Dritzehen died after putting 300 florins into the project, "an enormous sum in those days." Gutenberg duly offered to pay off Andrew's brother Nicholas, who instead wanted to join the business. Gutenberg, perhaps to save the money, agreed. Heilmann, the third partner, protested and apparently accused Gutenberg of hiding "certain arts" even from him. He also objected to having the ambitious relative at the secret skunkworks; Gutenberg sent a "servant" to tell Nicholas to break up "four forms placed in a press." Bouchet, *The Book*, 17.

21. Steinberg, *Five Hundred Years*, 26–27.

22. "Brief History of Early Printing," 20501; Mosley, "Enigma," 16.

23. Frederick G. Kilgour, *The Evolution of the Book* (New York: Oxford University Press, 1998), 85; McMurtrie, *Gutenberg Documents*, 37.

24. McMurtrie, *Gutenberg Documents*, 33.

25. McMurtrie, *Gutenberg Documents*, 36; Chappell, *Short History*, 59–60; Bouchet, *The Book*, 90, 10–11. Coster also printed and sold a Latin work called *Ars Moriendi*, "a kind of dialogue between an angel and the devil at the bedside of a dying person." The story remained in demand at least until 1480.

26. Bouchet, *The Book*, 19–20; McMurtrie, *Gutenberg Documents*, 37; Chappell, *Short History*, 60–61. The only firsthand accounts of what happened in Gutenberg's shop came from interviews with Schoeffer, conducted long after the fact. Schoeffer's reminiscences are in *The Spanheim Chronicles of 1495–1509*, a general history of Germany written by Jacob Wimpheling, who claimed to have interviewed Schoeffer in 1515. Schoeffer, in turn, said that he and Gutenberg eventually perfected their press in Mainz, regardless of the work Gutenberg had done previously in Strassbourg. Mosley, "Enigma," 13–28.

27. Ing, *Johann Gutenberg*, 69. Ing estimates Gutenberg produced 150 to 180 copies.

28. Kilgour, *Evolution*, 91; Bouchet, *The Book*, 20–21.

29. Chappell, *Short History*, 85.

30. Bouchet, *The Book*, 22.

4

A CERTAIN SCRAMBLING

Schoeffer and Fust lost no time. By the end of 1455, they had finished Gutenberg's Bible and were selling it. Perhaps alive to the willingness of the wealthy to pay for things like letters of indulgence, they used the type they had taken from Gutenberg to publish an expensive two-color prayer book, the Mainz Psalter, in 1457. It may have been printed privately for a few churchmen or patricians.[1]

Aiming at different Church buyers, Fust and Schoeffer followed it up with less elaborate religious books in 1457 and 1459. In 1460, they published a pamphlet greeting a new pope. Then Fust took to the road, showing up in several towns during the next years, selling mechanically written books. Others took notice.

In Strasbourg, the type threader Johannes Mentelin brought out a printed Bible, about a third smaller, to compete with the Gutenberg/Fust/Schoeffer edition on the market.[2] Using some equipment apparently repossessed from Gutenberg in yet another bankruptcy, an artisan named Albrecht Pfister produced a book in Bamberg in 1461. At least one more press was built in Mainz by then. There were perhaps as many as four.

Then Europe's feral tribal politics intervened and effectively spread the practice farther. Angered by the independence of Mainz's clerical leader, the pope sicced a bellicose archbishop, Adolph of Nassau, on the town in 1462. Adolph's army conquered it handily, sacked it, rousted the local priests, and displaced the guilds for the moment. Amid the flames, the bishop generously offered to spare Fust's life if he agreed not to use his press anymore. (The device, according to one account, was already burned and ruined anyway; according to another, Schoeffer had removed it safely to Bamberg.)[3] The other printers in town, less than reassured by the archbishop's show of mercy, fled.

Like the Chinese papermakers seven hundred years before, they took their craft with them. A Mainz printer named Berthold Ruppel fled to Basel, for example, where he was reproducing writing again by 1466. A Schoeffer employee and his associate ran to a Benedictine monastery near Rome, where they too built a Gutenberg machine and began to print. "Itinerant Germans" set up Spain's first press in Valencia. Similar devices were in Cologne by 1466, Venice by 1467, Augsburg by 1468, in Paris and Nuremberg and Westminster by 1470, and in Stockholm by 1483. About a hundred cities in Europe abruptly had printing, forty-seven of them in Italy, perhaps two dozen in France. By 1500, there were forty-five printers in France, fifty in Germany, seventy-three in Italy. In all, as many as 1,000 printers were at work on the continent. They churned out an estimated 6 million copies of 30,000 different titles in the medium's first decades.[4]

Their first books were almost wholly Christian and usually mystical in content. Almost all (about 75 percent of them) were in Latin. The prayerful *The Book of Hours* became a staple, as did long chronicles of demonic struggles and saintly perseverance. The first printed novels—*Edelstein* by Ulrich Bonner and *Ackermann aus Böhmen* by Johannes von Tepl—were similar moralizing tales. Schoeffer, competing now with Mentelin, brought out an even more compact Latin Bible in 1462, using new, cleaner type. Fust finally published a nonreligious book in 1465, *De Officiis* by Cicero. But almost all the popular books during the printed word's infancy were overtly pious, full of dramatically demonstrated virtue. The first best-selling novel was *Imitation of Christ* by Thomas à Kempis, printed in Augsburg. An initial book-length infatuation in France was *Dances of Death*. It featured Death "taking the great ones of the earth, torturing alike pope, emperor, constable or minstrel, grimacing at youth, majesty and love."[5]

These books, another historian later marveled, all maintained that "life, from cradle to grave, is a miserable, vulnerable affair; man's sins are too many to count, but the main ones are pride, luxury and gluttony; men in general obey the promptings of the flesh and ignore those of the spirit; the church itself is full of simony and pompous worldlings."[6]

Books, however, were not the only—or most important—products of the curious new factories. Short, seemingly innocent secular printed works appeared in increasing numbers. Pamphlets about medicines and laws, as well as the directives of certain burghers, clerical leaders, and noblemen, multiplied wherever printing spread. So did odd new interpretations of directives and treatments. Some instructed laymen how to perform previously unknowable tasks. Some led to questions.

Math, weight, and price tables, for example, appeared. Until that moment, decimal arithmetic had been an arcane, mostly forgotten skill from ancient Greece. Only court dukes and burghers could use it. Most of the world, in truth, had gotten along fine without it. In a barter economy, there was little need to calculate much more exactly than the raw numbers of loaves you delivered or what could be carried in the span of your arms. It became helpful to measure things more finely only as the money economy stirred in the decades leading up to Gutenberg's invention. Few, however, knew how. The simple new sheets with simple charts helped. An illiterate trader could now tell how much something was supposed to weigh without needing to perform calculations.[7]

Commerce became less complicated, faster, open to less-educated people. Then more printed conveniences appeared: bills of exchange and letters of credit that, properly reproduced and filed with a guild, could legally prove that a merchant had delivered something and could force the buyer to pay him. The papers gave the burghers' transactions a crucial security that had never before been available. Thanks to a new series of works from an Italian named Luca Paciolo, there was even something called double-entry bookkeeping to track money, find fraud, and, perhaps even more indicative of the day's changes, calculate profit.[8]

With faster commerce, people needed to change price lists more often. Archimedes, Pythagoras, and algebra were exhumed to help. With algebra came notions of calculating larger values, of putting them in order, and, soon, of different kinds of value. Plato, dusted off a few decades earlier by sophisticates in Italy, caused a sensation among those who, now that they could read him, were interested in such questions of both value and order. Thought provoked thought. In Florence, the humanist Marsilio Ficino wondered if, maybe, there was an order in nature as well as a divine order in the universe, and began to win converts among students who, until that day, had learned by rote repeating of Scripture. Accurate versions of Aristotle appeared. In 1469 came Pliny's *Natural History*. Cicero and St. Augustine and Boccaccio, whose ideas could well cause still more questioning among the led, were all available in multiple copies of print to multitudes of readers by 1473. Little of it had existed, inside or outside the closed private rooms of a few individuals, just a few years before.

Copies of printed directions and pictures—maps—also began to circulate in the 1460s and 1470s, with unintended consequences. Both sea and land navigation in Europe had been awful since about 400, when mapmaking, once marginally organized and cataloged by the Romans, fell to disparate fiefdoms and adventurers who did not talk to each other, much less share information. For a thousand years, maps occasionally were traced and, in the process, corrupted by various copyists' shaky hands or fertile imaginations. New maps often stayed private, the property of whoever initially drew them. They also were hard to use. In the twelfth century, the Arab geographer al-Idrisi published a map of the world, notable because no one with credible information, scholarly energy, or as much skill had ever tried such a thing before. He needed seventy charts to do it. Only a few copies of each one were made. By about 1300, there was at last a sizable map repository at the University of Vienna.[9] Yet accurate copies of them were rare and inaccessible to most travelers.

Now, as presses spread, maps were cheap to produce and easy to update with users' comments, experiences, and measurements. In the heartbeat of a couple of decades, growing numbers of common travelers, traders, and royally commissioned soldiers alike suddenly moved more easily, cheaply, and rapidly than any of the generations of *Homo sapiens* that had preceded them. And they, more actively and vividly than any of their predecessors, could now imagine that something might exist beyond the horizon.

In 1493, for example, an eight-page pamphlet was printed in Spain. It reported that someone had found a whole new world, way beyond the ocean. Within two years, hundreds of copies of the report about Christopher Columbus's journey had been reprinted in Rome, Paris, Basel, Antwerp, and Tuscany.[10] In London, Lisbon, Paris, and other places, a certain scrambling began.

So it was that in the last half of the fifteenth century an abrupt new communications tool lobbed scores of ideas into unfamiliar environments. Human memory seemed to expand. As had happened in Egypt when papyrus and hieratic were invented and in Greece when a new alphabet made writing easier, minute and soon wild mutations of thought and behavior followed the invention of the printed word in Europe. Suddenly more people saw more things, heard about tools, demons, techniques, dangers, everything. Most came from beyond the economic, geographic, and political obstacles that had stopped facts from reaching them in the past. A new fact altered a belief here. A foreign impression fused to a question there, and changed it. One was the "idea of an open-ended investigatory process pressing against ever-advancing ideas."[11] Science.

That idea too had laid dormant, unseen, and mostly unused since the second century, when the Greek Galen had taught the importance of experiment and observation—in effect, the scientific method.

The Greek Democritus, by suggesting that even the four known life materials of earth, wind, fire, and water might be made up of smaller building blocks, had long before formed what led to atomic theory. In the 1200s, Syrian physician Ibn al-Nafis had offered a theory that blood circulates through the body. In the mid-1300s, Roger Bacon had posited a law of inertia at Oxford. Nicholas of Oresme made a case that the world itself turned on an axis in the late 1300s.[12] Norwegians had braved the North Atlantic's huge swells back in the eleventh century.

But like everyone else in Europe at the time, the Norwegians had an oral culture and word of their adventure obviously was never printed. It thus died away as the first settlements and the first audiences that heard the tale died away in the thirteenth century and faded into the folklore of an isolated people. Bright notions like Nicholas's and Bacon's and Amenhotep's, which had not happened to reach the ear of someone who saw utility in them, similarly fell into disuse or into circles of small, uncommunicative elites.

Now, borne on sheets of paper, they rattled via cart across Europe. The amount of information available to a literate European by 1500, one enterprising geologist figured centuries later, grew by a factor of 1 million in about fifty years. The press, in short, "expanded data pools beyond all previous limits."[13]

With the new mass of information came speed. As in the subatomic world, the meeting of speed and matter loosed more energy: new kinds of crops, the barometer, and the gimbaled compass appeared within fifty years of the new medium's invention. So did deep mining techniques. Safer, more efficient Italian construction methods showed up in England. Syrian medical theory appeared in Spain. In the rapid "upward spiral in knowledge," sailing ships were redesigned, made faster, more easily navigable and capable of traversing still greater distances.[14]

Europe's ninety-year depression, not coincidentally, ended. The amount of land under cultivation during the late 1400s expanded for the first time since 1370. The number of cottagers—people who baked or sewed or shaped or glued raw materials in their homes at the direction of merchants who sold the finished goods—apparently increased as well. And as the "minutely fragmented sovereignties" that had impeded trade in the feudal countryside became less able to impose their will on commerce, trading blocks became larger.[15] Still more useful goods from distant trading partners again began to show up on the rising tide.

Another reason prosperity returned, of course, was that an important new industry—printing—had been created. People who had been mere artisans and calligraphers could, miraculously, generate and accumulate wealth.

Gutenberg himself was not among them. When Fust foreclosed on him in 1456, his precious technical secrets, his designs, his tools, his press, and the support he needed to exploit them all were lost. Desperate again, he borrowed still more money. He lost that too. In 1458, he stopped paying even the interest on his 1442 loan from the Chapter of St. Thomas in Strasbourg, and the next year his new equipment was foreclosed upon by the aforementioned Albrecht Pfister, who eventually fled with it to Bamberg. In 1459, yet another dreamer, a Mainz lawyer named Konrad Humery, took a flyer on the artisan. Gutenberg used the money to publish yet another Latin grammar text, *Catholicon*. Behind its title page, Gutenberg impressed the only printed words ever attributed directly to him. The passage thanked God and claimed "this book was perfected without the usual help of pen or style, but by the admirable linking of formes and types."[16] It too failed to lift him from poverty.

He apparently was out of printing for good after that, a bystander amid the accelerating bustle. He owned only some pieces of type and, it seems, rapidly deteriorating eyesight. Possibly through Humery's court connections, the new archbishop took a liking to the aging inventor and, for reasons that are even more obscure, actually granted him a pension. Gutenberg was given a new garment, some wheat, wine, and the right to eat at the archbishop's palace.

Apparently sustained only by the meager pension and Humery's ongoing charity, the inventor died blind in 1468. Humery generously placed a tombstone at the grave, citing Gutenberg as the inventor of the printed word. But the church at which he was buried, as well his grave, was lost to redevelopment in 1742.[17]

He was not the only lost soul. In the early 1460s, just as two refugee German printers set up shop near Rome, the aging Cosimo d'Medici resolved to build one last monument in his handcrafted republic of Florence. It would be a vast library. Bulging with two hundred volumes, it would challenge the world's largest collections, which at that time rarely exceeded three hundred books.

To supply them he called in the greatest copyist of the day: Vespasiano di Bisticci. Vespasiano had trained with the legendary Frederick of Montefeltro, and his clients included two popes and the richest noble families of the land. His scribes were famous for producing beautiful works quickly.

They delivered bound manuscripts on paper to commoners, on vellum to the nobility.

But when Cosimo, in his seventies and anxious to have his library, suggested that Vespasiano might use one of the fast, new German paper-stamping machines to fill the massive order, Vespasiano recoiled. Perhaps Cosimo was joking? The great copyist Frederick, Vespasiano scolded, "would have been ashamed to own a printed book." He assured the elder that, in return for a daily fee, his copyists could easily produce the two hundred volumes in just twenty-two months. They would, he added, be far more beautiful than anything the creaky, violent contraptions from the north could possibly manufacture.

Vespasiano was not wrong. His shop produced elegantly penned, often gorgeously illuminated works, taking "care to show honor to the contents of a book by the beauty of its outward form." A gentleman, he counseled his students, would never foul a proper library with a roughly inked, manufactured book on coarse rag paper. And since gentlemen had until that moment been the only people to buy Vespasiano's books, he no doubt saw little reason to resort to a device to grind out ugly tracts that his customers would never deign—or *should* never deign—to purchase.[18]

His snobbery was not entirely laughable. Everything before and around him in late medieval Europe told Vespasiano that art must in its order, tone, content, and appearance reflect the order, tone, content, and appearance of God, the Church, even the eventual cure for mankind's grim mortal condition. Good art demonstrated its maker's true faith, strict morals, and virtue. (That art had to be moral remained a rule among the growing intellectual and scientific communities until the late 1600s, when the regulation of the printed word happened to sag in some places, and then in the nineteenth century when the price of information fell precipitously again.) Vespasiano was not going to wreck his reputation or imperil his soul just because his client wanted fast delivery.[19]

But, in retrospect, his encounter was not with virtue. It was with commercial capitalism, a new and still unnamed phenomenon. By the time the pamphlet reporting Columbus's journey was printed in 1493, of course, Vespasiano and his craft had tut-tutted their way nearly to oblivion. The last of the manuscript copyists probably disappeared in the early 1500s. (Needless to say, hand copyists of business documents, later called scriveners and secretaries, continued to work until about 1900.)

Vespasiano's horror at the new, however, became a historic tradition. In the ages to come, the very best and most honorable artists, craftsmen, and business and word people energetically scoffed at new technology, at the quality of the work the new tools produced, and at the taste of the people who would buy such shoddy workmanship. "Printing," a press owner would lament in 1817, soon after a phenomenal new steam press debuted in London and replaced the screw- and lever-driven press Gutenberg had invented, "was born perfect and has degenerated ever since." When mechanical type composition—the technology that Lou Felicio would use—threatened to replace the artful, knowledgeable, complex humans who laid out letters in the 1880s, alarms about the damage machine type would cause to the eye and to the culture arose throughout the industry. In 1948, a Linotype company spokesman interviewed about the revolutionary photo type devices, fax machines, "jumping inks," and teletypes then threatening Linotype's supremacy, sniffed that "none of the new machines measure up to the machine casting method of producing type." By 1970, the marriage of phototype, offset printing, and the computer brought on a rude and meaner age. The freakish combination, a longtime printer and writer warned, produced a mere "*imitation* of printing, a picture of type that is not tactile in either form or expression." It could not possibly yield a "desirable" reading experience. A professor of printing added that typing through a cathode ray tube, just then becoming feasible, produced only an unreadable "stair-step effect" in the letters when they were printed. By 1996, a technical writer found the startling software that allowed people to compose colorful documents on their computer screens had only a "lamentable" ability to hyphenate and justify lines. He was scandalized that designers were clamoring for ways to apply the same pathetic standards to "the magnificent-and-hellish World Wide Web." "All printing is," counseled a retired Southern California printer two years later, "is getting the eye to go where you want it to go. But take typography from 50, 60 years ago, and compare it with today. *Terrible!*" His voice rising in exclamation, he asked his interviewer, "Do you know why everyone went to color printing? It's because typography got so bad that they had to do *something* to make (images) visible." And, less than sixty days before the third millennium began, two massive companies announced a plan to publish electronic books on the Internet. "Are you thinking that [e-books] will be accepted by the masses?" the owner of a copy shop in San Francisco incredulously asked fellow printers in an e-mail discussion group. "I sure hope not. Don't you think after sitting in front of a computer all day people will want a break and still read the old-fashioned way? I think and hope e-books will be a flop."[20]

Scoffers through the ages worried about what improvements in speed and memory tools meant for humankind. Everything about us—learning skills, motor skills, civic values—seemed to be endangered. Socrates, on confronting the just minted Greek alphabet and the strange new practice of using it to write things down, supposedly saw nothing but despair. The memory skills of the teacher who imparted knowledge by speaking would soon decay, he mourned. The magical growth of understanding that came from the face-to-face interchange of teacher and student would wilt and be lost.

And in the first decades of the printed word, even the growing stream of sacred literature alarmed many people like Vespasiano. Scriptural documents created out of mechanical yanking and probably not a little profanity were, it was said, "a debasement of the manuscript."[21]

Needless to say the aesthetes of the 1400s, like the dissenters of later centuries, also knew the new machine threatened more than virtue. It imperiled their livelihoods.

In 1457, the first appearance of Fust's elaborate *Mainz Psalter* "gave rise to protest from the calligraphers." Organized into guilds in many towns, the copyists explicitly denied membership to the interloping artificial writers. They invoked "charter rights"—royal permissions to serve as the sole reproducers of writing—wherever they had them, thus allowing nonmembers who tried to reproduce words without them to be arrested and fined. They could be violent too. In 1465, Fust arrived in Paris with a cart full of books to sell, only to be accused of witchcraft. The proof was in his inventory. His products were the work of the devil, his accusers said shortly before they tried to run him out of town. Fust was forced to hide. One historian speculates the copyists' guild was behind the hysteria.[22]

But compelling economics were at work against the old guard. Machine knowledge was dramatically cheaper to produce than handwritten knowledge.

For one thing, the word stampers used a new rag paper that was easier to make than parchment, and far less expensive than vellum. Copyists, a scholar later estimated, would have needed the skins of two hundred sheep—the herd of a wealthy person in medieval Europe—for the vellum to reproduce *each* of Gutenberg's 150 or so printed Bibles.[23]

A copyist still working in Paris in 1485 thus charged the father of Francois I of France the modern equivalent of $4,000 for three hand-penned books.[24] Fust sold machine-made books in the same town for sixty crowns each, apparently something near a dollar today. He could charge less, of course, because his artificial writing was far less labor intensive than writing by hand. In Italy, Vespasiano employed as many as fifty-five people to produce the Medicis' two hundred books. They manufactured less than four copies per person. Gutenberg, Schoeffer, and a succession of assistants produced about fifty copies of the Mainz Bible per person. But only one worker could produce scores of copies of a map or a flier or a prayer sheet or a math table.

Despite the copyists' hostility, Peter Schoeffer founded a printing business that lasted another sixty years. Johannes Mentelin, now privy to Gutenberg's secrets, was succeeded by sons-in-law and then grandchildren and then great-grandchildren in a business that lasted until 1548. They quickly learned to exploit the new technology profitably too. Schoeffer could turn out several hundred copies of an official proclamation at a time by 1470. By 1498, a printer in Barcelona could produce 18,000 letters of indulgence in a month. Sales and distribution channels grew too. At Frankfurt, a market in hand-copied books mushroomed into a booming printed book fair, drawing artisans and shopkeepers from all over central Europe. Copycat markets arose, usually in and around the percolating trading, shipping, and banking centers.[25]

A printed word business thus began to emerge. A priest, doctor, schoolmaster, and printer hooked up in Milan in 1472 to form what might have been the world's first company designed to choose, manufacture, and distribute knowledge. Three years later, a patrician, punch cutter, printer, and university administrator joined to print textbooks and sell them to a captive market of students at the university at Perugia, Italy. In Paris, a prosperous family of master butchers invested in and then ran one of the city's first successful printing operations. While Fust funded Schoeffer, the ruling family of the duchy of Modena helped finance what would become the legendary Venice printing business of Aldus Manutius.[26]

And in another of history's silent developments, these printers began to adapt their technology to their buyers' broader tastes and needs. Still more perverse consequences would follow.

During the printed word's first decades of life, most documents and books were designed to look like the hand-copied manuscripts they replaced. Gutenberg's and then Schoeffer's first type styles were images of handwritten letters, aping their formalities and idiosyncrasies. At worst, "the letters were crabbed and obscured by a thicket of curlicues and scribal flourishes that made reading very difficult."[27] The idea, perhaps, was to fool readers into thinking they were buying hand-copied works, or at least to create something that looked familiar to them.

But now, in the 1480s, some German, Italian, and then French printers began using type styles so different that they might be called a different alphabet. In retrospect, these second-generation printers probably aimed to make their words more commercial, easier to read, and easier to manufacture. As they fiddled with type, however, the industry and soon human knowledge took a drastic turn toward the modern. The new styles—as a group called "Roman," "Antigua," or later "Aldine" type faces—were simple, with clean, clear lines. Their letters were easily distinguishable from each other. And there were fewer of them. Gutenberg's thick "black letter" or "Gothic" type had about three hundred characters, including purposefully combined images (called ligatures, which came out of Greek) like œ, §, æ, ff, and fl. Roman styles, by contrast, had only about forty.[28]

Once again, less proved to be more. Print lovers these days look back on roman type's invention as an Eden-like graphic miracle. They revere the great early type designers—Nicolas Jenson, then Francisco Griffo and Claude Garamond, William Caslon and John Baskerville—as artful engineers capable of producing fine, subtle lines out of molten metal.

And they moved us into light. As with the simplified alphabets of Egypt and Greece, their new styles of type made knowledge more accessible to more people. Now they became symbols of the still larger shifts in the species that grew from the phenomenon of cheap information.

In Venice, for example, a man named Aldus Manutius married into what had been a Vespasiano-like printing family, but one that had adopted the new technology. Aldus imagined that the new tool's shaky, smudged output could somehow be made to look more like Vespasiano's elegant works, and upon entering the business, hired the Frenchman Nicolas Jenson to design something better. Roman type was the result.

Aldus used it "not because it was beautiful but because it suited his commercial intentions in that it was condensed and narrow and therefore made the most economic use of the type area."[29]

Aldus and the growing numbers of second-generation printers, moreover, attracted subversive admirers. Like many thinkers and social critics of the 1890s, 1960s, and 1990s, the malcontents of the late 1400s—shut out of the expensive guild and Church-controlled scriptoria that had until then manufactured all human writing in Europe—flocked to a new communication technology. Relatively young and disgusted with the status quo in education, religion, and politics, they were the early adopters of printing, clean type, and helpful illustrations. Many were heirs of those faddish Italian merchant princes and awakened scholars. They had continued to pursue ancient texts, and by Aldus's time had elevated the pursuit into an ideology, a thirst for knowledge for its own sake. To them, the Greek and Roman pasts were veins of pure wonder. Reading Aristotle, Plato, Euclid, even the Gospels in their original Greek, they found the terrible mistakes in translation and interpretation that copyists, self-interested clerics, and ignorant rulers had made during the centuries. Great, absurd scholastic debates had cascaded from the errors. Since 1229, for instance, a commonly used Latin grammar text based on inept translations had listed "salt" as a synonym for "priest," "dog" as a synonym for "vile" and "deny," and "heretic" for "stick." Not a few students and theologians thus spent many good brain cells trying to figure out why "the heretical dog denies God and sticks to his heresy." At the University of Paris, similar goofs filled the theology classes with questions of whether God could have come back as an ox or an ass if He wished, and whether a donkey could be crucified.[30]

The thinkers who adapted the new technology in the late 1400s found a completely different world in the original ancient texts. In medieval Europe, man had become a depraved and originally flawed beast who might be saved only through faith and mortification of the flesh. He learned the inflexible, unchangeable rules of the universe by rote and prescribed teacherly beatings. The purpose of life was clear: endure the current misery, please the lords and the Lord, and you'll reach a specific, closed, perhaps happier end. Schools of the day did not bother to teach history. The world, after all, had always been the same and always would be.

In the newly available classical texts, by contrast, the Renaissance scholars encountered humans sired by powerful gods, offspring who inherited some of their parents' strength, cunning, and abilities. These mortal creatures could create beauty as well as violence, achieve speed and grace, build and improve as well as act capriciously. They speculated. They changed the gods' minds, defied fate, created unscripted ends.

Such defiant thoughts had been around northern Italy for a hundred years. But now Aldus and his fellow second-generation printers reproduced the premedieval works again and again, in revolutionary, easy-to-read type. They published the classical writers in their original Greek for people to read themselves. Then they published modern writers like Marsilio Ficino, Giovanni Pico della Mirandola, and Erasmus, who interpreted, extended, and applied classical thought to the late 1400s and early 1500s. Their cheap words, thanks to the new tools, spread far beyond the lavish private libraries and monkish chapels where ideas used to stall.

So, from the north, English and German and French humanists showed up at the Renaissance printers' doors in Venice and Florence. People like Aldus created "chairs" in Greek for them and printed more of their works. Then printers at the Sorbonne, in Louvain, London, Basel, Strasbourg, and, fatefully, Wittenberg noticed the heady success of these easily digested, provocative works. More importantly, with them spread a general belief that individuals could and should read for themselves. Having someone interpret words for you was not always necessary and was rarely desirable.

Early in the trajectory of the printed word, roman letters thus came to be the alphabet, or at least the style, of new thinkers, of "independent" thinking, of a world in which a person was supposed to think for him- or herself. As happened in Greece the last time an alphabet became more accessible and practical, a great intellectual explosion marked the next centuries of human experience. The alphabet itself came to represent even broader things: the whole tree of liberal Western thought, of those who saw knowledge—and eventually human grace—as the result of an individual's pursuit, not only as a received gift from above.

On the other hand, the black letter Latin or Gothic typestyles of received Holy Writ—knowledge that was meant to be heard and not seen—symbolically came to be the official, unquestioned language of remote, implacable, centralized authority. It would be so during the great explosions immediately following this new phenomenon of lower-priced knowledge. It would be so well into the future.

NOTES

1. Henri Bouchet, *The Book: Its Printers, Illustrators, and Binders from Gutenberg to the Present Time* (New York: Scribner & Welford, 1890), 31–32, 38. A 1609 book recounts how Fust arrived in Paris in the early 1460s with books to sell for sixty crowns each, claiming they were made by a copyist factory back across the Rhine. Both the price and the boast enraged "the corporate scribes of the university" at the Sorbonne, and they formally charged him with being a devil, a capital offense in those days. But because no records of such a charge exist from the time, most scholars suspect the story is a fable. Bouchet, *The Book*, 37.

2. S. H. Steinberg, *Five Hundred Years of Printing* (New York: Criterion, 1959), 41.

3. Steinberg, *Five Hundred Years*, 75–80; "A Brief History of Early Printing," *Scientific American*, July 7, 1900, 20501.

4. George N. Gordon, *The Communications Revolution: A History of Mass Media in the United States* (New York: Hastings House, 1977), 7–8; Steinberg, *Five Hundred Years*, 98–101; Cor Knops, *Book History Chronology*, November 1998, www.xs4all.nl/-knops/index3.htm (accessed November 3, 1999). The Schoeffer employee was Konrad Swenheym. Warren Chappell, *A Short History of the Printed Word* (New York: Knopf, 1970), 64–65; Chappell, *Short History*, 73; J. R. Hale, *Renaissance Europe, 1480–1520*, 2nd ed. (Malden, Mass.: Blackwell, 2000), 143, 214.

5. Steinberg, *Five Hundred Years*, 84. Both *Edelstein* and *Ackermann* were printed in German, and Steinberg maintains that the "content of non-Latin books (was) important because they suggest the taste of reading classes that had no Latin." In this case, the content were "moralizing tales." Steinberg, *Five Hundred Years*, 100;

Bouchet, *The Book*, 100; Chappell, *Short History*, 63; Willi Mengel, *Ottmar Mergenthaler and the Printing Revolution* (Brooklyn, N.Y: Mergenthaler Linotype Company, 1954), 16.

6. Hale, *Renaissance Europe*, 178. In Germany, sniffed a Frenchman writing in 1890, at a time when hatred between France and Germany was again running high, "bad taste and prodigality already began to be apparent" in German books of the latter part of the fifteen century. Bouchet, *The Book*, 102.

7. Elizabeth Eisenstein, *The Printing Press as Agent of Change* (Cambridge: Cambridge University Press, 1979), 467.

8. Paul Kennedy, *The Rise and Fall of the Great Powers* (New York: Random House, 1987), 19; Paul Strathern, *A Brief History of Economic Genius* (New York: Texere, 2001), 46.

9. Eisenstein, *Printing Press*, 483.

10. Paul Levinson, *The Soft Edge: A Natural History and Future of the Information Revolution* (London: Routledge, 1997), 27.

11. Eisenstein, *Printing Press*, 258–59.

12. Nathan Rosenberg and L. E. Birdzell, *How the West Grew Rich* (New York: Basic, 1986), 254–55; Norman F. Cantor, *Medieval History: The Life and Death of a Civilization* (London: Macmillan, 1969), 536; Bernard Lewis, *What Went Wrong* (New York: HarperCollins, 2002). 79.

13. Douglas S. Robertson, *The Next Renaissance*, as cited in Bob Davis, "Think Big," *Wall Street Journal*, January 11, 1999, R 14; Eisenstein, *Printing Press*, 258–59.

14. Kennedy, *Great Powers*, 29. A Spaniard named Andrea Alpago translated the Syrian Ibn al-Nafis's blood circulation theory into Spanish. It came to the attention of Michael Servetus, who ultimately popularized a European theory. Ibn al-Nafis's theory, left unpublished in his native land, was more or less ignored in the Arab world. Servetus was burned at the stake for his Catholicism in Protestant Geneva in 1553, but his writings survived to inspire William Harvey, who in 1628 proved through experimentation that blood does circulate. Lewis, *What Went Wrong*, 79–80.

15. Karl Polanyi, *The Great Transformation: The Political and Economic Origins of Our Time* (Boston: Beacon, 1944). 73–74; Rosenberg and Birdzell, *How the West Grew Rich*, 91.

16. Douglas C. McMurtrie, *The Gutenberg Documents* (New York: Oxford University Press, 1941), 37; Bouchet, *The Book*, 32–33. The *Catholicon* was a book of Latin grammar and religious terms authored by John Balbus of Genoa.

17. Janet Ing, *Johann Gutenberg and His Bible: A Historical Study* (New York: Typophiles, 1988). Ing speculates that the pension might have been in belated recognition of Gutenberg's production of a Bible. Chappell, *Short History*, 64.

18. Jakob Burkhardt, cited in Chappell, *Short History*, 35–37.

19. Jacques Barzun, *From Dawn to Decadence: 500 Years of Western Cultural Life* (New York: HarperCollins, 2000), 67.

20. J. C. Squire, "The Revival of Printing," *Publishers Weekly*, April 4, 1931, 1818; J. Howard Rutledge, "New Machines Promise to Outdate Newspaper Methods, Simplify Jobs," *Wall Street Journal*, January 13, 1948, 1; Chappell, *Short History*, 241–42; Kathleen Spangler, "New Technologies Challenge Classical Typography," in *Technological Changes in Printing and Publishing*, ed. Lowell H. Hattery and George P. Bush (Mt. Airy, Md.: Lomond, 1973), 40; Conrad Taylor, "What Has WYSIWYG Done to Us?" *Seybold Report on Publishing Systems*, September 30, 1996, 26. Gerald L. Bigalk, interview, October 9, 1998; discussion group message from lance@let-us .com LET US! Copy Inc. San Francisco, CA, www.let-us.com, on www.printshare @printweb.com (accessed on November 5, 1999).

21. Levinson, *Soft Edge*, 23. Levinson sees stigmatizing new media through the ages as a predictable part of the appearance of pioneering technology.

22. Bouchet, *The Book*, 33; Frederick W. Hamilton, *A Brief History of Printing, Part II* (Chicago: United Typothetae of America, 1918), 30.

23. Alberto Manguel, *A History of Reading* (New York: Viking, 1996), 135.

24. The calligrapher was Antony Verard, who produced the works—the *Romance of Tristan* and two other secular works—in 1485 for Charles de Valois-Angouleme, father of Francois I. They were bound in dark velvet, with the duke's coat of arms. Bouchet, *The Book*, 94.

25. Steinberg, *Five Hundred Years*, 49. The speedy Barcelona printer was Johann Luschner, who reproduced the 18,000 letters of indulgence for the abbey of Montserrat. Individual abbeys used the letters to raise money, and by the end of the fifteenth century they had begun to print them in ever larger quantities. The average press run for these letters was probably about two hundred copies. Steinberg, *Five Hundred Years*, 100, 38–39.

26. Steinberg, *Five Hundred Years*, 92; Hale, *Renaissance Europe*, 140–41. "The capital outlay on press and founts and the delay between the printing of an edition and its sale at the outlets of a slow and costly distributive system," Hale pointed out, "meant that only a prosperous man, like the Parisian Jean Petit, who came from a family of master butchers, could set one up on his own." The dukes who invested in Aldus's press were the family of the brilliant polymath Pico della Mirandola, whose writings Aldus then faithfully published.

27. Charles L. Mee, *Erasmus: The Eye of the Hurricane* (New York: Coward, McCann & Geoghegan, 1974), 56.

28. Steinberg, *Five Hundred Years*, 32. Although Italian printers often lay claim to the Antigua style, it was first cut in Strasbourg in 1467.

29. Steinberg, *Five Hundred Years*, 32, 34.

30. The grammar text was by Englishman Ioannes de Garlandia, who taught at the University of Toulouse. Much of the confusion derived from Garlandia's faulty reading of an Old Testament episode in which King Saul asked David if he'd come out of his house after "a dead dog." The translator eventually solved the curious meaning of the question by deciding the word "heretic" was derived from the Latin

hacret. George Faludy, *Erasmus* (New York: Stein & Day, 1970), 22. The following were among the other debate topics at Paris: If God is omnipotent, can He make black into white? If God has a completely free will, can He contradict Himself? If He can make black into white and if He can contradict Himself, then can He not also make right into wrong and wrong into right? Justice into injustice? A damned man into a saved one . . . And if He cannot, then surely He is not omnipotent?" Mee, *Erasmus*, 29–30.

5

A HAPPY MAN, CONCERNED

In 1929, the Mergenthaler Linotype Company was a colossus in the printing industry. From its headquarters and factory in Brooklyn, where at that moment young Lou Felicio was growing up, it dispatched machines, parts, type fonts, salespeople, trainers, and even printers around the world. The famous company had some meaningful competition but dominated the industry. Gutenberg's print medium, despite wireless telegraphs and the recent appearance of commercial radio, remained the most important, frequently used, and admired form of mass communication.

It was in that year that Linotype sent an effusive New York salesman named Reginald Orcutt to Germany. Based in what he thought was a comically formal office in Berlin, he was to sell Linotypes to a continent that was still struggling in the aftermath of another brutal, paralyzing spasm of warfare.

Orcutt loved much. He loved his wife and daughter, parties, and especially travel. As a child, he'd been mesmerized by books about foreign lands. As an adult in 1921, he took the Mergenthaler job in part because it promised travel. But once in the company this sentimental man, a sucker for a good story, swooned again, this time for "the romance of the Linotype." For the rest of his life, he saw the Lino as "a machine of many tongues, composing the news of the world every day and every night in newspaper plants from Iceland to the South Seas . . . carrying speed for the printed word beyond all the oceans and across every frontier."[1]

His love for it started in what he thought of as a jail. Before it let him out on the road, the company sentenced him to a classroom for six months, for training. Orcutt was a little antsy. He recalls sitting by the window, looking out toward the places he wanted to go. He did rise dutifully at one point in the class to follow the instructor to a case full of metal letters. The instructor first pointed at a character that, to the impatient Orcutt, looked "like a letter *d* playing the violin." It was, the teacher explained, a lower case Icelandic *edh*. The *edh*, in turn, would soon be bound across the sea "with its companion *thot* as standard equipment of a Linotype for the Government Printing Office in Reykjavik." Then there was "a new font of Tataro-Bashkhir for Kazan and Tiflis, where tens of thousands of people are now at last beginning to learn to read."

Orcutt had never given type characters much thought. But these seemed to be something momentous, the seeds of change, of progress. Then his class went to watch the type designers. Orcutt, perhaps readily impressed, was impressed. The designers soon loomed as giants, artists who could create beauty out of engineering and philosophy. Their work had meaning.

"More than the layman may find it easy to appreciate," he said in his memoir, "every good type letter is fraught with human spirit. Whether its essence stems from the Humanists of the Renaissance, or comes from the artistic expression of tomorrow morning, its beauty and clarity—and thus its legibility and function—stem from the genius and personality of the artist who designed it and the craftsman who brought it into being." Orcutt concocted as many excuses as possible to hang around the craftsmen-engineers who could magically "recapture truly and completely in cold metal every characteristic touch and nuance of feeling of the artist."[2]

Orcutt thus found himself in a job that gave him everything: money, travel, passion, purpose. To him, his first sales trip to Iraq, birthplace of cuneiform four thousand years before, promised not just profit but geopolitical change, even human evolution. But the Arab world, the intellectual center of the world in 1300, was not the idea factory it used to be. The Ottoman Empire, which had included Iraq, bought its first press late, in 1710. Even then, its output was thin. Apparently under pressure from the calligraphers guild, the sultan forbade using the press to print Qur'anic Arabic script for a while. During the next thirty-one years his machine clanked out only seventeen books, most printed in Armenian or Greek type. It then was left unused for the next forty-three years. The family that bought it from the sultanate ran it for twelve years, producing five titles before going out of business in 1796. As revolutionary France bristled with two hundred fervid new newspapers in 1795, a Turkish engineering school quietly bought the empire's second press. There was not an operational press in Persia, modern-day Iran, from the late 1500s through the first half of the 1800s. Then, almost four hundred years after printed European news began, the *Ottoman Monitor* and the *Egyptian Gazette*, the first Middle Eastern newspapers, appeared. However, most remained "tools of Turkish authorities or foreign embassies" until the Ottoman Empire collapsed little more than a decade before Orcutt's arrival. As he checked into his hotel, Egypt had the closest thing to a well-established free press in the region. Morocco, Algeria, Tunisia, Syria, and Lebanon had newer, somewhat independent papers. In the British colonies like Palestine and Iraq, controlled newspapers generally existed to promote British imperial policy.[3]

Orcutt saw his mission in similar terms. "The securing of Persian oil [for the West] required the speeding of communications by road and plane, and this increasing contact with the world of progress inevitably meant bettering the standard of living, education, literacy, and the printed word. And of all of this the Linotype was an essential part."

Iraq's Government Printing Office in 1929 was in an old Turkish palace, run by an Englishman. "Here, by Allah, in the romantic heart of the ancient capital of Haroun al Raschid, was just such a place as that in which the stories of the Arabian Nights were originally told. And I must say that [the supervisor's] crisp English voice and rough tweeds seemed less of a heresy than the batteries of Arabic Linotypes that stood in the very structure that once housed exotic *houris* and odalisques. Silvery chatter had once mingled in these rooms with the plash of fountains and now, inappropriately, was replaced by the mechanical tinkle of Linotype matrices dropping to their assembly."[4]

When he got back to Europe, however, he discovered that something weird had begun to happen. Politicians suddenly were paying attention to Orcutt's beloved types, recruiting, altering, exalting, and exiling them for political purposes.

Austria had just forbidden its newspapers to use type larger than about a half-inch high. The government thus hoped to avoid "disturbing" its restive people. In Norway, authorities intent on reaffirming their twenty-year-old independence from Denmark forced the streetcar company in Bergen to repaint its signs, using a Norwegian *o* (which has an umlaut over it) instead of a Danish *o* (o, with a slash through the middle). They also changed the name of the capital city from Christiania (once a tribute to Denmark's King Christian IV) to Oslo, an ancient Norse word. In the Soviet Union, Josef Stalin forbade the use of native alphabets in Central Asia, reducing what were supposed to be allied republics into colonies of the Russian speakers. His blunt new government then "tore two characters out of the Tsar's Cyrillic alphabet and sent them into absolute banishment." The opposition White Russian press in Belgrade, Paris, and New York defiantly kept them in their dispatches. Turkey, this time because it was intent on westernizing, banned printing in Arabic letters again. In Yugoslavia, there was armed conflict between proponents of the Cyrillic alphabet, which represented the Orthodox Church, and of the roman alphabet of the Catholics.[5]

Well beneath the international leagues, official rapproachments and ambitious treaties that defined the era's diplomatic history, Orcutt realized that civilization's tiniest symbols and dots were in violent upheaval. It had happened before. Vain, ambitious men—even entire countries—had fiddled with type and letter styles to reflect their own glory ever since Gutenberg and Schoeffer invented them. As modern corporations strained to invent special logotypes to differentiate themselves from their competitors, so entire cultures used type to differentiate themselves from enemies and from their own pasts. They altered languages and banned words to isolate opponents. They promoted fonts to suggest grandeur, specialness, superiority. In 1556, French nationalism inspired Robert Granjon to establish a national type. (Called Civilite, it never caught on as a readable font for body text.) In 1692, nationalists tried again. Louis XIV, advancing France's campaign to outshine the Netherlands as the continent's preeminent power, commissioned the design of *Romain du roi*, a type that would exhibit "the cold brilliance[,] the absolute monarchy and logical mind of France." (Appropriately, he hired engineers, not artists, to fashion it. From above, they dictated that France's official letters had to fit in a rectangle divisible by 2,304 equal units.) The style, not coincidentally, came to reflect the remote, soulless autocracy itself. During the French Revolution years later, it was actively repressed as a symbol of inhumane government. At the same time, Italian monarchist Giambattista Bodoni designed a typeface that is in wide use today, but in fitfully nationalist Italy had far too much kingly "solemnity" and "pomposity" to become immediately popular. England's most common type styles, designed in the eighteenth century by William Caslon and John Baskerville, came to reflect (at least to the English mind) the fine English values of legibility, common sense, and adaptability. They had the "great virtue of unobtrusiveness combined with eminent readability." Their zenith coincided with Britain's rise as an efficient, adaptable, utilitarian industrial and imperial power. As England grew wealthier, German intellectuals at the beginning of the nineteenth century wondered why. They soon got to the subject of type styles. "Judicious men had . . . come to see that the stubborn adherence to gothic [black letter] type was a main obstacle to Germany's full share in the life of the civilized world." It also explained, they said, why the rest of the world had been too dull to adopt German culture. One gram-marian thought Gothic-style type was "undoubtedly the reason that pre-vents other nations from learning our language, and thus deprives them of the many good books produced in Germany." Traditionalists, however, kept the nation proudly tied to black letter type into the 1800s. On the other hand, the "nationalistic associations of 'German' script" led the German-fearing Scandinavian countries to develop their own roman typestyles.[6]

When Reginald Orcutt visited Belgium in 1929, he found political storms raging over whether to use Flemish or French on street signs. In Fin-land, students rioted over whether classes should be taught in Finnish or Swedish. In Orcutt's home base of Germany, there was a wholesale purge of foreign words. The telephone became the *Fernsprecher*. The elevator or lift, "hatefully English" words, became a *Fahrstuhl*, or "traveling seat." Sauce be-came *Tunke*, "a German word so ancient and obscure that even very few Germans knew what it meant." Followers of the rising Adolf Hitler swore militant allegiance to the ancient German black letters.

To Orcutt, who had a fondness for champagne and good jokes and in-teresting people, the wordplay was ominous. He wasn't sure why.

In the early 1940s, Hitler switched his thinking about letters. Seeking to promote Nazi science to the world, he decided gothic type was a "Jewish invention" and decreed that it never be used again.

But by then World War II was raging and Orcutt was far away, con-fined to Linotype's Brooklyn headquarters to wait out the horror. He could only look out his office window longingly, this time toward the distant slaughter and fire emptying and obliterating the charming neighborhoods and palaces he'd visited in Europe, the Middle East, and Africa. Friends were dead. Their kids were dead. Coworkers, loan officers, competitors, interns, publishers too poor to buy from him: all might well be dead. Many of his beloved machines probably were mangled, inoperable, gone.

Perhaps to temper his sadness, Reginald Orcutt began his memoir. At his desk, trapped by war, he cheered himself by writing about happier times. But when he got to the later 1920s, he finally saw what the confusing lan-guage and type reforms had meant. When the shapes, sounds, speed, and dis-tribution of information changed, larger things changed. "What seeds of hate and antagonism were being planted in those days," he reflected, "even among the very letters of the words that would sometime again cause the guns to speak—the guns that are so much more careless of their accents."[7]

NOTES

1. Reginald Orcutt, *Merchant of Alphabets* (Garden City, N.Y.: Doubleday, 1945), 6, 11.

2. Orcutt, *Merchant*, 10.

3. Bernard Lewis, *What Went Wrong: The Clash between Islam and Modernity in the Middle East* (New York: HarperCollins, 2002), 142–43; Said Essoulami, "The Press in the Arab World: 100 Years of Suppressed Freedom," Centre for Media Freedom, www.cmfmena.org/magazine/features/100_years.htm (accessed January 11, 2005).

4. Orcutt, *Merchant*, 53, 63.

5. Orcutt, *Merchant*, 13, 31–32; S. H. Steinberg, *Five Hundred Years of Printing* (New York: Criterion, 1959), 208, 210.

6. Steinberg, *Five Hundred Years*, 35, 120–21, 137, 127, 126, 128.

7. Orcutt, *Merchant*, 32.

6

THE TERRIBLE CONTAGION

As Reginald Orcutt pondered the chaos around him, the Linotype machine was barely fifty years old. Most of its oft revised alphabets were far younger. The languages they formed, moreover, were mutating. Phrases and words—much less concepts—like birth control, insulin, jazz, and tractors had not existed thirty years before. A historian of Orcutt's time pointed out that in 1900 "'drive' meant only an agreeable experience with a horse." By the time Orcutt was selling Linos internationally three decades later, that and hundreds of new words had been added to the language just to account for the automobile. At least 1,000 new words had been invented to describe the various sounds, parts, and habits associated with the radio. Aviation, a notion as fanciful in 1900 as time travel is today, had sprouted more hundreds of dictionary entries.[1]

Though Orcutt could not fully appreciate it in those first decades after his Linotype had revved up communication again, great empires already were falling and new forms of government were rising. Science was accumulating faster, and many of us were coming to understand human behavior and history as products of psychology, biology, and economics, as opposed to the state of men's souls. Self-consciously different, historically affluent youths were aggressively challenging venerated dogmas and making up new ones. Military power was shifting; incredible weapons were appearing. Transportation, education, literature, law, math, commercial organization, finance, and architecture were undergoing intense reform and rethinking. Radio was arriving as a popular medium, causing the whirlwind to accelerate again. New trade routes—like Orcutt's from Brooklyn to Berlin to Baghdad—were cheaper to exploit. Wealth was accruing among recent immigrants.

As in the first generations after the appearance of artificial writing and the new alphabets that made the printed word practical in the fifteenth century, not everyone was enthusiastic about these changed arts, altered technologies, half-understood threats, and lost virtues.

Had he been around, Orcutt would have seen how an abrupt speeding of information seemed to coincide with similar phenomena in the late 1400s. Fifteenth-century rulers, traders, and guardians of spiritual mystery—like their twentieth-century successors—also sensed danger amid letters' changing shapes and sounds. They lashed out in similar ways too. In 1462 the new archbishop of Mainz, for example, simply forbade reproducing letters by machine. Shortly thereafter, the University of Cologne forbade non-Latin letters in theological works. When that didn't restore their sense of calm, they demanded to review not only religious works but also secular documents that related to church affairs before letting common folk see them.[2]

They reasoned that between the lines in the new "vernacular" German, French, English, Italian, Spanish, and other native language works was the notion that congregants might interpret prayerful or political sentences in untutored, disruptive, and probably sinful ways.

Frankfurt and Mainz soon outdid Cologne, setting up a joint censorship office to regulate all secular books, regardless of language. And in 1487, Pope Innocent VII issued the first papal bull against "objectionable" books, generally meaning those that were not in Latin.[3]

Ultimately, the roaring in and around fifteen- and sixteenth-century Europe became no less awesome, literal, or murderous than the roaring Reginald Orcutt described in twentieth-century Europe. In new words and images, people in the late 1400s suddenly could create information more cheaply than ever before. It spread faster as well. Instead of one teacher reading aloud to many from a secret, incomprehensible text, now hundreds of writers and promoters spoke to thousands and then tens of thousands, privately. Perhaps not coincidentally, the wrenching realignments of Europe's tribes soon accelerated and deepened. Herds grew larger. They jostled for newly discovered commercial opportunities and trade routes, for newly valuable food supplies, raw materials, and, maybe to justify it all, for new ideas of what God had really meant.

New forms of government began to develop, with fiefdoms ceding to kingdoms and kingdoms, in turn, evolving into modern "national monarchies" capable of establishing order over the accelerating whirl of impressions and events. They wrested control over once subdivided England, Sweden, Austria, France, and Spain from old feudal aristocrats or, in Spain, foreign conquerors. Powerful nationalist notions also arose in the Holy Roman Empire's German duchies and the various states of Italy. Europe, once organized as a *republica christiana* where a group of select lords shepherded the dull flocks through secular affairs on Jesus' behalf, was becoming a *republica literarium* "in which every nation exerts its proportionate influence." At least in theory the royal ministers of the new monarchies crafted policy by a new and secular standard: the needs of the state. It was the "moral state," not the Church, "that stood between us and chaos."[4]

Needless to say, kings were more powerful than spiritual leaders in such states. Many were now richer and stronger than most local Church leaders, not least because they had partnered with the vibrant new merchant classes swamping or taking over the guilds. Nonnoble landowners and merchants played a crucial role in helping Henry VII consolidate his hundred-year Tudor dynasty in England. And the new monarchs, with their newly learned barristers, quickly memorialized their status in temporal law across Europe in the 1500s: even holy men were now subject to the laws of the monarchy. The monarchial state would take over interpreting and being guided by the laws of heaven.[5] (Absolute monarchs, of course, argued that whatever they happened to think was, because they happened to think it, the will of heaven.) Everything—armies, intellectual prowess, art, products, and beauty—came to be judged as reflections of a monarch's and a nation's glory. Ideas—languages, gods—beyond the nation's borders were bad. The ones inside the borders were good.

These were, in effect, unprecedented kinds of "imagined communities." In the metastasizing books and pamphlets, printed less and less in Latin and more frequently in readers' native languages, the printed word "helped fuse the idea of a distinct national language with a sense of common identity." Printing did not create national monarchies, but it made them possible in ways that had not existed in the past. Now, as generals would find in later centuries, broader communications made it possible to command larger swaths of territory. "Put simply," a scholar who otherwise put nothing simply later wrote, "the mental equipment that people drew upon in imagining and symbolizing forms of community itself underwent fundamental change."[6]

Charles of Valois, for instance, was one of several contenders for French territory. His "house" had controlled the throne for almost a century, but, in what eventually came to be called the Hundred Years War, he had fitfully lost territory to other feudal families and schemers struggling for tax money and land. The English, who supplied the muscle for the other families, were his most important rivals. England had occupied Paris just a few decades before, and retained a claim to it and several other provinces. It also had the support of much of the Church. The highborn clerics of the Sorbonne sent a sympathetic theologian to Rouen to judge and ultimately torture the confusing Joan d'Arc, who in the 1430s claimed God Himself was on Charles's side. After the public spectacle of Joan's trial, moreover, Charles found himself symbolizing something bigger. Public maps memorialized his advances; wider groups of people actually saw a nation for the first time. A real, "recognizably modern 'France'" was suddenly visible, far bigger and more important that the collection self-interested *monarchies petits*, regions and priests Charles was then fighting. [7]

It was a view at least as revolutionary as the first photos of the planet Earth, taken from space in the 1960s, which enlarged and redefined our view of our habitat. Our place in the universe literally looked different. Similarly, the maps of the 1400s did more than make transportation easier. They encouraged a different perspective of Europe's—and soon the world's—landscape. Historians and media theorists see it as nothing less than a change in our "spatial biases" that resulted in "a more rigid identification of political space."[8] It was understandable, flat, linear, and very different from the unknowable desires of God.

According to legend, Charles also liked these new maps. In 1458, he supposedly sent one Nicholas Jenson to Mainz to learn about the strange new artificial writing tool and perhaps its propaganda uses. Some historians doubt he ever dispatched Jenson, who soon showed up in Italy, but one of the newfangled machines did appear at the Sorbonne in 1470. From it and its companions poured what would become a rich river of thought. It floated the nationalist legends of Joan, of distinctly French values, distinctly French quality, and even distinctly French printing. It was an entity, a common and divinely created culture, a certain quality of outlook and talent that even internal enemies shared. Charles, or at least his followers, stoked the idea by celebrating Joan's behavior in song, sermon, and flier. The size of the idea doubled in two years (1481 and 1482), and its three hundred varieties of coinage finally unified into one. The productive tax system and well-organized military of the Valois gradually rolled the old feudal system of local privileges firmly into the control of their central royal administration in Paris. In 1484, the Estates General met to approve the new systems, the emergence of a French nation, and the monarchy's close identity with it. The legislature then adjourned, to meet again in some 150 years.[9]

Similar upheavals happened elsewhere. The English aristocrats whom Charles defeated returned home angry, threatened, and spiteful. Doing what they did best, they took up arms again. Out of their terrible civil war, now known as the War of the Roses, Henry VII emerged with control of a national throne. The Tudor kings, like the Valois kings, established a smaller, more efficient, overtly national court.[10] It, in turn, solidified internal control over its neighbors on the island, and gradually brought its fiefdoms and churches under its permanent sway. In Spain, Ferdinand and Isabella similarly united smaller kingdoms (initially through their marriage) and gradually subjugated feudal authorities by winning the right to appoint the grand masters of wealthy military orders, then title to more land, then control over the old royal councils.

They too used the printed word. Rulers' commands, once just posted or literally cried out in the streets, were now organized in books. England produced its first printed law books in the 1480s, a few short years after machine printing reached the island. The impact was monumental. The law itself—the rules that defined the state—changed from a loose collection of spoken commandments into an integrated, analyzed, changeable body of thought. Soon each new edict had to relate in some explainable way in philosophy and application to all previous edicts, now cataloged and open to trained lawyers.[11] England's approach, of course, grew in a different direction than the legal philosophies growing out of the new law books in France, which differed from Spain's. Each came alive, forming the spirit and DNA of each state's special identity.

We soon began putting other things into a new, printed order. In the late 1400s, we began using alphabetical indexes in books and dictionaries for the first time. We divided them into discrete sections. Ideas thus became easier to find and use. (Prior dictionaries listed words in no universal order at all.) Chronologies, useless in a society that did not teach history, appeared then too. There were "treatises, treatises, treatises" that for the first time set rules for architecture (by Ghiberti and Alberti), for constructing buildings (by Palladio and Piero della Francesca), for accurately portraying the human form and perspective in art (by Dürer), for goldsmithing and sculpture (by Cellini), for geometry and design (Leonardo). Bestiaries, planetary observations, business transactions, agreements, and accounting rules followed. Music, once copied by hand and written as successively added layers of sound, was now printed and written in the relatively new language of chords. A new level of complexity, the musical score, thus first appeared in the 1480s. All could then be readily handed down, readily built on, and readily improved for the first time in human history. All came from "the same new impulse to parse, to regularize in some sort of visual, linear order."[12]

Even individual identities changed. Where in feudal times the rich marked themselves with visual symbols and heraldic shields, now people

began to use surnames. They more commonly identified themselves by occupation (miller, smith), ancestry (Christopherson, or son of Christopher),
rank (burgher), or by where they lived (woods, hill). It might not be too
much to read into these names an expansion of a sense of self, of mattering
to—or at least redefining one's place within—the larger community.[13]

It was more than a fad. Some see a profound shift in this reorganizing
frenzy. Hundreds of years later Marshall McLuhan, the University of
Toronto media theorist, saw the arrival of the printed word as the very moment when the species junked its millennia-old oral and hearing culture for
an historic new linear culture. It was, he wrote, the dawning of Typographic
Man.[14]

All the reordering of territory, words, kingdoms, sight, and intellectual
capacities led to a similar rejiggering of our relationship to the heavens, or
at least to heaven's representatives. Kings began winning their century-long
effort to subdue their clergies as they had subdued their secular, dynastic rivals. Amid nationalist appeals similar to Charles's, for example, Ferdinand
and Isabella had mobilized emotion as well as troops to claim ever greater
parts of Spain from the Moors, and finally pushed them off the Iberian
Peninsula completely in 1493. The next year, they won the title "Catholic
Kings," which meant they could appoint their own bishops. Their successor, Philip II, later asserted his control over the Spanish clergy in part by
printing an awesome 15,000 copies of a Spanish-language breviary for
priests to use in their services. Philip thus claimed a privilege—determining
parts of a church ritual—that had once been the exclusive right of popes.[15]

In France, Charles's successors used similar literary tools in gaining an
upper hand over the clergy. They "deliberately severed the traditional bond
of religion and politics, and made the novel concept of *raison d'etat* their
guiding principle." Much of the next two hundred years of Western history,
in fact, can be understood as making "religious beliefs, orthodox or heretical, increasingly confined to the sphere of personal conviction and individual choice (while) public affairs were directed by a *raison d'etat* which no
longer needed and used supernatural arguments for the pursuit of worldly
ends."[16]

In England the second Tudor king, Henry VIII, crushed his realm's
Catholic clergy more violently, but not before emasculating it by giving certain lay printers the right to duplicate rituals, liturgy, and canon law for common parishioners. Soon the churches in most of the new kingdoms lost control over the production of prayer books. The new Hapsburg, Valois, and
Tudor kings in Germany, France, and England granted laymen exclusive
privileges to print for the clergy.[17] They, not the church bureaucracy, thus

could influence the books' content and slant. If religion was the opiate of the people, secular authority determined its grade, cut, and street-corner sales.

The new monarchs loved the press at least as much as they came to hate it. With it, they were able to subdue once independent groups, command larger territories, and mobilize sentiment. In 1483, John II of Portugal licensed book imports "because (they are) good for the commonwealth." In Austria, Maximilian appointed a court printer to drum up support for his fight against the advancing Turks, both among other kings and among his own subjects. France's book-loving Francois I (1515–1547)—he insisted on taking his huge library with him on trips to review his expanding empire—also seems to have had a sense of the invention's public relations uses. In 1527, he issued what may have been mankind's first policy paper, a public document that explained a truly convoluted policy toward Rome.[18]

But the newborn monarchies pushed, shoved, and brawled with each other just as often as the bickering, greedy local sovereignties they had superseded. Nicolo Machiavelli, writing in Italy in the early 1500s, famously described the era's politics as deeply cynical, murderous, increasingly and often proudly detached from any moral considerations. Consequently, citing reasons of state, Henry VIII could legitimately file trumped-up charges against wives, internal opponents, popes, and foreign colleagues. Henry, Charles V of the Holy Roman Empire, Francois I of France, the Spanish kings, the popes, independent German and Dutch city-states, and Maximilian of Austria daily slipped in and out of alliances with each other. They married their relatives to each other's relatives. They attacked each other. They arranged truces, celebrated with expensive processions and specially built castles, which now rarely lasted a year. Everything—friendship, blood feuds, maps, control over land and trading routes—gained speed. They differed at this time from their feudal predecessors mostly in that their holdings were bigger, their armies were more lethal, their courts wealthier, and their communications were printed and thus far more potent than the usually ill-distributed spoken or copied word.

Their printed, lighter-than-air claims and rationalizations, however, ricocheted off of metal and ideas in quick, unpredictable ways. The kingly reordering of Europe's newly mapped borders and the subjugating of the clergy rarely went according to plan, and often snapped out of control.

In the 1490s, a mordantly funny Dutch hypochondriac named Erasmus slowly gained a reputation among a tiny circle of priests and academics as an agile writer, thorough scholar, sharp thinker, and skilled puncturer of hypocrisy. Erasmus's favorite target was the then dominant method of learning called "scholasticism." An unpublished treatise of his deftly disassembled the scholastic "barbarians" within the church and the schools. Many of those who saw it loved it.

But impressing small circles of friends and patrons did not pay well. Erasmus managed to make some money as a scholar for hire and a translator, and did especially well when he visited England. There he met Thomas More and other New Men—later called humanists—who arranged paying teaching stints for him. But the king's taxmen confiscated his earnings when he boarded a boat for home. Angry and desperate for cash, he slapped together some eight hundred sayings in the space of two weeks during 1499. He called the collection *Adagia* ("adages"). He hoped to sell enough to reduce his debts and see him through until he could cadge another paying job.

To his surprise, the book took off. Erasmus, complex thinker, became famous for listing lame truisms no weightier than "Where there is smoke there is fire."[19]

As quickly as he could, he moved to more challenging works. There were elegant shreddings of scholastic education, satires of modern follies, and impassioned arguments in favor of knowledge for its own sake, of individuals' responsibility for their fellows' well-being, and of peace. (Those who found war sweet, he wrote, had never tasted it.) When he needed more money, he reissued enlarged editions of his *Adagia*. (One was written on deadline on a table at Aldus's print shop in Venice, where the visiting Erasmus hoped to gain "true immortality" and wider readership by having his work printed in Aldus's clean, roman type styles.)[20] He was soon among the first to actually make a living from writing the printed word. He was also among the first to explicitly recognize its uses for education and politics. Some called him "the conscience of Europe."

Like other humanists, he had by then made a profession out of his pursuit of knowledge. The favored method was to study Greek, Hebrew, and Latin texts, date them, seek out corruptions, and then, using both history and common sense, compare the different readings of them. Something valuable, they believed, always resulted.[21] Now famous, Erasmus decided to use the method to examine the original Greek texts of the Bible then being used by the Catholic Church.

He got the idea from a handwritten manuscript by a historian and grammarian named Lorenzo Valla. In works sparingly reproduced by hand, Valla had claimed there were "hundreds" of translation errors in the current Latin Bible.[22] Erasmus had long been intrigued by the assertion, and, now with the historically unprecedented need to produce writing to sell, set out to comb through the Scriptures to see for himself.

He found over four hundred "mistakes" by the time he finished. He found them, moreover, just after an age of script in which a list of bad translations might have been passed around a small circle of people and then, like Valla's work, largely forgotten. But Erasmus's lists were machine duplicated, distributed, and reduplicated. They were easy to see, discuss, and debate. While scholars later determined that a good number of the mistakes Erasmus identified were not errors after all, they caused a stir at the time. Not a few of his contemporaries wanted the book burned. A couple wanted Erasmus burned. But by then he was so famous and had so many friends in high places (including Pope Leo X, a Medici who was a patron of the humanists) that he escaped punishment.

Thus the book glanced off in another direction, eastward. In 1516, a copy made it to the German town of Wittenberg, where it came to the attention of a stout, soul-wracked monk named Martin Luther. Already a combative free thinker and a dramatic, often profane speaker, he was especially shocked by Erasmus's questioning of the Greek word *metanoia*. The word had made it into the Latin version of the Gospel of Matthew as "penance." Erasmus, consulting other Greek manuscripts, determined it was mistranslated. It really meant "to change one's mind" or "to come to oneself," not "to do penance."

To Luther, the world stopped. If one only had to change one's mind or make peace with one's heart to be saved, he figured the Church's whole system of penance and mortification was pointless. Faith could be individual, achieved by each sinner him- or herself. The Church's sales of indulgences, meant to excuse buyers from performing acts of penance, suddenly looked to Luther like a colossal waste at best, a manipulative and fraudulent money-raising scheme at worst.[23]

Luther's outrage over penance, in turn, led him to still more questions about priestly practices and theologies. He soon had ninety-five questions to debate with his Church superiors. Much like grad students of later times, young monks of Luther's era were supposed to earn their professional chops by presenting questions and propositions—theses—to their superiors. Luther was not, however, the type to discuss these urgent issues in private. With a flair for the kind of theater that might ensure public exposure for the hoped-for debate, he asked a printer in Nuremberg to reproduce them. The Nuremberg printer turned him down, but two others agreed to take the job. Fifteen days after Luther posted his ninety-five theses on a church door in Wittenberg, his primitive marketing team had translated the work into German and sent thousands of copies of it all over the Holy Roman Empire. They had what amounted to a mailing list. Erasmus, then in Basel, got one. According to his biographers, the Dutchman found the theses "mildly interesting" and sent them for comment to his friend Thomas More in England.[24] The chain reaction continued.

Most of this now heating reaction's components, it should be noted, had been around for a long time. Attacking the church was an old tradition by then. Dissidents had questioned clerical authority at least as far back as the year 100, when disappointed early Christians were trying to figure out what to do after Jesus had not returned as expected at the turn of the first century. Since then there had been at least a half dozen boiling theological controversies over the bishop of Rome's primacy, the Vatican's sacraments, its ownership of material possessions and ultimately its judging of human souls' qualifications for getting into heaven. In response the Church established the Inquisition in the 1200s to purge critics and literally wiped out the Provençal civilization of southern France, home to the "heretical" Albigensians. The 1300s were even more tumultuous, rife with theological controversy and bloody contests between Church and sovereigns. They led to the splitting of the papacy for a few years. In the early 1400s, Jan Hus led a brutal religious revolt in Bohemia, trying to break free of One Christianity. The first printed best-seller, *Imitation of Christ*, was in fact a criticism of hypocritical priests.[25]

"There is nothing, or almost nothing, in the writings of Martin Luther or any of the Protestant reformers of the sixteenth century that could not be found in fourteenth century literature," a chronicler of the period contends. "The question is not why the Protestant Revolt and schism came in the sixteenth century, but why it did not come a hundred and fifty years earlier."[26]

One reason was that, like the Egyptian priests who had refused to distribute the idea of One God for more than a century, the priests of the Catholic Church "always had better internal lines of communication than [their] challengers."[27] But now Luther, armed with a press that his forebears lacked or hadn't discovered how to use effectively, was outcommunicating everyone.

Within seven years after first publishing his theses in 1517, his pamphlets were everywhere. Thanks to Luther himself, German press output increased by 530 percent in that short time. He personally penned some 2,000 pamphlets from 1520 to 1526, and kept three printers working almost exclusively for him. Other authors, mostly dissidents, wrote another 5,500 pamphlets. (By comparison, German printers had produced only about 2,500 pamphlets during the previous twenty years.) By 1546, some 3.1 million copies of Luther's writings were in print, most of them in speedily distributed, avidly read German-language pamphlets accurately called "flying writings." They were "handy, relatively cheap, readily concealed and transported." Readers paid about a penny a page for them. A typical pamphlet cost about a third of their daily wages, approximately the same as the price of a hen.[28]

Books came out too. German presses printed about forty book titles a year before Luther. Two years after Wittenberg, their annual output had nearly tripled, to 111 titles. Within another two years, they were up to 211. In 1525, they printed 498. Luther allegedly wrote 183 of them while his colleagues authored another 215. Where Wittenberg's printers had produced nine titles—totaling perhaps 5,000 copies—during the first ten years of the century, one of Luther's printers manufactured 100,000 copies of just the monk's German translation of the Bible in ten years.[29]

Luther's Catholic German opponents, by contrast, authored twenty books. In all, reformers published five times as many books as the counter-Reformationists during Luther's lifetime.[30] It was not a fair contest.

Unlike the rare copies of codes, tales, and assertions that had been squirreled away, worshiped, and sometimes forgotten through the ages, moreover, the cheap neonate printed bodies of legal, commercial, and now religious thought built on themselves. New tracts replied to, tested, added to, and replaced other new tracts. Notions mutated in months, not centuries. Luther's, among others, grew ever more extreme. He first took on a few Catholic practices, then Church hierarchy, then the pope personally and the papacy in general, the sacraments, the relationship between church and secular ruler, and, finally, the ways to conduct secular rule.

Catholic Europe's responses to this abrupt flood of words and ideas were confused, sputtering, and violent. Luther's works were being officially burned by 1521. That same year, Catholic France warred with the increasingly Protestant Holy Roman Empire. Within the empire's German provinces, a Protestant led an armed attack on Trier. Catholics and Protestants were soon at war in most of the cities of the Swiss Confederation. Lutherans smashed church statuary and popularized the peculiar technique of pushing opponents through windows to their death. Men of conscience—from anonymous German burghers to articulate statesmen like More—condemned other men of conscience to be burned alive. In 1523, for example, Parisian judges burned a man at the stake for speculating that Joseph, not God, was Jesus' father.[31]

The flames literally grew higher. Whole armies of zealots took the field against other armies of zealots. Finally, some ten years after Luther posted and began publicizing his ninety-five debate topics, a German army entered and sacked Rome, shouting "Luther for pope" in front of the Vatican. Then it camped in St. Peter's Square for six threatening months.

The siege ended the Renaissance. The humanism that reached back to find truths in the past and apply them, regardless of the consequences, was finally inundated by the consequences, it seemed, of unfettered ideas. Luther, a devotee of the New Learning, had become an armed avenger. ("If such a spirit [of resistance] dwells in the peasants," he said in siding with the nobles in crushing a peasant revolt in southern Germany, "it is high time they were slaughtered like mad dogs."[32] An estimated 100,000 people, almost all peasants, were soon dead.) Erasmus, the conscience of Europe, had become a mere moderate, derided by Lutheran and Catholic alike. (Protestants condemned his last book, an almost heartbreakingly naive plea for the combatants to be reasonable. The next year, after his death, the Catholic Inquisition proscribed it too.) In England, humanists Bishop John Fisher and More had, like Erasmus, encouraged learning while holding on to the idea of One Christendom. By 1535, they had been executed. Both were sentenced to be hanged until they lost consciousness, then revived to witness the severing of their penises, which were then to be stuffed into their mouths. Still alive, they next were to be disemboweled. Their miseries finally would end when they were at last beheaded.[33]

Some historians see this gruesome maelstrom as the first revolution of written ideas. The printed word had in fact become a terrible contagion, something that (as Jonathan Swift would later complain) "feeding and engendering on itself, turns all into excrement and venom."[34] To the era's witnesses, the discord it spread must have looked like the unchecked plague that had stolen lives overnight, time and again, for more than one hundred years.

To those of us who now know better, it's easy to see that printed words themselves never eviscerated a thinker or slaughtered a child. Europeans had been butchering each other long before Gutenberg. But this new communications medium was now conducting bolts of energy that, for good or ill, pulsed through this one colony of *Homo sapiens*. They shorted out old understandings, lit up dark corners, scrambled traditions and left these tribes, in many ways, in chaos.

Medieval clergymen, of course, had warned that the new habit of reading for oneself led to heresy. And reading did directly lead to individual, often unprecedented and eccentric views not only of God, but also of government, commerce, health, and the physical properties of bodies as large as suns and as small as sparks. Holy, historic notions of astronomy, botany, anatomy, medicine, mathematics, law, and romance were similarly over-turned. Few that conformed to the always comfortable, sometimes capricious, imposed from above views of old remained by the time the groups that had assumed power finally found a way to bring the damnable virus under control.

NOTES

1. Mark Sullivan, *Our Times*, 6 vols. (New York: Scribner's, 1926–1935), 29–31.

2. S. H. Steinberg, *Five Hundred Years of Printing* (New York: Criterion, 1959), 186; Elizabeth Eisenstein, *The Printing Press as Agent of Change* (Cambridge: Cambridge University Press, 1979), 347; J. R. Hale, *Renaissance Europe, 1480–1520*, 2nd ed. (Malden, Mass.: Blackwell, 2000), 176. In 1475, the pope authorized the University of Cologne to investigate not only books but also their readers. In 1486, he authorized Archbishop Berthold of Mainz to supervise books printed there. In 1501, Pope Alexander VI's bull *Inter Multiplices* instructed German printers to submit all their books to their local archbishop for licensing.

3. Frederick W. Hamilton, *A Brief History of Printing, Part II* (Chicago: United Typothetae of America, 1918), 27.

4. Steinberg, *Five Hundred Years*, 82; Norman F. Cantor, *Medieval History: The Life and Death of a Civilization* (London: Macmillan, 1969), 542.

5. Karl Polanyi, *The Great Transformation: The Political and Economic Origins of Our Time* (Boston: Beacon, 1944), 111. Needless to say, we were not yet up to figuring out what do if the nation itself misbehaved. "Only in the 1700s did we—or at least Townsend, Hegel, Ricardo and Jefferson—begin to assert persuasively that the state should be subjected to its own laws, too." The idea of nation was limited. "Except for commanders and staff, the armies that fought each other for the kings of France and Spain were neither French nor Spanish but German and Swiss." Jacques Barzun, *From Dawn to Decadence: 500 Years of Western Cultural Life* (New York: HarperCollins, 2000), 93; Hale, *Renaissance Europe*, 50.

6. Ronald J. Deibert, *Parchment, Printing, and Hypermedia: Communication in World Order Transformation* (New York: Columbia University Press, 1997), 104. The percentage of titles published in Latin in Europe declined steadily from the 1460s and 1470s. Before 1500, 75 percent of "all printed matter" was in Latin, 8 percent in German, and 8 percent in Italian. (Almost all books in Spain and England were in the native language, however.) By 1650, the ratio of Latin to German books at the Leipzig book fair was still 71 to 29. It was 38 to 62 in 1700, 28 to 72 in 1740, and 4 to 96 in 1800. Steinberg, *Five Hundred Years*, 84. In regard to "mental equipment," see John Conrad Ruggie, "Territoriality and Beyond: Problematizing Modernity in International Relations," *International Organization*, Winter 1993, 139–74, cited in Deibert, *Parchment*, 157. Sovereigns had claimed to embody larger states in the past.

But the idea was not common during the Middle Ages. In the heyday of feudalism people toiled and fought for God, out of duty to lords, against evil. In general, the leader who sent them to war and taxed and protected them was local. By Gutenberg's day, the system had more or less collapsed amid the inferno of plague, war, heresy, magical devils, anti-Semitism, weapons technology, the bourgeoisie's fitful advances, and the declining status of patricians. All sorts of now forgotten noblemen, bishops, would-be kings, and warlords competed for the spoils: Norman F. Cantor, *Medieval History: The Life and Death of a Civilization* (London: Macmillan, 1969), 543. On the economic partnership between kings and merchants, see Polanyi, *Great Transformation*, 73–74. On monetary reform, see Deibert, *Parchment*, 81–84.

7. George Faludy, *Erasmus* (New York: Stein & Day, 1970), 59–60; Cantor, *Medieval History*, 542; Hale, *Renaissance Europe*, 45.

8. Deibert, *Parchment*, 101–3.

9. Henri Bouchet, *The Book: Its Printers, Illustrators, and Binders from Gutenberg to the Present Time*, ed. H. Grevel (New York: Scribner & Welford, 1890), 53.

10. Cantor, *Medieval History*, 542; Hale, *Renaissance Europe*, 49–50.

11. Eisenstein, *Printing Press*, 103–4. A man named W. de Machlinia probably was England's first law printer, followed by others, including Richard Pynson, who was Henry VIII's official legal printer until 1529. Pynson was one of the first of the official, "privileged" legal printers. He had the exclusive right to print the nation's expanding library of parliamentary law books. Bouchet, *The Book*, 53. Committing laws to print also made them "more irrevocable." Before machine printing, the Magna Charta was by law proclaimed twice a year in every shire. By 1237, however, it already was corrupted in some places. Since being set in the Great Boke of Statutes in 1533, by contrast, it has remained happily static. Eisenstein, *Printing Press*, 119.

12. Barzun, *Dawn to Decadence*, 67–68; Hale, *Renaissance Europe*, 190; Deibert, *Parchment*, 101–3.

13. Barzun, *Dawn to Decadence*, 114.

14. Marshall McLuhan, *Understanding Media: The Extensions of Man* (New York: Simon & Schuster, 1967), 157.

15. Hale, *Renaissance Europe*, 46–49; Eisenstein, *Printing Press*, 118.

16. S. H. Steinberg, *The Thirty Years War and the Conflict for European Hegemony, 1600–1660* (New York: Norton, 1966), 99.

17. Eisenstein, *Printing Press*, 118.

18. Mark U. Edwards Jr., *Printing, Propaganda, and Martin Luther* (Berkeley: University of California Press, 1994), 16–17; Steinberg, *Five Hundred Years*, 66; Edwards, *Printing Propaganda*, 16–17. Later, Charles I of France had his official printer (a Calvinist named Robert Estienne) publish another, this one justifying his shocking Catholic alliance with Muslim Turks and Protestant princes and against the even more hated English. When Dominicans in Germany organized mobs to seize and destroy Jewish writings, the none too tolerant Hapsburgs, wanting to keep internal

tensions at a minimum while they were off making war against the Vatican, also used printed propaganda. They issued their protests against anti-Semitism in officially printed pamphlets. On John II of Portugal, see Hale, *Renaissance Europe*, 214.

19. To be fair, many such sayings, long buried in unread ancient scrolls, were not lame in 1499. Erasmus's adages, some scholars point out, appeared in a world in which educators, many priests, and almost all kings solemnly warned that reading Scripture or classics or law for oneself inevitably led to heresy. So did human initiative in religious services, judging authority, or thinking for oneself. It was foolhardy even to try, for all of Europe's schools were under the sway of Thomas Aquinas and the scholastics. Aquinas maintained that all we can know of the world is what God left behind. Since we cannot possibly know the mind of God, speculating about the nature of his physical work is useless and perhaps sinful. The scholastics who followed him believed that true learning amounted to nothing more than memorizing the unchanging truths of life by rote. Study of the physical properties of things and metaphysics was abandoned and finally forbidden, as was the study of the past. The leading scholastics of Erasmus's day were an Englishman named Occam, who "insisted that men's reason could not begin to understand the mystery of God," and Duns Scotus, an educator who thought that "truth was revealed more in the contradictions and paradoxes of dialogue" than in the study of physical things. The emphasis on oral debate provided Erasmus and the humanists with their favorite scholastic targets: the windy, fruitless debates over whether an omnipotent God could change black into white. "If God has a completely free will," they then wondered, "can He contradict Himself? If He can make black into white and if He can contradict Himself, then can He not also make right into wrong and wrong into right? Justice into injustice? A damned man into a saved one? And if He cannot, then surely He is not omnipotent?" Among the other questions debated at the Sorbonne during Erasmus's stay included the following: Was God more likely to hear your prayer if you prayed for five minutes for five consecutive days or for twenty consecutive minutes on one day? In that environment, Erasmus's helpful observations and tiny truths—all gleaned from the private, slightly subversive act of reading—apparently struck a humanist chord across Europe. Thomas Charles L. Mee, *Erasmus: The Eye of the Hurricane* (New York: Coward, McCann & Geoghegan, 1974), 26–30; Faludy, *Erasmus*, 60.

20. Faludy, *Erasmus*, 116–19; Mee, *Erasmus*, 56; Bouchet, *The Book*, 110.

21. Faludy, *Erasmus*, 20.

22. Mee, *Erasmus*, 53–54.

23. Mee, *Erasmus*, 82–83.

24. Steinberg, *Five Hundred Years*, 39; Diebert, *Parchment*, 71; Mee, *Erasmus*, 84.

25. Deibert, *Parchment*, 69; Stephen Jay Gould, *Leonardo's Mountain of Clams and the Diet of Worms: Essays on Natural History* (New York: Harmony, 1998), 255.

26. Cantor, *Medieval History*, 538.

27. James Curran, "Communications, Power, and Social Order," in *Culture, Society, and the Media*, ed. Michael Gurevitch et al. (London: Routledge, 1982), 82. "In

the first place," historian Norman Cantor adds in explaining why sixteenth-century dissidents succeeded in breaking away from Rome, Luther's predecessors "did not have the printing press . . . It was very hard for the heretical theorists to disseminate their doctrines." But periodic economic depression as well as the regular visits of plague also contributed to a widespread apathy about religious matters. Moreover, "the papacy was so weak in the 14th century that it didn't fight heresy well, and thus let it run its course." Cantor, *Medieval History*, 538–39. "With the rapid dissemination and publication afforded by printing," adds Ronald Deibert, another historian, "heretical movements had a much better chance of spreading their message beyond the locality in which they emerged, making it much more difficult for the Church to take effective countermeasures." Deibert, *Parchment*, 69.

28. Deibert, *Parchment*, 71; Edwards, *Printing Propaganda*, 17. Luther first had Johann Rhau in Wittenberg, then Melchior Lotter in Leipzig, then Lotter's son (also named Melchior) in Wittenberg and then another local printer named Hans Lufft printing for him, sometimes all at once. Colin Clair, *A History of European Printing* (London: Academic, 1976), 130; Edwards, *Printing Propaganda*, 39. The contemporary term for "flying writings," which were eight to thirty-two pages long, was *Flugschriften*. The pieces were also called *libellus* or *Büchlein*, meaning "booklet." Edwards, *Printing Propaganda*, 16; Deibert, *Parchment*, 76.

29. The remaining eighty titles in 1525 were secular. Steinberg, *Five Hundred Years*, 81; Clair, *European Printing*, 129.

30. Deibert, *Parchment*, 73. The books sold very well too. In a time when a printer might turn out 1,200 copies of a work he expected to be a blockbuster, Luther's treatise about the existence of a German nation sold 4,000 copies in five days. His first edition of the German New Testament in 1522 sold out in three months. Clair, *European Printing*, 123.

31. Mee, *Erasmus*, 103. According to the Edict of Worms, "We want all of Luther's books to be universally prohibited and forbidden, and we also want them to be burned . . . This is well done, since if we are not allowed to eat meat containing just one drop of poison because of the danger of bodily infection, then we surely should leave out every doctrine (even if it is good) which has in it the poison of heresy and error, which infects and corrupts and destroys under the cover of charity everything that is good." Gould, *Leonardo's Mountain*, 254. Throwing people out of windows, though rare, had become something of a tradition among Church opponents. In 1419, followers of the recently martyred Jan Hus apparently pioneered the method when they threw three anti-Hus Catholic consuls (and seven other citizens) out the window of Prague's New Town Hall. Catholic rule was restored in the city in 1483, but not before an opposing mob threw the Catholic mayor out of a window. This technique became increasingly popular during the Reformation and the seventeenth century, especially in Central Europe. Gould, *Leonardo's Mountain*, 257.

32. Mee, *Erasmus*, 105–6; Gould, *Leonardo's Mountain*, 256. With his "little book" *On the Jew and Their Lies*, Luther urged keeping Jews out of cities, burning their

books and synagogues, and deporting as many as possible to Palestine. Erasmus's last book was called *On the Sweet Concord of the Church*. Mee, *Erasmus*, 116.

33. Fisher had been archbishop of Canterbury and was a favorite of Henry VIII's until he refused to support Henry's efforts to annul his marriage to Catherine of Aragon and marry Anne Bolyn. When Henry declared himself leader of the Church in England, Fisher's resistance stiffened. Henry imprisoned and then killed him, as well as other subjects who held to the Vatican's leadership of Christianity. More, Henry's former high chancellor, was another believer. In light of his long service, however, Henry foreshortened More's torture to a simple beheading.

34. In Swift's era (1667–1745), there was what a later historian (Clara Reeve) would called a "chaos of the circulating library" that seemed to fuel dissent. Cited in Gregory V. Laugero, "Infrastructures of Enlightenment: Road-making, the Circulation of Print, and the Emergence of Literature in the Eighteenth and Early Nineteenth Centuries" (Ph.D. diss., State University of New York at Stony Brook, 1994), 220, v.

7

FASTER THAN ASPARAGUS

Martin Luther was an extraordinarily passionate believer in reading the Bible for oneself. Laypeople, he insisted, should interpret it on their own, free of the dark bureaucratic spins of self-interested clerics.[1] Accordingly, he translated the Latin Bible into German for the masses in 1522.

A sensation, the book made him more famous and revered than ever. But Luther himself was immediately enraged by the way some of his readers, now happily free of the dark spins of self-interested clerics, had interpreted his words. The author, like all authors, could not believe they could be so wrong.

He was livid. His critics were fools, devils, worse. He called Erasmus, now appalled by Luther's spiraling radicalism, a "piece of shit." When his close comrade Ulrich Zwingli disagreed with him about certain rituals, Luther urged the duke of Prussia to expel first Zwingli and then all Zwinglians from the realm. He urged the expulsion of stubbornly Catholic residents from newly Protestant lands. Beating back still other learned readers, he asked the duke of Saxony to impose capital punishment for heresy, which was now defined as misinterpreting Luther.[2]

This too happened each time the printed word gained momentum. When in later centuries steam presses improved the word's speed, and when Linotypes and then computers reduced its cost, violent attempts to control the threatening energies loosed by the new communicators and readers quickly followed. They often aimed to maintain monopolies over crucial political, commercial, spiritual, or military information that had, until the moment before, been rare and expensive and the very crux of some interest group's power. Sometimes the efforts were to control the word's production and distribution. Sometimes they were to exterminate those who read on their own.

Clerics, who had the monopoly on understanding how the universe worked, had the most to lose when machine-printed words appeared in Europe. Their positions, of course, had rested largely on their being the only qualified interpreters and, when it was written, readers of God's will. They had been jealously guarding their source material since at least 849, burning the writings and finally the flesh of those who speculated about it inconveniently.[3] Now, letting others read it in their own, easy languages and, worse yet, letting them decide what it meant compromised the clergymen's most marketable services. Not least, it threatened their status in both this and the next life. They thus battled, as we've seen, to keep now readily reproduced Bibles obscure. Initially focused on Scripture, they even let racy materials enter the market through the late 1400s. In 1501, Pope Alexander VI tried to broaden Church censorship, but the masters at the University of Cologne, where the screws on biblical language were first tightened, warned the Vatican to keep its eyes strictly on heresies, and to leave the rest alone for the time being. Two years later, the Vatican began to censor books of bad "literary quality" anyway. In 1508, it required printers who had licenses to operate in their homelands to get a "privilege"—permission to print—from the pope too. And at the landmark Lateran Council meeting in 1515, Pope Leo X condemned printers who offered books that might promote errors in faith. He insisted too that bishops approve all translations from Hebrew, Greek, Arabic, and Persian into Latin. In France, the Sorbonne, the Parliament of Paris, the police, and the director-general of the book trade all adopted the Lateran rules. Like other secular authorities—although the lines between church and state did not always exist—they began to condemn books on their own, citing the Lateran Council as their authority. In 1518, the Spanish *Cortes* used them to ban a romance called *Amadis*. But then, like now, the censors only whetted the public appetite. The illicit *Amadis* quickly became one of the era's most popular books.[4]

Then Luther raised the stakes. For both Catholics and Protestants, he put humans' souls, monarchies, and the awesome New World wealth arriving from abroad at risk. The crackdown on the printed word got rougher, meaner, more unforgiving.

In England, Henry VIII moved first to suppress Protestant works and then, after taking England out of the Catholic Church, Catholic works. In 1529, he officially limited the printing, importing, or reading of certain books. The penalty was nothing less than imprisonment or death. Six years later France's Francis I, desperate to control Protestant heretics, momentarily banned the printing of *all* books in his realm. The penalty there too was hanging. Twenty-four Protestants soon were executed. In 1546 the

Church, now more convinced than ever that reading for oneself was dangerous, officially banned the printing of non-Latin Bibles. The pope would excommunicate violators; secular authorities were to punish them physically. Police in Lyon promptly arrested a printer named Sebastian Greyff and his most popular humanist author, and dutifully burned them. Censors in Paris, their torches lit, tracked down the printer of an offensive Zwinglian book of biblical notes, only to find it was one Robert Estienne, the king's own printer. Francis himself forbade his arrest. But when Francis died in 1547, Estienne sagely fled to Protestant Geneva. It was the same year that the Inquisition, unsure that all secular authorities would be as zealous as the French, took charge of censoring and punishing printers in Catholic countries.[5]

The dissidents were equally severe. In Geneva, Calvinists burned a Catholic printer at the stake in 1553, feeding the fire with his books. (Later placed in a museum, the lone book saved from the pyre had the author's fatal pro-papacy phrases highlighted by his accuser. It "still bears traces of fire on its leaves," a French writer of the late nineteenth century reported.)[6]

In 1571, Pope Pius V created an official list of banned books, the *Index Expurgatorious*. Readers who sampled its contents faced eternal damnation. Inquisitions could reach across oceans to find them too. The operator of the only press allowed into Mexico by its Spanish conquerors produced a book in 1572 that the distant inquisitors deemed insufficiently Catholic. They imprisoned him for two years.[7]

But authority's radical cures didn't always work. The medium was irresistibly simple, cheap, and profitable. Short of using totalitarian tools that would not be invented for another couple of centuries, there was little the reeling institutions of 1500 could do to stop the hundreds of printers who fired these pathogens into the body politic. Stopping masses of people from sampling the mounting piles of information was impossible. Consequently more books were produced during the final thirty years of the fifteen century than during the previous nine hundred years. Thirty-five thousand different titles appeared. There were as many as 20 million copies of them. Some 110 towns had presses by 1480, 236 by 1500. They became increasingly busy too. Venice produced nine times as many titles in 1495 as it had in 1482 (when it put out about 52). In all, European presses churned out 1,821 titles in the year of 1495. From 1480 to 1482, they had produced 519. More than twice as many towns, in other words, produced almost three times as many book titles. Counting the epidemic of pamphlets, maps, fliers, lists, and price sheets coming off the new machines, France alone had an "an enormous commerce" in printing by 1500.[8] Then came the dramatic spiraling of print during the Reformation, which one observer centuries later called the new technology's "killer application."

The disorder continued too because it was a physiological event, a spurt of change in our habitat that was well beyond politicians' or even an army's ability to control. Threatened rulers might stop someone from printing words that could be inconveniently interpreted. But they were powerless to halt readers' need to align their beliefs and behavior with a suddenly altered, wider environment. Europeans' world in the 1500s was full of just discovered oceans, exotic foreigners, invisible forces that made objects drop, lightweight fabrics, salts, strong metals, cheap coal, money, explanations of when to plant crops that God used to blight for insufficient piety, maps that showed the way to distant jungle monsters and reportedly effervescent minerals. It was possible to ignore all these new forces in the environment, but those who adapted to them produced more food, warmth, wealth, immunities, children, everything. Those who were slow or were prevented or simply refused to adapt literally fell economic (and even biological) prey to competitors who, say, shaped new metals into stronger plows. As twentieth-century Lou Felicio stumbled toward professional hell when he did not learn the computer, so did sixteenth-century Europeans who failed to account for the new materials and visions of heaven and earth. Failing to adapt carried consequences. So for many of us, finding regimes to fit—or at least allow us to meet—our new realities thus was something of a survival instinct.

It is said that optimism, not despair, causes revolutions.[9] Rising expectations—the idea that something more comfortable or at least less painful actually may be possible—preceded all the last millennium's great upheavals. (Conversely, the most downtrodden and dispirited classes of peasants, serfs, slaves, and workers typically were among the most conservative supporters of the moment's status quo.) By the time authority saw that some of the printed words abruptly circulating through Europe might be inspiring destructive glimpses into brighter worlds and wider environments, it was too late. Millions of germs were already out of the bag. *They* caused the discord, not the punished printers and writers.

Something in the nature of the little print shops themselves also helped make the printed word resistant to cures. They were in many ways hearty little social organisms highly adapted to the new, more fluid economy and environment. These merchants had sophisticated equipment, a physical plant, and more than one employee; this was a radically different business model than many burghers used for their cottage industries. The printers also were among the first to depend on volume. To move unheard-of quantities of books, pamphlets, maps, and fliers in short periods of time, the best ones learned the skills later enshrined in management books: to organize raw materials, assess markets, drive a workforce, manage risk, and balance their constant need for capital against a constantly shifting market. "To be a successful publisher," a historian of the business later explained, "necessitated the outlay of considerable sums in advance against a problematical profit at an indeterminate date." Their manufacturing too was complex. Each document required its own arrangement of type, its own remixing of ink, its own paper, and, from time to time, its own channels of distribution. In an era when most industrial plants were small (textiles was the Continent's biggest trade), some print shops were using advanced organizational techniques in which "the design of presses, the lay-out of fonts, the arrangements of the shops were all designed to speed output without sacrificing accuracy." A skilled, literate workforce developed.[10] It too was a source of wealth and stability that old businesses did not enjoy. Although merchants soon regarded their workers mostly as a costly source of endless trouble, skilled workers were powerful ballasts amid the constant attacks on the print shops. They constituted a new economic and political force—a part of an emerging urban working class—that bosses, kings, and clerics could not ignore or, when all else failed, burn en masse.

But for all its highly adapted behavior, the new industry also had political weaknesses. In the past, guilds had protected merchants from patricians and kept competitors out of their business. But machine printers did not fit easily into guilds. Craft guilds were designed to manage businesses involving a single skill, something like sewing or shoeing or baking. This new enterprise, by contrast, combined new crafts—press operator, engraver, compositor, press assistant—with old ones like binder, shopkeeper, illustrator, teamster, banker. Not surprisingly, guilds of calligraphers and copyists often refused to admit the new printer competitors anyway. As a result, many printers and publishers became "industrial outlaws." Parts of their operations, from securing raw materials to advertising finished books, remained unregulated and thus vulnerable to repeated interruptions by royal or clerical whim, by hostile laborers, by plagiarists and thieves and, most commonly, by each other.[11]

For they competed viciously with each other. Where guildsmen could not start, say, another wheat mill in town without securing a hard-to-get license from the millers' guild, printers had few competitive rules. Almost anyone with capital could enter the business and then try to elbow his way into the market. Like Gutenberg redoing Coster's most popular works, many continued to help themselves to each other's property. In his introduction to his new book a printer in Parma, for example, apologized for the new work's shoddy appearance. A competitor, he explained, had stolen his idea. Rushing to finish the book first, he had printed it "more quickly than asparagus can be cooked."[12]

Stealing ideas was easy. With printing cheap and transportation costs high, it was often smarter to reprint a title in a distant town than it was to ship it there. If a Wittenberg book sold well in Strasbourg, for example, "it was more common for a printer in Strasbourg to reprint the work than it was for the printer in Wittenberg to ship a large number of copies to Strasbourg." But the reprintings were not always authorized. Spain's Jacob Cronberger thus instructed his employee in Mexico City to melt down type after finishing each title so that competitors could not steal it to use to print their own version. In 1518, Erasmus discovered a stranger had printed one of his books without permission, and was selling it very successfully. He was far from the only victim. Luther's 1522 book about German nationhood sold out repeatedly, and he commissioned fourteen reprintings within two years. By then, pirates had produced sixty-six unauthorized editions. Unauthorized copies of the book ultimately outnumbered authorized ones by 90 to 1. The problem only got worse. A Frankfurt printer was selling a bootleg version of Gallileo's historic astronomy book a few months after it came out in Venice. Its inaccuracies were dutifully reproduced in unauthorized editions of the pirated version throughout Europe until at least 1683.[13]

Without protective copyright laws or guilds, the printers tried using distinctive printers' marks to identify their books as authorized or accurate, but pirates simply copied and reprinted the marks. Bootleggers in England even counterfeited Parliament's licenses to print its legislative proceedings. Looking for extra revenue, press operators secretly printed extra copies of their own shop's works and sold them on their own without sharing the proceeds with authors, publishers, or tax authorities.[14] In this, they were often happily aided by organized and otherwise respectable bookbinders and booksellers.

Many printers tried to make life more predictable by attaching themselves to churches, courts, and universities. But when certain sects or noble clans buckled in the era's uncertainty, so did they. Their captive presses, moreover, had to compete in the same commercially lawless arenas as secular presses. All were vulnerable as well, to their adopted sponsors' tastes. In 1501, printers in Cologne protested to Rome that its new printing prohibitions were "driving their business out of the city." In 1524, a Catholic duke in Germany, appalled by the religious chaos engulfing his realm, angrily forbade local printers to sell Lutheran words. The printers thus quickly found themselves with unsalable inventory on their hands. In their boiling German markets, they complained that Catholic work was "desired by no one and cannot be given away." They added they were in danger of losing "house, home and all their livelihood" while their competitors were cleaning up.[15] Heresy—or at least books and pamphlets that played to the moment's theological obsessions—was a booming, lucrative business. Luther's partner printers ended up as "spectacular" successes; wealthy, with multiple shops in different towns and ultimately political power. More independent printers did well too. The Basel printer who produced Erasmus's fateful 1516 translation of the Greek word *metanoia*—the one that provoked Luther to question the notion of penance—soon had seven presses cranking out some 250 works. His shop became "the meeting place of the literary world of his day."[16]

Yet even that shop, for all its mighty economic weight, wobbled when the Protestant revolt reached Basel. Like the threatened churchmen, lords, and academicians around them, many of the printer-merchants pined for the peace necessary to secure their investments and exploit their markets.

Nobody had much stake in the status quo. Secular and religious leaders yearned to control the destructive, half-understood threats the increasingly wealthy knowledge trades posed. And the tradespeople, like all businesspeople in all ages, yearned mostly to reduce risk, to control their costs, resources, prices, and clientele, and to impose a predictable order in their marketplaces.

When those two groups began to meet each other's needs in the middle of the sixteenth century, the contagion at last began to submit to still larger forces of human behavior.

Just about every would-be king or queen of the late 1400s and early 1500s had a printer or two on retainer or formally attached to the court. While the printers might produce celebratory poems, proclamations, and vanities, some soon branched into the more serious communications work of government. They were not, however, always acting out of a profound belief in their sponsors' causes. William Caxton, who set up England's first press, printed for the last, murderous kings of the House of York as well as the first murderous Tudor kings who defeated the Yorks.

But Henry VII, the first Tudor king, hit on an idea. He granted a "privilege"—a license—to a printer to sell the legal proceedings coming out of the Court of Common Pleas. Better yet, the printer would have a monopoly on the documents, which barristers needed to buy. Needless to say, the official grant proved to be enormously lucrative. Although it was split into ever finer privileges in future years—for different courts, for different kinds of laws—the official approval effectively eliminated the printer's competition and gave customers the choice of buying his books or none at all.[17]

Popes and local councils, it's true, had given privileges to printers before, but they had usually concerned the specific book or pamphlet the printer hoped to publish. The privilege typically meant a ruler had approved the content, and that the printer could be reasonably sure he would not be burned at the stake for producing it. Henry's privilege, however, amounted to advance permission to print an entire type of content and to enjoy the heavy commercial benefits that surely would follow. The printer, he apparently figured, was not likely to produce things that offended his benefactor or jeopardized his own income. Henry would get literary peace and collect taxes from the newly wealthy tradesman.

Henry VIII, the next Tudor, went farther. In 1529 he granted patents, which were legally stronger versions of privileges, to more printers. Officially, the printers had the monarch's "personal favor" to produce, for example, Latin schoolbooks, primers, psalters, cosmologies, and even classical works not just in a fiefdom or a region, but throughout the realm. (It was not strictly a favor; printers had to pay for the patents.) Legally too they got the use of police powers to manage their workers and to force those who dared to compete with them out of business.[18]

Henry knew what he was doing. By supplying printers with opportunities and keeping their customers' choices small (all the kingdom's hymnals, for example, came from the same business), he overtly aimed to turn these printers into "a new grade of tradesman . . . wealthy and powerful within the book trade but directly dependent on crown favor." In 1530, he added decrees that required licensees to submit their content to censors for approval before printing it. Few of the prosperous gentlemen printers objected then or a few years later, when Henry made them replace all their holy Catholic text with holy Church of England text.[19]

Other monarchs also adopted the tactic, selling the sole rights to produce all their Bibles, naval documents, math textbooks, and more. Portugal's king sold a patent to Jacob Cronberger, who had a press in Seville, to print royal laws. To that profitable franchise Cronberger soon added commissions from the Spanish royal family and finally the exclusive right to own presses (and 80 percent of the presses' revenues left after deducting his distant press operator's bare living expenses) in the Spanish colony of Mexico.[20]

In France the court formed its own professional association of printers, booksellers, and artists to govern and rationalize the business in 1487. It lasted until 1513, when Louis XII formed a more potent "community of printers." This may have been the first of a new era of state-sponsored licensing agencies as licensed "master printers" set and enforced industrial standards in the court's name. They also pledged to be heroic promoters of the monarchy and Catholicism. They kept heresy and sedition—two notions that could be redefined in an instant—out of their products by meeting with church and court censors to edit manuscripts they planned on publishing. Their executive committee fixed wages and prices, and kept members from copying and selling each other's works. The state, in turn, kept nonmember printers out of their markets.[21]

Venice organized a similar Guild of Printers and Booksellers in 1549. It quickly established trade conventions for itself and, in return for monopolies, helped the state and church control the presses' output.[22]

In 1557, Queen Mary chartered the Company of Stationers. The stationers, first formed as a copyists and bookbinders guild in 1403, now became a "company" whose members had exclusive rights to oversee the "art and mystery" of all printing and bookselling in England. Catholic Mary explicitly charged the stationers with promoting "Romish" work. The next year newly crowned Elizabeth reconfirmed the stationers' charter but changed its focus to promoting Protestant work. During the next 150 years of fitful dynastic struggle, the stationers remained remarkably flexible. Without abrupt changes in leadership or even memberships the company did the work of the Stuarts, the Commonwealth, the Stuarts again, and the Whigs as they took their often violent turns at governing. That is because the printers, despite their occasional paeans to free speech and condemnations of censorship during the ensuing years, were primarily concerned about maintaining their monopolies and minimizing interference in their affairs. While printers in Europe's unregulated free markets clawed at each other, dodged religious missiles (and missals), and scrambled to protect their investments in crowded and seemingly chaotic marketplaces, privileged printers tended to accept any government that would work with them to ensure order. Nor did monarchs, on the other hand, always care about their printers' character, religion, or political beliefs. They tended to accept any printer willing to work with them to ensure order and, perhaps just as importantly, pay the price. For English monarchs in particular needed money too. Even as they rose, Parliament gradually limited their powers to raise taxes, and the sums monopoly printers (along with monopoly street sweepers and other tradesmen) paid for their privileges were an important alternative source of revenue for monarchs during the stationers' golden age. As a result, with one partner regulating competition and another regulating content, the stationers became a phenomenally successful regulatory agency. The company looked much like the country itself. Although it admitted all qualified members of the trade, it concentrated power at the top in a committee called the Table of Assistants. Where everyone from "the meanest book-binder to the king's printers" jousted in the guilds that had less effectively tried to control the business before, now a tiny band (only 10 in 1550; 26 in 1684) of the craft's gentleman-aristocrats were assistants. Only they could vote on stationers' affairs. Though they all served at the monarch's whim, few were ever fired. Assistants, however, had to be nominated by their colleagues and be wealthy enough to buy their way up (for about £20, better than a year's average pay in the late 1500s) from liveryman, the next step down on the ladder. That class too was exclusive; there were only twenty to thirty liverymen in the Stationers Company at a time. When a liveryman was lucky enough to be tapped to become an assistant, he as-cended with an elaborate, ritualized dinner for his new peers. It might be on the stationers' own barge on the Thames, where like media barons of later eras the bookmen conducted grand, ostentatious balls and ceremonies. With similar pomp, they oversaw the industry's social and financial affairs. They provided pensions, rented out tenements, and loaned money to each other. Below the assistants and liverymen were the trade's numerous freemen or yeomen, who might be bookstall owners, laborers, or clerks. Many had served at least seven years as still lower apprentices before being admitted to the company.[23]

While being a member often meant wealth (in the 1600s, the company itself, as opposed to individual members, owned several lucrative patents; the proceeds ultimately were split among some of the members), not being a member meant not being able to print. Operating an unlicensed press in England brought the offender a year in prison. Printing an unlicensed book meant six months behind bars. Binding one cost three months. At the sta-tioners' behest, the authorities could and did seize presses, destroy them, melt down type, and appropriate the competitor's property so he might never do such business again. With the authorities manning the island king-dom's ports, the company "almost immediately" halted the importing of cheaper books from Holland and France, which had been cutting into their members' sales.

Individual stationers also worked closely with each other, sometimes having different members work on different parts of a single title. The shar-ing kept all printers busy during slow times. It also kept counterfeiters at bay. Because no one printing house would have the entire text in hand, the sharing kept pirate pressmen from producing extra copies to sell after hours.[24]

When it suited their needs, in short, they could control the numbers of printed words in ways that violent authority could not have imagined. They cut the number of printing businesses in London to twenty-five in 1586, twenty-three in 1637, and twenty in 1662. The stationers allowed each to have only a few (eventually three) presses. In their rulers' name they actively kept a press out of York until 1642, when Charles I took the city and, significantly enough, unilaterally set one up to aid him in his Civil War.[25] France's community of printers already had reduced the number of competitors in Paris to seventy-six in 1618, when the king replaced the community with a centralized *chambre des syndicats*. After that, the printers decided to allow thirty-six printers to work in Paris, eighteen in Lyon and Rouen, and twelve in Bordeaux.[26]

The new castes of elite, licensed printers even managed to slow the technology's spread to other cultures. Where the contagion had rocketed from duchy to kingdom to island to city-state into some 110 locales during its first forty years, only ten new countries adopted machine printing during the 1500s. A mere eight adopted it during the 1600s.[27]

Thus slowed the great careening increases in printed knowledge—which had fueled Europe's bloody lurches from oral to written culture, from feudal to national monarchies and from spiritual to man-made understandings of our world during the technology's first decades. With his commercial conventions and controls, it was the state-supported Catholic printer, not the Church itself, who ultimately kept Protestant works out of France and other Catholic lands. State-supported Protestant printers, not soldiers, were the ones who effectively damned and dammed Catholic works in their lands. The contagion of unofficial thought, while still abroad in the body politic, could all at once be more easily isolated and muted. More than brute censorship, boring and bloodless regulation did the trick. In that, printers themselves were active, enthusiastic and well-rewarded conspirators.

In today's terms, they had dramatically increased the costs of entering the business. The regulated printers wove a thick web of expensive licenses, penalties, organizational ritual, training requirements, taxes and fees to block newcomers' access to the technology. By the end of the sixteenth century, only those born into a press-owning family or those blessed by royal favor could become successful printers in most European countries or the broad foreign lands they were colonizing. The printed word and printed knowledge had become the property of a privileged producer caste, made rich by a rigged market.

As the costs of entering the market climbed, so did profits for those already in it. The agencies fixed both prices and wages. At a time when the gold and silver being extracted from newly conquered lands in the Americas pushed Europe's commodity prices up by 100 percent, retail printing prices maintained a "remarkable stability" from 1560 until 1640. Printers' labor costs, in turn, remained low. Their laws tilted the marketplace against their workers, who were forbidden to combine, leave one employer for another for higher pay, or even directly ask for customary guild wages.[28]

So great printing enterprises arose, and printers themselves became "great personages." By 1538, the licensed printing firm of Godart and Merlin in Paris employed two hundred people. Licensed printers in Lyon, Strasbourg, and Florence started what became princely industrial families. After the Mentelins and Schoeffers of the technology's first generation came not only Venice's Aldus Manutius—now so exalted that he was called Aldus Magnus, or Aldus the Great—and Spain's Cronberger, but nearly noble merchant families like England's Barker, which grew rich manufacturing law books in England. In the Spanish-ruled Low Country, generations of families like Plantin, Elsevier, and Blaeu came to power. The Elseviers' business still exists today as a multinational publishing company. At his death in 1589, Christophe Plantin had a huge plant in Antwerp with seventeen presses, and branches in Paris and Leyden. His business lasted eight generations, until 1875. Spain's royal printing overseers in 1621 licensed and sent Geronimo de Contreras to be Peru's monopoly printer. There he became the "progenitor of one of the most famous of all Latin American printing families." It monopolized the area for 158 years, until 1779. By the early 1600s, Willem Blaeu was an aristocrat of Amsterdam. His presses—which he set up in a row and named after the Muses—were famous for producing beautiful gilt-plate atlases and maps that were worldwide bestsellers. Rubens painted his family's portraits on birthdays, and office seekers sought his blessing much as they used to seek the favor of the now displaced patricians.[29]

Life for printers was tougher in unregulated places. In subdivided Germany, not yet a national monarchy, the worried German Diet in 1570 again tried to do something about the war of words that seemed to be prolonging the war of religions around it. It proclaimed that, from then on, new presses would be allowed only in certain princely state capitals, directly under authority's watchful eye. The proclamation, alas, went out to an area already rife with scores of presses. Without the common, enforceable regulatory conventions flourishing in unified England and France, they simply continued to multiply. Reprinting was rampant and licenses difficult to enforce. Printers in the German states, not coincidentally, generally remained "poor," or at least far less prosperous than their peers in next-door Holland, where the industry was organized by printers reporting to the Hapsburgs (who then ruled Holland).[30]

And the contagion reappeared when the regulatory systems stalled or failed from time to time. Licensing was in effect in England, for example, for all but 9 of the 140 years from 1556 through 1696. Whenever it lapsed, "pamphlets and piracies seemed to flourish," one historian reports. So did pressure, competition, and all the other uncomfortable, unpredictable by-products of freer enterprise. English authors and printers reacted nervously, playing prominent supporting roles in each resumption of various licensing acts into the late 1600s. Few supported outright bans of content, and some of authority's crudest censorships provoked some of history's most inspiring rebuttals. "He who destroys a good book," poet John Milton warned Parliament in 1644, "kills Reason itself." Author Daniel Dafoe, on the other hand, later thought piracy a worse evil than regulation and, in his "Essay on the Regulation of the Press," the *Robinson Crusoe* author proposed that it be reinstated.[31]

When general commercial controls slipped out of hand in France in the early 1600s, fifty new commercial shops opened immediately on the Pont Neuf, six of them printers. Many survived until 1618, when licensed printers, the Church, and the Crown replaced the sagging community of printers with the more effective *chambre des syndicats*.[32]

These were, however, no Dark Ages. As regulatory and government controls waxed and waned, a fabulous flow of challenging, even socially disruptive ideas leaked from the presses. The regulated 1500s, 1600s, and early 1700s were an age of terrific scientific discovery, wholesale rethinking of nature and animal behavior, an ongoing turning of the Western mind from an inflexible, divinely ordered universe to one yet to be discovered and continuously reshaped by reason, then method, and the meeting of human folly and physical law. Orthodoxy was short-lived. Decades after Copernicus overturned traditional astronomy, Galileo amended Copernicus. In England, the stern religious reaction of the Dissidents came and went in mere decades. On the continent, Descartes overturned the ancient Aristotle, only to be succeeded, enhanced, supplemented, and occasionally refuted by Thomas Hobbes, Isaac Newton, and John Locke, all within fifty years after Descartes first published. Scores of others—from George Berkeley to Leibnitz, Spinoza, and Scarlatti, among them—were to follow in the run-up to the Enlightenment (which, with the writings of Montesquieu, Voltaire, Hume, Bentham, Rousseau, and others, blossomed after regulation weakened in France and England in the 1700s). All published in lands where, before 1450, such revelations happened only every three hundred or five hundred years. They happened, moreover, only on the infrequent arrival of teachers so compelling and rhetorically powerful that their admirers, perhaps thinking of them as prophets and seers, might repeat and spread their thoughts. Now great teachers needed only distributors.

And, often thanks to their printer-regulators, they needed permission. Permission to publish, unfortunately, could be capricious. Galileo was the most famous victim. He cautiously secured advance Church approval to publish his landmark *Dialogio* in 1632. Printed with the pope's imprimatur, it was nonetheless immediately banned. The Inquisition promptly brought him to trial for heresy, sparing his life only after he recanted all his proofs. (Copernicus, whose theories Galileo expanded, had escaped persecution in 1543 by dying within hours of publication.) Word of Galileo's fate (he was sentenced to house arrest and died six months later) reached Holland just as Rene Descartes finished his first work of physics, called *Le monde, ou traité de la lumière*. Frightened, he put the work away and directed that it not be published until after his death. It was not.

Hobbes, fearing arrest after the publication of his book in 1650, fled to Paris. But the next year he published *Leviathan*, his most famous work, and French authorities quickly condemned its attack on the papacy. Hobbes fled back to England. He successfully ducked prison until 1660, when Charles II, his former math student, took the throne and offered protection. Yet six years later, Parliament included *Leviathan* on a list of books to be investigated for atheism, panicking Hobbes into burning his papers and delaying the publication of three more books. Locke, Hobbes's philosophical opposite, fared little better. His two *Treatises on Government* were written in 1679 and 1680, but he withheld them from publication until 1690, when the political climate was marginally friendlier to notions of states writing a contract between the people and their rulers. Indeed, many—most—of the great minds of these generations censored themselves, butted up against censors, fled, or were periodically suppressed as political and regulatory winds shifted: Daniel Defoe, David Hume, Denis Diderot, Voltaire. So did lesser talents.

For politicians, the problem both during and between the times when regulation worked well, remained that infernal questioning seemed to resurface wherever certain printed words were allowed to appear. "Books," Milton contended in his famous speech to Parliament, "are as lively and as vigorously productive as those fabulous dragon's teeth and, being sown up and down, may change to spring up armed men." That, to the politicians, was the problem in a nutshell. "Even the farmers concern themselves with political affairs," the Privy Council of Brandenburg groused when it raised import duties to try to keep relatively free Dutch newspapers out of Germany.[33]

The newspapers then appearing throughout Europe were new and especially troublesome kinds of printed words. Single news sheets and newsbooks began showing up as early as 1512, when one called the *Treu Encountre* appeared to describe the downfall of a prior king in England. It then vanished. Still more current bulletins followed. In 1531, a newspaper costing a *gazeta* appeared in Venice. (While its fate is unknown, it did contribute the word "gazette" to the newspaper world.) The New World's first "news" publication, a pamphlet about the threat posed by the pirate Sir Richard Hawkins, appeared in Peru in 1594. These things had immediate impact on the conduct of daily life. When in 1588 Spain sent its massive armada to England, a "war of nerves" and wild, destructive rumors convulsed Britain. "Elizabeth," the romantic Reginald Orcutt sang of the power of this new kind of printed word, "organized what amounted to an office of war information. She commanded printer Christopher Barker to go print a daily newspaper called the *English Mercurie* to report events and calm her panicky subjects."[34]

In Amsterdam, the first newspaper to list the market prices of certain commodities came out and proved to be too useful to businesspeople to let fail. Until then, such market information had appeared in a number of private "news letters," usually penned by a "correspondent" paid by small groups of business people to report both commodity and important political news. In 1609, a Hapsburg prince started *Aviso*, the first German newspaper. By virtue of its connection to the royal family seated in Prague, readers looked to it for firsthand political intelligence critical to surviving the vicious daily intrigues of French, German, English, Swedish, and Polish pretenders blundering through what later became known as the Thirty Years War. Two more papers, in Strasbourg and Cologne, followed to track the war. Taking advantage of the same opportunity, Dutch publishers began papers simultaneously printed in Dutch, French, and English.[35]

The regulatory agencies did not include this potent new medium at first. And it too threatened to start chain reactions that could readily spin out of political control. Once again, authority struck back against the threat with heavy-handed measures.

In 1625 in England, Charles I simply banned all news sheets, including a revolutionary new multisheet paper started in 1621 by Nathaniel Butter, Nicholas Bourne, and Thomas Archer. The king thought the paper far too anti-Hapsburg, the Spanish–German dynasty Charles then wanted as an ally.

They were allowed to restart the paper under tighter regulation in 1638, but Oliver Cromwell blasted them and their competitors out of existence when he came to power. When Charles II drove Cromwell out, he found the same regulatory answer for the newspaper contagion as his predecessors had for the book and pamphlet contagion: he appointed a licenser for all papers. The licenser, a military man named Robert L'Estrange, immediately began his own paper in 1663, and then, like his counterparts in the commercial and book press, halted a competitor's venture.[36]

France regulated its newspapers earlier. Its very first, in 1605, appeared annually. It was not until 1631 that a weekly appeared in Paris. Within five months, the monarchy expropriated it and gave to the king's doctor to run under a license granted to Cardinal Richelieu. *Nouvelles ordinaires de divers endoits* lasted for 150 years, printing bland recitations of official news, appointments, and paeans to absolutism. Equally regulated but more useful was the *Journal des savans*, run by the ecclesiastical counselor to the Estates General. It reviewed all books published in Europe, ran obituaries, covered the sciences, and recorded court decisions. It was, an admiring and less constrained foreign publisher later recounted, imitated in the British colonies in North America as one of the first papers of record.[37] Among the solutions to the newspaper contagion floated in Germany were making printers state employees and suppressing newfangled newspapers by royal decree.[38]

"I thank God we have not free schools nor printing," sighed the governor of the new colony of Virginia even as the first of the British America's presses was en route to Massachusetts from England. "Learning has brought disobedience and heresy and sects into the world, and printing has divulged libels against the government."[39]

But even there, libels and the raw numbers of printed words would fluctuate with the effectiveness of printers' regulation, until, at last, the cost of information fell again.

NOTES

1. Charles L. Mee, *Erasmus: The Eye of the Hurricane* (New York: Coward, McCann & Geoghegan, 1974), 89–92.

2. Mark U. Edwards Jr., *Printing, Propaganda, and Martin Luther* (Berkeley: University of California Press, 1994), 28; George Faludy, *Erasmus* (New York: Stein & Day, 1970), 229.

3. In 849, the archbishop of Rheims imprisoned the German monk Gottschalk for writing arguments contradicting St. Augustine; George Haven Putnam, *The*

Censorship of the Church of Rome (New York: Putnam's, 1906), 1:64–76. Other censorship actions were also taken by the Church before the advent of the printed word; in 1050, the Synod of Vercelli condemned a treatise by Berenger of Tours about the Last Supper. Nine years later it forced him to burn not only the treatise but also a document he wrote to defend himself. The Synod of Scissons forced Abelard to burn his works in 1120, and Innocent III ordered copies of his writings burned in 1140. Amaury of Chartes was already dead in 1209 when the Synod of Paris condemned his writings, so the Synod ordered his remains dug up and his followers burned at the stake. Writers Gherado Segarelli of Parma (1300), Cecco d'Ascoli (1328), and Jan Hus (1416), among others, followed Amaury to the stake, along with their works. The works, but not bodies, of Scotus Erigena (1225), Nicholas de Ultricuria (1348), and John Wyclif (1387) were similarly incinerated. John XXII condemned writings of the late Petrus Johannes Oliva in 1328, dug up his bones, and reburied them with his writings. There they stayed until 1471, when Sixtus IV declared Oliva's ideas sound, disinterred his bones, and gave them a third, proper burial. Jewish writings fared even worse. Various popes and kings ordered the collection and burning of the Talmud and other Jewish writings in 1239, 1244, 1254. 1267, 1415, 1555 (twice), 1559 (when Sixtus, who rehabilitated Oliva, proudly reported he destroyed 12,000 Hebrew volumes), 1565, 1592, and 1775 (when Pope Clement XIV forbade the possession of Talmudic and Cabbalistic books by rabbis and Jews in general and set a penalty of a hundred scudi and seven years in prison).

4. S. H. Steinberg, *Five Hundred Years of Printing* (New York: Criterion, 1959), 186, 191; Frederick W. Hamilton, *A Brief History of Printing, Part II* (Chicago: United Typothetae of America, 1918), 27–28, 31; Elizabeth Eisenstein, *The Printing Press as Agent of Change* (Cambridge: Cambridge University Press, 1979), 347. Later Cervantes's *Don Quixote* and Hobbes's *Leviathan* also profited from censorship. In 1656 a Dutch publisher, disappointed by the initial reception of his *Bibliotheca patrum polonorum*, asked local authorities to censor the book, thinking the notoriety would help sales. The authorities refused. Almost four hundred years after *Amadis*, a Catholic churchman condemned the "scientific liberty" and "anarchism and nihilism" of fifteenth-century books. "The foulest and most pernicious of all," he said, were "the unwholesome romances of the day." Joseph Hilgers, *Der Index der verbotenen Bücher* (1904), cited in Putnam, *Censorship*, 79.

5. Mee, *Erasmus*, 114; Steinberg, *Five Hundred Years*, 188. Vernacular Bibles were banned at the Council of Trent. The Church's ruling, one historian maintains, amounted to "a deliberate cultivation of mystery, an insistence on withholding pearls of wisdom from the swinish multitude and more emphatic distinctions between educated clergy and uninformed laity." Eisenstein, *Printing Press*, 344–45. On Estienne, see Henri Bouchet, *The Book: Its Printers, Illustrators, and Binders from Gutenberg to the Present Time*, ed. H. Grevel (New York: Scribner & Welford, 1890), 136–39.

6. Bouchet, *The Book*, 160; Steinberg, *Five Hundred Years*, 68–69. Greyff's popular humanist author was Etienne Dolet.

7. Hamilton, *A Brief History*, 27–28. The printer was Pedro Ocharte, who was born in France around 1549. In 1561 or 1562, he emigrated to Mexico and married the daughter of Mexico's first (and only) printer. Ocharte inherited the press and printed the offending book in 1572. "Ocharte's Gallic *espirit* probably annoyed the intolerant minions of the Inquisition more than any overt heresy." Lawrence S. Thompson, *Printing in Colonial Spanish America* (Hamden, Conn.: Archon, 1962), 27.

8. Frederick G. Kilgour, *The Evolution of the Book* (New York: Oxford University Press, 1998), 82, 85; Alberto Manguel, *A History of Reading* (New York: Viking, 1996), 134. Scholars' estimates vary widely. In 1935, historian John Lenhart fixed the number printed during the last third of the century at exactly 20,047,500. Lucien Lebe and Henri-Jean Martin, while figuring they couldn't know the precise numbers, agreed that Lenhart was generally correct. In 1970, writer Warren Chappell put the number at 12 million. Eleven years later, historian Richard Rouse revised the estimate to 12–15 million books printed during that short time. Kilgour, *Evolution*, 93; Bouchet, *The Book*, 12.

9. The leading advocate of optimism as a revolutionary force was probably Professor Crane Brinton, who, hoping to find what sparked social upheaval, studied five prerevolutionary societies. He found they all had several things in common, including a sense of rising expectations among certain classes of people. Upheaval came not when hope was gone, but when it was perceived that the government was preventing expected improvements. Crane Brinton, *The Anatomy of a Revolution* (New York: Random House, 1965).

10. Colin Clair, *A History of European Printing* (London: Academic, 1976), 126; J. R. Hale, *Renaissance Europe, 1480–1520*, 2nd ed. (Malden, Mass.: Blackwell, 2000), 114. Printing was one of the few trades in which calculation and business science were practiced. Anton Koberger's shop in Nuremburg grew to a workforce of one hundred.

11. Hamilton, *Brief History*, 43, 46.

12. Steinberg, *Five Hundred Years*, 84; Thompson, *Colonial Spanish America*, 13.

13. Erasmus's book was *Colloquia* (or "friendly conversations"), one of his most popular. Mee, *Erasmus*, 110–11; Clair, *European Printing*, 123; Adrian Johns, *The Nature of the Book: Print and Knowledge in the Making* (Chicago: University of Chicago Press. 1998), 31, 22.

14. Johns, *Nature of the Book*, 173.

15. Putnam, *Censorship*, 78; Ronald J. Deibert, *Parchment, Printing, and Hypermedia: Communication in World Order Transformation* (New York: Columbia University Press, 1997), 74.

16. Hans Lufft sold 100,000 Lutheran Bibles and had branches in Wittenberg and Konigsburg. Melchior Lotter first printed Luther's pamphlets from his shop in Catholic Leipzig, but then shrewdly sent one son (also named Melchior) and then another (Michael) to open a shop in Wittenburg. Melchior, the son, ended up as a power in Wittenburg, Lufft as its burgomeister. Erasmus's Basel printer was Johann Froben, a scholar-printer much like Aldus Magnus in Italy. Clair, *European Printing*, 130, 180.

17. Steinberg, *Five Hundred Years*, 74. Caxton printed about ninety titles, seventy-four of them in English. Most were "books that strongly appealed to the English upper classes at the end of the fifteenth century."

18. George N. Gordon, *The Communications Revolution: A History of Mass Media in the United States* (New York: Hastings House, 1977), 7.

19. Johns, *Nature of the Book*, 248–50.

20. Steinberg, *Five Hundred Years*, 71; Thompson, *Colonial Spanish America*, 12–13. The ten-year deal was struck in 1539, when Cronberger hired Juan Pablos to take a press, printing supplies, Juan Pablos's wife, a pressman named Gil Barbero, and a slave to Mexico City. Cronberger ordered them to turn out 3,000 sheets per day, "a fantastically high number" that they never achieved. Pressman Barbero was to get 5.5 ducats per month. The slave, of course, was to get nothing. After a decade, Cronberger would deduct all transportation, wages, living and depreciation costs from whatever profits the operation managed to produce and pay Pablos 20 percent of the remainder.

21. Bouchet, *The Book*, 122–25; Hamilton, *Brief History*, 49–50; Johns, *Nature of the Book*, 201.

22. Hamilton, *Brief History*, 29.

23. Harry Hillman Chartrand, *Cultural Economics: The Collected Works of Harry Hillman Chartrand* (Saskatoon: Compiler, 2000), culturaleconomics.atfreeweb.com/cpa_b.htm (accessed November 5, 1999); Johns, *Nature of the Book*, 59, 201, 204–12; Clair, *European Printing*, 269.

24. Caroline Davis, History of Publishing, apm.brookes.ac.uk/publishing/contexts/elizabet/legislat.htm (accessed November 5, 1999). In 1559 and 1571, Elizabeth forbade writing or printing texts that questioned her ecclesiastical or temporal authority. The practice of sharing the printing of single titles was called "concurrent printing." Johns, *Nature of the Book*, 99. Holland began creating English language works in the late 1400s when the relatively few English presses could not produce enough low-priced books to satisfy demand. Clair, *European Printing*, 269.

25. Steinberg, *Five Hundred Years*, 145. By contrast, the number of printers in London had grown from five to twenty-five during the first fifty years of the sixteenth century. Clair, *European Printing*, 256; Worshipful Company of Stationers, *History* (London: Worshipful Company of Stationers, 2001), www.stationers.org/history/earlycent.htm (accessed November 6, 1999).

26. Hamilton, *Brief History*, 50; Steinberg, *Five Hundred Years*, 136. The number of master printers in France was reduced from eighty-three in 1636 to seventy-five in 1644 and fifty-one in 1701. Robert Darnton, *The Great Cat Massacre and Other Episodes in French Cultural History* (New York: Basic, 1984), 79.

27. The ten countries that adopted machine printing were Turkey in 1503, Romania in 1508, Greece in 1515, Mexico in 1534, Ireland in 1550, Russia in 1553, India in 1556, Palestine in 1563, Peru in 1584, Japan in 1590. Of those, three (Mexico, Ireland, and Peru) were under the direct sway of the European self-regulating bodies. Warren Chappell, *A Short History of the Printed Word* (New York: Knopf,

1970), 84. Regarding adoptions in the 1600s, the Philippines in 1602, Lebanon and Boliva in 1610, the British colonies in North America in 1639, Iran in 1640, Finland in 1642, Norway in 1643, and China in 1644. Steinberg, *Five Hundred Years,* 113.

28. Hamilton, *Brief History,* 45; Steinberg, *Five Hundred Years,* 141.

29. Bouchet, *The Book,* 155–57; Hamilton, *Brief History,* 72; Steinberg, *Five Hundred Years,* 130–31, 150; Thompson, *Colonial Spanish America,* 42; Johns, *Nature of the Book,* 84–85.

30. Steinberg, *Five Hundred Years,* 20; Svend Dahl, *History of the Book* (Metuchen, N.J.: Scarecrow, 1968), 177. Some German printers formed a guild to regulate the trade but it, like England's old guild for text writers and illuminators, admitted bookbinders, journeymen, papermakers, and all sorts of others with conflicting economic interests. Johns, *Nature of the Book,* 201.

31. Steinberg, *Five Hundred Years,* 234; Chappell, *Short History,* 111; Johns, *Nature of the Book,* 234.

32. Bouchet, *The Book,* 180–81.

33. Chappell, *Short History,* 111–12; Willi Mengel, *Ottmar Mergenthaler and the Printing Revolution* (Brooklyn, N.Y.: Mergenthaler Linotype Company, 1954), 23; Thompson, *Colonial Spanish America,* 38.

34. Mengel, *Mergenthaler,* 16; Isaiah Thomas, *The History of Printing in America,* ed. Marcus A. McCorison (1810; New York: Weathervance, 1970), 11–12; Orcutt, *Merchant of Alphabets* (Garden City, N.Y: Doubleday, 1945), 114; P. M. Handover, *Printing in London: From Caxton to Modern Times* (Cambridge: Harvard University Press, 1960), 98–102; Bob Harris, *Politics and the Rise of the Press* (London: Routledge, 1996), 7–8.

35. S. H. Steinberg, *The Thirty Years War and the Conflict for European Hegemony, 1600–1660* (New York: Norton, 1966), 120–21.

36. Steinberg, *Thirty Years War,* 120; Chappell, *Short History,* 130–31. L'Estrange eventually allowed the usurper, Henry Muddiman, to set up a paper at Oxford in 1665 after he joined the licensing program.

37. Chappell, *Short History,* 129. The admiring foreign publisher was Isaiah Thomas, a leading printer in the British colonies during the later 1700s. Thomas, *Printing in America,* 11–12.

38. Steinberg, *Five Hundred Years,* 196; Chappell, *Short History,* 127–28.

39. Chappell, *Short History,* 139.

II

THE TYPE AGE:
FROM LEVER TO MACHINE

8

CAT TROUBLES

In 1638, well before things cracked open again, a "wealthy dissenting clergyman in England" named Joseph Glover chafed. Life was dark. To Glover and his fellow Dissenters, the monarchy and all of England had turned hellish, mired in profligacy, ostentation, and heresy. In a few years Glover's colleagues would be at war to cleanse the country, ultimately bringing Oliver Cromwell to power and relieving the king of his head. For now, however, Glover was itching to escape sinful England for a more reverent place. By letters ferried back and forth across the forbidding North Atlantic, he asked the overseers of the new oasis of piety in Massachusetts for permission to take refuge among them.

He also asked to bring a printing press with him. With it, he promised to produce material for struggling Harvard College, then making do with expensive books imported from England. His would be the first such contraption in British America.

When permission arrived, he bought a press and hired a laborer to run it. He then herded his wife, two sons, the press, the assistant, and a not immodest household of five servants onto a ship for the treacherous journey to America and a more innocent life.[1]

But Glover's fate, in the end, "was similar to that of Moses, who, although zealously engaged in conducting the children of Israel from Egypt to Canaan . . . never reached the land of promise himself." He died during the rough passage. His bereaved wife and children arrived in the chill autumn of 1638 without him, friendless in the new land. Winter approached. All they had was the press, some paper, some type, and obligations to care for the people they'd brought with them, including the worker who had none too accurately told Glover he knew how to print.[2]

After a decent mourning period, a suitor—Henry Dunster, first president of Harvard College—came to court the widow Glover. By the time he got Mrs. Glover to the altar in 1641, the college already had taken in the press and Stephen Daye, the laborer-printer who had come from England with the family. Daye had had the press running for two years, and had coaxed out *Freeman's Oath, an almanack.* It was the first book produced on the North American continent.

It was awful. The historic tome was so badly printed that many of the colony's writers resumed sending their work to London to be published. Shipping them abroad might be expensive and slow but was preferable to submitting them to Daye's deadly care. Daye himself managed to become "embarrassed with debts" within four years. He was jailed briefly before sailing home to England, leaving the colony to scramble to replace him. In 1649, Harvard's overseers found a replacement in a large empty cask, the only shelter an immigrant named Samuel Green could find for himself and his family. Green was honest enough to admit he'd have to learn how to run the press and got the job.[3]

Industrious, he studied the craft and was doing good, reliable printing in the colony by 1660, when a religious society in England commissioned Harvard to produce a Bible to try to convert nearby Indians. To help, the society sent Green 150 sheets of paper, an assistant named Marmaduke Johnson, and what amounted to the new medium's next labor problem.

Johnson proved to be "very idle." By September 1662, he hadn't shown up at work for six months, leaving the Bible half done. He'd also strayed: the married assistant was indicted in 1662 for "alluring the daughter of Samuel Green, printer," fined £5 and ordered to go home to England to his wife. Apparently in heat, he stayed anyway and was soon fined £20 for threatening to kill a competitor for Ms. Green's attention. Somehow still in Massachusetts in October 1663, he was fined yet another £20. This time, the court itself booked him on a ship due to leave in six weeks. Remarkably, Johnson again evaded deportation, although a fire destroyed the court records that might have explained how. "His wife might have died," a historian speculated, or "he had influential friends, and he made his peace with Green." In the labor-short colony, the masochistic Green even rehired Johnson, although now he prudently paid him for each sheet he finished printing instead of with a regular salary. But little improved. His "demeanor hath not been suitable," Harvard ruled before firing him again. And so it went. For the next nine years, managers kept hiring and firing the resilient slacker to help print a project here, a project there. In 1670 he married again, although not to Ms. Green. Perhaps heartened by this show of stability, the colony's overseers appointed him as, of all things, Cambridge's constable. He nevertheless remained "poor, and rather indolent." Shortly after he died in 1675, Harvard sued his estate and finally recovered some press parts it had suspected him of hoarding even during his years in law enforcement.[4]

Thus the printed word's first day on American shores was also the first day that labor became a distracting, often controlling force in the new land's communications business.

And labor would grow into a (sometimes *the*) major regulator of the medium in both the new and old worlds, exercising a powerful voice in determining the printed word's cost, scope, and speed.

Thanks to the potent regulatory agencies emerging out of a newfangled merchant economy, knowledge already had become more expensive and complicated to manufacture than it had been in the first generations of printing. Printed knowledge now traded at the same deliberate, ritualistic pace as the businesses that physically produced it. The gentlemanly, state-sanctioned monopolies that produced it, in turn, moved only as fast as the people who worked at them.

Samuel Green gradually became regulated royalty; official printer to both the college and the colony, owner of three hundred wilderness acres on the west side of Haverhill. He also found the time to produce, among 192 books and pamphlets and flyers, nineteen children. Not a few followed him into the trade. Printing Greens eventually settled in Connecticut and Maryland. Until 1775, Boston itself "was not without one or more printers by the name of Green." All descended from Samuel.

Clucking over his work, in a rough copy of the way things worked in Europe, were licensers. To avoid "contentions and heresies" and, in the process, to preserve the market for Green, regulators prohibited anyone else from printing in and around Cambridge for a while. (The penalty: authorities would expropriate the offender's press.) From time to time, the four licensors—the president of Harvard, which owned the press, and three other community leaders—censored "some small religious treatises . . . which the general court or some of the ruling clergy judged rather too liberal." One such review led them to suspend Green for a short while. Another time, they rejected Green's request to print *Imitation of Christ*, the perennial European best-seller by Thomas à Kempis. (The Protestant censors regarded the author as "a popish minister.") When they needed to, they also passed extra laws to limit trade. In 1671, for example, a Cambridge bookseller applied to the regulators to publish a local statute book. Green was to do the printing, aided by Marmaduke Johnson. But the bookseller feared that

Johnson "might print [and sell] additional copies for himself." At the book-seller's request, the censors wrote two ordinances to give the bookseller the exclusive right to sell the law book in the area. Green proceeded to print that and scores of other works during his long tenure, becoming a pillar of the community, captain of the Cambridge militia, and something of a priv-ileged figure even in sternly antiprivilege Massachusetts. As a feeble old man, he "insisted on being carried in his chair [to oversee the militia] on days of muster, that he might review and exercise his company." He died in 1702, at the age of eighty-seven.[5]

How Green's occasional employees viewed him is not known, but workers in the printing businesses in other regulated countries by then ac-tively, even proudly, hated owners.

Class divisions in those more mature nations were deep. "All the work-ers" a former apprentice named Nicolas Contat wrote of his time in a Paris printing house in the 1730s, "were in league against the masters." An ap-prentice only had "to speak badly of (the masters) to be esteemed by the whole assembly of typographers."[6]

Usually, however, the typographers—they were also called printers, compositors, "typos," and other, less complimentary names—were as deter-minedly hostile toward the younger workers as they were toward their bosses. To the senior printers, apprentices were threats. Someday apprentices would take their jobs. Hoping to humiliate them out of the business, the journeymen often made newcomers like Contat bow to them or even pay them before entering the shop. They regularly hazed them and at intervals put them through still more elaborate rites before allowing them a few pro-fessional "privileges." The rites bore a striking resemblance to the more ex-pensive costume parties and *haute* ceremonies of their masters, who also marked their grudging passages toward full competition with each other with feasts, ritual pledges, tolls, and last-ditch schemes to keep their num-bers small.

Before they could actually earn a living as printers, apprentices like Contat faced years of demanding tests of their obedience and their man-hood. In Germany, junior printers endured a decade-long series of hazings full of dark death and resurrection themes before they could take their better-paid place among the journeymen. Everyone except the apprentices in Contat's shop in Paris exchanged secret, ceremonial greetings, ate together, and nonchalantly used the rookies' property as their own. After as many as three years of ostracism, the elder printers put an apprentice through the next initiation rite, the "taking of the apron." Usually at a tavern, the boy—probably now in his early or middle teens—swore never to work for less than a standard wage and to stand by his colleagues. If he betrayed them, he'd be blacklisted from the shop, and his name would be sent to all other shops. All other senior printers would refuse to work with him. After taking the apron, the apprentice finally would learn some printing skills.[7] When he wasn't off doing domestic chores, he was allowed to dampen paper, ink presses, move type from composing sticks into forms and wheel carriages into place. After four more years, the fellow might at last become a journeyman and at last earn a living wage.

In the meantime, Contat and his fellow apprentices on the Rue Saint-Severen in Paris "slept in a filthy, freezing room, rose before dawn, ran errands [for both the master and the master's family] while dodging insults from the journeymen and abuse from the master, and received nothing but slops to eat." The household cats lived well by comparison. The master's doting wife fed them better than the apprentices, sometimes giving them leftovers that the boys coveted. They slept in better quarters and were much better loved. The mistress of Contat's household required everyone in the business to serve them. Preparing to leave for the country with her family, she apparently went over the line one day, scolding and reinstructing the hungry boys how to coddle the cats properly. After she left, one of Contat's fellow apprentices, by now drunk, snatched the mistress's favorite pet and, in a savage impulse that was never explained, killed it.

Looking on, something wild and primal flashed in Contat and the other apprentices, and they began to run. They rampaged through the house, chasing the other cats, and, sometimes after inflicting maximum pain, killing them. They spilled into the street next, racing toward neighbors' pets. They captured a number of them, tortured them, and slaughtered them too.

The bloody pogrom, the sociologist who later translated Contat's autobiography observed, suggested more than just the episodic insanity of badly nurtured teenage boys. It was class hatred; an impure acid that, exposed to certain levels of heat and pressure, seemed to ignite. A little more dryly, an economist later noted "cultural stresses of high intensity" had developed in workplaces throughout Western society at the time. They were highest wherever political controls were tight, and political controls were especially acute in absolutist and often terrifying Paris. Above cold shops like Contat's rose grim prisons, the Bastille and the Chatelet, which were full of "ordinary Parisians . . . confined without warrant and punished without trial." City hall hosted weekly public torturing of such criminals for the masses' edification and, it's not hard to imagine, brutalization. Few were safe from the nobility's punitive whims. It was during this era that much of our modern vocabulary of spying—"espionage" and "surveillance," among other words—was invented and employed by the monarchy's agents against citizens great and small. Trapped beneath the more fortunate social classes that sat heavily on the merchants (it was during this era that words like "millionaire" were coined to describe, usually disdainfully, the bourgeoisie's ostentatious flaunting of riches gained from the nation's speculative gold bubble) who pushed them around, Contat and his fellow apprentices festered a long time before they ultimately ran amok. In the aftermath, however, they were not sure what to do with the animals' carcasses. The mistress of the house finally found her beloved gray cat several days after the riot, partially dismembered and decaying, at the bottom of a shaft behind her house.[8]

After enduring years of exploitation and meanness, apprentices who actually reached the profession's state of adulthood did not have a much healthier environment. "Anything is permitted" for the journeymen, Contat reported. "Excessive drinking is considered a good quality, gallantry and debauchery as youthful feats, indebtedness a sign of wit, irreligion as sincerity. It's a free and republican territory in which everything is permitted. Live as you like, but be an honest man. No hypocrisy."[9]

Their drinking, moreover, was epic.

"We had an alehouse boy who attended always in the house to supply the workmen," the young Benjamin Franklin recalled of a time in the mid-1720s when, stranded in England, he worked in a London printing business. "My companion at the press drank every day a pint before breakfast, a pint at breakfast with his bread and cheese, a pint between breakfast and dinner, a pint in the afternoon about six o'clock, and another when he had done his day's work." The prodigious drinking made Franklin, hardly prudish but distinctly more industrious, uncomfortable. He soon transferred from the pressroom to the presumably more sober compositors' room. There, however, his new mates charged him an "initiation fee" of five shillings. They used it to buy liquor for themselves.[10]

Class divisions back in Franklin's Boston and Philadelphia, where press owners now competed with each other for business as well as for labor in a more open market, seemed less pronounced. Workers did not necessarily think of themselves as stuck. Franklin himself was mobile, jumping from shop to shop and ultimately class to class. His initial Philadelphia job included a request to gather competitive intelligence on the town's second printer for its first. He left that position at the behest of a sponsor who, free to compete with the other two printers in town, offered to set him up with a press of his own. (The sponsor's offer turned out to be empty, but Franklin did not find out until he went all the way to England to pick up the promised funds and press. He was left there almost penniless, and he took the job at the sodden London print shop to make enough money to get home.) He soon managed to become a press owner anyway. Needing no regulatory permission, he scraped together capital and equipment by partnering with a friend. His class-bound counterparts in Europe would have found his upward mobility an absurd fantasy. In the early 1700s, presses could be had in London for "the relatively small sum of £5 each." (At the time, the average Londoner earned about £30 per year.) But buying one required official permission as well as money. And the only way a journeyman in France, England, Switzerland, Italy, Holland, and Spain could get permission was to join the "oligarchy of masters" who, by handing out state-sponsored permissions, controlled the industry. The only way to join the oligarchy, in turn, was to marry a master's daughter. It was unlikely.[11]

He was thus a permanent worker, consigned to set type, feed paper, pull levers, stack sheets, and compete with young boys for as long as he could please his masters, avoid the attention of the authorities, and keep his health. (Health was iffy. The fastest, most skilled workers were renowned for holding type in their mouths as they set it and, as often as not, breaking to eat without benefit of washing their ink-stained, metal-flecked hands.) He tended his presses and type in a "theater," often dark, dirty, and ill ventilated, in or next to the master's house. Not surprisingly, the whole domicile/business often moved to family-like rhythms and language. The shop's oldest worker was called "father." In France, the most accomplished journeyman was "mother." Clerks in the retail book shops that often were part of the house called each other "brother." All bossed each other around or deferred to each other according to their familial titles and roles. They sometimes teased and exploited each other like families too. Older "brothers" forced younger ones to pay them a "solace"—usually a small amount of money— to rectify a mistake or even join them at a pub. And all deferred to the master printer. Even in North America, the master printer "in parental fashion . . . punished small crimes and insubordination" with fines, cold shoulders, and beatings. There he might also "protect his youngsters from external dangers from sheriff's deputies to village ruffians." In Europe, the journeymen sometimes provided the protection. But pitting a worker's interest against those of the head of the business was like defying a father, and just as legally impossible in many shops. There were consequences: the withholding of attention, the denial of respect, the cutting of pay, the stripping of privilege, and banishment and the loss of protection from the long, unpredictable arm of the state. Being fired often meant being evicted from one's home.[12]

Class divisions, in short, had deepened into a permanent, expensive, inflexible state of distrust in the belly of the maturing printed word industry in Europe. America would soon follow, and the divisions would remain deep forever more. The animosity grew as printing became a heavy machine industry into the 1800s and 1900s. (It waned near the end of the twentieth century, when easier presses, alphabets, and finally computers made manufacturing the printed word into a typeless light industry with no further use for manufacturing specialists.) Masters always connived to bring in cheaper labor, and expensive labor always connived to stop them. Everybody strained to improve his or her own lots. To the masters, that made the printer "lazy, flighty, dissolute and unreliable." To the printers, it made the master a "bourgeois" who "ate different food, kept different hours, and talked a different language. His wife and daughters dallied with worldly abbes. They kept pets. Clearly, the bourgeois belonged to a different subculture, one which meant above all that he did not work."[13] As each managed to reserve another slice of the money or another moment of respite that made printing something take longer, the costs of producing the printed word ratcheted upward again.

Closing the divide was rarely encouraged and almost never proposed. From above, politicians were not interested. As long as the industry itself kept dangerous communications from circulating and kept tax and tithe money coming, they stood aside. They stepped in only when content threatened them, when untaxed merchandise appeared, or when competitors threatened the official printers they sponsored. Both masters and workers were comfortable enough with the system to avoid taking many chances. Both classes took turns actively suppressing real or imagined changes in most of the trade's labor relations, content, customs, and tools.

Sometimes it was the masters who felt threatened and beat back changes. When Dutchman Willam Blaeu improved Gutenberg's lever press in 1620, it was largely opposed in England by press owners who, snug in their monopolies, had little incentive to invest in it. In 1721, a master printer in Jena shouted down "the damned hellish fiend" who had offered a technical improvement that would, by virtue of altering work flow, disturb "the well-established state of repose of the printers."

Sometimes it was the workers: In 1772, workers in Basel got the city to ban the use of Wilhelm Haas's big new press capable of imprinting the entire side of a sheet with one pull of the lever. The thing could well eliminate jobs.[14]

Sometimes both masters and laborers, members of the same regulatory agency in many areas, combined to inhibit technical as well as commercial innovations. For the workers, it was often for fear that better tools would imperil their jobs. For the masters, it was for fear that better tools would encourage new competition.[15]

Between them, both classes managed to keep the technology as well as the trade almost stagnant during what were the otherwise inventive centuries of the Enlightenment. The hurricane lamp, the toilet, the adding machine, the hot air balloon, telescope, pendulum clock, piano, and steam turbine, among hundreds of other wonders, were invented in this era. While Gutenberg's lever-operated press remained relatively untouched, sailing ships, music, construction techniques, firearms, and even the culinary arts virtually were reinvented. Strong metal screws, it's true, replaced wood screws in the contraptions in the 1500s. Engravers also began etching images into metal instead of wood at about the same time, making for a more durable image to print. In the early 1600s, Blaeu engineered his easer-to-use version of Gutenberg's device, which also sprouted "friskets" and "tympans" and other melodically named parts that improved quality. People learned to sew as well as glue pages together into book form. To the primarily wooden presses, iron parts finally were added in the 1700s. The presses gradually became bigger, sweatier. To French workers, the brawny machines became "bears"; to English workers, "horses." Yet technically, as one elegiac writer put it, all amounted to just "a new, metallic hymn in honor of Gutenberg."[16]

NOTES

1. Joseph Blumenthal, *The Printed Book in America* (Boston: Godine, 1977), 1–2. Blumenthal suggests that Glover may have made an earlier trip to Massachusetts to prepare the way for his and his brood's arrival.

2. Isaiah Thomas, *The History of Printing in America*, ed. Marcus A. McCorison (1810; New York: Weathervane, 1979), 42.

3. Thomas, *History*, 50–53; Blumenthal, *Printed Book*, 1–2.

4. Thomas, *History*, 69, 71–75.

5. Thomas, *History*, 69; Blumenthal, *Printed Book*, 2.

6. Robert Darnton, *The Great Cat Massacre and Other Episodes in French Cultural History* (New York: Basic, 1984), 79.

7. Adrian Johns, *The Nature of the Book: Print and Knowledge in the Making* (Chicago: University of Chicago Press, 1998), 95; Darnton, *Cat Massacre*, 88.

8. Darnton, *Cat Massacre*, 75–79; David Hackett Fischer, *The Great Wave: Price Revolutions and the Rhythm of History* (New York: Oxford University Press, 1996), 135, 118. Fischer's Paris of the 1730s was a place of both "extravagant wealth and grotesque poverty . . . Many lived like animals on close-built bridges above the river Seine, while the great families of France resided in magnificent mansions only a few streets away." Moreover, it was "also a capital of despotic darkness. It was the controlling center of an absolutism that ruled by terror, cunning and brutal force." On the word "millionaire," see Paul Strathern, *A Brief History of Economic Genius* (New York: Texare, 2001), 47.

9. Darnton, *Cat Massacre*, 88–89.

10. Johns, *Nature of the Book*, 96–97.

11. Douglas C. McMurtrie, *A History of Printing in the United States*, vol. 2, *Middle and South Atlantic States* (New York: Burt Franklin, 1969), 27–28; Johns, *Nature of the Book*, 76; Darnton, *Cat Massacre*, 79–80.

12. Johns, *Nature of the Book*, 75; Walker Rumble, *The Swifts: Printers in the Age of Typesetting Races* (Charlottesville: University of Virginia Press, 2003), 181, 6–7.

13. Darnton, *Cat Massacre*, 81.

14. Colin Clair, *A History of European Printing* (London: Academic, 1976), 358; S. H. Steinberg, *Five Hundred Years of Printing* (New York: Criterion, 1959), 198.

15. Svend Dahl, *History of the Book* (Metuchen, N.J.: Scarecrow, 1968), 176.

16. Henri Bouchet, *The Book: Its Printers, Illustrators, and Binders from Gutenberg to the Present Time*, ed. H. Grevel (New York: Scribner & Welford, 1890), 157; Pierre de la Marre, "An Industry Born," *Printers World*, April 21, 1997, as reproduced at www.dotprint.com (accessed January 2, 1999). The frisket was a piece of parchment cut to expose the text to be printed and to help keep ink from getting onto the surfaces that were not supposed to be printed. A tympan was a piece of soft fabric that helped keep the type level when it was impressed onto the paper. Both the frisket and the tympan were parts of the double-hinged case that actually held the type and was itself introduced in about 1570. Johns, *Nature of the Book*, 92–93; Willi Mengel, *Ottmar Mergenthaler and the Printing Revolution* (Brooklyn, N.Y.: Mergenthaler Linotype, 1954), 12.

9

TRICKLE, STREAM,
TORRENT, WAVE . . .

In the early 1700s, an unfortunate era of terrible price inflation and "heroic" government borrowing began in Europe and North America. As if some new age was beginning to boil up from the deep, speculative bubbles rose and burst spectacularly in England and France. (The first had been in Holland in the early 1600s.) Dislocations followed throughout the century. Work in some English rural villages mysteriously stopped and disappeared, sometimes in a day. Thousands of shocked residents were moving, leaving their generational homes for distant, unfamiliar mills and factories that promised to forestall starvation. They sometimes did not fulfill their promises, and they were often horrible and inhumane places. Populations throughout Europe grew dramatically. Violent crime became epidemic as wealth increasingly concentrated in fewer hands, and a mean, overcrowded lifestyle developed in the narrow streets of the half thought-out warrens of prole housing hurriedly glommed onto the edges of many cities. There, in a metaphor of what was happening to the way money was starting to circulate, old rules of behavior no longer applied. "Chastity," Adam Smith later wrote of how the upper classes viewed the goings-on in the dangerous industrial slums, "is breached." Western institutions labored under the strain until its governments began to fail. Armed insurrections roiled Geneva, Russia, the Netherlands, Corsica, Ireland, and finally British America. Bread prices in Paris, in one of history's few neat coincidences, peaked on the day the Bastille fell in 1789.[1]

France's great coincidence was only the bloodiest example of how the regulated merchant elites were losing control of the trades they oversaw. Sixty years of rising costs, declining demand for their goods, and the sheer uncertainty that came with social upheaval had dulled the masters' instincts.

The politicians who provided the muscle to suppress their competitors were increasingly enmeshed in conflicts between their mandate to preserve the status quo and their need to upset the status quo in order to raise more money.

In France self-doubting politicians, flailing to keep their impoverished institutions from collapsing, were panicked by crushing national debts and egged on by grand theories of how to cure them. Some economic philosophers, like Bernard Mandeville, counseled that self-interest was the key to both getting out of debt and achieving social progress. Encourage self-interest, and you'll create wealth. Others, like François Quesnay, argued the quickest was to prosperity was to adopt laissez-faire policies; keep the regulators' hands off commerce as much as possible. The great eccentric Adam Smith (a wildly knowledgeable man living with his mother who was occasionally found on the street staring thoughtfully at and muttering toward the sky; he resolutely and painfully plunged into the winter sea for the sake of his health before heading back to his desk to record insight after insight for ten long years) delivered *The Wealth of Nations* in 1776. Its explanations of "natural" economic mechanics and unseen hands of the marketplace were immediately translated into many foreign languages and folded into policy in many of Europe's chambers. It thought regulation was ill advised.

So some members of the ruling classes decided regulation in general and censorship in particular were an obstacle. They agreed that censoring expression obviously was an important way to maintain order, but it was not an unalloyed good. Sometimes, they said, it amounted to limiting commerce. When you limited any commerce and trade, including the print trade, you frustrated self-interest. You thus also violated natural law and, put another way, God's mechanical laws of rewarding the smartest, most blessed people among us. Worse yet, you also deprived the state of needed revenues.

Elite printers, on the other hand, disagreed. They remained solidly in favor of censoring unlicensed authors and manufacturers. To them, censorship was central to the system that had created their wealth, and they complained that while the Royal Court and the Parlement of Paris were debating the niceties of censorship, the disheartened police who normally confiscated competitors' works were doing halfhearted work and wrecking the system. Whenever the censors looked away, in fact, dammed-up and usually unlicensed books, pamphlets, and ideas burst out of Avignon, Geneva, Neufchatel, and Lyon. From London and Amsterdam, they increasingly slipped by the book police.

When the government fell in 1789, the thirty-six licensed printers of the Paris Book Guild were finally inundated in the great egalitarian swell. There were calls to abolish *all* the professional oligarchies that had ruled the nation's economy for centuries. Almost immediately, two hundred new newspapers appeared in France. In Paris alone, the two hundred presses operating in 1789 grew to seven hundred by 1795. By 1810, there were 137 printing shops and 588 booksellers in town. And out of a French business community straining to produce unprecedented numbers of printed sheets came, at last, technical innovations to help produce them faster: a press that required but one pull of a lever to imprint a large sheet of paper; a process that minimized the need to reset type over and over again. In the now unregulated commercial scramble to satisfy demand, Nicolas Jean Robert, a Frenchman living in England, invented a radical new papermaking process that increased output by a factor of ten. It dropped the cost of paper, long the printed word's most expensive component, by a third.[2]

England's controls on the printed word already were compromised. Freedom of religion had battered them first. Stationers, ever sustained by the automatic, mandated sales of official church hymnals and prayer books, had kept their monopolies even as governments changed from requiring them to print all Church of England books to printing all Catholic to all Protestant to all Catholic books again. The type of content didn't matter, but the volume and diversity of it did. As England became more tolerant, parishioners scattered freely into Anglican, Catholic, and other institutions during the latter half of the seventeenth century. Each hierarchy, in turn, needed its own hymnals and books. Each found its own stationer printer. Where all hymnal revenues in the land used to go to one lucky printer, now many split the money. Power within the stationers company split accordingly.

Similar problems arose as readers' tastes in romance, business, and politics became more diverse. Risk averse and fat, the company's coddled master printers did not—or could not—redeploy their capital or their workers fast enough to satisfy the tastes of their more numerous and frustratingly fickle customers. It was one thing to print all the king's books. It was another to produce, say, the burgeoning numbers of official Whig, proregulation, and/or laissez-faire titles at the same time, and then not be sure they could be sold. The demand strained the suppliers. In modern terms, the master printers did not have the savvy or production capacity to satisfy readers' now frantic pursuit of law, commerce, science, education, news, and even fantasy. Competing in an open market required speed, finding and enforcing operational efficiencies, assessing and taking risk, and more speed. The master printers of regulated England never had to learn those skills. They readily lost sales to competitors who did.

Booksellers, once minor members of the Stationers Company, were the toughest competitors. They had a better street-level sense than the printers of what people would buy, and they nimbly wooed popular authors on their own. They, not printers, now bought manuscripts to publish. Increasingly prosperous, they soon got the upper hand in the company. Their fondest wish was for more and better materials to sell. Preserving the master printers' rights to be the exclusive manufacturers of certain titles was hardly a priority for them. On the contrary, such rights often drove up the costs of buying books to stock in their shops and limited their supply. In 1695, when the press restrictions that had sustained the company for 139 years came up for renewal, the booksellers—eventually to be called publishers—supported the reformers in Parliament.

The restrictions were in political trouble anyway. As England steered away from royal authority, reformers saw the rules that reserved certain trades for certain kingly supporters as potent political symbols of dreaded privilege. The old licenses and patents had played a central role in Parliament and the monarchy's 150-year battle for power. As Parliament chipped away at royalty's authority to tax people directly, the Crown's sales of monopolies over different kinds of businesses and specific book titles had been an important source of money. But by the late 1600s, its authority to sell such things was gone too. When Parliament finally stripped the royal court of its power to tax people directly in the Glorious Revolution of 1689, the stationers was the last of the twelve monopoly "companies"—the self-regulating trade groups that Mary, Elizabeth, and their successors had formed to raise money—that still had some original powers. Its hold on its profession, moreover, did not last much longer. In 1695, the laws supporting the stationers' monopolies came up for renewal. Parliament's triumphant Whigs at last had the votes to eviscerate them too.[3]

Now the Stationers Company was left as a mere registrar, almost toothless. Printers still had to register all books with the company, helping the government keep track of what was on the market. But the stationers could no longer fine, seize, and destroy (or, according to some scandalmongers, secretly resell) nonmembers' work. Competitors, some of them able to raise unprecedented amounts of capital through new joint-stock companies, were now free to multiply and produce almost whatever printed words they thought they could sell.[4] The number of booksellers in London quickly increased by 25 percent (to 188) in the next five years. The number of commercial printers grew even faster, from twenty-three in 1695 to sixty-two in 1705 and seventy-four in 1725.[5]

Not surprisingly, the new competition proved to be as chaotic, mean, risky, and larcenous as the unregulated competition of the Renaissance and Reformation. Pirated books multiplied, especially from unregulated Scotland. Desperate stationers begged Parliament to restore their regulatory powers. But, rejecting the stationers' pleas to reinstate the restrictions and prepublication censorship that had secured the printed word business in the past, Parliament came up with something new.

In 1709, it adopted the world's first modern copyright law. The law for the first time gave authors, not printers or their state sponsors, formal economic rights to their work. They could profit from them for fourteen years after their death. Now authors in effect hired printers to manufacture and publishers to sell their work. If someone copied it without their permission, the author—as opposed to the state or the printers' association—could take the offender to court. By collecting taxes on author-authorized work, Parliament profited by stimulating sales, not restricting them.

Other nations also adopted copyright laws (the United States in 1776, France in 1793, the German states starting in 1839), formally granting inventors and authors—as opposed to kings, manufacturers, distributors, and sellers—ownership of the ideas they created and letting the market regulate what was available to read.[6]

"A torrent of books and pamphlets materialized" after each copyright law, each regulatory change, and each flirtation with freedom of the press. Jeremy Bentham, Rousseau, David Hume, Adam Smith, Gibbon's *Rise and Fall of the Roman Empire*, newspapers, popular novels, Shelley, encyclopedias in France and in Britain, and more, appeared. As there had been a quickening of the Renaissance after the printed word became possible, now there was a quickening of thought, later categorized as the Enlightenment, after the printed word was freed to circulate faster again. As Renaissance-era works promoted the idea of a nation bigger than any one fiefdom or region, some work now promoted, for the first time, the idea of a "civilization" larger than any one nation.[7] Similarly whole economies, like trade itself, looked larger than any one nation.

Many years later another economist saw it as a turning point. Consulting whatever data he could find, he parsed the past 1,000 years into economic eras and found periods of inflation and falling productivity, followed by periods of price equilibrium. During the "waves" of price equilibrium, real prices dropped. Population growth and productivity seemed to change in concert with each other. All kinds of wealth—food, money, shelter—multiplied more rapidly than the numbers of people. There was more to go around.[8]

One of the long, prosperous "price equilibrium" waves began during Gutenberg's time in the fifteenth century. Another would rise at the end of the nineteenth century and still another at the end of the twentieth. With each, there were great technical changes in the printed word that lowered the cost of information. As costs dropped, print merchants obviously could earn more money on each book or newspaper they produced without raising the prices they charged customers. Hence they printed more.

One such wave rose during the decades just before and just after 1800, and it swamped the old restraints on both the manufacturers and authors of the printed word. By the time it receded the merchant system itself, increasingly weighty in the rising industrial tide, was gone.

The long, slow stasis of printed knowledge was ending at last. Activity in the corners of the craft began to look as frantic as it had in the first half of the fifteenth century, when Gutenberg, Coster, Castaldi, and many of Europe's other inventors turned, as if by some mystical agreement, to working on similar notions at the same time. In addition to the papermaking and type-quickening innovations, the escalating demand led a German printer named Jakob LeBlon to exotically apply the lessons of Isaac Newton's *Opticks* to try to print in color. His shop failed, but as his century ended imitators were adapting his work into what would soon be the basis of all color printing to come. Phillipe-Denis Pierres fashioned a press on which the lever returned automatically to its starting point. Erasmus Darwin (Charles's grandfather) and James Watt, the inventor of the steam engine, both came up with "copying presses" that could reproduce a few copies of recent originals with special ink in the late 1770s. (Watt's actually worked and was used to copy business documents for a century.) More radically, Alois Senefelder, a Bavarian writer who couldn't get his plays published, decided to sell them himself. Without a clue of how to copy them, he concocted a a way to print with stones, wax, and water. (Descendants of his technique, called lithography, remain widely used.) Joseph-Marie Jacquard, Charles Babbage, and Thomas de Colmar tinkered with ways to produce words out of calculated signals to machines, ideas that would one day morph into computers. William Nicholson designed new ways to deliver ink to the type on a press. Nicolas Robert and John Dickinson reinvented papermaking into a machine-driven art. A hydraulic press appeared.

In the first decade of the 1800s came carbon paper and, to help a blind contessa in Italy, a typewriter. An American (Adam Ramage) and an Englishman (Lord Stanhope) almost simultaneously built great iron presses. (The American version flopped; the British one was a terrific success.) In London, a group of bankers, anxious to communicate more rapidly, arranged to have war news delivered to them by carrier pigeon. In 1815, they got early news of Wellington's victory across the channel at Waterloo and used it to make a killing on the market.[9]

Still more new tools soon spilled out of the unregulated disorder. They arrived with purposes that had nothing to do with keeping political, spiritual, or national order, but they too had outcomes no one could think how to direct.[10] Social gears seemed to be slipping in the process.

NOTES

1. David Hackett Fischer, *The Great Wave: Price Revolutions and the Rhythm of History* (New York: Oxford University Press, 1996), 120–41; Nathan Rosenberg and L. E. Birdzell Jr., *How the West Grew Rich* (New York: Basic, 1986), 7–8.

2. Raymond Birn, "Malesherbes and the Call for a Free Press," in Robert Darnton and Daniel Roche, eds., *Revolution in Print: The Press in France, 1775–1800* (Berkeley: University of California Press, 1989), 50, 56; Carla Hesse, "Economic Upheavals in Publishing," in Darnton and Roche, eds., *Revolution in Print*, 78, 92; Phillippe Minard, "Agitation in the Work Force," in Darnton and Roche, eds., *Revolution in Print*, 107; Paul Strathern, *A Brief History of Economic Genius* (New York: Taxere, 2001), 63–66, 72–75. The inventor of the single-pull press was Francois Ambroise. In 1799, Firmin Didot welded together types of a form so that he wouldn't have to recompose it for the next printing, a process he called stereotyping. Henri Bouchet, *The Book: Its Printers, Illustrators, and Binders from Gutenberg to the Present Time*, ed. H. Grevel (New York: Scribner & Welford, 1890), 232; S. H. Steinberg, *Five Hundred Years of Printing* (New York: Criterion, 1959), 199.

3. Harry Hillman Chartrand, *Cultural Economics: The Collected Works of Harry Hillman Chartrand* (Saskatoon: Compiler, 2000), culturaleconomics.atfreeweb.com/cpu_b.htm (accessed January 7, 2002).

4. By 1695, moreover, England's economy was being transformed into something different. Some £4.25 million—almost 13 percent of the nation's industrial wealth—was invested in the fairly new joint-stock companies that exploited the era's fluid money flows more effectively than traditional chartered companies did. The amount in joint-stock companies doubled in the next eight years. James E. Thorold Rogers, *Industrial and Commercial History of England* (London: Macmillan, 1869), 125.

5. P. M. Handover, *Printing in London* (Cambridge: Harvard University Press, 1960), 68–70; Adrian Johns, *The Nature of the Book: Knowledge in the Making* (Chicago: University of Chicago Press, 1998), 66, 72.

6. The first American copyright law, adopted at the confederation's birth in 1776, gave copyright protection to books by American authors or to foreign books revised by Americans. It sent American printers off on a wholesale campaign to revise foreign works in order to gain legal protection. Rosalind Remer, *Printers and Men of Capital: Philadelphia Book Publishers in the New Republic* (Philadelphia: University of Pennsylvania Press, 1996), 58–61. In 1870, Germany granted authors literary ownership rights for thirty years after owner's death. Svend Dahl, *History of the Book* (Metuchen, N.J.: Scarecrow, 1968), 228. Europe's nations agreed to make

copyrights reciprocal at the Berne convention in 1886. Steinberg, *Five Hundred Years of Printing* (New York: Criterion, 1958), 211–12.

7. Jacques Barzun, *From Dawn to Decadence: 500 Years of Western Cultural Life* (New York: HarperCollins, 2000), 422.

8. Fischer, *Great Wave*, 57.

9. Pigeons remained a staple of financial communications for decades. In 1850, Paul Julius Reuters founded his Reuters news company with a fleet of forty-five pigeons. Exchanging news between investors in Belgium and Germany, the pigeons could beat trains by four hours.

10. "In well-ordered societies, political authority is dedicated to stability, security and the status quo." But a society's technical capabilities are "bound to be degraded if control of either scientific inquiry or innovation is located at points of political or religious authority that combine an interest in controlling the outcome . . . with the power to restrict or direct experiment." Rosenberg and Birdzell, *The West*, 265.

10

EXTREME CHEAPNESS

On the night of November 28, 1814, John Walter, proprietor of the *Times of London*, walked into his pressroom on Printing House Square to tell his workers they'd have to wait to start printing the next edition. His reporters and type compositors were running late, awaiting dramatic news from abroad. He'd keep the pressmen apprised.

Walter returned in a couple of hours but had different news: the pressmen were fired. All of them. Protest "was useless," he warned. The paper already had been printed on a new kind of press; a fast, steam-powered machine that had been secretly assembled in a locked building next door. It was so wonderful that, once the type was set, "there was little more for a man to attend upon" to produce a newspaper. The *Times* consequently had no further use for men who pulled levers. They should go home. The armed guards who had appeared at the doors would make sure they left safely.[1]

The men reportedly were dumbfounded, almost silent at first. Walter had to be worried about what would happen next. Tensions between owners and workers were historically high. As Walter's own paper put it, a labor war had been raging in England since 1810, starting in the nation's hosiery business. In those days the industry's knitters worked on frames, sometimes in their own homes, that they rented from their bosses. Their bosses, anxious to cut costs, recently had introduced wider frames. Easier and faster to use, the frames translated into fewer paid hours for the workers. Worse yet, the owners had raised the rent on them, abolished the practice of posting what they'd pay for finished work, and sometimes paid workers in scrip useable only at expensive, company-owned stores. Similar problems afflicted the Northlands region, where steam-powered looms were being introduced in centralized cotton- and wool-weaving factories. Unorganized and dispersed, workers began making formal pleas to manufacturers and to Parliament for relief. Their appeals, however, went nowhere. Then, in a bit of industrial theater, someone cut wires out of several frames and locked them up as "hostages" in a church until the manufacturers improved working conditions. Still, nothing changed. Much like the cat-mutilating apprentices of Paris, the knitters and weavers brooded until February 1811, when they gathered in an angry meeting. The militia broke it up, and inevitably violence escalated. Under cover of night, more knitting frames were sabotaged. During the next two years of conflict, mobs—knitters and weavers as well as a large cast of supporters—frequently attacked and destroyed the now despised manufacturers's property.. They often started their attack with threatening letters from a "General Ned Ludd." No one knows who Ludd was or if he existed merely as the nom de guerre of several labor leaders. Walter's *Times* reported the threats, reprisals, and eventual destruction of looms and buildings not as a labor dispute but as a rejection of technology. The Luddite Rebellion, the papers wrote, imperiled one of the era's central beliefs, progress. To crush the uprisings, an outraged Parliament made machine breaking punishable by death in 1812. Twenty-three Luddites were executed the same year, while thirteen were deported to Australia. The violence continued sporadically until 1817 and was still common when Walter conspired to add steam to the printing press much as the knitting industry had added steam to its looms.[2] But, under the watchful eye of armed guards and prodded with Walter's promise to pay them until they found new jobs, the fired hand pressmen filed peacefully out of the building.

Walter had turned literally and figuratively toward a new world. Today he and his father, who started the paper, would be called early adopters; people brave enough to be the first to try expensive new ideas and tools. In their own day, they were pioneers of the new art of making an industrial product out of the printed word.

They were inveterate innovators. Hoping to make type composition faster, the senior Walter many years before had invested in "logography," in which he cast the type of whole common words in metal to be used again and again. The process proved to be cumbersome but Walter went on to start the *Daily Universal Register*. He changed its name to *The Times of London* in 1785. To distinguish its content, he built an unprecedented foreign news service. To keep its quality high, he next invented the modern editor, responsible for both content and informed comment. To make it more timely and cheaper to produce, he bought "a battalion" of Lord Stanhope's faster, more stable, all-iron but unproven printing presses in 1803. Each was capable of printing 250 sheets per hour, up from 100.[3]

His equally aggressive son, John Walter II, took over the paper in 1810, and, much like the publishers and printers who got invitations to the Linotype-Hell demonstration of 1993, found himself at a new technology presentation, this time at a workshop on White Cross Street. All he saw was "a massive assemblage of gears." But its inventors promised it would be different. Instead of pressing sheets to a flat piece of iron (called a platen), it rolled paper through cylinders. The cylinders brought the paper to meet type, which itself had been moved along to it on a belt. Where apprentices used to ink the type by pressing on it with ink-filled leather balls, this contraption would store ink in a central reservoir. With those novel cylinders, it would dab at the ink and roll it smoothly over paper, untouched by humans. Better still, it would be powered not by men yanking on levers but by steam. The forty-year-old codesigner of the press—a German immigrant named Friedrich Koenig—estimated that if he could build it successfully, it would print eight hundred sheets per hour, 220 percent faster than the *Times*'s relatively new iron presses. When all was said and done, it would cost a hefty £11,000.[4] Walter, according to legend, bought two on the spot.

Friedrich Koenig, like Johannes Gutenberg, had migrated toward opportunity. Born in Germany in 1774, he was an apprentice in Leipzig before deciding in 1802 that he could build a better printing press. Steam power was being applied to everything at the time, and Koenig figured it could work for a press too. At his new workshop in Suhl, he envisioned steam raising and lowering iron, moving the press bed and making ink flow with cylinders all at once. He did soon develop the Suhler press, which was fast but not very good. Sure he was on to something, he left for St. Petersburg and ultimately London to find investors. England, one historian says, was attractive because it had copyright and patent protection laws that Germany did not, meaning that no one could easily appropriate his work. Three London printers soon agreed to fund his efforts and by 1810, Koenig and Andreas Bauer, another immigrant German engineer, patented their first press. One of their printer-backers used it to publish a directory but then apparently abandoned the project.[5]

The other investors, however, soldiered on, still hoping to print books by steam. One of them invited Walter—a newspaperman, not a book printer who might compete with them—to their skunkworks. By November 1814, the presses were built and installed.

Koenig and Bauer went on to produce another steam-powered press that could print on both sides of a sheet of paper at a time. But they too ran afoul of money men. While they wanted to sell their inventions broadly, their investors—print shop owners—objected to selling steam presses to competing printers. The engineers left in a huff, returning to Germany where they started a press manufacturing company called Koenig & Bauer, which endured into the twenty-first century.[6]

Their steam press was too expensive for most book and document printers anyway. It was newspaper and periodical publishers who bought most of the steam machines during the first half of the nineteenth century.[7] For them, it was too compelling not to adopt. Walters's new presses, for example, were six times faster than his old muscle-powered devices, and they immediately lowered his production costs by a hefty 25 percent. (The paper saved 250 guineas a year by eliminating the jobs of the compositors who set duplicate forms so multiple presses could print the same page at the same time.)

It was nothing less than "the beginning of modern printing."[8]

And the *Times* quickly roared into a rich new era. When it took an hour to print 250 sheets on a lever press, there was not the time, manpower, or money to produce a lot of copies of a lot of pages on short news deadlines. Newspapers of the day were limited to a few pages, and most kept the number of copies they printed to around 1,000. When they limited the number of each edition's pages, however, they also limited the number of ads they could run. Papers in Europe and North America thus had to get most of their money from political parties and interest groups, who subsidized them in an effort to assemble and wield power. But now Walter, who could print more papers faster and more cheaply than anyone else, rapidly increased the size, circulation, and amount of ad revenue the *Times* could harvest. Subsequently Walter, enriched, refused all political subsidies. The *Times*, at first alone among newspapers, was a uniquely independent voice.[9]

By 1816 it was so engorged with ads that the paper, thanks to a system that taxed papers by the number of sheets in each edition, bulked up to cost seven pence. It was "a price no workingman could afford." Thus up sprang the *Political Register*, a daily open letter printed on one sheet in order to escape the tax on multipage papers. It soon hit a "stupendous" circulation of 40,000. By way of comparison, London's biggest paper in 1802 had had a circulation of 1,700.[10]

Across the Atlantic, a Boston inventor named Treadwell demonstrated his own steam press in 1822. There, however, Walter's Luddite nightmare came true. The shop where Treadwell built it was destroyed "by a fire attributed to hand pressmen who were intensely hostile to his invention."[11]

The *New York Daily Advertiser* was the first American paper to install the Koenig steam press in 1825, at a cost of $4,000–$5,000. Unconstrained by the kind of taxes that slowed British papers, news periodicals in the United States multiplied freely. In New York alone, the *Sun* opened in 1833, followed by the *Herald* in 1841, and the *Tribune* in 1851. The first German penny newspaper appeared in 1833. By then, there were even mightier new steam presses on the market. American Richard Hoe built a press that could produce a fantastic 4,000 sheets an hour. Two engineers the *Times* had hired to replace Koenig and Bauer built a still faster version. Koenig and Bauer, meanwhile, were improving and speeding up their own machine.[12] In all cases, newspapers' circulations grew as their production costs fell.

Then innovations in paper and distribution further reduced the cost of information. In those years, one economist observed, the "hardest part of the [business] equation was the supply of raw materials." Supplies were expensive. Getting them was often arduous, subject to the vagaries of shipping. If they arrived, there was little guarantee they were any good. Ever since the Middle Ages, another historian added, "prices were determined above all by transport costs." Thanks to tolls and taxes levied at each crossing into a different province and to the sheer manpower and time needed to cart goods from place to place, grain prices rose 75 percent by the time they traveled the 650 miles from Archangel to Moscow. While the new nation-states had eliminated most of the internal tolls that made transportation so expensive, shipping remained a labor-intensive, costly problem.[13] But the same commercial and technological fervor that sped up presses now revolutionized the cost, availability, and reliability of the printing business's raw materials.

Out in the colonial frontier town of Pittsburgh, for instance, a pioneer printer named John Scull had struggled mightily for years to collect subscription money from readers, find sources for articles, scrounge up financing, and even keep coworkers alive. (One assistant succumbed to "a short illness" soon after joining him. Within a month of emigrating from Philadelphia to take the dead man's place, his successor committed suicide.) Not least among Scull's problems was getting paper over the rugged, nearly roadless Allegheny Mountains. When he couldn't get it, he had to buy difficult "cartridge paper" from nearby Fort Pitt. But when a paper mill opened in the vicinity in 1797, his problems and transportation costs eased dramatically. He cut his subscription prices, and soon his *Gazette* became stable and presumably profitable.[14]

More dramatically, in 1803 the Frenchman Nicolas Louis Robert set up a mechanized mill in England to make paper out of wood pulp instead of rags. By 1824, the price of paper was 33 percent lower than it had been when Robert arrived. By 1843, it was 50 percent cheaper. A hundred years earlier, paper had accounted for about 25 percent of the cost of producing the printed word. By 1910, it would represent only 7.1 percent.[15]

Type was also expensive, although "letter founding"—the manufacturing of the metal alphabets compositors used—was automated in 1822. The numbers of letters that could be cast jumped from 7,000 to 12,000 per day. They too accelerated "the process of cheapening and diffusing the printed word."[16]

Finally, distribution costs dropped. Sophisticated postal systems had developed throughout the West. In the United States, the new government started giving a special discount to newspapers in 1789, "hastening the rapid growth of the press." The new nation, moreover, had sixty-nine post offices and stations, one for every 22,000 "free inhabitants." It was an unusually high number. Publishers paid about 1.5 cents to mail their newspapers between them, but, given that they could send their materials collect to their subscribers, they often didn't even pay that much. (Mail carriers were notoriously bad about collecting postage when they delivered to subscribers and helped ensure that the postal system always lost money on delivering the printed word.) While Congress kept strengthening the system with acts in 1790, 1791, 1792, and beyond, postage rates fell to 3.8 cents by 1863. The system expanded almost ceaselessly thereafter, too, as delivery times shortened. In 1790 it took forty days to get a letter from Portland, Maine, to Savannah, Georgia. It took only twenty-seven days in 1810 and twelve in 1839. The speeds between Philadelphia and Lexington, Massachusetts, increased by 50 percent between 1790 and 1812 and again from 1812 to 1839. By then, the government had an express post that delivered at twice the speed of regular mail for triple the price of normal postage. In 1829, newspaper reports of Andrew Jackson's message to Congress zipped from Washington to Baltimore in 1.5 hours, to Philadelphia in 10 hours and to New York in 20 hours. All were the fastest printed communications ever recorded.[17]

American newspapers and books also traveled fast and cheaply because they bore a relatively light tax burden. England, by contrast, had since 1712 required manufacturers to affix a stamp to each printed work, indicating that they had paid tax on it. Parliament had in part intended to control the spread of information or at least restrict it to classes that could afford it. It worked. By the 1830s, one in thirty-six Britons bought newspapers. In tax-free Pennsylvania, one in four citizens bought newspapers.[18] "The extreme cheapness with which newspapers are conveyed by the mail in the United States . . . unencumbered with a stamp duty or any other public restriction . . . renders their circulation more convenient and general than in any other country," a printer of the time conceded.[19]

The price printers and publishers charged their readers for information, moreover, often fell with their production costs. Pamphlets and circulars—cheap to produce, mail, and, when necessary, hide—remained the printed word's least expensive forms. The price of popular books started to come down again with the appearance of the first "remainder houses" in the 1780s. French publishers began producing rough-hewn books on notably blue paper for their least affluent readers. In 1800, when the average worker's wage was five to six shillings a day, one "self-consciously sumptuous" edition of Sir Walter Scott's novels sold for thirty-one shillings, six pence in England. By 1836, Charles Dickens's *Pickwick Papers* was selling by installment at one shilling each.[20]

The price of newspapers—the primary beneficiaries of the steam press—fell to a penny in the United States by 1830. The first successful penny newspaper was started on a lever press in 1833 by a printer named Benjamin Day. Day, not having enough work to do in the shop, none too logically priced it at a penny. It was a hit, and Day quickly hired three men. Each worked for twenty minutes "and pulled like a horse at the hand press until he was played out, and then another took his place," a fellow printer recalled decades later. "They got out 400 or 500 copies an hour."

In 1836 in Washington, D.C., aspiring publisher Daniel Fanshaw used different technology. He brought a donkey to work each morning and hoisted the beast up to his third-floor office with a pulley. There, he hooked the donkey to his press. The donkey, walking a treadmill, made the gears of his hand press move.[21]

Most typically, though, it was the steam press that drove a remarkable drop in newspapers's prices and an explosion in the number of papers, especially in the United States. *Average* newspaper prices fell from six cents in 1810 to a penny in the 1830s. The number of papers increased by a factor of ten, from 235 to 2,300, from 1800 to 1850. Some 16 million newspapers passed through the U.S. mail in 1831 alone. In England, stamp taxes continued to keep newspaper prices higher than they were in North America (the *London Times* paid £68,000 in stamp taxes in 1828), but numerous penny magazines and trade journals appeared to report about families, boys and girls, agriculture, mining, botany, engineering, and the revolutionary new railroads.[22]

Printing, now almost entirely divorced from the selecting and selling of creative work, was becoming a business of heavy machinery. New kinds of owners and new kinds of workers were needed to run it. "It was not the coming of the machine as such but the invention of elaborate and therefore specific machinery and plant which completely changed the relationship of the merchant to production," an observer of the era explained.[23] An expensive tool like a steam press, for example, was too big for the old-style shop on the ground floor of a master's house. Its output was too voluminous for a one- or two-man or even family enterprise to sell efficiently enough to make a profit. Its increasingly complex revenue streams—from advertisers, readers, booksellers, rural subscription agents, and so on— required specialists to manage them. Content was now more timely and perishable than ever and was in constant demand. New kinds of writing professionals—reporters and diarists and specialists in various technical pursuits—were taking their places next to the novelists, clerics, philosophers, and clerks who traditionally filled newspaper columns. All were likely to go to work not at a converted house, but at a factory, a place adapted not to families but to production.

The factories obliterated the last of the old oligarchies like France's Community of Printers and England's Stationers Company. "Local and regional markets," an economic historian observes, were "being replaced by nationwide markets" served by faster information, powered ships, and, increasingly, railroads. "Local monopolies disintegrated" upon the arrival of cheaper, better competitors from afar.[24] In many places, no new tools for regulating markets replaced them for quite a while.

Print was not the only business going through tectonic shifts in production methods, in its needs for capital and new kinds of ownership to manage it, or even in the vast increase in the numbers of customers it served. But, as the only mass communication we had at the time, it clearly reflected—and helped spread—the broad changes then transforming the West's markets. Consequently, wide changes in the organization of our markets were "accompanied by a change in the organization of society itself."[25]

Nations continued to balloon and realign. During the first decades of the machine age, England's population shot from 9 million to 13.7 million. France grew to 36.5 million people in 1850, up from 26.9 million in 1800. As the United States built its industrializing momentum, its population would double from 1860 to 1890.[26] France went from absolutist monarchy to republic to empire to monarchy again; acquiring, selling, trading, and sometimes losing Italian, North American, Austrian, German, and Russian territories. The Ottoman Empire receded from Europe's borders. The Russian empire expanded. British North America became a republic, while Britain subjugated its monarchs to the will of Parliament. Perversely, the

United States developed a stronger central government even as it allowed for more direct election of local governors.

Philosophers of the era, in grand and overarching attempts to understand what was going on, began to borrow metaphors from the new means of production reshaping the world. We were subject now to the working of gears, regulators, cycles, and implacable countervailing forces. To William Townsend, who inspired Malthus and Darwin, "it is the quantity of food which regulates the number of the human species." Adam Smith had in the 1770s written of the mechanistic origins of wealth. In 1778, Robert Malthus, viewing the weed-like growth of a desperate working class around him, wrote of the mechanistic origins of poverty. (Food production, he said, could not possibly increase as fast as the population could multiply.) Jeremy Bentham and Edmund Burke argued that the market's laws were the same as the mechanistic laws of nature. In 1812, Georg Wilhelm Friedrich Hegel published his explanation of dialectical reasoning and the conflict of extremes until, like some weighted machine part settling into a manufactured space, one idea tripped another into motion, physically nudging science and history and humans themselves toward some inevitable end. In 1817, David Ricardo argued that all the mechanistic clanking was heading in a catastrophic direction. In another few years, Karl Marx exiled himself in the British Library to apply the same mechanical model to the interplay of labor and capital, foreseeing a paradise beyond the horizon. To pessimists like Ricardo and Malthus, these great machines eventually produced sobering results, most of which could be gleaned from Edward Gibbons's *Rise and Fall of the Roman Empire*, published in 1776, then and now considered a seminal description of how great power eventually dissipates. The new era's fantastic growth in production simply had to taper off, they maintained. Science and logic made it inevitable. But population would continue to grow, and, with production failing, soon would run out of the resources it needed to sustain itself. The era's optimists—Smith, Condorcet, Bentham, Burke, Jefferson—were not so sure. They saw different mechanisms at work. If we would free labor to find its own price on the market, let goods to move across borders, and allow capital to find its highest, most efficient use, wealth and population would find their own equilibrium.[27] The pessimists of the day tended to favor despots, thinking them the only authority strong enough to curb and appropriate resources for the long-term good. The optimists favored minimalist governments that would let the great machines run. While the definitions of who was a pessimist and who was an optimist changed often during the next two hundred years, the argument outlasted the machine age itself.

Newspapers and the printed word, one theory goes, helped drive all this. They now "expressed new ideas from a previously inert or silent part of the population."[28] They also brought knowledge to previously silent citizens.

But the steam press and the other new communications tools of the early nineteenth century continued to labor under one powerful, daunting physical restraint. When it was solved, the reign of Lou Felicio began.

NOTES

1. Elizabeth Faulkner Baker, *Printers and Technology: A History of the International Printing Pressmen and Assistants Union* (Westport, Conn.: Greenwood, 1974), 15–16.

2. Felix Silverio, The Luddites, www.gober.net/victorian/reports/luddites.html (accessed December 13, 2003). Tensions ran high in other industries too, for England's entire economy was troubled. Real wages across the country—its trade with the Continent cut off by Napoleon; its trade with North America threatened by impending war with the United States—fell by about 50 percent in 1811 alone. Prices were up 87 percent since 1790. Sales of everything, including hosiery, were depressed.

3. Walter and Benjamin Franklin corresponded about logography. Henri Bouchet, *The Book: Its Printers, Illustrators, and Binders from Gutenberg to the Present Time*, ed. H. Grevel (New York: Scribner & Welford, 1890), 226–27. The Walters' willingness to invest in new technology was carried on by John Walter III, who in the 1860s oversaw the development of a rotary press and type composition machine experiments. "Walter, John, III," www.britannica.com/eb/article?eu=78018 (accessed January 10, 2004); P. M. Handover, *Printing in London: From Caxton to Modern Times* (Cambridge: Harvard University Press, 1960), 154; Frederick G. Kilgour, *The Evolution of the Book* (New York: Oxford University Press, 1998), 101. Stanhope, who invented the press, engineered it from principles sketched out three hundred years before by Leonardo da Vinci. S. H. Steinberg, *Five Hundred Years of Printing* (New York: Criterion, 1959), 201; Handover, *Printing in London*, 152.

4. Handover, *Printing in London*, 152; Colin Clair, *A History of European Printing* (London: Academic, 1976), 361.

5. Warren Chappell, *A Short History of The Printed Word* (New York: Knopf, 1970), 174. In another example of how inventors in this era borrowed heavily from each other, William Nicholson had first proposed using cylinders in presses a decade earlier. Kilgour, *The Book*, 103; Clair, *History*, 360–61.

6. Kilgour, *The Book*, 105; Clair, *History*, 362.

7. Clair, *History*, 356. It was not until 1826 that the first books were printed on a steam press in Leipzig. Steinberg, *Five Hundred Years*, 201.

8. Steinberg, *Five Hundred Years*, 201; Kilgour, *The Book*, 103; Chappell, *Short History*, 174.

9. Handover, *Printing in London*, 154.

10. Handover, *Printing in London*, 154–55. Parliament closed the single-sheet tax loophole in 1819, after which less prosperous Londoners confined themselves to buying Sunday newspapers for the time being.

11. Baker, *Printers and Technology*, 16.

12. Frank Luther Mott, *American Journalism A History: 1690–1960*, 3rd ed. (New York: Macmillan, 1962), 204; Chappell, *Short History*, 199; Clair, *History*, 356. The engineers who replaced Koenig and Bauer were Augustus Applegath and Edward Cowper, whose new steam press was installed in 1828. Handover, *Printing in London*, 158.

13. Karl Polanyi, *The Great Transformation: The Political and Economic Origins of Our Time* (Boston: Beacon, 1944), 74. During the Middle Ages, there were fifteen tolls to pay between Paris and Rouen, a cost that increased grain prices by 33 percent. To travel the 150 miles from Nuremberg to Frankfurt, one had to pass through four fiefdoms. Each required travelers to pay for an escort through its territory. Frankfurt levied another charge at its gate. J. R. Hale, *Renaissance Europe, 1480–1520*, 2nd ed. (Malden, Mass.: Blackwell, 2000), 102.

14. Audrey Abbott Iacone, "Early Printing in Pittsburgh, 1786–1856," *Pittsburgh History Summer 1990* (Pittsburgh: Carnegie Library, 1990), clpgh.org/exhibit/neighborhoods/downtown/down_ n43.html (accessed January 10, 2004). Cartridge paper was used to load bullets into guns and was unsuitable for printing. A finer version is used by artists for sketching.

15. Steinberg, *Five Hundred Years*, 199.

16. Steinberg, *Five Hundred Years*, 201.

17. Richard R. John, *Spreading the News: The American Postal System from Franklin to Morse* (Cambridge: Harvard University Press, 1995), 31, 26; Richard Burket Kielbowicz, *Origins of the Second-Class Mail Category and the Business of Policymaking, 1863–1879*, Journalism Monographs no. 96 (Columbia: Association for Education in Journalism and Mass Communications, University of South Carolina, 1986), 3; U.S. Postal Service, History of the U.S. Postal Service, www.usps.com/history/his1_5.htm (accessed September 7, 2002); John, *Spreading the News*, 17–18; Mott, *American Journalism*, 193–94.

18. Kilgore, *The Book*, 123; Chappell, *Short History*, 199.

19. Isaiah Thomas, *The History of Printing in America*, ed. Marcus A. McCorison (1810; New York: Weathervane, 1970), 18–19.

20. Rosalind Remer, *Printers and Men of Capital: Philadelphia Book Publishers in the New Republic* (Philadelphia: University of Pennsylvania Press, 1996), 61; Kilgour, *The Book*, 114.

21. "A Morning with Theodore L. De Vinne," *Scientific American*, November 14, 1903, 339–40.

22. Ben H. Bagdikian, *The Information Machines: Their Impact on Men and the Media* (New York: Harper & Row, 1971), 8; John, *Spreading the News*, 3. Magazines included *Family* and *Boys and Girls Penny Magazine* in 1832. Handover, *Printing in London*, 160.

23. Polanyi, *Great Transformation*, 74–75.

24. Harold G. Vatter, *The Drive to Industrial Maturity: The U.S. Economy, 1860–1914* (Westport, Conn.: Greenwood, 1975), 60.

25. Polanyi, *Great Transformation*, 75.

26. Clair, *History*, 355; George Corben Goble, *The Obituary of a Machine: The Rise and Fall of Ottmar Mergenthaler's Linotype at U.S. Newspapers* (Bloomington: Indiana University Mass Communications Program, 1984), 14–15.

27. Nathan Rosenberg and L. E. Birdzell Jr., *How the West Grew Rich* (New York: Basic, 1986), 7–8, Polanyi, *Great Transformation*, 135.

28. Bagdikian, *Information Machines*, 9.

11

THE DAM'S LAST BRICK

On a January day in 1885 Melville Stone, a onetime reporter who had clawed his way up to become editor and part owner of the *Chicago Daily News*, got a tip that a promising new technology was taking shape at a repair shop in Baltimore. If it ever worked, it would surely be worth a fortune. One contemporary estimated the payoff as nothing less than "the wealth of a Croesus and a place in the temple of fame."[1] Making the invention work, however, was proving to be hard. The first wave of investors in the device and the German immigrant who was trying to coax it to life had run out of money. More investors were needed.

As interested as Stone—whose first paper was proudly "Republican in everything and independent in nothing"—was in the possible riches, he was attracted to what the device aimed to do: mechanically pick and arrange the letters that, in turn, were fed to the presses to print.[2]

Arranging the letters (and spaces and paragraphs) that appeared in print—composition—remained the slowest, costliest, and most primitive part of the increasingly industrial printed word business. To some, it was more than that: composition was the one last brick holding back the vast, accumulating weight of the inventive force of nineteenth-century communications.

"What makes our books and newspapers expensive," a German technical journal writer complained, "is neither paper nor printing; it is the composition."[3] "Presswork," a leading American printer of the day concurred, "is the profitable branch of the business. It is the composition that is the great sinkhole. It is in types and wages of compositors that the profits of the house are lost."

Stone and the other titans of the printed word business still set type the way they did in the days of cat massacres. Amid the bellowing racket of power presses and the tapping of telegraph operators, their compositors sat or stood by cases full of letters. With an eight-inch "composing stick" in one hand and a handwritten manuscript in front of him, the compositor picked metal letters out of the cases and placed them, with a distinctive *tick*, on the composing stick. Character by character, the best compositors worked on about six words at a time, finally assembling eight or nine lines' worth of words and spaces. Then he or an assistant carefully transferred the lines from the sticks to a metal frame where, building a few lines at a time, a page full of type eventually took shape through the hours. Mistakes were common. Correcting them was hard. Inserting a missed letter or word sometimes meant rearranging a whole page to free space for it.[4]

And it was expensive. At about the time Stone got his tip, the *New York World* spent $300,000 a year on composition, devoting its entire thirteenth floor to workers clattering and ticking at 230 cases of type. The *New York Times* employed a hundred hand compositors. The *Chicago Herald* had 150, working in a "hall of compositors" filling 150 frames.[5]

These artisans, moreover, remained a breed apart. Their reputation as arrogant, obstreperous, willful, and hard-drinking people was well developed by then, and often deserved. Many, it was said, alienated their coworkers. Among the world's most literate and opinionated workers, they often managed the less educated press operators and other production workers in many shops.[6] They were not exactly proletarian brothers-in-arms. Their bosses had not come to love them much better since the cat massacre days, either. They had fantastic abilities to calculate line lengths by sight, spell well, and use correct grammar. They were dexterous enough to fill large frames with small metal letters and strong enough to lift them. They best ones were fast enough to beat last-minute deadlines and often edited the copy they were creating. But they had always been difficult, and they remained that way. They disrupted operations often. Sometimes it was for abrupt, temperamental, notoriously self-assigned breaks from work. Sometimes it was with demands for raises or job security. Sometimes it was with angry group demands for managers to resolve a slight. (Too many times, it was for one of their ceaseless intramural baseball games; warning that responsible compositors had no business risking their valuable time or fingers playing ball, one union member grudgingly admitted that some players on the two Government Printing Office lunchtime teams had "startling" skills at the plate.)[7] They were among the few craftsmen to successfully organize themselves into an effective union in those days. They often proved to be skilled, hard-nosed negotiators. To folks like Stone and his fellow press owners, they were unbearably maddening and impossibly overpaid. As one owner put it, "The foremen [often compositors, often unionized] are tyrants. They go around and . . . say 'we want this proposition carried so and so,' and they go to the men and the man finds his [job] depends on [agreeing to] it. I know personally where men have been coerced to go in favor of measures which their judgment condemned."[8] Appeasing them was expensive. Replacing them was a fond dream.

The owners tried hard to make it come true. Attempts to bring in cheaper, nonunion workers were constant, if not always successful. The "first [printing labor] disputes of any consequence" in the burgeoning new sprawl of Chicago arose during the summer of 1863, as the Civil War was steeply pushing up all workers' wages. The fed-up publisher of the *Chicago Times*, acting in secret, paid a Milwaukee printer to provide him with an entire nonunion workforce to put out his paper. He sneaked the new workers in by boat one summer morning, marched them to the newspaper, and, not unlike John Walters's dramatic pressroom *coup* of 1814, theatrically dismissed the unionists. As they filed out, he put the new arrivals in charge of the composing room. But they proved to be "so outrageously incompetent" that the manager was "compelled to send for his former compositors the very next day."[9]

Still squirming under inflationary pressures and an unprecedented demand for war news a few months later, the city's newspaper publishers agreed to try again. This time, they'd do it together. They fired 25 percent of their current compositors in one grand swoop and set out to replace them with cheaper people. Replacements, however, proved hard to find; the war had drained away most of the city's unemployed laborers. Unable to get their papers out on the street or reap the advertising windfalls that came with wartime's boom circulations, they again admitted defeat and rehired their former compositors.[10]

But they did not give up. Next they surreptitiously hired a Mrs. Blatchford to train, at a secret place somewhere west of Chicago, about forty nonunion women "into the mysteries of the art of composition." Once prepared, the women would replace the noxious unionists. But word of the new labor training camp leaked out in 1864, when one city paper, the *Morning Post*, ran a cautionary series of stories "that typesetting was properly a woman's vocation." The *Post*'s union compositors, after setting the story, demanded to know if the paper meant to fire them again. "The union," the paper's business manager replied to the type men massed inside his office, "can go to hell." It did. The workers went on strike and within a month permanently lost their jobs to some of Mrs. Blatchford's protégés.[11]

Some of her other students joined a second, better-trained wave of Milwaukee printers who showed up at the *Chicago Times* one day that fall. The "first intimation [the union compositors] received" that labor strife had reignited at the paper was "when they came as usual to begin their day's labor" and were told they had been replaced. This time, they were not rehired.[12]

Similar union-busting dramas, sometimes successful but usually not, played out in New York, Pittsburgh, Leavenworth, Topeka, Little Rock, and other towns during the next twenty-five years. "Many employers," the day's leading industry trade journal understated, "entertain strong feelings of antipathy against the typographical union."[13]

But human compositors—union or not, male or female—would always be slow, unreliable, and more costly than a machine, and the producers of the printed word hoped to replace them all with technology. One publisher estimated that, between 1865 and the time Stone got his tip, investors had put some $10 million into various mechanical typesetting schemes and ventures. Among them was the author Mark Twain, who sank $190,000—probably equivalent to about $5.7 million today, almost his entire fortune—into a contraption that had 18,000 moving parts and would, he predicted, "do everything in a newspaper office but spit, swear, and go out on strike." After six years of development, the machine flopped. Twain had to return to writing to dig his way out of debt.[14]

Twain's was hardly the only failure. In 1833, a rich Hungarian landowner named Josef Kliegl had staked everything he had to open the world's first composing machine factory. It died quickly, and Kliegl lived out his days as a music teacher. In 1855, a Danish inventor won a prestigious gold medal at a Paris expo for his typesetting machine design. But the device proved cumbersome in practice, and the inventor eventually had to pawn his medal for food. He died in poverty. Russian inventor Peter Paul Knjagininski, emotionally broken by the collapse of his composing machine effort, became a drunk. Reportedly weakened by years of building and rebuilding failed prototypes, an American named Timothy Alden unveiled what proved to be a workable design for a machine in 1857, only to hear another inventor had just introduced a similar one. He collapsed and died six months later.

Other inventors who threw themselves at the problem met less dramatic endings. In 1822, Bostonian William Church, for example, patented a type machine that could theoretically put up to 5,000 characters per hour in their proper order, compared to about 1,500 that hand compositors could do. Once built, the machines based on Church's design turned out to be slower in practice. Someone had to even out, or justify, the resulting letters and words on each line. By the time the lines were justified and the pieces of type returned to their original cases, the whole process was no faster than hand composition. Similar problems afflicted an 1840 machine built by Henry Bessemer (who more famously went on to revolutionize steel furnaces) and two partners. In 1842 came an English–French amalgam called the Pianotyp that apparently looked like a piano and, in the end, set type like one too. New York's largest printing company installed a Mitchel machine in 1853 to create newfangled city directories. It performed serviceably.[15]

Yet newspaper and other kinds of printers found the Mitchel impractical, and the pace of experimenting accelerated. "From 1850 on," one historian reported, "no year passed in which a new (composing) machine was not announced." Between 1870 and 1900, 127 different composing machines were invented out of 1,500 patents. Only three machines sold over three units.[16]

Several English publishers, for example, tested a Hattersley machine. Instead of cranky and expensive hand compositors, they had "boys and girls" feed mechanically produced type to a low-wage typist. But it didn't work out. The kids kept clogging what proved to be a fragile machine. "Breakdowns were constant." ("After a long and fair trial," a visiting American compositor subsequently reported, "the machine was discarded.")[17] In 1869, the ever adventurous *London Times* adopted a machine designed by Swiss engineer Charles Kastenbein. It proved to be better than most, but other publishers found it inadequate. Timothy Alden's invention, later acquired by two more sets of investors who renamed it first the Green machine and then the Burr machine after themselves, won trials at several New York print shops and newspapers but proved fragile in production. The city's generally frustrated publishers collectively offered a $500,000 prize for any typesetting idea that could save them 30 percent off the cost of hand composition. Groups of inventors and financiers formed to capture the prize, but the publishers never found a worthy idea.[18]

"Some of the best inventive genius in the United States has been devoted to the solution of the typesetting problem," *Scientific American* noted in reporting about yet another patented design. But in spite of all the money and experimenting, an economist marveled many years later, "probably no other handicraft employing such a large number of persons underwent as little change during this period, so full of industrial reconstruction."[19]

Even as Stone got his tip, rumors and news of still more composing machines continued to swirl. An inventor named Tolbert Lanston supposedly had come up with a machine that could both produce and justify

12,000 characters per hour. A Thorn machine was out but needed two workers to operate. An Empire machine, on the market since 1872, also required two workers, plus a third to work another machine devoted to forging the type letters. In Germany, an engineer remembered only as Herr Fischer was perfecting a device that shot prearranged letters down perpendicular pipes to a compositor, who then picked out the type with his fingers.[20]

So Stone, whose portrayal of his role in the coming days of Typographic Man's ascension was not modest, could be forgiven for being skeptical that his exploratory side trip to see an immigrant's new machine in Baltimore was going to be worthwhile. A fellow publisher whom he told of the trip sniffed that the invention's backers were merely a "number of stenographers" and that the machine sounded like it was in "a crude state." Stone himself "had spent . . . time studying upon the subject, and had investigated the machine in which Mark Twain was interested and in which he had lost so much of his fortune." His mood could not have improved much as he was led through the city to a modest-looking machine shop. "In a little upper room," he later told an interviewer of this nativity scene, "I found the machine and the inventor."[21]

And he saw that they were good.

The inventor turned out to be one Ottmar Mergenthaler. He'd arrived in Washington thirteen years before as a callow eighteen-year-old from the same region of southwestern Germany that had produced Johannes Gutenberg. Already a natively skilled draftsman, the young man's chances of getting an engineering job near home were bad; legions of soldiers were returning from the Franco-Prussian War and glutting the job market. With thin prospects and about to be drafted like his two older brothers, Mergenthaler set off for Washington, D.C., armed with $30 and the name and address of a distant relative he had never met. The relative, August Hahl, hired him as an apprentice at his machine shop in 1872, committing him to work for three years in return for room, board, and a practical education in the mechanical arts.[22]

The shop produced precision instruments like watches and clocks (mostly for what was to become the U.S. Weather Service) and built working models of designs customers would use to apply for a patent at the nearby U.S. Patent Office. Hahl's apprentice turned out to be talented (when the apprenticeship ended, he made the young man his foreman), but the economy soon turned sour. The Panic of 1873 dried up much of his business, and Hahl moved the shop, his family, and the young Ottmar Mergenthaler to Baltimore to start fresh.

In 1876, two customers from Washington brought in a design for a device they called a writing machine. It would, they hoped, revolutionize court reporting by printing directly onto a piece of paper. Mergenthaler thought the thing needed some redesign. Hahl agreed to build a prototype for a not inconsiderable fee of $1,600.[23]

Mergenthaler was right about the device. Still, the two men who hatched the idea—an engineer named Charles T. Moore and James Clephane, once a stenographer to U.S. Secretary of State William Seward and an energetic court reporter who'd made a fortune perfecting stenographic technologies—were as smitten with mechanical composing as the long line of dreamers who had preceded them. Time and again during the next six years they reappeared with new designs and a few more investors. Clephane liked Mergenthaler in particular, occasionally hiring him as a consultant, and, when money got tight, offering him equity in a company that he swore would be huge if an invention ever came to pass. That venture went broke, but by then Mergenthaler also had become obsessed with the idea and kept working on it without pay. His type machine designs, like the others before them, never quite played out. He recalled tearing up a set of drawings in 1879 "in a fit of anger brought about by the extreme financial straits" into which Clephane had led him. In 1883, Clephane came back with yet another set of investors and convinced Mergenthaler to leave August Hahl to set up his own shop to pursue the idea still further.[24] By late 1884, most of those investors were at the end of their patience too. The remaining dreamers—as convinced as Alden, Bessemer, Knjagininiski, Kliegl, Twain, and all the others that they might at last be near success—went looking for new investors to join them.

To drum up interest, they asked potential investors to come to a demonstration at Mergenthaler's shop in Baltimore, first in July 1884 and then in January 1885. Melville Stone was in the second group.[25]

The visit achieved the status of myth in the retelling. Everyone remembered it a little differently. When Stone recounted being secreted to this technological manger, he suggested he was alone. "The invention," he solemnly recalled, "impressed me very greatly." Seemingly without delay, he asked fellow publishers from the *New York Tribune*, Rand McNally, and the Associated Press to come to Baltimore. They "were as impressed as I was." Mergenthaler remembered all the publishers—plus Stilson Hutchins of the *Washington Post*—as being there at once. All, in any case, pledged to put up money and call in still more publisher colleagues to fund the machine and bring it to market.[26]

So, 109 years before Lou Felicio walked into the Linotype-Hell open house at a suburban Denver hotel, another group of potential investors, buyers, salespeople, and a few curious associates passed through the commercial carnage of February 1885 into the Chamberlain Hotel in Washington, D.C.[27] They, like Lou, would see a strange-looking product demonstrated.

They would also get to rub shoulders with Washington celebrities. Lame duck President Chester A. Arthur attended. So did James G. Blaine, recent presidential candidate and the once and future U.S. secretary of state. Cabinet member and future Supreme Court Justice L. Q. C. Lamar was there too. Still more politicians came to the celebratory banquet, where Mergenthaler addressed the room and afterward entertained offers.

More investors—forming a group Mergenthalter subsequently called the "syndicate"—promptly signed on. They set up a new company, forced out a couple of previous Washington backers, gave themselves discounts on the new company's prospective product, reserved the exclusive rights to use the machine in their own cities, swore everyone to secrecy, and bought 7,000 of the new company's 40,000 shares. Their stake cost them about $300,000, an amount that Mergenthaler himself estimated was the largest ever paid for an invention that did not yet work. In early twenty-first-century money, it would be the equivalent to about $9 million.[28]

The money, at least according to Stone, went to buying a patent for a part that Mergenthaler used in his design and to Mergenthaler to set up a shop to build a dozen machines. There would be more money for the inventor, sanguine new investors told him once again. If he did manage to perfect a machine, he would get $50 for each one sold. Some day, Whitelaw Reid dreamily told Mergenthaler, the inventor would return to Germany a rich man and live in "one of the noted and beautiful castles on the Rhine."[29]

About a year later Reid began denying, occasionally to people who had never asked, that he and his colleagues had at last found the printed word's holy grail. Yes, there was something special brewing, he told an editor's meeting. But no, it was not yet for sale.[30]

When it was at last time, on July 3, 1886, he invited editors, investors, publishers, and some of New York's most influential people up to his *New York Tribune*'s ninth-floor composing room to meet a great inventor and see a great invention. He had the machine hoisted in a crate nine floors up the side of his building. "The arrival," one of Reid's printers recalled of the big day, "made a big stir. All of us who could manage to, crowded around for a good look at it."[31]

Reid put on a show. As Mergenthaler finished demonstrating the invention, Reid supposedly leaned over, clapped him on the back, and said loudly, "Why, Ottmar, you've cast a line 'o type." They decided to call the machine the Linotype.[32]

NOTES

1. Walker Rumble, *The Swifts: Printers in the Age of Typesetting Races* (Charlottesville: University of Virginia Press, 2003), 46.

2. It was not uncommon in those partisan days for newspapers to declare their party loyalty in their mastheads. A. H. Belo's new *Dallas Morning News* was dedicated to "Democratic principles in a wide and general sense, holding free to combat the use of power wherever found." Sidney Kobre, *Development of American Journalism* (Dubuque: Brown, 1969), 471. At that time, being Republican meant supporting high tariffs to protect American industries from foreign competition. Stone grew up in Chicago, where he was a teenage reporter for the *Chicago Tribune*. In 1872, he became editor of the Chicago *Republican*, renamed it the *Inter-Ocean*, and established his reputation as an inflexible Republican. He was demoted eventually, however, and resumed reporting until 1876, when he cofounded the *Chicago Daily News*, the city's first penny newspaper. It too was soon on shaky financial ground. Victor Lawson, Stone's former high school classmate and owner of the company that printed the *News*, bought a majority stake by assuming its debts (many of which were to his own printing company) and agreeing to add capital. Together, he and Stone made the paper a terrific success. Stone sold the rest of the paper to Lawson in 1888 and went on to become the first general manager of the Associated Press. Frank Luther Mott, *American Journalism A History: 1690–1960*, 3rd ed. (New York: Macmillan, 1962), 463–65, 510; Kobre, *American Journalism*, 449.

3. From the technical journal *Deutsche Buck- und Steindrucker*, February 1889, cited in Willi Mengel, *Ottmar Mergenthaler and the Printing Revolution* (Brooklyn, N.Y.: Mergenthaler Linotype Company, 1954), 41. From a speech by Theodore L. DeVinne to the National Editorial Association, as cited in Elizabeth Faulkner Baker, *Printers and Technology: A History of the International Printing Pressmen and Assistants Union* (Westport, Conn.: Greenwood, 1974), 69.

4. Pierre de la Marre, "The Literary Era," *Printing World*, April 25, 1997.

5. George Corben Goble, *The Obituary of a Machine: The Rise and Fall of Ottmar Mergenthaler's Linotype at U.S. Newspapers* (Bloomington: Indiana University Mass Communications Program, 1984), 1, 29.

6. As one printer put it, "The average compositor knows as much geography as many school teachers, and more politics than many office holders." Hugh Wallace, "Linotype Operators," *Inland Printer*, April 1897, 45.

7. "Some very closely contested games have been played this season," the correspondent noted, even as he disapproved of the practice in an 1891 letter to a printing trade journal. Em Dash, "Letter from Washington, D.C.," *Inland Printer*, August 1891, 997. Compositors loved the game forever more. Taking a break from complaining about working conditions at two Baltimore newspapers in July 1891, "the compositors on the *American* and the morning *Herald* vied with each other on the base-ball field last week," another correspondent reported. "The *Herald* nine won with ease." Fidelities, "Letter from Baltimore," *Inland Printer*, August 1891, 993–94.

Their international union soon ran nationwide leagues and playoffs for the locals' teams. Seymour Martin Lipset, Martin A. Trow, and James S. Coleman, *Union Democracy: The Internal Politics of the International Typographical Union* (Glencoe, Ill.: Free Press, 1972), 69.

8. Baker, *Printers and Technology*, 66–70, 248.

9. "Personal Recollections and Observations: Being a Retrospective of the Printers and Printing Offices of Chicago to the year 1857," *Inland Printer*, May 1886, 499–500.

10. "Personal Recollections and Observations."

11. "Personal Recollections and Observations."

12. "Personal Recollections and Observations."

13. "Strikes and Lockouts," *Typographical Journal*, August 15, 1889, 1–2; "The Present State of the Typographical Industry," *Inland Printer*, March 1896, 628.

14. "Typesetting Machines," *Inland Printer*, February 1891, 415. Twain, whose real name was Samuel Clemens, struggled to perfect and get his Paige typesetter to market for years. By the time it debuted at the 1893 Columbian Exposition in Chicago, it was nine feet long, weighed three tons, and had a keyboard with 109 characters. Its price was $12,000. W. C. Roberts, "The Paige Typesetting Machine," *Inland Printer*, June 1893, 248–49; "Typesetting Machines," *Inland Printer*, September 1891, 1060; Harry Kelber and Carl Schlesinger, *Union Printers and Controlled Automation* (New York: Free Press, 1967), 3. Twain's interest in—or boredom with—hand composing began when he was a type apprentice in Missouri. "I worked not diligently, not willingly, but fretfully, lazily, repiningly, complainingly, disgustedly, and always shirking the work when I was not watched," he recalled. Dixon Wecter, *Sam Clemens of Hannibal* (Boston: Houghton Mifflin, 1952), 200.

15. Mengel, *Mergenthaler*, 133; Rumble, *The Swifts*, 46-51. The "other inventor" was W. H. Houston. Colin Clair, *A History of European Printing* (London: Academic, 1976), 377. The Pianotyp was patented in the United States by James Young and Adrien Delcambre. Rumble, *The Swifts*, 1516.

16. Kelber and Schlesinger, *Union Printers*, 3.

17. A. Spencer, "Type-setting Machines," *Typographical Journal*, September 15, 1889, 2.

18. Kelber and Schlesinger, *Union Printers*, 3; Clair, *History*, 377–79; Rumble, *The Swifts*, 50–55; Frank J. Romano, *Machine Writing and Typesetting* (Salem, N.H.: Gama, 1986), 23.

19. "A New Typesetting Machine," *Scientific American*, July 20, 1901, 38.

20. Kelber and Schlesinger, *Union Printers*, 3; "The Gutenberg Typesetter," *Inland Printer*, June 1886, 545.

21. The fellow publisher was Whitelaw Reid of the *New York Tribune*, who in the foreword to a book written by William H. Smith, yet another of Stone's cronies, took the lion's share of the credit for uncovering the Baltimore invention. Cited in Goble, *Obituary*, 111. The mere "stenographers" who had previously backed Mergenthaler were in fact an illustrious group that included Lemon G. Hine, one of

Washington's best-connected lawyers, the publisher of the *Washington Post*, a noted engineer, and, at their head, the inventive James Clephane, who had once been a stenographer to Secretary of State William Seward but had since brought a number of lucrative stenographic inventions to market. He had also been a confidante to President James Buchanan. In all, the investors had sunk more than $1 million into the venture before Stone and Reid met Mergenthaler. Goble, *Obituary*, 25. Melville E. Stone, "History of Linotype," *Colliers Weekly*, as reproduced by Type Associates at typeassociates.com/MelvilleStone.htm (accessed December 2, 1999).

22. Goble, *Obituary*, 47–48; Ottmar Mergenthaler, *Biography of Ottmar Mergenthaler and History of the Linotype* (Baltimore, Md., 1898), 3.

23. Mergenthaler, *Biography*, 5; Goble, *Obituary*, 49.

24. Goble, *Obituary*, 54–55. Moore left the partnership in 1884.

25. Mergenthaler, *Biography*, 16.

26. Joining Stone in Baltimore (at least according to Stone himself) were Whitelaw Reid of the *Tribune*, William H. Rand of Rand McNally, and William Henry Smith of the Associated Press. Stone, "History of Linotype"; Mergenthaler, *Biography*, 18.

27. Mergenthaler, *Biography*, 18; Romano, *Writing Machines*, 58.

28. Goble, *Obituary*, 114–15; Mergenthaler, *Biography*, 17–18, 20.

29. Mergenthaler, *Biography*, 21. J. W. Shuckers, former private secretary to U.S. Supreme Court Chief Justice Salmon P. Chase, had previously patented a "justifying apparatus" that Mergenthaler had in large part incorporated in his machine. Stone says he acquired the patent from Shuckers, who was then living in Atlantic City. Stone, "History of Linotype"; Goble, *Obituary*, 118. But in his biography Mergenthaler recounts that settling the Shuckers patent remained an internal company issue several years later. Mergenthaler, *Biography*, 63.

30. Mergenthaler, *Biography*, 42.

31. John E. Allen, "Veteran Machinists and Operators Recall Early Days of Linotype," *Linotype News*, August 1936, 3; Romano, *Machine Writing*, 63.

32. Goble, *Obituary*, 81. Reid's exclamation may be apocryphal. Mergenthaler claimed credit for naming the machine. In any case, ads for the machine did not include the "Linotype" name until 1887.

12

"THE HASTY APPROACH OF EVIL"

Unveiling the Linotype was hardly Whitelaw Reid's first publicity stunt. Newspaper publishers regularly made big deals out of their acquisitions or, better yet, new buildings. In New York, Reid moved the *Tribune* into a new thirteen-story "tall tower" in 1875. Not to be outdone, the *Times*, the *World*, and the *Herald* put up even grander office towers for themselves in 1889, 1890, and 1894. (The *Times's* building almost bankrupted the paper's owners; the *World's* 1890 opulent offices cost the modern-day equivalent of $75 million.) The *Philadelphia Times* built one in 1876, the *Philadelphia Record* in 1882. The *Boston Herald* erected its big new building in 1882. The *Chicago Herald* erected its building in 1891.[1]

They crowed no less about their news scoops, cartoons, and technological prowess. In 1862, for example, the *New York Times* called its new type machine nothing less than "THE invention of the Nineteenth Century." A "new era in newspaper publishing" was starting, the breathless writer reported.[2]

Oddly enough, readers seemed interested in such things. By the time of the first Linotype open house in the late 1880s, everything connected with the printed word was glamorous. Its writers frequently were celebrities, sometimes cast as courageous adventurers. (The *New York Times* sent Henry Morton Stanley with much fanfare to find the lost missionary Dr. David Livingstone in the Congo in 1869, and then loudly published his wincingly bully reports of beating and driving his servants through the jungle.) Its illustrators were politically powerful pundits. Caricaturist Thomas Nast helped take down the Tweed ring in New York from his pulpit at *Harper's Weekly*. Even its fastest hand compositors—called "swifts"—could draw large crowds to public typesetting races in Memphis, Chicago, Boston, and Philadelphia in 1886.[3] And its moguls, much like today's movie directors and network owners, were among the day's glitterati.

Reid belonged to this class of larger-than-life publishers like Horace Greeley, Joseph Medill, and soon Joseph Pulitzer and William Randolph Hearst. He cut a self-consciously dramatic figure as a dashing, self-made small-town Ohio editor, Civil War correspondent (his vivid accounts of the Battle of Gettysburg and then of the defeated South won him wide fame), editor, and then owner of New York's biggest paper, successful businessman, antilabor crusader, vice presidential candidate, putative president, and ambassador to France. Horace Greeley had hired Reid for the *Tribune* in 1868, making him editor when Greeley ran for president in 1872. He became the paper's owner when Greeley died, and proceeded to make it more popular and profitable than ever. (The paper was famous for titillating, questioning headlines. "Was It Murder, or Suicide?" "Did She Kill Him for Love?" "Will the President Sign It?" In a letter to the editor, one *Tribune* reader complained, "I am getting awfully tired of your questions. A great newspaper is supposed to know everything, and ought not to annoy its readers with needless inquiries. This morning you ask, 'Will Mr. Platt Consent?' How the h— do I know?")[4] He also embarked on a business course that could not have been more different than the notoriously labor-friendly Greeley's. He cut costs relentlessly. When his hand compositors struck in 1877, he broke the printers' union and began investing heavily in type inventions. (He ran three Burr machines amid his nonunion hand compositors). When those machines proved inadequate (the special type they used was too brittle for most heavy newspaper work), he readily joined—and, according to him, led—the investment group that, along with Melville Stone, went looking for better technology and ultimately found Mergenthaler in Baltimore. He became the new Mergenthaler company's first president as well. In the meantime he cut his news-gathering costs first by forming what became the Associated Press and then, quite illegally, conspiring to have the AP and its rival United Press share news and expenses. He was an early adopter of faster presses for similar reasons. He also campaigned hard against the International Typographical Union (ITU), which counted most of the compositors and many of the pressmen and bookbinders in the nation's biggest printing plants as members, and regularly encouraged other publishers' workers to secede from the union. Unionists hated him.[5]

That too was typical. The publishers were strident, polemical, and highly political. People either passionately admired or passionately reviled them.

And their newspapers were their cities' dominant, most visible sources of daily conversation. By then they were the world's first mass medium: the only means of talking to and entertaining huge groups of people all at once. It had never been possible to communicate ideas simultaneously to more than the number of people who could hear an unamplified human voice or could fit into a theater, a courtyard, or a cathedral. Even best-selling books—which had become "relatively expensive" in many parts of the world—rarely sold more than 1,000 copies in the 1700s and early 1800s. Immensely popular authors like George Sand and Victor Hugo sold "perhaps 500" copies a year in France, while poets were lucky to sell 250. Pamphlets typically came in lots of 1,500 or fewer. Newspapers appeared in relatively miserly editions of 1,200 or 1,400 until 1814, when Friedrich Koenig's new power press made producing more copies possible. After that the newspaper became a phenomenon, able to reach 10,000 and then a stunning 55,000 people a day by midcentury. By 1892, the *New York World* had a circulation of 374,000, and the *Chicago Daily News* 243,000. In France, *Le Petit Journal's* circulation was 750,000. The *London Daily Telegraph's* was 300,000, and its editors frankly dreamed of reaching a million readers one day soon.[6] Now masses of 300,000 or 750,000 people received similar impressions at the same time, were stimulated by the same print, and reacted with similar pride, shock, curiosity, puzzlement, outrage, or sadness all at once. As happened when the press first shot ideas at individuals in previously dark places, creating quick communities of informed (or duped) people had an impact. These ideas were not just larger than the individuals who read them. They were larger than the groups of people who read them. Reid and the others who put their names on them also were, for this brief moment in history before the advent of film and radio stars.

Their overwrought exclamations about cheap metal alphabets, however, actually came true. The Linotype, after some initial missteps, almost outstripped the hyperbole.[7]

Newspapers in St. Louis, St. Paul, Chicago, and Washington, D.C., installed machines almost immediately after the Lino appeared. Joseph Pulitzer's *New York World* printed its first machine edition in September 1890, and promptly announced it would order another hundred devices. (Consistent with its relentless exaggeration, it bought many of them during the next two years, but not one hundred.) The *Chicago Times* and the *Chicago Enquirer*, the *Boston Herald and Globe*, the *Philadelphia Bulletin*, the *Cleveland Plain Dealer*, the *Detroit News*, and the *Pittsburgh Chronicle-Telegraph* printed notices it would also buy some. By 1891, the *Providence Journal* had fourteen of them. The New Orleans *Times-Democrat* had fifteen. By 1892, twenty-three papers were running three hundred Mergenthalers. Then the *Atlanta Constitution* bought ten just for itself in 1893. In 1894, in the wake of a jarring financial panic, the *New York World* bought twenty more. By then, the Mergenthaler Company was selling Linotypes in Europe as well. Some 4,000 were in use in 1898. In 1904 there were 7,129 type machines in operation; 6,375 of them Linos and all but 500 of them in the United States.[8]

The reasons were not obscure. The machines did not break down often, and they were fast.

Very fast. Printers in those days measured the amount of type they set in ems (the width of the letter *m*, the widest letter in any type font). Some hand compositors were so dexterous and fast—one was called "the velocipede" by his admiring fans—that they could set more than a thousand ems of type per hour. Three months before Reid and Mergenthaler went public, the winner of hand typesetting's national championship in Philadelphia produced 2,277 ems of correctly spelled and spaced type per hour. "No one," it turned out, "would ever go faster." But a few years later, in 1891, pedestrian machine operators in New Orleans were doing 2,300 ems per hour. In 1893, the best Lino operator at Reid's *Tribune* put down 8,567 ems in an hour. It was "a week's work for a handsetting journeyman." By 1900, machine compositors were expected to average 5,000 ems per hour just to keep their jobs.[9]

Academic researchers rushed in to study the dramatic changes. At Johns Hopkins University, one expert calculated that Lino operators were four times as efficient as hand compositors. In 1895, Congress asked the country's labor commissioner to assess the impact of machinery on several different important industries, including printed communications. The government found that a hand print shop took 340 man-hours to set and print 100,000 railroad tickets. A machine print shop did the same job in twenty-five hours, thirty-eight minutes. It concluded that composing machines were 3.5 to 10 times more productive than humans.[10] The commissioner and the congressmen who accepted his report portrayed its findings as a defining triumph of American ingenuity.

To press owners, the hour of their final, defining triumph over their maddening unionized printers was at hand.

The leaders of the new Mergenthaler company—those who controlled it were almost all newspaper publishers—decided to try to outflank the union. They'd establish beachheads for the Lino at the edges of the industry, in nonunion job and book printing companies and at Reid's own nonunion

Tribune.[11] Then, once the machines were up and being run by nonunion workers in open shops, the technology would have enough data and economic force behind it to convince the country's biggest plants to endure the upheaval of dislodging their ITU member workers.

Reid gleefully predicted to his fellow Mergenthaler stockholders in 1887 that publishers who bought machines soon would be able to replace their union compositors with low-wage typists (meaning women) who could learn the machine "in a few hours." He considerately suggested that experienced printers—meaning members of the International Typographical Union—probably should be spared the inconvenience of even auditioning for such jobs. "The older and better a printer is, the less likely he is to relish being told that he has a new trade to learn in order to continue profitably at his old business."[12]

To tell the public about the coming transformation of the mass media workforce, The American Newspaper Publishers Association invited its members to cover a demonstration of the Mergenthaler and three of its competitors in Brooklyn. They found seemingly frail people at work. The *New York Times* "watched Miss J.J. Camp, a stenographer, operate successfully a type-setting machine." "Pretty girls," the *New York World* added lyrically, "gingerly lettered keys."[13]

The union-busting appeals were not subtle. The Thorne, an important Linotype competitor, advertised by sending publishers proofs of type "set on this machine by a lady operator." She had, moreover, set a jaw-dropping 47,000 ems of type in ten hours.[14] "Cheap Composition!" the Mergenthaler company exclaimed in its ads. Another Thorne ad promised buyers they could "save money at once," and that there was "no skilled machinist required in attendance."[15]

An unnamed Chicago newspaper made the first move against the union in late 1887. Soon after installing its first Lino, the paper (it was probably Stone's *News*) announced it wanted to amend the five-year contract it had just signed with the union. Specifically, it intended to have a nonunion worker operate the new machine at below-union wages. The ITU, needless to say, objected. It had no problem having a machine at the paper, but it wanted the publisher to give union members first crack at operating it. The arbitrator called in to resolve the conflict sided with the publisher, ruling the labor contract of earlier in the year clearly covered only hand setting.[16] The path to freedom appeared to open wide for publishers everywhere.

For many workers, all paths abruptly looked blocked by "the hasty approach of evil." One unionist forecast that in St. Louis alone machines would force "40 to 60 percent" of the union compositor/printers out of jobs.[17]

Even objective observers agreed machines could leave thousands of people permanently unemployed. American prosperity would die away. "New processes of manufacture will continue," the U.S. commissioner of labor warned in 1885, "but will not afford the remunerative employment for the vast amounts of capital which have been created during that period."[18]

"Every few days the 'machine scare' comes up in our office," a compositor reported to the union's journal. "If an increase in the (union wage) scale is asked for, 'we can't pay it and will put in machines if the demand is insisted on,' is the answer we get."[19] At the *Washington Post*, the ITU squared off against publisher and Mergenthaler stockholder Stilson Hutchins for what it figured to be a landmark contract dispute in 1888 over the use of type machines.[20]

In Sacramento, *Bee* publisher V. S. McClatchy bought his first type machine and began advertising in San Francisco for "young" workers to come to Sacramento to run it. Testifying to a federal commission, one unionist claimed that publishers with new machines "frequently" were opting for "less highly trained and less skillful workmen; in many cases to the replacing of skilled artisans with poorly paid women and children operatives."[21]

"The Mergenthalers are here," a union hand compositor in San Francisco later wrote, and "conditions are alarming." He reported the *Chronicle* planned to lay off forty hand compositors and the *Examiner* seventy-five in the coming months. Two other papers in the city already had shed a total of twenty-six. Across the country, on July 22, 1889, the publishers of the New York *Sun*, *World*, and *Times*, otherwise bitter competitors, abruptly posted notices in their composing room that they all were reducing wages as of that day. (A strike ensued, ending a week later when the publishers withdrew their edict.) The next month, publishers in Little Rock, Leavenworth, and Topeka all announced that they too would bring in machines if they could not cut their hand compositors' wages.[22]

In Edinburgh, Scotland, the *Evening News* ordered seven Linos after its initial experiments worked out well. "And when these get into full swing," a unionist there mourned, "alas for poor Typo!"[23]

Publishers everywhere during the first decade of the Linotype era were using the new technology—or the threat of new technology—to cut their labor costs. In Montgomery, Alabama, the nonunion *Advertiser* reduced printers' wages from 15 cents to 10 cents per thousand ems of type. In Oil City, Pennsylvania, "the printing business . . . is at a standstill, the introduction of type-setting machines having dispensed with the use of all extra men, although the same number of regulars are employed." In Atlanta, publishers broke the union altogether. In New York, "the introduction of type-setting machines has set in strongly in this city, and is creating a revolution in the trade. Numbers of compositors are idle." In North Dakota, country papers invested cooperatively in machines as "the means of throwing out a large number of good men."[24]

Not a few of the good men suspected the printed word itself, at least as they knew it, was dying. It seemed time to quit. In letters to both the trade magazines and the union's own *Typographical Journal*, this most literate of industrial workforces floated ideas to push colleagues to leave the industry. One suggested paying members a bounty of $75 to change careers. A Baltimore compositor suggested his colleagues retrain themselves, exactly as Lou Felicio would do one hundred years later when he put his pride in his pocket, "as janitors in office buildings, watchmen in banking institutions or salesmen in stationery stores."[25]

Others were defiant, challenging the dumb machines to fights. A Boston printer offered to pit three hand compositors against a machine to see who could set the most type.[26]

Others proposed to outthink them. "In all machines," said one, "the same operations are repeated from time to time, whereas [hand compositors] may be at work for years and may not once perform exactly similar motions for five minutes together. [Not having] a piece of mechanism that can think, and the numerous efforts to secure this phenomenon, prove the sure foundation on which the compositor's art is based."[27]

And still others contended there was nothing to worry about because machine type was too ugly to succeed. "It cannot and never will be used in the production of first-class work, either for newspaper or other classes of printing," another correspondent asserted, unknowingly echoing the fifteenth-century delusions of Vespasiano di Bisticci. But then again, throughout history "critics of the new media have usually been defenders of the elite, attempting to bar the new onslaught of the masses."[28]

Most printers, however, fully understood they could not win. "Looking at the type-setting machines of to-day, one . . . foresees the time when such machines will be a complete success," said one.[29]

The International Typographical Union knew it too. Its president counseled that "those familiar with the productiveness of machines are agreed that handwork cannot begin to compete with them."[30]

But something was wrong. The union was supposed to be the machine's greatest foe, but its leaders were saying nice things about it. They didn't stop with compliments, either: the ITU was soon one of the technology's loudest supporters. And as it touted the machines, it was the master printers, not the unionists, who found themselves being outflanked.

As early as June 1888—pretty much as soon as papers began installing Linotypes—the ITU officially encouraged hand compositors to learn how to use them. It did so, moreover, with a sophisticated understanding of how economies can work. In an eerie prelude to the supply-side economics that would enjoy a vogue a hundred years later, the union argued that everyone, including its members, would profit from the industry's unprecedented new production speed. Anything that improved capacity and profits ultimately would be good for the worker.

In the past faster presses, cutters, feeders, and other machines had "all led to more work and better pay," one member pointed out. "May not the dreaded typesetting machine prove equally advantageous in a very short time?" Another predicted that the labor-saving machines would actually double the number of jobs for compositors within five years. Machines may look scary at first, said another union correspondent, but they have a way of working out for the best. "We as printers are not more favorably impressed with the iron compositor than were our friends the teamsters of a half century ago with the iron horse," he counseled as he recalled the history of technological upheaval. "There was a time the seamsters prophesized [doom] because [sewing machine inventor Elias] Howe had struck a new note in the song of the shirt. But somehow these cataclysms were side-tracked and turned into blessing, and this new compositor will not prove an exception."[31]

The *Inland Printer*, the industry's major trade journal at the time, recalled that labor was supposed to "be decimated" back when Koenig's steam press replaced the hand press. But in practice the new capacity "brought the cost of printing within the reach of a larger mass of the public" and engendered still more newspapers, printed words, and jobs. "Every measurable reduction in the cost of production has increased the consumption in a ratio that about equalizes matters all around in the end."[32]

So a major labor organization, faced with a dreaded new technology, decided to remake itself. The decision may not have had a precedent. In the late 1880s and early 1890s, relatively new industries were full of angry, uneducated people new to factories. Many were new to English and the United States. Almost all were new to their impossibly polluted and often unlivable cities (New York was just completing its first park; Chicago did not have one yet and lived under a poisonous, yellow sky of coal smoke) and to the unnerving, constant threat of physical and financial harm. They were often managed, moreover, by a generation of industrialists who came out of the militarist training of the Civil War and were fed on an ideology that said they were succeeding precisely because they were fitter and stronger than their workers. Conflict in this confused, combustible environment was common. American farmers were in open revolt against railroads and ephemeral monetary innovations, organizing grange strikes and struggling to create their own political movement. Private and state militias were shooting and killing railroad and coal workers striking to preserve their jobs against labor-saving technologies. But the International Typographical Union, probably alone among the dissidents and advocates of "Single Tax" clubs and fledgling multi-industry unions mobilizing to shut down the whole country if they needed to, decided instead to adopt the new tools that threatened it. It would become a union of people with markedly different sets of skills. Toward that end, the Indianapolis local sent two people to the *Standard Union* in Brooklyn to learn as much about the machines as possible. They concluded, "unions should in no way discourage their use, but should insist their members be employed." Both the Cincinnati and Philadelphia locals bought their own Mergenthalers to train their members. At the *Milwaukee Sentinel*, "the printers here seem willing, and a great many of them anxious, to see the advent of these machines, the sooner the better."[33]

Officially the union even resolved to support master printers who adopted the fabulous new machines, offering to help by taking less pay during "training periods." In return, however, the ITU wanted only its own experienced journeymen workers to run the machines. When they were fully trained, moreover, they should run them at full union wages. The machines' speed, the union conceded, probably made being paid by the number of "ems" impractical. Pay therefore should be by the hour, not the em. Yet because working at a machine could be such drudgery, cause so much eyestrain, and be so physically demanding, the union wanted to cut work days to nine or even eight hours.[34]

There were, of course, those within the International Typographical Union who remained convinced that accepting the machines in any form was suicidal, if not cowardly. "The typesetting machine," a Buffalo unionist insisted, "decreases the number of hands and the cost of the work but does not increase the number of newspapers to an extent that will be any relief."[35]

Getting people like him to adopt the machines set off a vast struggle within the union. The relatively new national ITU leadership—the organization had not even had a national office until recently—struggled to get its distant locals to stop fighting the new metal. In the process, it began to wrest organizational power from the locals' representatives, preparing to strong-arm stubborn compositors into learning the machines if necessary.[36] Their future depended on it.

NOTES

1. Frank Luther Mott, *American Journalism: A History, 1690–1960*, 3rd ed. (New York: Macmillan, 1962), 497.

2. Walker Rumble, *The Swifts: Printers in the Age of Typesetting Races* (Charlottesville University of Virginia Press, 2003), 55.

3. Rumble, *The Swifts*, 86.

4. "Mr. Reid's Question Answered," *Inland Printer*, June 1896, 291.

5. George Corben Goble, *The Obituary of a Machine: The Rise and Fall of Ottmar Mergenthaler's Linotype at U.S. Newspapers* (Bloomington: Indiana University Mass Communications Program, 1984), 110–11, 113; Rumble, *The Swifts*, 144, 142; Reid wielded what one ITU vice president angrily called a "lusty pen" against the workingman. Elizabeth Faulkner Baker, *Printers and Technology: A History of the International Printing Pressmen and Assistants Union* (Westport, Conn.: Greenwood, 1974), 92.

6. David J. Russo, "The Origins of Local News in the U.S. Country Press, 1840s–1870," *Journalism Monographs*, February 1980, 1; Henri Bouchet, *The Book: Its Printers, Illustrators, and Binders from Gutenberg to the Present Time*, ed. H. Grevel (New York: Scribner & Welford, 1890), 238. In 1854, the *London Times* sold 55,000 copies daily, far outdistancing its five competitors in the city, whose circulations ranged from 2,500 to 6,600. P. M. Handover, *Printing in London: From Caxton to Modern Times* (Cambridge: Harvard University Press, 1960), 162. In 1830, the 650 weeklies and 65 dailies in the United States had an average circulation of 1,200 readers. Ten years later, the country's 1,141 weeklies and 138 dailies averaged 2,200. Some papers obviously were bigger; the *New York Sun* sold 15,000 copies a day by 1835. Rumble, *The Swifts*, 8–9; Mott, *American Journalism*, 167.

7. The 1886 model initially fell short of its investors' impossibly high expectations. Though Mergenthaler didn't believe it, the *Louisville Courier-Journal* and Stone's *Chicago Daily News* apparently complained that type broke easily and sometimes ended up positioned higher or lower than other characters on a line. At the *New York Tribune*, Whitelaw Reid found the machine unsuitable for setting certain kinds of copy. Goble, *Obituary*, 111; Mergenthaler, *Biography*, 31. Mergenthaler believed Reid's troubling reports were false, part of a plan to force Mergenthaler from the company. A trade journal added that reports of the first model's efficiency were "rubbish," rumors propagated by "smart alecks of the New York press." Rumble, *The Swifts*, 140. And some—although not all—union compositors were ostentatiously critical of the machine's work. The Lino, one sniffed in a report to the union in 1889, gave type a "miserable appearance." A. Spencer, "Type-setting Machines," *Typographical Journal*, September 15, 1889, 2. "The menacing horror," another union

writer added, "was not absolutely perfected and might never be." J. W. Sullivan in *Union Printer*, the journal of ITU Local no. 6, as cited in Goble, *Obituary*, 212. In 1887, the *Manchester Guardian* adopted a new Thorne machine. Like many mechanical typesetters, it broke down often enough to negate the advantages gained from its terrific speed. J. Southward, "Type Composing Machines" (1891), as cited in Colin Clair, *A History of European Printing* (London: Academic, 1976), 379. Added the president of the District of Columbia ITU local, "Printers are never alarmed nowadays when they hear that machines are to be introduced in an office. They know that the machine has not yet been invented that will universally, or to say considerable extent, supplant hand composition." "President Kennedy on the Position of Unionists Toward Type-setting Machines," *Typographical Journal*, August 1, 1891, 5. No one, however, was more disappointed than Mergenthaler, who could not properly regulate the temperature of the machine's molten lead and begged Reid and the others to stop selling it until he could improve it. Reid, however, pressed on and had Mergenthaler build 212 of the often malfunctioning machines. Goble, *Obituary*, 82, 84, 87. It was Mergenthaler's second model, offered in 1889 after Reid left the company, that took off.

8. J. G. Reeves, "The Rogers Typograph," *Typographical Journal*, November 1, 1890, 5; St. Louis Notes, *Inland Printer*, August 1891, 1021; Phil Corcoran, "Provisional Membership," *Typographical Journal*, November 16, 1889, 1; "The Type-setting Machine," *Typographical Journal*, February 2, 1891, 4; "Machine Work in New Orleans," *Typographical Journal*, November 2, 1891, 2; Rumble, *The Swifts*, 147; James R. Slider, "Atlanta and the Printing Interest," *Inland Printer*, September 1893, 482; "Notes on Typesetting Machines," *Inland Printer*, July 1894, 364; Mergenthaler, *Biography*, 71; G. E. Barnett, "The Introduction of the Linotype: The Displacement Of Labor," *Yale Review*, November 1904, 251–52.

9. "Machine Work in New Orleans," *Typographical Journal*, November 2, 1891, 2; Rumble, *The Swifts*, 135, 151, 153.

10. Barnett, "Introduction," 251–73; Carroll D. Wright, *Hand and Machine Labor* (Washington, D.C.: U.S. Bureau of Labor, 1898), 359–61; Harry Kelber and Carl Schlesinger, *Union Printers and Controlled Automation* (New York: Free Press, 1967), 11.

11. Basil Kahan, *Ottmar Mergenthaler: The Man and His Machine* (New Castle, Del.: Oak Knoll, 2000), 27–28. *Washington Post* publisher Stilson Hutchins initially recruited Reid into the Linotype investment group not only because of Reid was prominent and wealthy, but because his nonunion paper would prove a less contentious place to introduce the machine than Hutchins's *Post*. Hutchins was particularly worried about the pressure union compositors from the nearby Government Printing Office would put on him if he was the first to install a machine.

12. Goble, *Obituary*, 213.

13. Goble, *Obituary*, 271–72. Camp was a favorite of Mergenthaler, who had been employing her to demonstrate his machines since at least 1883. Mergenthaler, *Biography*, 15.

14. A. Spencer, "Type-setting Machines," *Typographical Journal*, September 15, 1889, 2.

15. Ads in *Inland Printer*, August 1895, 576; July 1895, 220.

16. "Type-setting Machines: An Arbitrator Decides That the Chicago Agreement Does Not Apply," *Typographical Journal*, September 1, 1891, 4.

17. Phil Corcoran, "Provisional Membership," *Typographical Journal*, December 16, 1889, 1.

18. Eric A. Johnson, "We're Not Washed Up," *Reader's Digest*, November 1943, 11–16. Johnson was president of the U.S. Chamber of Commerce.

19. C. H. Gilman, "Modern Mechanism: Will Type-setting Machines Have a Good or Demoralizing Influence?" *Typographical Journal*, December 1, 1891, 1.

20. Kahan, *Mergenthaler*, 68. Hutchins ultimately brought in the first generation "blower" Linotypes but later got rid of them "because of disputes with the union and maintenance problems."

21. Barnett, "Introduction," 271–72.

22. Editorial, *Typographical Journal*, July 1, 1895, 1; "Strikes and Lockouts," *Typographical Journal*, August 15, 1889, 1–2.

23. Samuel Kinnear, "Reception of the Linotype in Edinburgh," *Inland Printer*, May 1896, 182.

24. Goble, *Obituary*, 237; "Correspondence from Oil City," *Typographical Journal*, April 1, 1892, 5; James R. Slider, "Atlanta and the Printing Interest," *Inland Printer*, September 1893, 482; Leonidas, "From New York," *Inland Printer*, August 1891, 994; R. M. Tuttle, "Out of Work Printers," *Inland Printer*, October 1895, 55.

25. Will H. Winn, "A Cheerfully Optimistic View: Everything Rounded for the Best, Even the Machine a Blessing," *Typographical Journal*, February 1, 1896.

26. Myrick Waites, "The Typograph vs. Hand Composition," *Typographical Journal*, December 1, 1890, 1.

27. Rumble, *The Swifts*, 145.

28. E. B. Williams, "The Linotype," *Inland Printer*, June 1891, 790–91; Paul Levinson, *The Soft Edge: A Natural History and Future of the Information Revolution* (London: Routledge, 1997), 56–57.

29. A. Spencer, "Type-setting Machines," *Typographical Journal*, September 15, 1889, 2.

30. Barnett, "Introduction," 261.

31. An Old-Time Printer, "We Want More Labor-Saving Devices and Materials," *Inland Printer*, September 1891, 1043; J. G. Reeves, "The Rogers Typograph," *Typographical Journal*, November 1, 1890, 5; Winn, "Optimistic View," *Typographical Journal*, February 1, 1896.

32. "Typesetting Machines," *Inland Printer*, September 1891, 1061.

33. "Miscellaneous Notes," *Typographical Journal*, February 16, 1891, 6; "Type-setting Machines. An Outline of the Report of the Delegates Sent East by no. 1," *Typographical Journal*, March 2, 1891, 1; "Notes on Typesetting Machines," *Inland Printer*, July 1894, 364; H. S., "From Milwaukee," *Inland Printer*, August 1891, 994.

As time passed, unionists grew more insistent that the machines would be a boon for them. "It is the experienced and practical printer who will derive the benefits of the machine, and not the novice, as many would believe," one printer believed. C. H. Gilman, "Modern Mechanism: Will Type-setting Machines Have a Good or Demoralizing Influence?" *Typographical Journal*, December 1, 1891, 1.

34. Barnett, "Introduction," 260–61.

35. Hugh Wallace, "Typesetting Machines and Union Legislation," *Inland Printer*, September 1895, 603.

36. Barnett, "Introduction," 260.

13

COMPLACENCY'S TRIUMPH

While workers lobbied and tried to shame their colleagues into supporting the union's controversial stance, their bosses mobilized to fire every one of them. Many owners excitedly saw themselves at the end of a long, difficult, expensive—perhaps the modern-day equivalent of $300 million in total investments since the Civil War—battle to cut their labor expenses. Now they had the machine to do it. They had the strategy and the money to get it up and running. And they were organized. Victory was in sight at last.

They called their antiunion groups Franklin Clubs (in honor of their secular saint, Benjamin Franklin) or Typothetae (a dusty German word for "type placers"). Some had been around since 1833, when Philadelphia owners, hoping to drive discount printers from town, tried to fix the prices they would charge customers. Like the stationers, they'd fine members who charged less. Similar self-regulatory clubs and groups cropped up in New York City, western New York State, Chicago, St. Louis, Milwaukee, Memphis, Louisville, St. Paul, Grand Rapids, Baltimore, Harrisburg, Boston, Columbus, and Cincinnati. When they failed to control competition by fixing prices, they tried to control costs by negotiating as a group with their paper and ink suppliers. But without the enforcement powers of a state-sponsored employers' group like the Stationers Company or Paris Book Guild, their efforts were only fitfully successful. Finally, as the ITU grew into a powerful bargaining opponent, they decided to transform themselves into a united employers' front to confront the workers' front. In 1887, just as the Lino started selling, sixty-eight delegates coalesced into a nationwide United Typothetae.[1]

Some thought themselves massing for Armageddon. The most radical delegates resolved to purge the nonbelievers: Typothetae members, they said, had to be union-free. Those who still negotiated with workers' groups should get rid of their unions right away, while they were retooling their composing rooms and the iron was hot. If that meant firing longtime employees, hiring replacement workers to work the new machines, and enduring the ongoing community anger such actions usually caused, so be it. If they weren't up to it, they would be barred from the Typothetae.

More moderate delegates defeated the purge, but even they were spoiling for a fight. They promised to help each other defeat the ITU effort to shorten the workday to nine hours. They also approved efforts to try to weaken their opponents by keeping print shop and newspaper compositors physically separate from each other and forbidding the foremen in their shops to belong to a union.[2]

The initial skirmishes were encouraging. Back home after the meeting, member companies promptly defeated ITU strikes to win a nine-hour day in Chicago and New York. They strung out a strike in Pittsburgh over the same issue for two years, with other Typothetae chapters sending financial support to keep the struck printing plants operating.[3]

But their war to get rid of the hand compositors union, like their efforts to fix prices and strong-arm suppliers, didn't go as well. The reasons were many: the employers' strength and will, like the workers', varied from place to place. Some negotiated better than others. Some, moreover, were less hostile to unions than their colleagues. To them, the International Typographical Union was an often troublesome but expert provider of crucial services, effectively acting as personnel departments for their companies. The union recruited workers, trained them, made sure there was always someone manning a station through illnesses and inclement weather, and even disciplined unreliable or unethical colleagues. Often angry with their workers and disgusted by their demands, many employers nevertheless treated the union as a necessary and not altogether wasteful cost of doing business. They also were wary of the cost—to say nothing of the painful personal ordeal—of trying to force the ITU out of their shops and newspapers.

And they had opponents. Like the owners, the workers were in a fighting mood. The owners met to form the United Typothetae the same year that a champion "steel-drivin' man" named John Henry challenged a steam drill to a contest to build a train tunnel near Birmingham, Alabama. Henry supposedly worked and worked and laid more steel than the newfangled machine but then, having proved some unclear principle, collapsed and died. True or not, the oft-repeated story had a powerful impact in a time when cold metal was replacing warm-blooded men in scores of professions.

"Hammer songs" about the legend were becoming popular just as press owners began buying type machines at the end of the 1880s. Defensive and perhaps humming the tunes, hand compositors were not above issuing their own challenges to the mute type machines showing up in their offices. The ITU hated the very idea of the foolish contests, since they would help make the case that the machines were better to use than humans. It regularly warned members not to engage the metal one on one (and flatly prohibited the contests in 1900). But workers, none too compliant even in the best of times, often ignored them.

And, oddly enough, workers often beat the machines. In 1889, for example, a hand compositor at the *New York Herald* squared off in a John Henry–like race against an "expert typewriter" working a Lino. In the first heat, the machine "far outstripped" the hand printer in speed. The hand printer's copy, however, was cleaner and much more accurate. After making the corrections, the hand printer had set more useable type in less time than the machine. In the next heat six weeks later, the stenographer's speed was still better, but his accuracy had not improved. Again, the experienced hand printer won.[4]

The industry's inexperienced replacements, in short, simply were not working out. Setting type on deadline always had involved much more than putting letters in the right order. And the messianic machine proved not all that easy to use. The machine "is complicated," one unionist reassured his colleagues. It had a special keyboard, organized differently from the qwerty typewriter stenographers used. "In addition to the mechanical knowledge required, the operator must have some knowledge of spelling, punctuation, division of words, capitalization and style." The unionist estimated it took up to six months to learn to operate it efficiently. "The machine, at present, is complicated, delicate, and a good brand of common sense on the part of the operator is necessary," another added.[5]

The literate machinist also needed to have a working familiarity with mechanics and, probably more important, be deadline savvy. The pressure in shops could be intense, and the margin for error was small.

A Dayton Typothetae member told of hiring a nonunion foreman who soon was desperately scrambling to keep the machines running and get type to the presses. The foreman used a traditional remedy. "To keep his courage up," the master printer added, he "resorted to quaffing diligently of the cup that cheers but also inebriates." He was quickly fired, replaced by a union foreman.[6]

In St. Louis, the publisher of the *Star-Sayings* also found himself unable to get someone to run his new Mergenthaler effectively. He too agreed to train his ITU compositors on it, although not before what a printer reported as "a good deal of difficulty in coming to terms as to compensation for the operators." Skeptical workers saw such negotiating, repeated in city after city, as a "cunning effort to find out how little the journeymen printers can afford to work for."[7] They were, no doubt, correct. But it also was a sign that publishers still needed competent professionals, and some of them realized the ITU remained the best place to find them.

Even the United Typothetae of America's president soon became a believer. "It is a mistake to have a machine which costs thousands of dollars to be managed by an incompetent pressman. The superior performance of the qualified workman fairly justifies his higher wages."[8]

Thus moguls across the industry found it more economical to train hand compositors who already knew printing to run the machines than to hire typists who did not. In spite of self-serving articles about filling their composing rooms with typists, newspaper publishers did not replace many of their union compositors with cheaper, less-skilled, nonunion workers, male or female. While women compositors did work during this era, most were not formally trained. They generally worked at unorganized, low-paying, hand print shops, and typically stayed in the profession for less than five years. One reason may have been the pay. The five hundred women setting type in Chicago in 1899—the great majority at non-newspaper "job shops"—earned about $8 per week; men averaged $14 per week. In New York, nonunion women earned $7 to $12 per week. The ITU had admitted women since the 1870s and always had insisted they be paid the same wages as men. But few women ever joined, effectively stymied by the union's long apprenticeship requirements and its gruff composing room culture. "Only a few women have the courage to do this," the head of the New York ITU local told the *Ladies Home Journal* of the rough six-year apprenticeships full of physical indignities, extended absences from home, and elaborately demeaning rituals that violated most of the social conventions governing young girls at the time. Of the 5,500 union printer/compositors in New York when machine type appeared, for example, only about one hundred were women.[9] Publishers, in any case, had little interest in replacing expensive and troublesome union men with equally expensive union women.

Yet even with union typographers on the machines, newspaper publishers happily watched the costs of producing the printed word drop like a stone.

Adolph Ochs of the *Chattanooga Times* (and soon of the *New York Times*) estimated his new composing machines saved him about 80 percent of his hand composition costs. In 1890, the *New York World* reported that the $173.01 it used to spend to set a page by hand had fallen to $62.22 to set a page by machine. The *Providence Journal* said its composing room costs were dramatically lower, while the *Louisville Courier-Journal's* composition costs were "nearly one half lower" and the *Chicago Daily News's* were down "from one-half to two-thirds" in 1890. The next year another (unnamed) newspaper foreman told his assembled union compositors that each machine was doing the work of four workers, at one-third the cost to the company. In 1894, the Mergenthaler Company advertised that the 140 dailies then using the machine (up from 70 in 1893) were spending only 50 percent of what they'd paid for hand composition. In 1895, the U.S. Bureau .of Labor released its study showing that the total number of man-hours needed to produce a unit of printing had fallen since 1885, despite the higher hourly wages that machine operators were getting. By 1904, the New York Press Association estimated that the technology had cut publishers' labor costs in half.[10]

And when costs dropped, the sheer numbers of printed words skyrocketed again. Despite a chaotically depressed economy, sales soared dramatically in the first years of the machine era. The amateur economists of the ITU, in short, had been right. When productivity boomed, printing boomed. When printing boomed, the number of jobs boomed.

With its new machines, for example, the *New York World* could make and fill the space for more advertising. When it—and all papers—could physically produce only so many typeset pages in the amount of time it had to produce each daily edition, it actually had to turn away ads. It just didn't have the ability to set more ads and more news between the ads. The machines changed all that overnight. Now publishers could sell as many ads as possible, confident that they could produce extra sheets on time. The *World*, for one, began printing 50 percent more pages in each edition shortly after converting to machine type. Its circulation hit a million in 1897, up from 374,000 in 1892, while the *New York Herald* made $1 million in profits in 1897, a huge sum for the day. Kansas City's four dailies not only increased the number of pages they printed but also spawned an evening paper to harvest the newly available ad revenue. In Scotland, type machines similarly enabled newspapers to run more pages and accept more ads, and the number of presses used to print daily newspapers doubled from thirty to sixty in five years. Newspapers in the United States began printing Sunday magazines and supplements as a way to package still more of the pages they could produce and, more importantly, accept still more ad revenue. Some had grown to 120 pages per week by 1903.[11]

The printed word had been expanding steadily and impressively in the United States for more than a hundred years. But now print, freed of its old commercial and financial restraints, took off. There was a tremendous expansion in newspaper, book, and commercial printing almost immediately after the Linotype and two other practical composing machines hit the market. While economic census figures for 1889 are primitive, they suggest the industry grew massively during the 1890s. It continued to expand, faster still, into the first decades of the next century. Newspaper advertising in the United States tripled between 1892 and 1914. Advertising *and* circulation revenues in newspapers rose from $143 million (in nineteenth-century dollars) in 1890 to $166 million in 1899 to $280 million in 1904.[12]

Like the starry-eyed tulip, gold, and stock speculators that came before and after them, the day's entrepreneurs rushed into the bonanza. There were 1,650 dailies in 1892, 2,250 by 1914. Their average circulations doubled during that time, although the population did not. In 1911, media mogul E. W. Scripps said that all you needed to start a paper was "the use of a basement, enough means to get a second-hand press, four linotype machines, and the crusading spirit." He was being modest about the money: in truth it took about $1 million to start a big-city paper and maybe $30,000 to start a small-city one, amounts that would be worth roughly $30 million and $900,000 in the early twenty-first century. Scripps was more accurate about the community power and celebrity a "crusading spirit" could get. Would-be titans were attracted to not only the payoffs but also being part of the day's most visible and prosperous medium. Those who could not afford to start dailies started twice-weekly papers, which multiplied from two hundred titles in 1892 to six hundred in 1914, or weeklies, which increased to 12,500 in 1914 from 11,000 in 1892. The annual amount of second-class mail—newspapers and magazines delivered at special discount rates—increased by almost 20 percent in the century's final four years. News had become, as one historian called it, a leviathan business, closed to the entry of all but the very rich.[13]

Books became a bigger industry too. The United States produced 4,559 new book titles in 1890. Ten years later, it was turning out 6,356 titles per year. It was up to 12,012 by 1914. Books also became increasingly accessible, falling from the equivalent in 1800 of an average American worker's pay ($1.00) to, in some cases, a dime by 1900. And they became a central part of the country's social life. Book clubs became common weekend gatherings, where people swapped and debated books and postcards as they would later swap and debate music and film titles. The Boston Society of Arts and Crafts was the most famous, oft mimicked den of popular thought for the rapidly expanding urban middle class. A magazine, the *Dial*, became popular by leading book clubs in each month's national literary debate. Another, the *Philistine*, had a circulation of 200,000 readers a month.[14]

The book publishing industry, like the newspaper industry, changed under the new pressure of serving bigger audiences with more products. Notoriously civil, bookish editors abruptly found themselves making money a bigger part of their decisions about whether to publish a given work. For the first time, they started assigning marketable subjects to authors (as opposed to waiting for authors to come to them with ideas), creating whole new categories of books like home improvement for whole new classes of people who for the first time actually had the time and money to improve their homes. "As the century ended, the criterion of salability was paramount. Publishing might still be a gentleman's business, but it was a business," one historian recounts. Some sold out under the pressure. Noted logophile J. P. Morgan, for example, took control of the venerable Harper's house in 1899.[15]

Some guardians of public taste—even those in the book business—were less than pleased about the changes. They cringed as bookstores filled with "cap and sword" romances and thrillers turning on "the assassin's dagger, blood and the horrors of the tomb." Popular culture with its lurid, drooling murders and obsessive sex, they warned, was sending civilization straight to hell. Jumping from newspaper to magazine article to book caused "mental desultoriness," the editor of the *New York Post* maintained. Another editor, who founded the nation's first journalism school, claimed it led to "enfeebling of memory [and] dissipation of mind and thought." Even Whitelaw Reid was sure too much reading induced "an intellectual state of oyster-like consciousness"[16]

But "now the book is essentially a mechanical product," counseled the editor of a leading literary magazine of the day, and it was high time the literati got used to it. "The astonishing increase of late years in the number of readers is one of the great literary facts of the time," he warned them in 1901. "It might be expected that the tastes and standards of old readers have been swamped in the surge of demand from so tremendous a newly-risen clientele."[17]

Magazines also got cheaper, thanks to the new production techniques, and grew exponentially. A "great general illustrated magazine era" bloomed. By the turn of the century 175,000 were reading each issue of *Harper's*; 300,000 were reading *Cosmopolitan*, 739,000 reading the *Ladies Home Journal*, and 1.2 million were reading a magazine called *Comfort*, based in Maine. Specialty publications like the *People's Home Journal* went to 315,000 people, the *Delineator* to 500,000, the *Hearthstone* to 600,000. *McClure's*, started in 1893, had a circulation of 300,000 four years later.[18] Costing ten cents per issue, the racy *Munsey's Magazine*—which published a full novel every month—had a readership of 700,000. In all, the nation's six leading general circulation magazines enjoyed a 148 percent increase in readership during the 1890s.[19]

But all kinds of printed words multiplied. States' average spending on their government printing increased 76 percent from 1880 to 1904. "Advertising forms"—what we'd called marketing materials today—represented about 43 percent of the $347 million in finished printing sold in the United States in 1900. To produce it, the number of printing and publishing enterprises of all kinds in the country had increased from 17,724 in 1889, the year the improved Linotype hit the market, to 23,814 in 1899, a 34 percent increase. They increased by yet another third in the following decade.[20]

Print was everywhere. Citizens of the United Kingdom sent 178 pieces of mail—including printed matter—per thousand citizens. In the United States, it was 94 pieces of mail. (The French sent 62 pieces of mail per thousand people, the Germans 58, the Canadians 38, and the Japanese 34.) Books were ubiquitous. The number of public libraries in the United States increased by 25 percent, from 4,000 to 5,000, in the century's last four years. The number of volumes in them increased by 21 percent, to 40 million. It amounted to a little more than one book available, for free, for every adult in the country. While there are no numbers available for circulars, flyers, invoices, memos, banners, packages, or printed sheets produced at the time, we do know that in the United States the fifty biggest newspapers printed an average of twenty pages per day in 1900 (Hearst's New York *Journal* averaged 80 pages a day), and had an average circulation of 600,000. That would amount to 12 million newspaper sheets circulated a day, or about one for every adult in the country. By then, there was one whole daily newspaper in circulation for every American family.[21]

New jobs sprang up all over. By 1895, more people were employed in machine shops than in hand composition shops. (The year before, the union had estimated that 10 percent of its members were out of work, probably an aftershock of the devastating 1893 economic depression.) By 1899, ITU President Samuel B. Donnelly told the U.S. Industrial Commission that there would be as many printers employed by 1900 as there had been before the Lino had been introduced.[22]

But he understated the case. When the gains and losses were counted up more than a decade after these cheaper, metallic alphabets arrived on the scene, researchers flatly concluded that "linotypes . . . did not displace any hand compositors."[23]

Yet they too underestimated the size of the printing boom. The ITU—which converted its own hefty *Typographical Journal* to machine type in 1900—grew by 69 percent from 1888, when evil first hastily approached, to 1900. Almost 210,000 people—both union and nonunion—worked in the printing industry by then, 163,000 of them in production. In all, the number of wage earners in America's energized printing industry increased by 21 percent from 1889 to 1899. And they made more money. Compositors were now averaging $19.50 a week, up more than a third from $14.50 ten years earlier. The value they added to the materials that passed through their hands and machines had increased by 26 percent. In 1900, the industry pumped $176 million—equivalent to something like $5.2 billion today—into the economy in wages, salaries, and purchases. It sold its wares for $374 million, or about $11 billion today. Sales grew by *another* 46 percent during the next five years, to $546 million. It was the country's fastest-growing big business in terms of sales increases.[24]

The printed word was once again in flood. At the turn of the century there were, for example, some 2,394 printers, compositors, pressmen, lithographers, and bookbinders for every million people in the United States, a ninefold increase since 1850 for a population that had increased twofold. But there were still not enough of them to meet the demand. When the City of New York in 1900 plaintively asked the union to supply 150 machine compositors to set type, the ITU could come up with only 100.[25]

Adopting this last mechanical piece in the printed word's ascendance, in sum, was ·faster, more peaceful, and more profitable than anyone had dared expect. If nothing else, it let the ancient rivalry between workers and owners lapse into civility for a brief moment. In 1895, for example, the master printers of the United Typothetae graciously invited the enemy ITU to its annual convention, where they passed a resolution thanking the union for its "complacency" in helping them weather not only the recent economic depression but the profitable retooling of their businesses.[26]

Once again, something more than a printing boom seemed to be unfolding.

Once again, alphabets and type fell into the hands of previously voiceless competitors as they got cheaper to produce. Those who owned information before had feared it would happen. At a publishers' meeting in 1889, even some "prominent" newspaper owners had opposed adopting machines precisely because it "would ultimately so cheapen type" that just about anyone could start a publication. And, in fact, penniless immigrants like Samuel S. McClure and Joseph Pulitzer, "poverty-stricken" farm boys like Frank

Munsey, ministers' sons like George Horace Lorimer and even stock speculators like John Brisbane Walker founded (or revived) the day's most popular newspapers and periodicals. Former printer's devil Adolph Ochs borrowed $250 and assumed $1,500 in debts to buy half interest in the tiny *Chattanooga Times*, which he ultimately parlayed into ownership of the *New York Times*. Fremont Older, born in a log cabin, got editorial control of the *San Francisco Examiner*. Bartender and curio shop owner Harry Tammen, librarian Harvey Scott, and serial entrepreneur William Rockhill Nelson wheedled their way into ownership stakes and eventually daily newspaper fortunes in Denver, Portland (Oregon), and Kansas City.[27]

In them came reports of unfamiliar new phenomena, as if from an alien culture arising: pictures that moved, radiation, chain stores, genetics, neon light, terrestrial stationary waves, self-service, modernism, insulin, tractors, jazz, birth control, lipstick, separate but equal, cafeteria, crossword puzzle, and, as the era ground to its horrific stalemate in the trenches of Europe in the new century's second decade, "no-man's land." Words, the basic building blocks of human communications, were literally multiplying. Some 1,000 words were added to the dictionary during the next twenty-five years merely to describe the new radio. Hundreds were invented to describe the automobile; more hundreds for the shocking new wonder of flight.[28] All of these words represented concepts, whims, and life forces that had not existed in 1890. They made some people, including Ottmar Mergenthaler, very uncomfortable.

NOTES

1. The word "typothetae" dates back at least to 1470, when Emperor Frederick II of Germany used it to describe the printers guild. It hoped to foster trade, shield members from "unjust and unlawful exactions," produce uniform trade practices, disseminate technical knowledge, and "arrive at mutual understandings with employees." Frederick W. Hamilton, *A Brief History of Printing in America* (Chicago: United Typothetae of America, 1918), 73, 80–81; Elizabeth Faulkner Baker, *Printers and Technology: A History of the International Printing Pressmen and Assistants Union* (Westport, Conn.: Greenwood, 1974), 33.

2. Baker, *Printers and Technology*, 242, 246.

3. Baker, *Printers and Technology*, 255.

4. George Corben Goble, *The Obituary of a Machine: The Rise and Fall of Ottmar Mergenthaler's Linotype at U.S. Newspapers* (Bloomington: Indiana University Mass Communications Program, 1984), 239; "Type-setting Machines: An Outline of the Report of the Delegates Sent East by No. 1," *Typographical Journal*, March 2, 1889, 1.

5. E. B. Williams, "The Linotype," *Inland Printer*, June 1891, 791; Hugh Wallace, "Linotype Operators," *Inland Printer*, April 1897, 4546.

6. Baker, *Printers and Technology*, 253–55.

7. "St. Louis Notes," *Inland Printer*, August 1891, 1021; "The Typothetae and the Union," *Inland Printer*, September 1895, 594.

8. Baker, *Printers and Technology*, 69.

9. Harry Kelber and Carl Schlesinger, *Union Printers and Controlled Automation* (New York: Free Press, 1967), 8; G. E. Barnett, "The Introduction of the Linotype: The Displacement of Labor," *Yale Review*, November 1904, 271; "Lady Compositors," *Inland Printer*, November 1889, 109; Charles F. Dumar, "Women as Typesetters," *Inland Printer*, August 1891, 1001. The number of women typesetters both in and out of the union, moreover, declined precipitously right after the turn of the century. In 1900, there were 1,587 women printers and compositors, some 15 percent of all U.S. workers in the field. By 1904, their numbers fell to 520, only 5 percent of all machine operators. Kelber and Schlesinger, *Union Printers*, 8.

10. Goble, *Obituary*, 236, 267–68; Meyrick Waites, "The Typograph vs. Hand Composition," *Typographical Journal*, December 1, 1890, 1; Baker, *Printers and Technology*, 20; Leonidas, "From New York," *Inland Printer*, August 1891, 994; "The Linotype," *Inland Printer*, April 1893, 6; "The Linotype," *Inland Printer*, April 1894, 4; Kelber and Schlesinger, *Union Printers*, 7–8.

11. J. G. Reeves, "The Rogers Typograph," *Typographical Journal*, November 1, 1890, 5; Joseph Pulitzer, owner of the *World*, was prevented from buying a Lino by the Mergenthaler Company's main stockholders, who had reserved the use of machines for themselves in their home cities. In New York, Reid's *Tribune* had the Lino monopoly, which lasted until about 1892. In the meantime the *World* opted for a different machine, the Rogers Typograph. It was a worthy, cheaper competitor to the Lino until the Mergenthaler Company acquired the Rogers and the company that made it in 1895. Its inventor, Robert Rogers, served as Mergenthaler's chief engineer into the 1920s. Frank Luther Mott, *American Journalism A History: 1690–1960*, 3rd ed. (New York: Macmillan, 1962), 546; X.Y.Z., "Machine Gossip in the West," *Typographical Journal*, January 1, 1896, 59; "Pressmen versus Compositors," *Inland Printer*, June 1897, 289; "Modern Printing Methods," *Scientific American*, November 11, 1903.

12. Kelber and Schlesinger, *Union Printers*, 9; Sidney Kobre, *Development of American Journalism* (Dubuque: Brown, 1969), 518.

13. Kelber and Schlesinger, *Union Printers*, 9; Mott, *American Journalism*, 547, 549; C. H. Howard, "Publishers and the Postal Department," *Arena*, December 1901, 575.

14. Kelber and Schlesinger, *Union Printers*, 9–10; Paul Levinson, *The Soft Edge: A Natural History and Future of the Information Revolution* (London: Routledge, 1997), 82; Joseph Blumenthal, *The Printed Book in America* (Boston: Godine, 1977), 50.

15. John Tebbel, *Between Covers: The Rise and Transformation of Book Publishing in America* (New York: Oxford University Press, 1987), 82, 95.

16. Henri Bouchet, *The Book: Its Printers, Illustrators, and Binders from Gutenberg to the Present Time*, ed. H. Grevel (New York: Scribner & Welford, 1890), 238; Thomas C. Leonard, *News for All: America's Coming-of-Age with the Press* (New York: Oxford University Press, 1995), 9. E. L. Godkin was the editor of the *Post*; Walter Williams the founder of journalism school.

17. "Of Making Many Books," *Current Literature*, December 1901, 655.

18. Mott, *American Journalism*, 512; "Some Magazine Circulations," *Inland Printer*, June 1897, 290.

19. Frederick G. Kilgour, *The Evolution of the Book* (New York: Oxford University Press, 1998), 123.

20. Kelber and Schlesinger, *Union Printers*, 9–10; "Modern Printing Methods," *Scientific American*, November 11, 1903; Bureau of the Census, *Thirteenth Census of the United States, X: Manufactures, 1909* (Washington, D.C.: U.S. Dept of Commerce, 1910), 767.

21. B. R. Mitchell, *International Historical Statistics: The Americas, 1750–2000*, 5th ed. (New York: Palgrave Macmillan, 2003), 3, 6, 610–26; Mitchell, *International Historical Statistics, Europe 1750–2000*, 5th ed. (New York: Palgrave Macmillan, 2003), 3–4, 6, 8, 750–56; Mitchell, *International Historical Statistics, Africa, Asia, and Oceania, 1750–1993*, 3rd ed. (New York: Stockton, 1998), 3, 5–9, 781–93; Tebbel, *Between Covers*, 81; Leonard, *News for All*, 177.

22. Baker, *Printers and Technology*, 20; William Paschell, "The International Typographical Union," *Monthly Labor Review*, May 1952, 496. Paschell contends that type machines fed the unemployment, but his numbers—that the ITU had 30,000 members at the time—do not jibe with the union's own membership count. Goble, *Obituary*, 243.

23. Barnett, "Introduction," 255.

24. Goble, *Obituary*, 240. The union had 19,025 members in 1888, 32,105 in 1900. *A Study of the History of the International Typographical Union, 1852–1963*, vol. 1 (Colorado Springs: Executive Council of the International Typographical Union, 1964), 315; Carroll D. Wright, "Great Industrial Changes since 1893," *World's Work*, August 1901, 1109; Bureau of the Census, *Thirteenth Census*, 767; W. S. Rossiter, "Printing and Publishers: The Barometer Industry," *American Monthly Review of Reviews*, September 1906, 338.

25. There were 788 printers for every million Americans in 1850, 1,726 in 1880, and 2,394 in 1900. The country's population increased 2.33 times during the same period. U.S. Bureau of Labor Statistics, cited in Baker, *Printers and Technology*, 25. "Modern Printing Methods," *Scientific American*, November 11, 1903.

26. Baker, *Printers and Technology*, 247. By contrast, violent strikes had convulsed the railroad system in 1894.

27. Goble, *Obituary*, 272. Richard Digby-Junger, ed., Mass Market Magazine Revolution, Gale Encyclopedia of Popular Culture, www.findarticles.com/cf_0/g1epc/tov/2419100778/p4/article.jhtml?term= (accessed April 21, 2004); Mott, *American Journalism*, 549, 554, 572; Kobre, *Development*, 476, 490, 462.

28. Mark Sullivan, *Our Times*, cited in Richard Rhodes, ed., *Visions of Technology* (New York: Simon & Schuster, 1999), 29–30.

14

THE WORLD WITHOUT KINSHIP

The better he did, the more uneasy Ottmar Mergenthaler seemed to feel.

In most ways, he enjoyed a far better fate than Gutenberg, the last man who had caused trouble by making type cheaper and faster. By 1899, Mergenthaler had a grand house in a fashionable section of Baltimore, a wife, four children, many close friends, and an estate worth almost $500,000. (His family continued to receive royalties from his inventions for another twenty years.)[1] Personally, he was a lover of beer, cigars, and good jokes. By most accounts, he was a thoughtful and generous friend and a considerate employer more progressive than many of his peers.

But like Gutenberg, he was in many ways out of sync with his times. As a businessman, he lost power and faith in the company—and, more broadly, in the dramatically faster new industrial economy—he had helped create. By 1899, the end of his life, he was a rejected and resentful worker in what he saw as a mean, immoral commercial world. Many of the spirits loose in the economy, he knew, had been roaring toward some ill-defined conclusion for decades. Others inadvertently had been accelerated by Mergenthaler's own life's work. All saddened him.

"Promises made by a company," he wrote mournfully of the lessons of his business life, "are only made to be broken."[2]

He was thin-skinned by nature, but especially sensitive about his business affairs. Various relatives, Stone, Reid, and most of the executives who succeeded them as his business associates constantly upset and offended him in some way. They broke promises. They supposedly kept profits from him. They ignored his advice. They forgot to reply to him. He found it hard to forgive many of the slights, real or imagined.

He dated the betrayals from his birth as an entrepreneur, when August Hahl (actually his stepmother's brother's cousin) took a large share in a company formed to produce Mergenthaler's early machine designs. They quickened along with his machine's success. An incident in 1891 caused him "indescribable surprise and disgust." Another in 1892 and 1893 left him fuming that "of the many contemptible attempts . . . to take advantage of him, none left Mr. Mergenthaler with as much disgust as this one." The company's deals to sell Linotypes in Austria and Germany in 1894 amounted to personal "repudiation over and over again!" In 1895, company executives—by then as alienated as Mergenthaler was—proposed changing the company's name because, they said, the firm's clerks spent too much time writing out the word "Mergenthaler" hundreds of times a day. They wanted a shorter, more efficient name. "Of the many communications received," the inventor replied hurtfully, "I do not remember one which was made so painful an impression upon me as the one . . . advising me of the intention to strike my name from" the company.[3]

His health, moreover, was not good. Compositors in general were a sickly lot, typically working in badly ventilated, oxygen-short shops. Their rooms were often on the top floors of newspaper buildings; the *Baltimore Sun*'s composing room, for one, was "like a furnace in summer." They regularly suffered from maladies like "hang wrist"—which sounds like a precursor to carpal tunnel syndrome—and "lead colic," a gastrointestinal disease probably related to the lead they absorbed by handling and holding type in their mouths as they arranged words on their composing sticks. Even worse were the respiratory diseases, probably related to working in close quarters with benzene, which was used to clean type, and near gaslights. Mortality rates were scandalous. The average compositor in 1893 lived only 38.78 years, almost nine years less than the average American male in 1900.[4] Working over the molten metals of Mergenthaler's type plagued the new generations of compositors, and Mergenthaler himself was among the first victims.

His respiratory problems began in 1888, when he was almost too ill to make it to New York for Reid's demonstration at the *Tribune*. Later attacks were diagnosed as pleurisy. In 1896, now undeniably suffering from tuberculosis, he was finally forced from the heartaches of daily business life to recuperate—or at least to try to breathe more easily—in the dry climes of Arizona and New Mexico. "You'd hardly recognize me if I came back to Baltimore," he wrote to a friend. "I don't drink beer or smoke cigars anymore. Illness makes people moral."[5]

Little of his sardonic humor, however, showed up in his resentful autobiography, which he began in the desert. Writing formally in the third person, he determined to record all the unnecessary, wasteful, destructive insults he'd suffered at the hands of his big business overseers. He was nearly finished when a fire destroyed the New Mexico house he and his family occupied and, with it, his first and only draft. By then, his disease had reduced him to a mere 113 pounds. Literally struggling for breath, he limped home to Baltimore to start the thing all over again. He again chose to skip writing about his brave immigrant adventure, his wife, the traumatic death of a four-year-old son, his surviving children, the fantastic new age of invention, the wonders of electric power, the unprecedented boom in printed knowledge he had helped cause or even about the terrible fire that rousted his family and destroyed his recent work. Instead, he detailed how he close he would come to solving a difficult technical or production problem in the Lino's birth, only to have a colleague unfairly frustrate him. It happened again and again at each step of his professional life.

As if hanging on until he got those outrages on paper, he died soon after he finished. He was forty-five and had wasted away to one hundred pounds.[6]

He was not the first inventive spirit to be nurtured and then hurt by unfamiliar new business styles. Financier Johann Fust had hung over Gutenberg's shoulder, imposing the rigors and speed of a new age. He harried Gutenberg, exacerbated his debt, forced employees on him, and ultimately purged him from his own shop. Four hundred years later, Reid lent Mergenthaler money to buy stock in their new company and then held the obligation over the inventor's head for years. He saddled him with unwanted employees, most with corporate powers greater than Mergenthaler's. Desperate for Linotypes to sell, he cajoled Mergenthaler into quitting his ceaseless experimenting, since production delays were imperiling the company. Reid, who once promised Mergenthaler enough riches to live in a castle on the Rhine, ran out of patience much as Fust had run out of patience with Gutenberg. In 1887, barely a year after the company was formed, Reid began harassing the inventor in all sorts of ways, significant and petty. Among other things, he stopped responding to Mergenthaler directly and then moved the company's workshop to Brooklyn, effectively leaving the inventor in a satellite office in Baltimore.

Mergenthaler, needless to say, was offended. A dispute over royalty payments left him "ever wondering about Mr. Reid's queer ways of assisting him in building castles on the Rhine." When a foreign licensing agreement neglected to compensate him, Mergenthaler turned acid. "Another stone toward Mr. Reid's castle on the Rhine!" he spat. After those and other confrontations, Reid succeeded in purging Mergenthaler from the company for a time.[7]

In retrospect, many of the incidents that wounded Mergenthaler look like little more than the daily banal miscommunications, policy disputes, and production imbroglios common to every market-driven business. Yet Mergenthaler was not the only soul to find the new, increasingly industrial, overtly manipulative, market-driven business life of the day difficult to stomach. Whole classes of society thought its captains were often short-sighted, untrustworthy, and immoral. From the threatened American plains came the Populist movement, which sought to wrest the era's political and economic power away from the relentlessly expanding industrialists. From urban areas came progressivism, which hoped to blunt their power by broadening the vote, making more positions of authority—senators as well as judges—subject to popular vote, and hiring regulators to oversee transportation, food, and the emerging trusts. Factory and mine laborers, bringing the new country's first widespread union movements to a boil, insistently sought relief from the wages, expenses, and working conditions imposed by their powerful, often armed bosses. For dissenters throughout the West, the often cruel, organically mutating market itself had become the great political and moral issue of the time. Ricardo and Malthus contended that the laws of the unfettered market limited human possibility. Left unchecked, they led inevitably to starvation. Robert Owen argued that society itself limited human possibility, and now Karl Marx and Friedrich Engels argued that man, to be free, had to be free of the market altogether.[8]

The West, we now know, was then coming into full industrial flower. New, highly adapted business organisms fed off information, science, and capital. They prospered much as other highly adapted species prospered: they outran, out-muscled, out-ate, and out-reproduced their competitors. Their businesses ran not on the strength of their associations but on how much capital and information they could apply to a goal. They invented organizations that applied them better than their predecessors could. First stock companies, then corporations, oligopolies, and monopolies arose: Standard Oil, Union Pacific, Singer, Bell Telephone, Colt, DuPont, International Harvester. Andrew Carnegie's company produced more steel than all of England in 1901, and then sold itself into U.S. Steel, creating an even bigger company.[9] Then came Ford and mass production techniques. Often without the checks and balances of competitors to keep them honest or unions strong enough to challenge their internal policies, their power was becoming awesome and put them beyond the ability of local and state authority to control. Many built wealth that only national governments had achieved previously. They used it like governments too. They formalized their power in new laws and created regulatory agencies to ensure their market stability and minimize their competitive costs. They employed private militias, often to fight labor. When the physical environment got in the way, many simply altered the landscape.

As they obliterated physical and economic obstacles, they also obliterated the remains of the values that underpinned old mercantile system. Until the nineteenth century, people of consequence had identified themselves by their true faith and strict morals. To succeed, they took care to demonstrate those virtues publicly and repeatedly (if not always sincerely). Their work "must by its order mirror the hierarchical order of the world, which is moral order." They often worked, like Mergenthaler at the start of his career, in farms and shops run by relatives and in businesses controlled by small, close-knit, familial commercial groups and guilds. They did well by impressing the few people and gods who needed to approve of them. But now—amid the high-velocity crashes of images, words, and distant forces far from view—the value of art, products, ideas, and words had been cut "loose from moral significance, from regard for virtue in the maker's character, and from the expectations of the public."[10]

Refusing to accept it, Mergenthaler spent his last few breaths writing about fairness among colleagues, about looking beyond economic constraints to fine-tune his machine, and about being "morally compelled" to buy stock—even if it meant borrowing money from the dangerous Reid—in the new company the new-era industrialists had formed around him.[11]

But in reality Mergenthaler by then was tied to an organization peopled by strangers with no emotional or family ties to each other. In this context, his compunctions were at best dated niceties. At worst, they were unproductive, unprofitable, unquantifiable, and dramatically out of place in a modern, sophisticated company.

"The generation which fought the American Civil War in their twenties," as two economists put it, "invented that epitome of enterprise not based on kinship, the modern industrial corporation, in their forties."[12] War veteran Reid, for example, turned fifty the year he lent Mergenthaler $25,000 to buy stock in their new corporation.

He was only one of the veterans in his field. Harrison Gray Otis, a Union Army officer and then "a typical drifter of the time," scraped together $6,000 in 1882 to buy a new, barely breathing paper called the *Los Angeles Times*. He turned it into a publishing and corporate powerhouse by 1900. Alfred H. Belo, a colonel in the Confederate Army, migrated to Texas, where he soon acquired the *Galveston News* and started the *Dallas Morning*

News. Civil War veteran Charles Taylor managed to buy an interest in the struggling, neonate *Boston Globe*, and by 1900 was reaching 150,000 people a day and fending off offers from Joseph Pulitzer.[13]

Few generations in the ancient expanse of human history, moreover, were as wealthy, optimistic, and productive as Reid's. In just the last decades of the nineteenth century and the first of the twentieth, their powerful new commercial societies of strangers organized to pursue specific commercial goals had replaced miracles like indoor gaslights with new miracles like electric lights. Wealth flowed toward greater numbers of people, creating unprecedented classes of managers—like Mergenthaler himself—who had disposable income and disposable time, all unceasing and all disruptive. There were telegraphs and telephones, railroads and turnpikes. Invisible devils like water-borne disease had been discovered. Chicago meant to banish them by reversing the flow of its river, something only God could previously do. For New York City's children, there were capital blessings like fresh milk railroaded to them from faraway upstate Goshen, and freedom from the plagues that spread from the poisonous "swill milk" previously coaxed from tethered, unhealthy Brooklyn cows. We were moving from farm—often foreign farm—to city. We were armed with mind-boggling new weapons, large guns that fired over and over again without stopping and even one colossal 250,000-pound gun than could rain one-ton shells on enemies miles away. We lived and worked in tall structures that we'd learned to build seven, eight, nine stories above the ground. Soon we'd fly. Back on *terra firma*, we moved faster than humans had ever moved before, by rail. More and more frequently, we drove automobiles. (In 1900, there were 8,000 cars, 10 miles of paved roads, and 96 automobile deaths in the United States; by contrast, there were 115 lynching deaths.)[14] And there were products. The numbers of manufactured goods, great and small, grew wildly: instant coffee, vacuum tubes, Novocain, vitamins, the toaster, boxed cereal, and many, many more.

Mergenthaler wasn't the only person who felt a little alarmed. "Now comes the new menace from America," a British writer warned. "If it threatens England, it is equally dangerous to the recently victorious Teuton." Describing the flood of American products arriving on French shores, the editor of *Economiste francais* archly (and inaccurately) reassured his readers that "this class of commodities was received with less unanimous approval." In 1901, the *London Daily Mail* reported the typical Briton "rises in the morning from his New England folding-bed, shaves with American soap and a Yankee safety razor, pulls on his Boston boots over his socks from North Carolina, fastens his Connecticut braces, slips his Waltham or Waterbury watch in his pocket, and sits down to breakfast. There he congratulates his wife on the way her Illinois front-corset sets off her Massachusetts blouse."[15]

The United States was only one among several countries then transforming the international merchant system into an international industrial economy, but it was by then the leader. Its share of the world's manufacturing output had increased by more than 50 percent in the last twenty years of the nineteenth century, and now exceeded that of England and Germany, the traditional leading producers.[16]

Most Americans were impressed. "In truth," one economist confessed at the time, "it is hard to fully explain the stupendous increase [in wealth]. The results [of the census of 1905] suggest that the present period may be no mere alteration from depression to prosperity, but that the nation has come upon a mighty industrial era without precedent in the history of men."[17]

And many Americans were impressed with themselves. Reid and his peers were not coy about what they were doing. They excitedly cast the rise of their new organizations in rapturous, almost mystical terms. They wrote in their newspapers of a "manifest destiny" turned global, driven by recently evolved breeds of smart, courageous, sharp-edged men not unlike themselves. They were, as the social Darwinism of the day put it, more fit than others, rising above even their own customers. "I have constituted myself the advocate of that large majority of the people," said mogul and self-styled crusader E. W. Scripps, "who are not so rich in worldly goods and native intelligence as to make them equal, man for man, in the struggle with individuals of the wealthier and more intellectual class."[18]

The period from 1890 to 1910, a historian reflected more than half a century later, was "one of the most exciting two decades in which to live in [the industrial West's] history, by virtue of the optimism and hopes that a thinking person might reasonably expect of society as he looked in the future. The limitations of nature all seemed conquerable, if not by technology, then certainly by science."[19]

As when Gutenberg introduced movable type and sped up human communication, the human library of written works was again expanding at a fantastic rate. The number of people who could read it grew faster than ever before. About 86 percent of the American populace was literate by 1890, up from 80 percent in 1870.[20] It translated into an extra 4.5 million previously inarticulate readers in one society, suddenly able to witness the unprecedented, rapid massing of images, experiences, and viewpoints of the ensuing decades. A great excitement of molecules followed.

Strange things, we now know, happen when people and their leaders start getting information at the same time. Political power shifts. "Social reaction time is accelerated," as one learned researcher put it, "speeding the pace of developments for both leadership and electorate." Lower classes become less dependent on higher ones, who find that their old power "based exclusively on initial possession of information is destroyed." Large, mature institutions—by definition big, slow, and set in their ways—may fail to respond to the multiplying new social or economic or political demands in time.[21] As they lose the ability to manage community tensions, friction escalates and conflict may erupt. Centuries old and seemingly permanent, the Ottoman, Austro-Hungarian, Russian, English, French, German, Spanish, Japanese, and Chinese empires would be gone or nearly gone within the next fifty years. Some fell in little more than a decade after information accelerated again. Colonial regimes in China and South Africa collapsed sooner. The governments that survived were forced to assume new shapes, sharing power with arrivistes. In the United States new classes of people—mostly the ascendant bourgeoisie—forced their way into the political process with the direct election of senators and the invention of the referendum and the initiative. In the West, the nation-state finally and completely supplanted the national monarchy. In east Asia and the Americas, nationalist movements transformed once obedient, dependent populations into forces that would soon seize power from out-gunned, out-manned, and often out-informed old elites.

Political institutions were not the only ones in crisis. Others bent toward new spiritual inventions, the rise of new economic elites and classes, dramatic population shifts, altered military standings, wholesale changes in daily habits, and what must have looked to folks like Ottmar Mergenthaler like something bordering on chaos.

More ideas seemed to collide more frequently during the era, almost never predictably. On December 28, 1895, Wilhelm Roentgen published a paper telling of his discovery of an X-ray, which was neither solid nor liquid nor gas. A colleague reported on the paper at a professional conference, with Antoine Henri Becquerel in the audience. Becquerel took the knowledge back to his lab and, within a month of Roentgen's news, discovered that uranium emitted the same kind of rays. Three months later, the word went out that X-rays could burn. By the end of the year, they were used to take pictures and then, leaping to the legal system, to help determine guilt in a court case. They were used as diagnostic tools in U.S. Army hospitals in 1897. With such things in mind, Marie Curie discovered another element in 1898, which she called radium. She named this whole new ray-emitting process "radiation." Learning of Curie's investigative path, Paul Ulrich Villard identified gamma rays. In 1899 came alpha and beta rays. Radon was identified in 1904. That year, some of the new radioactive substances—all of them mostly invisible, confirmed as existing only by watching what they did and rigorously eliminating all other explanations of physical behavior—were used to shrink a cancerous tumor for the first time. In the largest of our imagined spaces Henri Poincaré was reexplaining celestial mechanics to better fit new the astronomical evidence of the movement of rays we recently had uncovered. In the tiniest of our imagined spaces, we came up with the Saturn model of an atom, with a big nucleus and smaller electrons orbiting around it.

And more: Albert Einstein, in one fertile year of 1905, came up with his special theory of relativity, a paper revolutionizing our understanding of how light radiated and a new proof of how mass and energy and speed related to each other. Freud popularized the notion that we had unconscious as well as conscious thoughts that, once understood, helped explain why we acted or why we did not. Now came theories that all our behavior derived from the nervous system and then from the neurons and synapses in our brain that influenced the nervous system itself. Emile Durkheim traced how behavior often reflected our immediate social groups. Ivan Pavlov documented reflexive learning and behavior. John Dewey and Maria Montessori demonstrated experiential learning in humans. We mapped the cortex in 1906. It relegated reason (until recently the standard we believed we could use to regulate society), pleasure, and pain to mere by-products of Freudian, Darwinian, and Nietzschean forces. In the philosophies of the day, nature itself—once a paradise we could only achieve by stripping ourselves of civilization or a cauldron we could endure only through faith—was now an organic, ever-evolving stew that produced neither sinners nor saints but survivors. The way we looked at things thus had to change: in art there were modernist and Ash Can schools; Max Weber, Arthur Dove, and George Luks. The visual arts became abstract, fractionated, distorted, and deliberately absurd. Art nouveau and modern architecture gave way to Frank Lloyd Wright and Charles McKim.[22] After we overlaid a map of global moisture and temperature patterns on a map of global plant life in 1907, God's grace seemed a less comprehensive explanation for the blooming of flowers and the thriving of certain kinds of crops. In botany, we mapped the distribution of plants against temperature—meaning unimpeded exposure to the rays of the sun—and moisture. From the new discipline of topography, we learned the Earth had a crust and a mantle beneath its surface, but no discernible hell. The received word, a universal moral code, and, as in the world of business itself, kin and family were now less useful tools for surviving the worlds around, above, or below us. At about the same moment (in 1912), we came to understand that continents themselves—the ground on which we literally stood—drifted, essentially unmoored, ever changing, and impermanent.

They had in that sense come to resemble the impermanent underpinnings of all our previous understandings of how and why we behaved, of the heavens and the earth, of evil, progress, pleasure, pain, death, and beauty. As the Reformation in Gutenberg's wake had recast divine order as the work of humans, now in Mergenthaler's wake human behavior and even nature were recast as the fruit and failures of knowledge.

Once again, an abrupt drop in the cost of information had coincided with a frantic period of discovery. The last, critical piece of the puzzle of manufacturing the printed word—fast, cheap type—had fed nothing less than a mushrooming of human knowledge and capabilities. The furious pace would continue for almost another hundred years in the West until, at last, type itself disappeared.

The great transition to industrial society was well under way—it was in fact almost complete—by the time Mergenthaler's cheap, fast alphabets precipitously lowered the cost of information. His alphabets were not even the only reason the price of the printed word was falling in the late nineteenth century. Steam-powered presses and inexpensive wood-fiber paper already had made each printed sheet less costly to produce. Lower postage rates, the expansion of the railroad, and the increasing concentration of the population in cities all made it easier, speedier, and cheaper to distribute knowledge than ever.

But his new hot-metal type was the last and arguably the most important innovation in the century-long transformation of the printed word into a mass medium. Similarly, it was the last and arguably the most important step in the evolution of the devoutly linear Typographic Man we grew to love and hate and then buried in the twentieth century.

The printed word turned out to be Typographic Man's medium. When it sped up, became more common, and reached its apogee, Typographic Man's life accelerated and hit its apogee. In the branches of its sentence structure, chapter subdivisions, disciplined outlines, dramatic progressions, thesis statements, and inverted pyramids, printed knowledge incorporated the order, romance, learning styles, contrivance, and method that scuttled the remains of many previous Western philosophies, orthodoxies, national monarchies, and international empires in the coming decades. At our best, we built overwhelming varieties of printed knowledge, all from methodically gathered and purposefully revealed evidence, character traits, or product features. Each was reconciled in the end to achieve a desired impression or result. Similarly, we built our individual understandings of the world and ourselves through the measured accumulation of observations, needs, impressions, and cosmic forces, all reconciled through conclusions and theories as plentiful and erasable as the sheets on which they were printed. Soon we came to see *ourselves* not as premolded beings fulfilling our fate according to some divine or kingly mechanism, but as the accumulation of our experiences, our needs, our heredity, and maybe even a few spiritual forces. We now read and thought individually, frequently, and for more reasons than our forebears. In part we came to value ourselves as roughly equivalent to the number of works we read, the amount of knowledge we collected from them, and the value of the thoughts we created because of them. In the golden age of Typographic Man energetic individuals, almost regardless of class, could accumulate knowledge. Much as we wrote and read, we could collect knowledge, organize it efficiently, apply it shrewdly, and harvest its results. Hence came wealth, value, and virtue.

By the start of the twentieth century, we could also gather knowledge from the telegraph and the telephone. There were photographs, ever more easily taken by growing legions of "Kodak maniacs," to record our experience more vividly and immediately than had ever been possible. There were even moving pictures.

But printed ideas remained Western civilization's primary medium at the time. There were far more printed works—not only books, newspapers, and periodical stories and articles, but the vast numbers of statistics, memos, invoices, flyers, packages, and orders borne on paper—than there were photographed images, telegraph messages, or maybe even telephone messages throughout the industrial West.[23]

None of the other media of the day, moreover, were as easy to create and use as the printed word. The telegraph used an obscure, hard to use, and expensive alphabet much like hieratic, beyond the reach of most people to understand and use. Moving pictures were the product of specialists far less numerous than the 10,000 scribes working in fifteenth-century France. Their communications, while widely distributed, were relatively few in number. Radio existed, but as yet only in labs and as sailing ship experiments, far from popular view or use. When it emerged, of course, the world would spin still faster and yet another reorientation would ensue. Ultimately, type would not keep up with other kinds of human communications and became among the most expensive ways we had to relay thoughts. Thus began its long slide.

NOTES

1. Basil Kahan, *Ottmar Mergenthaler:The Man and His Machine* (New Castle, Del.: Oak Knoll, 2000), 137.

2. Ottmar Mergenthaler, *Biography of Ottmar Mergenthaler and History of the Linotype* (Baltimore, Md., 1898), 53.

3. Mergenthaler, *Biography*, 60, 63, 68, 70.

4. Fidelities, "Letter from Baltimore," *Inland Printer*, August 1891, 993–94; Walker Rumble, *The Swifts: Printers in the Age of Typesetting Races* (Charlottesville: University of Virginia Press, 2003), 10, 181, 179.

5. Kahan, *Mergenthaler*, 129.

6. Kahan, *Mergenthaler*, 131.

7. Mergenthaler, *Biography*, 41, 67. The inventor returned to the reconstituted company after Reid became ambassador to France in 1889, but he never regained a position of controlling manufacturing or of convincing the company to bring his next innovations to market. He was replaced as the company's chief engineer in 1895.

8. Karl Polanyi, *The Great Transformation:The Political and Economic Origins of Our Time* (Boston: Beacon, 1944), 85.

9. Paul Kennedy, *The Rise and Fall of the Great Powers* (New York: Random House, 1987), 242.

10. Jacques Barzun, *From Dawn to Decadence: 500 Years of Western Cultural Life* (New York: HarperCollins, 2000), 67.

11. Mergenthaler, *Biography*, 23.

12. Nathan Rosenberg and L. E. Birdzell Jr., *How the West Grew Rich* (New York: Basic, 1986), 125.

13. Sidney Kobre, *The Development of American Journalism* (Dubuque: Brown, 1966), 472, 416.

14. Peggy Whitley, ed., American Cultural History, 1900–1909, www.nhmccd .edu/contracts/lrc/kc/decade00.html (accessed September 28, 2002).

15. "Our Commercial Supremacy: The Alarm over American Invasion of Foreign Markets," *Current Literature*, November 1901, 541. The British writer was Geo. B. Waldron.

16. Kennedy, *Great Powers*, 202, 244.

17. W. S. Rossiter, "Printing and Publishers: The Barometer Industry," *American Monthly Review of Reviews*, September 1906, 342.

18. Thomas C. Leonard, *News for All:America's Coming-of-Age with the Press* (New York: Oxford University Press, 1995), 151.

19. George N. Gordon, *The Communications Revolution: A History of Mass Media in the United States* (New York: Hastings House, 1977), 84.

20. Frank Luther Mott, *American Journalism:A History, 1690–1960*, 3rd ed. (New York: Macmillan, 1962), 507.

21. Ben H. Bagdikian, *The Information Machines: Their Impact on Men and the Media* (New York: Harper & Row, 1971), 1.

22. Whitley, American Cultural History.

23. In the United States in 1900, for example, there were 1.3 million telephones in use, fewer than one for every thousand people. The only other countries in the world that had phones at the time were Germany (306,000 telephones), France (80,000), Italy (17,000), Japan (12,000), and England (3,100). Only Germany had phone capacity as great as 1 percent of one phone for every thousand citizens. Telegrams were more common than phones. France sent .96 telegrams for every thousand people in its population around the turn of the twentieth century. The United States sent .83 telegrams, Japan .73, Germany .70, Egypt .54, and England .28 telegrams per thousand people within its borders. B. R. Mitchell, *International Historical Statistics: The Americas, 1750–2000*, 5th ed. (New York: Palgrave Macmillan, 2003); telephones in the United States and South America: 619–620, 623; radios in use: 626, 639; postal and telephone traffic: 610–612; population: 3, 6; Mitchell, *International Historical Statistics: Europe, 1750–2000*, 5th ed. (New York: Palgrave Macmillan, 2003); telephones: 765–68; radios in use: 775–78; postal and telephone traffic: 750–56; populations: 3–4, 6, 8; Mitchell, *International Historical Statistics, Africa, Asia and Oceania, 1750–1993*, 3rd ed. (New York: Stockton, 1998); telephones in use: 802, 808–9; radios in use: 814–15, 817; postal and telephone traffic: 781–93; populations: 3, 5–9.

III

THE END OF TYPE: FROM MACHINE TO MATH

15

FULL PANTRY, NO CAN OPENER

In 1944 and 1945, as World War II finally headed toward a climax, some Americans at last allowed themselves to speculate about what the world might be like after the shooting stopped. The landscape, they knew, was being radically altered, although no one could say exactly how.

Mainstream magazines spent a lot of ink guessing. "An amazing new world is in the making in the plants and laboratories now devoted to war," one writer reported brightly. He saw "almost perfectly elastic" glass springs for our watches. A new metal called aluminum promised lighter engine weights, fantastic savings, and cars that would run "sweeter and farther. You will have cheap electricity for luxuries like heating and cooking, for new gadgets that will fill your future home." Another article forecast that husbands soon might waste entire days sitting by a fantastic "television screen." There'd be a "pop up when done toaster," a two-hour workday, electric fireplaces, and "telenews." We would get cranky when "the jet-propelled transport is utterly jammed."[1]

The details varied, but everyone seemed to sense change; one era ending, another being born. In the media, leaders of great powers, small professions, and volunteer associations, among many others, anticipated important and usually ill-defined changes. Something was in the air even in the quiet of the Wesleyan University library. It was more a feeling than anything else, the university's librarian wrote in the Connecticut institution's *About Books* newsletter. But whatever it was, it was "upsetting the typesetter."

The library, she explained, had purchased its own Linotype machine a couple of years before, hoping to cut the time and money spent producing its own publications and journals. But so far, the machine only had gathered dust. With many of the nation's printers in the military, the university could not find anyone to install or run it.

Now she wondered if it would become obsolete before it was ever used.

She already knew, if only vaguely, about a "photo-lettering machine" that would appear in the coming peace. Used mostly for advertising, it "literally makes type lie down and roll over." The librarian (she was not given a byline in the newsletter) also had heard about laboratory devices that supposedly raised letters off paper and used electricity to stick ink to pages. "Still more intriguing is a sort of inverted x-ray device; the operator rolls a whole stack of sensitized sheets over a magic plate." People could copy things without a press, ink, heavy equipment, or even type.[2]

Miles away in Cincinnati, a compositor felt the same vibes, relaying "rumors . . . that some dreamer was trying to develop a machine that would replace the Linotype by composing type on film or sensitized paper."[3]

Hearing the same gossip, another writer reported "an impression that the printer is about to join the dinosaur in the tar pits of history."[4]

A few voices warned that "this great flood of new knowledge" about to follow victory might be more than we could handle.[5] The war itself had generated so many stupendous intellectual advances, an engineer named Vannevar Bush suggested, that we were running out of the brain room to track or recall it all. It was not a small problem, he added. Human evolution might sputter and slow.

Bush was no crackpot. Coordinator of almost all the military research funded by the federal government during the war, Vannevar (rhymes with *beaver*) Bush was a one-man "scientific cyclone." The press also dubbed him the "scientific generalissimo," the "Yankee scientist," and the "chief of staff" of a "vast scientific empire" that was, even by Bush's normally judicious public pronouncements, "the greatest scientific force in the world." Running on $3 million a week in an age when a loaf of bread cost nine cents, Bush organized some 7,000 intellectuals on 300 campuses to rethink, invent, and otherwise improve ideas that could be turned into products that, in turn, could win the war.[6] It was unprecedented. No nation ever had pursued a war by devoting so many of its resources to laboratory research.

But that too had been Bush's idea. Born in 1890 into a studious and liberal Massachusetts family—his father was a Universalist minister—Bush grew into the kind of aggressive, elaborately credentialed eastern establishment intellectual that Sunbelt politicians later loved to demonize. Schooled at Tufts, the Massachusetts Institute of Technology (MIT), and Harvard, he was already doing important antisubmarine research for the navy in his mid-twenties. While a professor and then a dean at MIT, he earned tens of patents. The most important was for a "differential analyzer" that did "the work of several score mathematicians" and was, as it turned out, a prede-cessor to the analog computer.[7] For that and other work, he began to ac-cumulate prizes. (He eventually would be cited by three presidents and the British Empire.)

In 1939, the Carnegie Institution in Washington, D.C., made him pres-ident of its far-flung network of researchers and scientists. Bush took to Washington. Alarmed by the war already raging across the oceans, he began inserting himself into government councils. He sent proposals to President Franklin Roosevelt for aviation projects and got himself appointed to an important military research committee. He then gathered the scientist-presidents of Harvard, MIT, and Cal Tech to offer to organize national re-search in the event of war. In 1940, Roosevelt let them. He created the Of-fice of Science and Research Development (OSRD) to create, ignite, and somehow manage what became a profound explosion of knowledge. From it would emerge tanks that could fire shells 2,000 yards, aluminum, am-phibious landers, vast advances in radio communications, and the perfection of radar. (The U.S. Army Signal Corps, which operated all the new radio wave equipment, itself had more men than Napoleon had at Waterloo.) There were cloaking devices and detection devices. Bush, for one, figured the war's tide had turned in 1943, not when Stalin turned Hitler around at Stalingrad, but when Bush's legion of eggheads came up with sonar tech-nology that effectively ended the German U-boat threat to Allied supply lines in the Atlantic. They engineered a way to mass-produce penicillin, a trick that cut the Allied death rate from wounds and disease to half of what it was in World War I. There was even a "mass differential analyzer" that, in surpassing Bush's own invention, could compute problems while weighing up to thirteen shifting variables. It allowed for the quick aiming of the army's new long-range cannons, performing trajectory analyses that, ac-cording to one account, otherwise would have taken a math whiz, much less a gunner off a Missouri farm, 715 years to calculate.[8] Not least among the great advances Bush oversaw, of course, was a top-secret project in New Mexico, where one of his groups was solving the problem of nuclear fission.

Not that anyone understood the big picture. "Bush's group, not really a team, in general works like a squad of golfers in which each player is handed a club, and told to shoot for a faraway green he cannot see," one ob-server complained.[9]

The OSRD chairman may have been the only one who had an overview. From "an immense paneled office" on 16th Street in Washington, he occasionally traveled the country in his own army plane, exercising "vir-tually unlimited" power in his expanding corner of the world. "He moves," a *Newsweek* story noted, "as if he were constantly receiving shocks, and you expect to see a fuse blow from overload at any second. 'Damns' and 'hells' intersperse his sentences like a superimposed Morse code." Another contemporary called it "jumpiness."[10]

He spent the war reviewing proposals for funding new investigations, checking on their progress, and recruiting new talent. A good number of the scientists on Bush's payroll were refugees, part of the European intelligentsia that Hitler dispossessed and ultimately sought to exterminate. Viewing the medical, industrial, and military inventions that they were producing under the Americans' protective wing, Bush predicted, "The Nazis will live to regret what they did to their scientists."

And of course they did. But as the war ended, Bush was as worried as he was impressed by the amazing leaps in human accomplishment during the global struggles for survival. There was just too much knowledge. We were sure to be overwhelmed by it, confused, so dizzied that we might not be able to use much of it. We were still trying to remember it all with the same tools—books, newspapers, indexes, and human memory—"used in the days of the square-rigged ships." In many ways "we seem to be worse off than before—for we can enormously extend the record [of human thought]; yet even in its present bulk we can hardly consult it." To Bush, we risked stalling as a species, compromising "the entire process by which man profits by his inheritance of acquired knowledge."[11] Learning.

In a basement room at the University of Pennsylvania in 1944, for example, a thirty-five-year-old engineer named J. Presper Eckert labored on one of the government's (although not Bush's) war science squads. He was trying to fabricate a circuit for an ambitious machine that would be able to calculate artillery trajectories faster and more accurately than even the mass differential analyzer. Eventually the machine became ENIAC, the world's first large computer, but at the time it was an unreliable collection of tubes and wires that Eckert knew needed this particular circuit to work. He was "frustrated," especially because he knew the solution to building the circuit already existed somewhere. "I always think of [the world's accumulated knowledge] as like having a nice larder or a pantry full of canned goods, and you don't have a can opener. Here's all this good stuff up there; you can't get into it . . . I remember I spent a lot of time looking in every language for solutions to that [circuit] problem, and never found a satisfactory solution." He eventually found it "in a French article . . . but [not soon enough] to be useful."[12] The machine could not be finished before the war ended.

Bush was convinced we needed to invent new ways to store knowledge and retrieve it out of our knowledge pantries at the right time. He figured we'd need to invent whole new "information management technologies" to do it. Bush already knew of some that held promise, although still too slow or unformed to help. There were facsimile transmitters and computational devices. He also cited a process that combined what he called microphotography and optical projection into some sort of coded speech. He dreamed up others on his own, including one he dubbed memex. It would consist of a viewing screen and a keyboard to help users ply helpful "trails" through information massed on a memory device, maybe microfilm.[13]

Another idea, not mentioned in his *Atlantic* article, was a kind of super typewriter that would cut out steps in the production of a printed page.[14] Bush had worked on it in 1938, mostly to help break codes, but soon ran out of time to develop it further.

As he too speculated about the postwar horizon one day in 1944, he suggested that "when peace returns it ought to be applied to something."[15]

At about the same time, in June 1944, two engineers in still unliberated Lyon—Rene Higonnet and his lab mate Louis Moyroud—were registering patents for a new type idea of their own.

Middle-aged Higonnet, employed at the Paris office of International Telephone & Telegraph (ITT) when the war broke out, reportedly was a reserved man, prone to long quiet periods when he thought about high-speed photography. For example, it ought to be possible to *create* type and words—not just photograph them—on paper by rapidly exposing chemically treated film to light. Trapped in France and thrown together during the war, Higonnet and the younger and more outgoing Moyroud, who had worked for another ITT subsidiary, found themselves responsible not only for maintaining a sector of telephonic operations at the shorthanded phone company, but for producing bulletins that informed coworkers of service and equipment problems.

They hated the latter job. It was an "appalling" bother. They needed to get the word of breakdowns out rapidly (if not instantaneously) but instead dictated and waited while linecasters and repair people and etchers laboriously prepared their bulletins for press.[16] There had to be a better way.

What had been a fourfold increase in speed in Ottmar Mergenthaler's day just fifty-some years before looked pokey in the age of blitzkriegs, picture radios, and atoms being shot through smoke chambers. Printing presses already were lighter, stronger, faster, and sometimes even cheaper than their iron forebears. Quick and more accurate offset presses were supplanting old letterpresses, which pressed paper to a tangible image to produce a printed sheet. In the 1920s and 1930s high-speed photography widened the eyes of many a laboratory fabulist and engineer. By 1931, as the science of optics blossomed, so did the means for photoengraving, which would replace the practice of physically etching images onto the metal plates that, in the end, would end up mounted on the presses. Some, like Higonnet, itched to adapt it to type.

People had been trying to mix photography and typesetting since at least 1856, in the same industrial chaos that ultimately produced Mergenthaler's Linotype. Nine years before Mergenthaler's hot-metal machine came to market, an American named Michael Alisoff adapted a photo process to transfer music symbols to paper, and the next year one George Drummond designed a system in which letters were imprinted in black on a white ribbon and then photographed. (To make italic letters, you stretched the ribbon before taking its picture.) The same year in which the Lino appeared, a British engineer named Thomas Bolas perfected a way to produce metal type from what amounted to photographic molds. Hungary, which produced a disproportionately large number of type tinkerers dating back at least to the bankrupted Josef Kliegl, produced another in 1894, when Eugen Porzsolt patented a design to link a keyboard to a photographic unit. At about the same time, cinematographer William Friese-Green found a way to expose entire lines of type to light at one time. Shortly thereafter, a terrifically determined American named William C. Heubner also designed a device, which ultimately proved unworkable, for setting type photographically. (Heubner was still turning out important inventions and processes in the 1950s after enduring decades of derision; his "jumping ink," or electrostatic, printing process became a big hit.)[17]

By the time the new century was two decades old, at least a half dozen more phototypesetters were in circulation. In the United Kingdom, both the Photoline (designed by Arthur Dutton) and the Bawtree machine (by Alfred Bawtree) were available. In 1925, Nobuo Morisawa fashioned a working phototypesetter that with refinements was still being marketed in Japan in the 1990s. Some heavyweight companies also got involved. Kodak financed a crucially important machine—it operated much like the ones that subsequently revolutionized the industry—called the Thothmic in 1921. Mergenthaler Linotype funded a prototype that would photographically drive a hot-metal machine in 1926. Lanston Monotype, one of Mergenthaler's most potent competitors, did the same thing, backing a Briton named George Westover in the 1930s. (Lanston Monotype subsequently got cold feet, forcing Westover into the arms of a more sympathetic tool company. Eventually it used his ideas in its Monophoto after World War II.) By the 1930s, yet another clever Hungarian engineer, Dyonis Uher, assembled his Corex Phototype Setting Machine and sold it to the mighty Man Corporation in Germany. Man was manufacturing the Uher type, which produced raised letters on a strip of cellophane, by 1936. Here, there, everywhere: a "fototypesetter" was being built at the G. F. Bagge Company in Cleveland. In New York, a man named Parker Hart registered patents for a "multi-cel photocomposing machine" before the war erupted.[18]

But the visions floating in Higonnet and Moyroud's heads, as they got serious about their tinkering, were different. The other phototype machines, an observer in the future would write, "were little more than hot-metal linecasters adapted to photographic techniques."[19] They produced film and tapes that were fed into the banging, ringing machines that actually cut and manufactured pieces of metal. The metal then was turned into an image of a page for the press to reproduce. In Lyon, the inventors were thinking about replacing the messy Linotypes entirely. They rigged together constantly rotating matrix disks, telephone circuits, and finally binary digital code to instruct lightning camera shutters when to open, close, and shoot light onto film at high speeds. It was heady stuff. But, soon after registering their patents in the wake of D-day, they found themselves without the corporate financial support they needed to produce a marketable machine. Higonnet and Moyroud had no money for research and no real prospects for any in the postwar moonscape that had been Europe.

By then Vannevar Bush, whose memex article would nettle the sleep of young engineers for the next twenty years, was a celebrity among smart people. Word of his scientific wonderland had spread rapidly among surviving intellectuals everywhere the Allied armies landed, including France. Even after the war, when he returned to the Carnegie Institution, scientists and entrepreneurs kept knocking on his door. Carnegie, needless to say, did not have the resources of an OSRD, but Bush was perhaps the most connected scientist in the world. (To keep the OSRD's potent momentum alive, Bush had hatched a plan for a peacetime version of the OSRD. It would be a sort of national science foundation, which is what it was eventually called when Congress created it a few years later). In part because of Bush's personal reputation, the United States continued to attract under-funded intellectuals.

Rene Higonnet was among them. He booked passage to New York to look for investors as soon as he could. Networking led him to William Garth, who owned a small printing supply company in Cambridge, Massachusetts, that was nearly bankrupt as a wartime military contract expired. By the fall of 1946, he desperately needed a new revenue stream. In New York to meet Higonnet, Garth immediately liked the inventor's idea. Like Johann Fust and John Walter and Melville Stone before him, he made an offer: if Higonnet and his partner Moyroud could build a working prototype back in France and assure him that he'd be the first to see it, Garth would pay for their voyage back to America. Higonnet agreed.[20]

Money men are often cast as mere exploiters in the history of science, but Garth—an MIT grad like Bush—was "a guy of great vision who recognized the potential of this technology," a colleague remembered many years later. "A near genius," Garth had "the remarkable talent of seeing the numbers three and three, and seeing when they added up to six, when they could be multiplied to make nine and when they should be raised by the power of three to make 27."[21]

Higonnet and Moyroud brought the prototype back in July 1948, and Garth collected trusted experts—one was a MIT engineer named Samuel Caldwell, a longtime Bush colleague; the other his own company's patent attorney—to poke at it, test it, and think about how it could be sold. He also showed it also to C. M. Flint, an engineer who had persuaded the American Newspaper Publishers Association (ANPA) to start a research fund to create new cost-cutting machines. Everyone was impressed. The ANPA engineer and Garth almost immediately went to Washington to that fount of research funding, Vannevar Bush, to discuss it.[22]

The scientific generalissimo, perhaps thinking about how to produce microfilm for all the world's accumulated knowledge for his imaginary memex machine, was similarly intrigued. At Garth's urging and impressed by the endorsement of his trusted wartime colleague Caldwell, Bush agreed to help. He'd lend his name to Garth and ANPA in their fund-raising efforts. And he would throw his own, almost forgotten typesetting patent—the one he thought ought to be applied someday—into the effort. If it worked, Bush's share of the profits would go to MIT. Higonnet and Moyroud would get to market it in Europe. Garth would have a healthy new business.[23] And, some five hundred years after Gutenberg, people would start printing words differently. What might happen as a result was not discussed.

NOTES

1. David O. Woodbury, "Your Life Tomorrow," *Colliers*, May 8, 1943, 40; Alan Dunn, "Utopia: 1955," *Saturday Evening Post*, December 30, 1944, 36–37.

2. "Upsetting the Typesetter: A Note on Anticipation," *Library Journal*, February 15, 1945, 77.

3. International Typographical Union, *125th Anniversary Commemorating the Founding of Cincinnati Typographical Union no. 3*, Special Collections, Norlin Library, University of Colorado–Boulder, First Accession, Box 7 (1971).

4. Freeman Champney, "Taft-Hartley and the Printers," *Antioch Review*, Spring 1947, International Typographical Union Collection, Special Collections, Norlin Library, University of Colorado–Boulder, Box 60, Notebook 2.

5. Woodbury, *Your Life*, 40.

6. "Scientific Cyclone," *Newsweek*, January 10, 1944, 50; "Chief of Staff," *New York Times Magazine*, January 23, 1944, 16; "Yankee Scientist," *Time*, April 3, 1944, 52; "He Knows Our Secret Weapons," *American*, April 1944, 128; "Scientific Generalissimo," *Scholastic*, May 15, 1944, 9.

7. "Chief of Staff," 17; G. Pascal Zachary, *Endless Frontier: Vannevar Bush, Engineer of the American Century* (New York: Free Press, 1997).

8. "Progress Report," *Time*, November 29, 1943, 40; "Yankee Scientist," 52; Christopher Keep and Tim McLaughlin, Notes from the Vannevar Bush Symposium sponsored by Brown University and the Massachusetts Institute of Technology, October 12–13, 1995, http://jefferson.village.virgina.edu/elab/hfl0034.html (accessed November 3, 1999).

9. "Yankee Scientist," 52.

10. "Scientific Cyclone," 50.

11. Vannever Bush, "As We May Think," *Atlantic Monthly*, July 1945, www.theatlantic.com/unbound/flashbks/computer/bushf.htm (accessed June 17, 2004).

12. The part was a filter circuit. David Allison, Division of Information Technology and Society, National Museum of American History, Smithsonian Institution; Peter Vogt, "Interview with J. Presper Eckert, Chief Engineer, ENIAC Computer," *Development of the ENIAC Interviews*, Record Unit 9537 (Washington, D.C.: Smithsonian Video History Collection, 1988).

13. Bush, "As We May Think."

14. Lithomat Corporation, "Proposal for Research in Graphic Arts through Photo-composition," January 16, 1949, Harry Ransom Humanities Research Center at the University of Texas, Box 5, Folder 13, 3.

15. Zachary, *Endless Frontier*, 272.

16. "Printing by Photograph Shown to Public," *New York Times*, September 16, 1949, 29; Alan Marshall, "Les origines de la photocomposition moderne," in *La Lumitype-Photon: Rene Higonnet, Louis Moyroud et l'invention de la photocompoition moderne* (Lyon: Musee de l'imprimerie et de la banque, 1994), 59–72.

17. Marshall, "Les origines," 59–72; Thomas Bolas, "Origination of Printing Types by Photographic Methods," *Scientific American*, supplement, March 10, 1900, 20231; Lawrence Wallis, "Hungarian Rhapsody," *Printing World*, March 14, 1994, 24; W. B. Wren, "Electric Printing," *Scientific American*, November 24, 1900, 324; Davidson et al., "Revolution in Printing: A Report for General Georges Doriot's Manufacturing Class," May 1953, Baker Library, Harvard Business School Archives and Special Collections, Manufacturing Files, Box 39, 36.

18. Marshall, "Les origines," 59–72; "Setting Type by Photograph," *Literary Digest*, April 11, 1931, 22.

19. "Modern Typesetting Turns Fifty," *Seybold Report on Publishing Systems* 23 (1994): 20.

20. Elizabeth MacIver Neiva, "Chain Building: The Consolidation of the American Newspaper Industry, 1953–1980," *Business History Review*, Spring 1996, 17–19.

21. Lou Rosenblum, interview by author, November 25, 1998.

22. Lithomat Corporation, "Proposal," 1; Neiva, "Chain Building," 17.

23. Lithomat Corporation, "Proposal," 1–3.

16

WAR AFTER THE WAR

At that moment, however, many of the master printers who might buy such futuristic gizmos seemed troubled and distracted. Unlike the pop magazines and books they produced, their own postwar visions seemed distinctly downbeat. In their trade journals, they sounded mostly like executives overseeing a mature, sophisticated, expensive, and intensely worried industry.

On the bright side, the public demand for printed information seemed insatiable. Daily newspaper readership had doubled during the past thirty years. Low-priced, mass-produced books were everywhere. For twenty-five cents, then ten cents, and finally five cents each, Emanuel Haldeman-Julius sold 300 million Little Blue Books—sixty-four-page books bound with staples—from 1919 through 1949. The Book of the Month Club appeared in 1926, garnering 47,000 members in its first year. Paperbacks in Britain started at sixpence (US$0.12). In 1938, four entrepreneurs started Pocket Books, and were happily fattened by selling almost 9 million copies of *The Good Earth* by Pearl Buck in their initial years.[1] Business generated hundreds of millions of tons of printed matter from year to year. As the New Deal and the war got under way, the American government and military joined the public as extravagant consumers of print.

Yet terrible things seemed to happen to the companies that manufactured these endless reams of printed materials. Publishers and shops had fallen amid increasingly ominous court rulings, rising paper and labor costs, and the massing competitive threat of new kinds of communications.

The death toll had run high. Almost a quarter of the nation's daily papers had gone out of business from 1909 through 1944. The number of weeklies fell from 13,903 to 10,504, another decline of almost 25 percent.

Since the start of the war, moreover, printers' raw materials had become scarce and expensive. All the combatant governments had strictly controlled the distribution of ink and paper, keeping the bulk of them for themselves during the war and creating shortages for everyone else. Books and news-papers had to shrink, cutting the numbers and even the sizes of pages to pre-serve the dwindling paper stocks. Kept from growing during the war, the master printers worried they'd be unable to grow after it. Costs remained historically high. Paper rationing continued in England until 1949, four years after Japan and Germany surrendered.[2]

Their revenues were dubious too. Advertising, the lifeblood of both newspapers and magazines, was essentially flat. Ad lineage (which is how pe-riodicals measure the advertising they sell) had dropped 58 percent during the Depression. Hobbled since Pearl Harbor by limits on the numbers of pages they could produce, publishers still hadn't gotten back to 1929 levels when the war ended. Radio, meanwhile, had become a formidable com-petitor. After falling immediately after 1929, radio advertising rose steadily even as newspaper ads declined. "A great part of radio's gain," a journalism historian eventually understated, "appears to have been at the expense of the newspaper." Print publishers had tried everything—threats, legislative lob-bying, lawsuits, third-party boycotts, and, perhaps most odious of all, busi-ness philosophy—to dismiss and then try to beat back radio's threat since the early 1920s. In one of the most egregious misreadings of a competitive threat in business history, a 1923 printing trade journal editorial scoffed that a New York radio station's radical plan to accept advertising was "loaded with insidious dangers." Listeners would "regard the advertising message as an unwarranted imposition on its time." If they "are obliged to listen to some advertiser exploit his wares, they will very properly resent it . . . An audience that has been wheedled into listening to a selfish message will nat-urally be offended. Its ill-will would be directed not only against the com-pany that delivered the story, but also against the advertiser who chose to talk shop at such an inopportune time." During the Depression years, news-papers first forbade wire services to sell news to radio, and then only if the stations broadcast no more than ten minutes of news a day. The prohibition more or less died by 1938, as radio became more popular and gained polit-ical power.[3]

And now as World War II ended, something new—television—was ready to come out of the lab.[4]

The new printing technology had not really helped the master print-ers control their rising costs. While worker productivity had increased (it shot up by 60 percent between 1914 and 1927), print owners could meet the growing demand only by hiring still more people to work at still more machines. In short, "both productivity and employment grew at the same time," a printing economist of the day observed. The industry never did fully get to save as much in labor costs as it spent on technology.[5]

"Basically," grumbled the *Chicago Daily News* publisher, "there have been no radical changes in the printing industry for generations." "A few spiral gears have replaced tooth gears," added the publisher of the *Raleigh News & Observer*, "but otherwise there has been no basic change in the hot-metal method of setting type in this century." In 1920 Gannett Newspapers had introduced "teletypesetting" at the Evanston (Ill.) *News-Record*. With it, an operator typed keys that punched code into paper tape and then ran the paper tape through a machine that cast the lines of type into metal. It made line casting much faster. One operator could run several Linos at once. But the compositors union quickly gained the sole right to run teletype machines and negated much of the savings publishers had hoped to gain.[6]

Such tools, moreover, were complex, expensive, and often onerous to run. "The difficulties of operating the equipment can be staggering even for those who can afford ownership," a historian explained. They drove many companies to merge. "The steady pressure toward consolidation that has created surviving newspaper empires is just as indicative of the rising costs in plant and operation as it is witness to the aggressiveness of owners."[7]

And their workers were as complex, expensive, and onerous as the machines. All American industries had "witnessed profound transformations in the labor market" when mass immigration from Europe stopped. New American workers in general were more assimilated and more focused on money issues than the bruised and brutalized generation of mostly foreign-born unionists had been. They forced "changes in workplace recruitment and management practices" that remained largely unresolved by the end of World War II. They were in that sense becoming more like the members of the International Typographical Union that oversaw the printing industry: generally born in this country; aware of their rights; politically savvy. (Even in 1910, when 70 percent of the union carpenters and 68 percent of the union masons in New York were foreign-born members, 69 percent of the New York ITU local were natives.)[8] Business in general didn't know what to expect from American workers after the war, but confrontations and violence in the auto, steel, and energy industries did not bode well. A telephone strike loomed. The Congress of Industrial Organizations (CIO) looked especially sinister. If it succeeded in organizing unions across the auto, steel, and mining industries, it would conceivably have the power to shut down the American economy at once if it didn't get its way.

The typographers union—which was not officially part of the CIO—had been battling, and often cowing, print owners for many years. [9] As the war ended, its power was substantial. Like the state-sponsored oligarchs of old, the ITU effectively decided who could enter the business and who could sell which printed products in the United States. It cornered and embarrassed nonunion producers. At most of the nation's biggest shops, it determined who got hired. Thanks to "work rules" it wrote into contracts, the union determined how much work could be done, when it could be done, how many people were needed to do it, how fast it could be delivered, and, among other things, who could deliver it. It, not managers, supervised the nation's biggest composing rooms. (Foremen were members of the union, on the side of workers instead of management.) As such, it controlled costs in the most sensitive, expensive parts of the industry. Its influence on the overall costs of producing printed information was huge.

Those work rules, of course, existed to create wages for its members, prevent accidents, maintain awareness, and minimize disruptions to both the employee and the production flow. But some were notorious. The union, for example, forbade employers to use any material typeset in another shop. When an advertiser brought in a finished ad to a newspaper, one of the paper's compositors would reset it before it could go to press. The original either was destroyed or returned to the advertiser. In the history of the printed word, the practice—called "reproduction" by the union brass, "bogus" by everyone else—may have been print owners' most maddening expense. (The *New York Times*, for one, had to reset almost six million lines of bogus advertising type in 1958.) Bogus was so infamous that it managed to jump the little-traveled divide between technical factory manual language and popular culture, soon becoming the definition of all things false and ridiculous. [10]

Other seemingly unfair work rules also raised the cost of printed information. In Detroit, compositors whose work extended a fraction into their lunch hours were paid time and a half wages for the whole break period. In San Francisco, compositors who worked a minute beyond 6:00 P.M. got premium night shift pay for their entire eight-hour shift. Three workers were needed to clean the ink fountains on the *Chicago Sun Times* presses, but the ITU contract required eight. Senior union members at some shops got as many as twenty-two paid holidays a year because, by the middle of the twentieth century, they were usually better organized and had more negotiating power than the master printers. "Against such practices," one appalled observer said, "most U.S. publishers can only shrug helplessly." [11]

Helpless or not, publishers and press owners were sure the often inane rules were hobbling them. From the union's perspective, of course, each rule had a good reason to exist. Overtime rules, for instance, were born of years of attempts to force people to work during break periods or after hours without extra—or sometimes any—pay. For people whose job included prolonged exposure to molten metals, heavy lifting, and exacting detail work under hourly deadlines, vacation was not just fun time off. It was a critical health issue. Publishers, moreover, were not really helpless. The union was hardly omnipotent. Its membership, while robust, was actually 7 percent lower in 1944 than it had been in 1921. And though the wage scales in union contracts had gone up, many press owners never actually paid the workers as much as the contracts allowed. Full eight- and nine-hour shifts were rare during the Depression, and ITU members' actual pay averaged 17.4 percent less than what their full-time wages were supposed to be. Even during the war, when full shifts were common and labor was scarce, more than 7 percent of the ITU's members still earned less than their full-time wages. Their real income—thanks to inflation, the government's suspension of many work rules, and its refusal to grant wage increases—declined during the war. Even in 1946–1947, when the business boomed again, less than 5 percent of the union's 70,000 workers made enough overtime to get more than a full-time wage.[12]

The owners, in sum, tended to exaggerate both the ITU's role in driving up their costs and its power at the bargaining table. Yet as they tried to concoct some way out of their jam as World War II ended, they were in fact not organized enough to make many changes. The guilds, kingly "communities of printers," and the price-fixing owner groups that had squashed competitors and regulated prices in the past were long gone. The old United Typothetae of America, which tried to use the Linotype as a lever to destroy the union fifty years before, was in disarray, lost among some 60 national and 250 local printing employer groups across the country. The groups rarely worked together. The Typothetae, reading the handwriting on the wall, voted itself out of existence in July 1945. In its place it formed a new (and ultimately more successful) group called the Printing Industry of America to try to represent print owners more effectively.[13]

In the meantime, most master printers were left to battle the union on their own. Some did it well. R.R. Donnelley & Sons, based in Chicago, was one of the largest commercial printers in the world, producing the Bell Telephone directories, encyclopedias (the *Encyclopedia Britannica* as well as Compton's and Funk & Wagnalls), catalogs for Firestone and B.F. Goodrich, textbooks for the city of Chicago, *Reader's Digest, Time, Farm Journal*, and all the books published by the American Bible Society, among many others. It was also innovative. It stepped in when *Time* cofounder Henry Luce nearly abandoned the idea of a weekly photo magazine called *Life* because he could not get complex images printed on tight weekly deadlines. With its enormous resources, Donnelley invented a new kind of ink that would dry quickly on a new kind of customized, slick paper, and Luce got to launch his magazine.[14]

And it was staunchly antiunion. Founded in Mergenthaler's era, the company publicly became a bitter ITU enemy on August 26, 1905, when workers came to work to find the following message posted on the door: "Hereafter this composing room will be operated as an open shop." Workers were given the choice to renounce their union membership or leave. The notice had been posted by T. E. Donnelley, son of the company's founder and its president. T. E., as he was called, fully expected union members to strike. And when they did, he immediately brought in trained workers to replace them, including low-wage "girl feeders" working at his presses. Security guards were there, trained and armed. His precise preparations paid off. The company, now staffed by competent nonunion employees working nine-hour shifts for less than union wages, continued to produce good work. The exiled unionists raged, picketed, sputtered, and, after years of trying, gave up applying for jobs there.[15]

"Probably no lockout in the whole history of the American labor movement was as nearly complete, as nearly perfect, as the lockout that Donnelley perpetrated on the printing crafts," a union lawyer later conceded. It lasted almost forty years.[16]

Donnelley worked hard to maintain it, refusing to hire applicants who had worked at union shops in the past. "If their references showed they worked in a union house, we assumed that they were union people," T. E. Donnelley once testified. They were disqualified. If Donnelley couldn't find a white nonunionist, he would "temporarily" hire a black nonunionist to fill the vacancy, "although on a Jim Crow basis." He had stenographers record union leaders' speeches, looking for hints of new organizing efforts at his plant or people who might try to pass themselves off as nonunion in order to infiltrate his operation. Sometimes he found them by accident. Once, for example, he recognized five of his employees in a newspaper photo of bowlers enjoying themselves at a Union Printers Bowling League tournament. Their secret ITU affiliation thus exposed, their lives soon turned. Although firing people because they belonged to a union was illegal by then, the union later reported that company managers repeatedly "taunted" two of the outed bowlers when they got back to the plant and for weeks after the picture appeared. The other three subsequently found themselves barred from earning enough merits to qualify for overtime pay.[17]

In 1933 the Wagner Act barred companies from refusing to employ people on the basis of their union affiliation, but the fearsome ITU still did not try to infiltrate Donnelley again until 1938, the year after the U.S. Supreme Court validated the act. Although Donnelley remained an open shop, by 1940 the union claimed it had "sure footholds" in several Donnelley departments, trying to get other workers to join and finally force the company to bargain with it. [18]

It still did not have enough members in 1942, when the company found itself with a big new contract to print the Sears Roebuck catalog. To get it, it had outbid a union printer that in turn thus had to lay off "several hundred" ITU workers. Donnelley, however, did not yet have the production capacity to do all its new work. For the long run, it would again train new, nonunion workers. In the short run, it would send its overflow work to union shops. To appease the conscience of the workers at the union shops who might then feel they were supporting the notoriously antiunion Donnelley, the company officially announced it was ending its thirty-eight-year-old lockout. [19] (Its policy of refusing to bargain collectively with a union, though, remained in place.)

Unionists in the city were hardly mollified. Enraged, they accused the company of asking them to help it wreck the union. They were filling in while it trained people for jobs Donnelley would not deign to interview them for. In August 1942, they asked all union printers in the country to refuse to accept any of Donnelley's overflow work. Other unions like the Teamsters and the Electrical Workers and Office Employees helped by refusing to work with or for companies that did business with Donnelley. To the government, which had special wartime powers to prohibit strikes and keep production going at all costs, it looked like big trouble was brewing in Chicago. Donnelley advised the government of a "threatened strike" against it, thus triggering a staggeringly slow series of official hearings, briefs, accusations, and counteraccusations while the printing work went ahead. A year later, the War Labor Board ruled the dispute had "become so serious that it may lead to substantial interference with the war effort." Lawsuits were filed. Hearings stretched into 1944, when Donnelley began to graduate trained nonunionists. [20]

In response, some 70,000 voting members of the ITU, many of them angered by the dispute, elected one of their most fiery, aggressive colleagues to lead them into the postwar world. [21]

Woodruff Randolph despised the typographers' appeasement policies of the Depression and World War II years. During the Depression, the union had shied away from conflict, careful not to push its troubled employers out of business. During the war it had, like most national unions, signed a no-strike pledge. As promised, it dutifully gave all its labor issues— including the problem at Donnelley—to the War Labor Board to resolve. The board, however, had proved unsympathetic much of the time, at one point rejecting the ITU request for a 15 percent wage hike after years of no increases. It also tended to favor owners when they argued that work rules inhibited their output, and often suspended the rules for the war's duration. ITU members' earning power, meanwhile, had continued to decay.

Randolph pledged to reverse the trends, although he might have known that historically wars had never been kind to unions. When World War I ended, for example, many American unions had been decimated by government hunts for communists and, more damaging still, by the rush of newly enriched businesses to cut costs. The ITU had fought them in 1919. Chicago and then New York print owners had posted surprise, Donnelley-like notices that they were reducing wages and keeping a forty-eight-hour work week. Strikes ensued, and publishers tried putting out their magazines on typewriters for a while. The union, at least in New York, ultimately won a forty-four-hour week but suffered a 12.5 percent wage cut.[22]

Now, as World War II careened toward an end, Randolph proclaimed there was only one solution for antilabor governments, decaying wages, and the machinations of companies like Donnelley: a general offensive. When the war ended, he said he'd strike if necessary to regain lost wages, support fellow unionists, and gain footholds where they had not had them before.

Almost immediately after taking office, he raised a $1 million fund to help union members pay for food and rent while they were out of work during the coming years of strife.[23]

For the print owners, costs (if not hell) seemed about to break loose again.

Randolph and the ITU lost no time. When the government lifted wartime wage freezes and the prohibitions against striking in 1945, ITU locals aggressively began asking for substantial salary increases in their new contracts. They struck thirty dailies almost immediately. Not a few employers, determined to make up sales lost to wartime production controls, surrendered quickly. Resisting, they figured, meant going out of business for a time. "You just did not want to take a strike because, if you did, you simply could not even attempt to publish," one publisher explained. "The unions just had you by the throat."[24]

Those who fought, suffered. In 1945, the publisher of the Quincy (Mass.) *Patriot Ledger* resisted his workers' pay demands and watched the union compositors walk out in protest. His efforts to bring in nonunion strikebreakers failed, and his newspaper was out of print for thirteen long weeks.[25]

Seattle was without a newspaper for eight weeks in 1945. Cleveland's papers were down for a month in 1946. Springfield, Massachusetts, had no paper for six months through March 1947. Shorter strikes unfolded in Rochester, New York, Washington, D.C., and Minneapolis.[26]

By one count, there were seventy-eight newspaper strikes from 1945 through 1947. Randolph and the ITU won most of them. Between 1945 and 1948, they forced up composing room costs at an average 50,000-circulation daily newspaper by a staggering 98 percent. At the *Dayton Journal*, production workers' wages doubled. The compositors' wage gains were "both absolutely and relatively greater than for manufacturing wages as a whole" after the war.[27]

The cost of producing printed information was rising quickly again. Indeed, from the end of World War I through the late 1950s, taxes, inflation, and rising costs of raw materials and wages inexorably reversed the trend started at the turn of the nineteenth century, of constantly falling costs.[28] The jolts in the late 1940s accounted for most of the increase.

Caught between rising production costs and a public that probably would not pay higher prices for their products, the master printers desperately turned to Congress for help. And, as it did at the end of World War I, the federal government again complied.

Allied with other worried industries (strikes had cost American businesses 3–6 million man days per month in 1946), the master printers helped draft many of the seventeen labor bills proposed on the first day of the Senate's session in 1947. The vast majority would give owners new tools to resist unions and thus to control their burgeoning costs.[29]

Out of the subsequent politicking—including the eventual overriding of a presidential veto—came the Taft-Hartley Act, which effectively gave back to industry many of the bargaining advantages it had lost during the Roosevelt administration and the New Deal of the 1930s. Among other things, it permitted states to outlaw "closed" (meaning all-union) shops. (Fourteen states did so by 1954.) To neutralize the CIO, it forbid industry-wide strikes. To negate the kind of weapons the ITU used to fight Donnelley, it banned secondary boycotts and strikes that had "unjustifiable objectives." For other kinds of walkouts, it gave the president the power to force strikers back to work for a "cooling off" period. To drive leftists out of the unions (although by then mobsters were a far bigger force in most unions than ideologues), it required union leaders to sign anticommunist pledges.

Needless to say, labor unions were outraged. The ITU, for one, fired back immediately. First, it called the anticommunism provisions a farce. "To proceed to the logical conclusion," it huffed in a hastily written pamphlet, "no Communist or other law violator could reasonably be permitted to represent any employer." If workers had to sign loyalty oaths, managers should too. At their 1947 convention, held just before the new law was to take effect, members resolved that they could not "accept as leaders those who associate themselves with communism." But they would not ask their leaders to sign the pledge. Instead, "we rely on the democratic principles of our country and the good sense of our people to keep those principles alive and functioning."[30]

The whole Taft-Hartley Act was "conceived in sin," CIO chief Phillip Murray thundered. To American Federation of Labor President William Green, it was "conceived in a spirit of vindictiveness against unions." Some 200,000 coal workers walked off their jobs in protest. Cosponsor Robert Taft, at his son's wedding the day the Senate overrode the president's veto of the bill, emerged from the church to see pickets across the street reading "The Tuff-Heartless Act" and "To the Groom: Congratulations to You.—To Your Old Man."[31] The unions' biggest objection, of course, was to the provisions outlawing contracts that required closed shops, minimizing their ability to appeal to the National Labor Relations to resolve issues without strikes, and then stacking the laws to keep unions from striking if they couldn't settle disputes otherwise.

Even some publishers were a little shocked by the new law's scope. "As a matter of fact," the secretary of the Chicago Publishers Association later told a congressional subcommittee, "most of the Chicago publishers, or all of the Chicago publishers, I would say, would prefer to continue a closed shop if it were legal."[32]

Leaders of the American Newspaper Publishers Association (ANPA)—the national version of the Chicago publishers group—rushed to meet with Randolph, hoping to avoid more strikes. They met eighteen times, sometimes inviting the mayor of Chicago, where the old pre-Taft contracts were due to expire at the end of 1947 and the first of the big post-Taft showdowns would begin. They pleaded with Randolph to accept open shops.[33]

But the pugnacious Randolph refused. Certain the law would be overturned during the next Congress, he told locals to not to sign any contracts at all. If there weren't any contracts, Randolph figured the union could not be violating laws that restricted what the contracts might say. Instead of contracts, ITU locals would work under their own "conditions of employment." The conditions, of course, included refusing to work with workers who didn't belong to the union. If the employer met the conditions, the ITU compositors would work. If the employer did not, the compositors would not work.

Print owners were flummoxed. They needed contracts as much as they needed compositors. At Chicago's six daily newspapers, which had been operating union-only composing rooms for fifty-five years, publishers insisted that contracts were crucial for them. Contracts defined what their operating costs were and how long they would remain stable. It was unthinkable to go forward while leaving them open to change and not having everyone's role cast in writing. The legal liability would be enormous; the threats of shutdowns constant. In Philadelphia, as in Chicago, print owners readily agreed to a "substantial" wage hike for their workers, but only if the ITU signed a contract. In New York's suburbs, the *Nassau Daily Review-Star* publisher offered a similar deal.

The ITU said yes to the wages, no to the contracts.

The master printers had no way to compel the ITU to sign anything. At their convention in Indiana, the employer members of the Printing Industries of America concluded "there appeared to be no method of forcing the local union to enter into a legal contract."[34] In the meantime, union Lino operators went on strike in Chicago, Philadelphia, and New York.

Print owners turned to the courts. In the past, the National Labor Relations Board (NLRB) had ruled that *companies* that refused to sign a contract were conducting unfair labor practices. Now a group of Baltimore commercial print shops claimed the union's no-contract policy constituted the same unfair labor practices as an employer's no-contract policy would. In Cincinnati, the Southern Newspaper Publishers Association sued 130 ITU locals on the same grounds. Printers from Pittsburgh, Philadelphia, Detroit, Newark, and St. Louis, among others, jointly protested the ITU's tactics to the NLRB. In Akron, print owners actually got the ITU local to defy Randolph and sign a contract. But the NLRB could not certify it until ITU's refusenik leaders signed the Taft-Hartley anticommunist pledge.[35]

Taking another tack, 242 magazine, book, and commercial print shops in New York—where printing and publishing was the city's second biggest industry—simultaneously posted notices on March 11, 1948, announcing that their 4,000 composing room employees' work week had been increased to forty hours (up from 36.25 hours).[36]

The ITU responded in kind. It struck the 242 New York printers and a total of forty-four newspapers in twenty-seven other cities in 1948.

When the NLRB ruled the no-contract policy was a "deliberate frustration of the bargaining process," the union switched tactics again. Randolph said the union would sign contracts, but only short-term ones that were immediately cancelable if, among other things, the ITU should find a nonunion worker at a plant. Needless to say the master printers, in dire need of stability in their shops, found the idea of having their operations stopped at the ITU's whim less than attractive.[37] The battle continued.

It was, the press said, a "'war' between publishers and their printers."[38] For the moment, it seemed unwinnable by anyone. The union was now up against not only individual employers but also the federal government. And despite their efforts to legislate their way out of their cost problems, the employers now found themselves up against an even more defiant, clever group of employees than they faced before they helped pass the Taft-Hartley Act.

As during the enormous run-up in the cost of printed information during and after the Civil War, some print owners again tried to invent their way out of their troubles. Perhaps they could find some cheaper way to get their materials into print.

NOTES

1. Frederick G. Kilgour, *The Evolution of the Book* (New York: Oxford University Press, 1998), 129.

2. There were 2,600 dailies in 1909, 2,006 in 1944. George Corben Goble, *The Obituary of a Machine: The Rise and Fall of Ottmar Mergenthaler's Linotype at U.S. Newspapers* (Bloomington: Indiana University Mass Communications Program, 1984), 342; Warren Chappell, *A Short History of the Printed Word* (New York: Knopf, 1970), 232.

3. Goble, *Obituary*, 342; Frank Luther Mott, *American Journalism: A History, 1690–1960*, 3rd ed. (New York: Macmillan, 1962), 679. New York's WEAF announced it would give advertisers ten minutes of airtime for $100. The editorial was from *Printer's Ink* magazine, "The Insidious Dangers of Radio Advertising," cited in Richard Rhodes, ed., *Visions of Technology* (New York: Simon & Schuster, 1999), 71; Ben H. Bagdikian, *The Information Machines: Their Impact on Men and the Media* (New York: Harper & Row, 1971), xxi.

4. Regular TV broadcasts began in New York in 1939, covering a thirty-mile radius. Aware of how radio had changed them, newspapers were not sitting idly by. The *St. Louis Post-Dispatch*, the *Sacramento Bee*, and the *Dallas Morning News* had experimented with sending out news stories by facsimile machine. Mott, *American Journalism*, 680–81.

5. Elizabeth F. Baker, "Unemployment and Technical Progress in Commercial Printing," *American Economic Review*, September 1930, 452–58.

6. John S. Knight, cited in David R. Davies, "An Industry in Transition: Major Trends in American Daily Newspapers, 1945–1955" (Ph.D. diss, University of Alabama, 1997), ocean.otr.usm.edu/~ddavies (accessed January 13, 1999); Goble, *Obituary*, 330.

7. Chappell, *Short History*, 228.

8. Gavin Wright and Paul A. David, "Early Twentieth-Century American Productivity Growth Dynamics: An Inquiry into the Economic History of 'Our Ignorance,'" Stanford Institute for Economic Policy Research, Discussion Paper no. 98-3, *Abstracts in Economic History*, April 1999; Charles R. Walker, "A National Council for the Printing Trades," *Monthly Labor Review*, January 1921, 33.

9. Charles Howard, a former ITU president, was the CIO's first secretary, but he served as an individual, not as an ITU representative. The ITU itself was a member of the rival American Federation of Labor. Seymour Martin Lipset, Martin A. Trow, and James S. Coleman, *Union Democracy: The Internal Politics of the International Typographical Union* (Glencoe, Ill.: Free Press, 1972), 50–51.

10. "Bogus Man," *Time*, May 11, 1959, 50. The ITU had been proposing bogus rules to make sure its members had plenty of work since at least June 1872, with varying success. But New York newspapers finally accepted them in 1896, and they became a standard feature in most major newspapers for the next seventy years. In the interim, bogus provided important revenue for many compositors. "Many of you," ITU President Elmer Brown noted in 1960, as the union considered abolishing bogus, "are reminiscing about the hungry '30s. The old-timers in my local tell me emphatically that, had it not been for reproduction [bogus], their bellies would have been touching their backbones on many occasions." Paul Jacobs, "Dead Horse and the Featherbed," *Harper's*, September 1962, 49; Harry Kelber and Carl Schlesinger, *Union Printers and Controlled Automation* (New York: Free Press, 1967), 19. The ITU ultimately began dropping bogus from its contracts in 1968.

11. "Bogus Man," 60.

12. Membership in 1921 was 72,758 and 67,474 in 1944. The decline could be traced in part to some former ITU printers splitting off to join more specialized printing unions. Goble, *Obituary*, 346; Freeman Champney, "Taft-Hartley and the Printers," *Antioch Review*, Spring 1947; Lipset et al., *Union Democracy*, 52.

13. Baker, *Printers and Technology: A History of the International Printing Pressmen and Assistants Union* (Westport, Conn.: Greenwood, 1974), 307–8.

14. *Brief on Behalf of the Unions before the Mediation Section of the National War Labor Board. In the Matter of R.R. Donnelley & Sons Company (Lakeside Press) and Organization Committee of Chicago Printing Trades Unions*, January 5, 1943, 20; George H. Waltz Jr., *The House That Quality Built* (Chicago: Lakeside, 1957), 26–27.

15. *Second Brief on Behalf of the Unions before the Mediation Section of the National War Labor Board. In the Matter of R.R. Donnelley & Sons Company (Lakeside Press) and Organization Committee of Chicago Printing Trades Unions*, February 24, 1943, 16. Donnelley and to a lesser extent an association called the Employing Printers of Chicago ultimately became so skilled at training competent nonunion printers and compos-

itors that they attracted almost two-thirds of New York's magazine printing business to lower-cost Chicago in the 1920s. Baker, *Printers and Technology*, 306.

16. War Labor Board, *Second Brief*, 13.

17. War Labor Board, *Second Brief*, 21, 28, 35–36.

18. War Labor Board, *Second Brief*, 5, 9.

19. War Labor Board, *Brief on Behalf of the Unions*, January 5, 1943, 21–22.

20. War Labor Board, *Brief on Behalf of the Unions*, January 5, 1943, 22; March 20, 1944, 17.

21. Lipset et al., *Union Democracy*, 50, 52.

22. "Adjustments in Printing," *Survey* 46, May 14, 1921, 198.

23. Mott, *American Journalism*, 780.

24. Mott, *American Journalism*, 781; Elizabeth MacIver Neiva, "Chain Building: The Consolidation of the American Newspaper Industry, 1953–1980," *Business History Review*, Spring 1996.

25. Neiva, "Chain Building," 12.

26. Mott, *American Journalism*, 780–81.

27. Davies, "Industry in Transition," 6; Champney, "Taft-Hartley," 8.

28. S. H. Steinberg, *Five Hundred Years of Printing* (New York: Criterion, 1959), 213.

29. James T. Patterson, *Mr. Republican: A Biography of Robert A. Taft* (Boston: Houghton Mifflin, 1972), 352.

30. International Typographical Union, "Come Let Us Reason Together on Some Taft-Hartley Subjects," Special Collections, Norlin Library, University of Colorado–Boulder, Box 60, 6.

31. Patterson, *Mr. Republican*, 362.

32. Testimony of John O'Keefe, secretary of Chicago Newspaper Publishers Association, before a subcommittee of the House Committee on Education and Labor, December 22, 1947, cited in International Typographical Union, "A Case for Repeal of the Taft-Hartley Act," Special Collections, Norlin Library, University of Colorado–Boulder, Box 60, Notebook 2.

33. "Taft-Hartley Strike Enters Second Year," *Business Week*, December 11, 1948, 96–99.

34. John Seybold, *The Philadelphia Printing Industry: A Case Study* (Philadelphia: University of Pennsylvania Press, 1949), 67, 70–71.

35. Willard Shelton, "Labor: First Fruits," *New Republic*, December 8, 1947. The Baltimore printers called themselves the Graphic Arts League. Seybold, *Case Study*, 71; "Printers Battle over Closed Shop," *U.S. News & World Report*, December 5, 1947, 35–37.

36. Kelber and Schlesinger, *Union Printers*, 42.

37. Davies, "Industry in Transition," 7; Kelber and Schlesinger, *Union Printers*, 44; Seybold, *Case Study*, 68.

38. "Printers Battle over Closed Shop," 35.

17

DREAMS OF GIRL TYPISTS

Linotype salesman Reginald Orcutt once found himself in Ankara, watching companies compete for a contract to sell 40,000 typewriters to the Turkish government. "A regiment of salesmen from America, Germany, Italy and France crowded the hotels, competing for the order," he recalled. Ultimately, most of the contract "went to . . . a somewhat obscure German firm, whose salesmanship was as old as the Garden of Eden. It was perfectly plain that his two young, beautiful, dizzy and very blonde demonstrators so dazzled the eyes and emotions of official Ankara that the order was soon in the German bag. Perhaps faces fell when it was realized that the blondes were not part of the standard equipment."[1]

Trying to make women part of the equipment was a tradition in the print industry. "Girl" and "inexpensive" were used interchangeably in labor and technology discussions. When women were cited in printing industry talk, it typically was to illustrate that a piece of machinery could be run by just about anyone. Skilled, expensive union workers like those in the ITU, regardless of gender, would no longer be necessary.

In 1840 young Henry Bessemer had promoted his new type machine as being cheap to operate and as "an excellent occupation for women." When the *London Times* sought to test if a different type machine could save it money, it hired "a young lady" to work it for ten hours a day, for six consecutive days. (It was then "bitterly attacked by the London compositors, who feared unemployment. It was opposed also because female, hence cheap, labour was employed on this machine," another historian recounted.) In 1864, the unfortunate Timothy Alden's machine was marketed as one that women could run. (One New York shop exclusively employed women on it.) When Whitelaw Reid sought to show that the new Mergenthaler

Linotype would cut costs in 1888, he had women work on it at a demonstration in Brooklyn. At the time, women's wages "were cheaper than men by as much as one-half to two-thirds."[2]

But few women ever got to run a Lino. The work was "heavy, dirty, and loud," and running a linecaster required training that women usually couldn't get. In Boston, at least according to the ITU, bosses eventually decided "that a woman was a great inconvenience" because she couldn't always lift her type case. The brass matrices for cast letters were weighty; women of the day commonly did not do much strength training. Added to union rules that required that Lino operators graduate from the rough six-year apprenticeship—which began, moreover, at an age when girls were not properly let out of their houses—before getting to run a machine, market conditions generally drove or kept women out of composing rooms during hot-metal type's long reign.[3]

Everyone who paid out high wages, however, kept having same repetitive dream of finding machines that cheap labor could operate.

When the cost of producing the printed word rose again at the conclusion of World War II, even the high-minded Vannevar Bush found himself transfixed at a demonstration of a new communications device one day, staring as "a girl stroked its keys." He too seemed stuck on the image. In speculating how his memex machine might work, he later fantasized about how a "girl strokes its keys languidly."[4]

He was hardly alone. As the print industry of the United States stumbled toward paralysis at midcentury, some publishers again thought they could make their dreams come true.

When the ITU struck the *St. Petersburg (Fla.) Times* in November 1945, for example, publisher Nelson Poynter brought in two new typesetting tools and hired women to run them. One was called the Verityper, the other the Underwood Electric Typewriter. With them, he managed to produce sixteen-page editions every day, keeping some money coming in while he hired and trained strikebreakers to replace his expensive union compositors on his hot-metal machines for the long run. By January 1946, the strike was over. Poynter was putting out his paper with nonunion compositors, and the ITU was defeated. His victory—one of few for the master printers—attracted "other publishers from around the country to observe."[5]

In Quincy, Massachusetts, it was too late for publisher Prescott Low. But he bought two of the cold-type machines Poynter had used and stored them in his basement against the day he might need them again.[6] It would come soon, he was sure.

In 1947, when the second round of postwar upheaval in the printed word business began, many other big-name print owners copied Poynter's battle plan from 1945. At several of the struck Chicago newspapers, "a single girl typist, working on a justifying typewriter, can turn out just about as much type as a highly skilled linotype or Intertype operator," one business magazine reported. The "girl" earned $1.25 to $1.50 per hour; union compositors got $2.36 to $3.03 an hour. The "justifying typewriter," the Verityper, had cost the newspaper $700 to buy. The hot-metal linecasters they replaced cost $4,000–$10,000.[7]

There were other cheap typist machines with names like Justowriter, Lithotype, and Electromatic, all ranging from $600 to $2,000 to buy. Linotype reportedly was testing a new keyboard so simple that "it might enable a girl typist to operate a Linotype machine with only a little practice." The long-desired revolution might be imminent. "Probably the past three years have produced more widespread initiative in printing inventions . . . than any period in a half century," a publishing trade magazine observed. An anonymous "newspaper executive" gushed that the new tools had "advanced the art of printing five or 10 years in a space of a few months" since the start of the Chicago Taft-Hartley strike. For the ITU, a business magazine noted hopefully, the machines "could mean a decline in power."[8]

By spring 1948—probably the midpoint of the Taft-Hartley strikes— master printers had purchased 279 Veritypers, 115 Electromatics, and 49 Royal condensed-type typewriters. Another 24 Veritypers and 35 IBM Electromatics reportedly were on order. Fourteen newspapers, at least according to stories later found to have been "planted" in a trade journal by the Publishers Association of New York, were about to install the devices. Some 770 typists and 660 proofreaders already had been hired and were being trained. They had produced 220 dummy pages a day at one paper. The *New York Daily News*, the journal reported, already had produced a full edition in dress rehearsal.[9]

These were "cold type" (as opposed to the Lino's hot-metal type) devices, and they were easy to use. A typist set stories in long, evenly justified columns. Another worker then cut apart the columns and pasted them onto a sheet to look just as they would in print. The worker then took a photograph of the pasted-up page and transferred the image to a printing plate. The plate would then go to the pressroom to be imprinted onto sheets.

But dreams, needless to say, are ephemeral. The cold-type newspapers looked horrible. Small-type classified, stock market, and radio program listings were especially tough to read. "The trouble with typewritten copy," *Publishers Weekly* noted, apparently without irony, "is that it looks typewritten." The machines were also slow. Observers estimated that it took two and a half hours to move a news story from copy desk to finished paper, about four times as long as with hot-metal type. Another estimate was that it took five hours to get a story on page one. By contrast, it took the *Wall Street Journal* fifteen minutes. "This kind of speed," a *Journal* reporter wrote, "puts the present emergency operation of the six struck Chicago dailies in the shade." Publishers found that "fewer words per page means [printing] more pages, and newsprint is still in short supply."[10] In the end the longer hours, smaller papers, and increased use of raw materials cost the publishers more than they could save by using nonunion labor.

As it did in the 1890s, hot type proved to be cheaper than cold. "Anybody who thinks that he is going to effect substantial savings in using the so-called substitute methods will be badly fooled," said the lead composition researcher for a master printers' trade group. "I don't care what method of keyboard setting you use, hot or cold, they all require a high degree of judgment. And that kind of skill costs money."[11]

"The best overall judgment," another observer found, "seems to be that daily newspaper can be put out without printers, but that the result is awkward, messy, wasteful of newsprint, and plays havoc with speedy news coverage."[12]

Finally even the struck cold-type publishers soon began angling to get union compositors back to run their Linos. In May 1949, the Chicago print owners offered a huge $100 a week raise, which amounted to anywhere from a 25 percent to a 34 percent increase, depending on a compositor's seniority. But the ITU, expecting that Congress would soon repeal the Taft-Hartley Act, rejected it.

This time, it was the union that was delusional. Congress beat back efforts to repeal the law during the summer, leaving Randolph crestfallen. It would, he knew, be at least two years before labor-friendly candidates could get to Washington to bail him out politically. He didn't have the money to wait that long. Struggling with huge strike expenses (the union had spent $13 million on benefits for striking members since 1945), he finally gave in.

In September, the ITU signed a contract in Chicago that included the raise and a pledge by publishers to provide "the maximum [job] security possible under the Taft-Hartley Law." Publishers in effect promised, although only with a handshake, not to hire nonunion help.[13] The newspapers then put away their cheap cold-type machines and returned to their powerful Linos. The surviving Chicago papers kept their union-only promise for decades, sometimes long after type itself disappeared from their pages.

The mighty International Typographical Union, now nearly 100,000 members strong, also abided by its truces with both the Taft-Hartley Act and new type tools. Although the public seemed to hate it—the nation was generally hostile to labor at the time, and the press often portrayed ITU moves as selfish, reactionary, and even traitorous—the union had done its job well. Against rich owners and potent federal agencies, it had won huge raises for its members, kept their jobs secure, and cosseted them with an array of services (health care, pensions, even a retirement home) not common for the time. But it also understood master printers were not about to stop trying to replace its members with machines run, as Woodruff Randolph put it, by yet another "flock of girls."[14]

Sure enough, print owners' resolve to get out from under the ITU had never been higher than after the midcentury war for control of the American printed word. They strengthened their national trade organizations, and many, like late-nineteenth-century publishers, pooled their resources to fund new inventions that might help them cut their production costs. Even before they put their primitive cold-type machines into storage, they came across another promising idea. It was the one from Cambridge, cosponsored in part by the famous Vannevar Bush.

The next machine, everyone now knew, probably would be a camera. Promoters of the new technology hyped "photographic typesetting" as an entirely different kind of process. It even made shops *look* good. Gerald Bigalk, a central California printer, recalls returning from war in 1946 to find out his old high school printing class teacher had become a salesman for the company that had installed one of the new devices in West Los Angeles. Bigalk asked his teacher to take him to see it and was duly impressed. The thing was much quieter and cleaner to operate than hot-metal machines. "When I saw it," he recalls, "I thought, 'here's a guy who's got carpeting on the floor!' It was *plush*."[15]

In practice, however, these photo machines' first applications "were so general as to be almost useless," remembered John Seybold, who with his sons went on to create both printing businesses and then influential graphic arts consulting practices during the second half of the twentieth century. The machine Bigalk saw, called the Fotosetter, was not always reliable, and was known to put type in unanticipated places on a page from time to time. Its own designer conceded the machines were "only a step removed from the old type-casting machines, merely substituting a camera unit for the metal-pot-and-casting assembly." He suspected, however, that it was "the forerunner of other, more radical phototypesetting machines."[16]

They would in fact be different; faster, more versatile, cheaper and, as Bigalk noted, cleaner to operate. Linotypes, of course, produced "slugs" of metal, perhaps two inches wide. Each was a line of type that, grouped with other slugs, would be arranged to form sentences, paragraphs, sections, stories, and finally whole pages of type. The new phototype machines, on the other hand, produced no metal or slugs. A phototype operator tapped out a story on a keyboard. After a few more steps, the result was a long strip of film on which paragraphs and words of different sizes were already arranged. A worker then applied wax to the film's back side, cut it, and arranged the pieces to form the image of what the page would look like, pasted the pieces of film into place, and took a picture of the page so that it could be made into a plate that would be put on the press.

The new machines had "yet to prove (they were) the next step forward in the Graphic Arts," conceded the leaders of Big Six, the ITU local in New York. "But one hundred years of experience coping with new methods of typesetting have taught the union many things. We realize that progress and change go together. The safest way to introduce new machinery into the trade is to have our union men operate it. This intelligent approach to mechanical problems should see Big Six through for at least another century."[17]

"I think we should be smart enough to see a development in the industry and prepare for it," Randolph added. Following the same strategy it had used to survive the switch from hand to machine type in the late nineteenth century, his union began volunteering its members to run the photo machines and bring others who might run them someday into its tent. In 1947, it invited the lithographers (the craftsmen who made press plates out of the metal type pages the compositors created and would be likely to run phototype machines) to join it.[18]

Vannevar Bush's phototype project, thanks largely to great public relations, appeared to be the machine most likely to succeed. It had good science, a celebrity front man in Bush, and a savvy marketer in businessman William Garth. It also appeared to have money behind it. With the American Newspaper Publishers Association (backed most prominently by the publishers of the *New York Times* and the *Boston Herald-Traveler*), Bush and Garth had raised $103,000 to finish developing Higonnet and Moyroud's phototype machine. (They had, however, hoped to raise about $450,000.) When done, they hoped to sell their machine for $5,000, about half the price of a Linotype. It would be five times faster than a Lino too. Garth predicted it would cut the cost of printing in half. Bush was no less sanguine. "Printing as it is now done," he said, "is an obsolete art."[19]

As the scientific team—Higonnet had chosen to stay in France while Moyroud had moved to the United States to join Samuel Caldwell as the project's lead engineers—perfected the invention, the business team dropped tantalizing hints of what was to come. In a careful promotional striptease, Bush and Garth first showed the device, called the "Lumitype" and later the "Photon," to "a few bookmen" in early 1949. (The event probably was more of an open house seeking investors than a sales pitch for the machine.) In September, they staged a public demonstration for a few chosen journalists in Cambridge. The next month, taking a page from the marketing strategy of instant photography pioneer Edwin Land, they pumped up the buzz another notch. They set up their machine at the Waldorf-Astoria Hotel in New York, headquarters of that year's American Newspaper Publishers Association convention, and made still more grand predictions. Bush, the scientific maestro of World War II, said that the Mergenthaler technology was "obviously on its way out." Garth was there too. Once a touch football opponent of MIT classmate and Polaroid executive Bill McCune, who, in turn, attended Land's dramatic publicity splash for his new one-step Polaroid camera at the Optical Society of America in February 1947, Garth announced his Photon in Polaroid-like terms. Using Land's words almost exactly, replacing only those related to photography, he told the master printers assembled at the Waldorf that his new machine "represents the first major development in printing, especially in composition, in seventy-five years." Land had offered filmless photography. Garth offered typeless printing.

"There's no question [Garth] was a superb publicist and marketer," an admiring engineer who later joined Garth's company observed. "I was present [at Land's announcement of the Polaroid Camera], and I think Garth saw the potential of that kind of publicity. I believe he used it at that show in 1949."[20]

In reality, his machine was not ready to be installed anywhere. It needed more development and, of course, more money to pay for the development. To raise funds, Garth sold his company's office duplicating supplies business.[21] To make the machine better, he called on more former MIT classmates.

Lou Rosenblum, for example, was an optics engineer at Polaroid who occasionally saw Garth at MIT alumni meetings in and around Cambridge. He liked and respected Garth but had little to do with him professionally until, seemingly out of the blue, "he walked up to me and asked 'what you do know about typesetting in Hebrew?' I, being a smart-aleck, said 'not much, but probably more than you do.' Then he asked me something like, 'do you know why vowels in Hebrew sometimes are placed on the left and sometimes on the right side of consonants?' And I said, 'Bill, maybe I *don't* know as much as you do about typesetting in Hebrew.'" He eventually "romanced me into leaving Polaroid, which took quite a bit of romancing because it was for less money."[22]

As in the 1450s and 1880s when disparate inventors raced to finish their versions of essentially the same idea, competitors did not idle while Garth, Rosenblum, Bush, Moyroud, Caldwell, and the others romanced and tinkered. Intertype unveiled an improved Fotosetter. The Mergenthaler company promised its own photocomposing machine soon (it finally introduced its Linofilm machine in 1954). 3M, McGraw-Hill, Heubner, and DuPont reportedly were developing phototypesetters or related phototype supplies.

And Garth flogged away too. He and his partners predicted, again and again, that their invention would be a "revolutionary way of doing things . . . to meet the dangers we now all face, a trend of rising costs—particularly composing room costs—rising prices, and dwindling profits."[23]

None too accurately, Garth abruptly announced he had sold ten Photons for 1950. He won laudatory stories in the technical press. (*Popular Science* called the Photon "one of the most promising photocomposition machines.") He used a Photon to typeset a promotional book, with the actual typesetting work being done by the obligatory "girl who hadn't had any Photon training at all." The sixteen different Photon typefaces and type sizes she used in the book, Garth added, would have cost "more than $25,000" on a Linotype. Vannevar Bush ceremoniously presented it to the president of MIT at a highly publicized luncheon. It was, he said, "proof of a successful competition with moveable type." It was nothing less than "a milestone in the graphic arts."[24]

By early 1953, Garth said he'd already sold sixty of the machines, leasing each at $400 a month.[25]

His count, however, was fanciful. He could not name an actual commercial installation of his machine until September 1954. Even then, it was a loaner to Preston Low, the Quincy *Patriot Ledger* publisher who in 1945 had conscientiously stored a Verityper in his basement for his next battle with the union. Low, trying the Photon out, readily joined Garth's publicity parade. He told the press the Photon would soon let him reduce his workforce by 30 percent. So far, he was doing great things with just one Photon operator. It was, of course, "a young lady, formerly a tele-typesetter operator."[26]

By the next spring, a grand total of four Photons were in operation: two at the *Patriot Ledger*, one at the Machine Composition Company in

Boston, and one at MIT's print shop. None had been sold; all were being used on a demonstration basis. The company had not turned a profit since 1950, when it claimed the proceeds of the sale of Garth's old business as revenue. Most recently, in 1954, it had lost $12,599. To raise more cash, it sold another 25,000 shares. With $617,000 in the bank from the stock sale, Garth confidently predicted that he'd lease out another twenty machines in 1955 and that Photon would become profitable in 1956. But it was not to be. The company lost another $356,000 in 1955. Although it sold five more machines, including one to Time, Inc., and one to the *New York Times*, it lost $1.7 million in 1956.[27]

The other brands of phototype machines—Intertype's reimproved Fotosetter and Mergenthaler's Linofilm—were not selling well, either. But each installation seemed to have a profound impact. In May 1954, the ITU reported that a Niagara Falls, New York, shop had cut its composing staff from eighty-five to nine after installing a phototype machine. If the master printers weren't paying attention, the union was. "It must be recognized that phototypesetting does have a real place in the industry," the union told members in a forty-eight-page pamphlet about the new technology. The ITU now foresaw "an era that may possibly prove to be as significant as the one which witnessed the introduction of the linecasting machine."[28]

"Like a stray comet speeding from space toward our cell of the universe," an ITU leader portentously observed, "so print shop automation seems—now distant but coming fast and for sure." On a grittier level, in 1956 the ITU predicted 30,000 members eventually could lose their jobs if it didn't act.[29]

Evil seemed to be approaching hastily again. "To steer our course to safety" the union resolved to put its members on phototype keyboards much as it had put them on Linotype keyboards some sixty years before.[30]

NOTES

1. Reginald Orcutt, *Merchant of Alphabets* (Garden City, N.Y.: Doubleday, Doran, 1945), 129.

2. Frederick G. Kilgour, *The Evolution of the Book* (New York: Oxford University Press, 1998), 115; Colin Clair, *A History of European Printing* (London: Academic, 1976), 378; Walker Rumble, *The Swifts: Printers in the Age of Typesetting Races* (Charlottesville: University of Virginia Press, 2003), 56–57; Donald Hoke, "The Woman and the Typewriter: A Case Study in Technological Innovation and Social Change," *Business and Economic History* 8 (1979): 79.

3. Rumble, *The Swifts*, 132; George Corben Goble, *The Obituary of a Machine: The Rise and Fall of Ottmar Mergenthaler's Linotype at U.S. Newspapers* (Bloomington: Indiana University Mass Communications Program, 1984), 25.

4. Vannever Bush, "As We May Think," *Atlantic Monthly*, July 1945, theatlantic .com/unbound/ flasshbks/computer/hushf.htm (accessed June 17, 2004).

5. David R. Davis, "An Industry in Transition: Major Trends in American Daily Newspapers, 1945–1955" (Ph.D. diss., University of Alabama, 1997), 7, http://ocean .otr.usm.edu/~ddavies (accessed January 13, 1999).

6. Elizabeth MacIver Neiva, "Chain Building: The Consolidation of the American Newspaper Industry, 1953–1980," *Business History Review*, Spring 1996, 13.

7. "Printing Faces a New Era," *Business Week*, March 13, 1948, 22.

8. "Two Composing Machines Make Their Bow," *Publishers Weekly*, May 1, 1948; "New Advances in Production," *Publishers Weekly*, September 24, 1949, 1506; "New Advances in Production," *Publishers Weekly*, September 24, 1949, 1506; "Printing Faces a New Era," *Business Week*, March 13, 1948, 22. Companies like Marshall Field, Jewell Tea, and BF Goodrich quickly adopted these new "cold type" machines to set their ads and, in some cases, internal newsletters. "Goodrich Uses Cold Type," *Business Week*, June 26, 1948, 23.

9. Frank Luther Mott, *American Journalism A History: 1690–1960*, 3rd ed. (New York: Macmillan, 1962), 42–44.

10. Daniel Melcher, "Can Important Economies Be Expected from New Developments in Typesetting?" *Publishers Weekly*, September 6, 1947, 1068–70; Freeman Champney, "Taft-Hartley and the Printers," *Antioch Review*, Spring 1947; J. Howard Rutledge, "New Machines Promise to Outdate Newspaper Methods, Simplify Jobs," *Wall Street Journal*, January 13, 1948, 6.

11. Bernard Snyder headed the Composition Research Committee of the Graphics Arts Industry. Harry Kelber and Carl Schlesinger, *Union Printers and Controlled Automation* (New York: Free Press, 1967), 49.

12. Champney, "Taft-Hartley."

13. William Paschell, "The International Typographical Union," *Monthly Labor Review*, May 1952, 496; "Chicago Printers Give In," *Business Week*, September 25, 1949), 110. Despite constant attempts to repeal and then amend it, the Taft-Hartley law remained on the books through the end of the hot type era. In 1961, the U.S. Supreme Court ruled in favor of a case that effectively gave the ITU some closed-shop rights under the act.

14. *Typographical Journal*, supplement, September 1955, 24.

15. Gerald Bigalk, telephone interview, October 9, 1998.

16. John Seybold, *Computers in Typesetting* (Washington, D.C: Government Printing Office, 1970), 12. Intertype, Linotype's main competitor in selling hot-metal machines, manufactured the Fotosetter. Its chief engineer was Herman Freund. "Printing: Ancient Craft Is stirring with New Inventions," *Fortune*, October 1949, 107.

17. Kelber and Schlesinger, *Union Printers*, 49.

18. Elizabeth Faulkner Baker, *Printers and Technology: A History of the International*

Printing Pressmen and Assistants' Union (Westport, Conn.: Greenwood, 1974), 436.

19. Lithomat Corporation, "Proposal for Research in Graphic Arts through Photo-composition," January 16, 1949, Alfred A. Knopf Collection, Harry Ransom Humanities Research Center, University of Texas–Austin, Box 5, Folder 13, 3; "Printing by Photo Is Shown to Public," *New York Times*, September 16, 1949, 29; Kelber and Schlesinger, *Union Printers*, 47; "Lithomat's Composing Machine," *Publishers Weekly*, September 24, 1949, 1503; "Printing without Type," *Business Week*, October 1, 1949, 57.

20. "Lithomat's Machine," 1503; "One-Step Camera," *Business Week*, March 1, 1947, 40; Lou Rosenblum, telephone interview, November 25, 1998.

21. He sold Lithomat's offset duplication business for $675,000 to the AB Dick Company. "Dick Buys Lithomat," *Business Week*, October 2, 1950, 20; "Duplicator Business Sold," *New York Times*, October 23, 1950, 34.

22. Lou Rosenblum, telephone interview.

23. "Printing Wakes Up to Modern Technology," *Business Week*, October 11, 1958, 94–96. The other fund-raisers on the trail for Garth were *Boston Herald* publisher Robert Choate and Houghton Mifflin president Henry Laughlin. Henry Laughlin to Alfred Knopf, letter, February 23, 1949, Alfred A. Knopf Collection, Harry Ransom Humanities Research Center, University of Texas–Austin, Box 51, Folder 13.

24. "Typewriter with a Memory Sets Type on Photo Filter," *Popular Science*, August 1950, 96. The book, the first set entirely by phototype, was called *The Wonderful World of Insects*. "Typeless Typesetting," *Business Week*, January 17, 1953, 53; "M.I.T. Gets a Book 'Set' by Photo Type," *New York Times*, February 6, 1953, 17; "M.I.T. to Get Book 'Set' without Type," *New York Times*, February 1, 1953, 74. The company's second promotional book was truly artful: the New Testament set "in cadence form." Designed by a conservator of fine prints, "it was by far the best photocomposed book." Lou Rosenblum, interview, November 25, 1998.

25. "M.I.T. to Get Book," *New York Times*, 4.

26. "New Printing Devices," September 16, 1954, 48; "Fantastic Photon," *Newsweek*, September 20, 1954, 60.

27. "Photon, Inc. Predicts Loss From Operations in 1955 But Profit in 1956," *Wall Street Journal*, May 23, 1955, 11; "Photon Sells Common Stock," *Wall Street Journal*, April 27, 1955, 16; "Photon Outlook Brightens," *Wall Street Journal*, January 24, 1957, 19; "Photon Says Its Sales Rate Is at One Machine a Week," *Wall Street Journal*, May 20, 1957, 10.

28. "For Printing: A Step Beyond the Linotype," *Business Week*, May 15, 1954, 66–69.

29. O. L. Crain, "Put Telescope on Distant But Quick-Coming Automation," *Typographical Journal*, December 1958, 203; "ITU Will Fight for Jurisdiction over Improved Printing Processes," *Business Week*, October 6, 1956, 77.

30. Crain, " Telescope," 203.

18

BUCK ROGERS STUFF

But things had changed since then. Sixty years before the ITU had represented virtually all the crafts involved in producing the printed word in the late nineteenth century. By 1912, it still oversaw close to 80 percent of the workers involved in the graphic arts, press operators, engravers, and even some reporters among them. But since then the various specialists had split off into their own bargaining groups and finally their own craft unions. By the mid-1950s pressmen, photoengravers, lithographers, artists, and the other workers belonged to more than a dozen different unions. At the time it decided to stake its claim on phototype, the ITU represented only 32 percent of the industry's workers.[1] And it was not the only union that wanted to run the new phototype machines. None too gently, all began to position themselves to reserve the machines for their own workers even before the technology was proven.

In 1955 Detroit's newspapers, for example, were not close to buying phototype. For one thing, no one knew if it could work at major metropolitan papers. The publishers also had other plans for their investment capital. Like others of the era, they remained wary of risking anything—including a fight with the ITU over a technological changeover—that would interrupt publishing or advertising sales for a prolonged time. When the ITU contract expired and their compositors went on strike in December 1954, the Detroit papers offered to raise compositors' wages by $3.75 a week. But the ITU refused to sign the contract unless the papers also agreed to let its members have the new pasteup and film stripper jobs that would be created if and when they adopted phototype. Before the publishers could respond, two other unions objected that *they* should hold these "unborn jobs." The impasse prolonged the strike an extra three weeks, until the papers promised everyone that, rather than choose a union to run the things, they would simply agree not to buy phototype during the new contract's two-year lifespan.[2]

"One major technological cause of trouble [between unions] has been the rise of phototypesetting," *Fortune* magazine soon reported. Phototype, after all, would "obviate the need for much of the work that followed the casting of the metal slug, for example, locking up the type, pulling reproduction proofs. These jobs were ordinarily done by ITU members, and so the ITU claims jurisdiction over the 'stripping' operation that has replaced them. But lithographers have traditionally done stripping. Stripping, in turn, is [formally] represented by the Photo Engravers."

To the unions, the stakes seemed enormous. Without the new phototype jobs, an ITU vice president warned, "the ITU many of us have known will cease to exist. Our opponents are playing for keeps—and they intend to pick up all of the marbles if they can."[3]

At its 1956 convention, the ITU thus budgeted $5 million to fight other unions over phototype jobs and also allocated money to train Lino operators to work phototype keyboards.[4]

The lithographers union tried to charm master printers into supporting its claim on the then hypothetical jobs. It invited 800 "representatives of management" to join 2,000 of its members at a New York hall for a closed circuit TV demonstration of new printing techniques. The message was that the lithographers—alone among the typographers, pressmen, paper workers, photoengravers, and even steelworkers unions claiming phototype—favored automation and cost-saving machines. "We don't view automation as something labor should fear," the lithographers' president proclaimed. The press loved it. The union's party "broke new ground in American industrial relations," the *New York Times* reported. "Here's a labor union," the *Wall Street Journal* added incredulously, "that pushes for more labor-saving devices." Pressing its advantage, the union went farther the next year, proposing a $2 million joint union–management fund to promote new printing tools. "This," a *Times* editorial cooed two days later, "is the true American economic credo." The day after that, the pacific union created another new fund, this time to fight the ITU and the pressmen's union for the phototype jobs.[5]

A free-for-all erupted. The printing pressmen's union sent an urgent letter to its locals to defend themselves against both the Lithographers and the ITU which, it said, wanted to steal their members. The photoengravers union, with 18,000 members, formally threatened to retaliate if the ITU kept trying to claim its people's jobs.[6]

Amid the posing and saber rattling, a few real jobs appeared. In 1956, the *New York Daily News* became the first newspaper to buy a Linofilm, the

Mergenthaler Company's phototype machine. The next year, the *New York Times* ordered a Photon. Both papers trained ITU members to use the new machines, and both judged the experiments successful. The *Times* bought a second Photon; the *News* bought two more Linofilms. Where the *Times* previously needed both a Linotype operator and a hand compositor to design, set, and arrange one of its ads, now it needed but one "skilled" Photon operator.[7]

The new day, in fact, appeared to be coming at last. "Today," a business journal noted, composing rooms were "a mechanical jungle of clankings, hissings and roars; tomorrow, thanks to all sorts of new photographic and electronic devices, it may be more like a quiet garden than a jungle." Thousands of raucous shops and small papers were ready to go quiet, especially those that had switched from the old letterpress to the increasingly popular offset presses. (In letterpress, letters and images were literally pressed onto a sheet of paper. In offset printing, letters and images were indirectly transferred onto paper over a series of rollers, all arranged on the simple chemical truth that oil, meaning ink, and water don't mix.) By the early 1960s 431 weekly newspapers and 41 small dailies were being produced on the cheaper and easier-to-use offset presses, and they were perfect for cold type.[8]

The publisher of the *Boston Herald-Traveler*—who happened to be a Photon investor—foresaw a different kind of garden. The cost of producing the printed word would fall drastically, he said. Then the number of newspapers in the United States would increase, perhaps not unlike the great viral spreading of the printed word in 1890s or the late fifteenth century.[9]

Still, the revolution dawdled. Phototype just would not take off. In the late 1950s, after years of being on the market, only a smattering of companies had bought it. Mergenthaler had trouble giving systems away. In 1957, it gave them to the *New York Daily News* and a commercial shop. Though the *News* kept its machine, the commercial shop stopped using its gift in 1959, saying "it didn't fit its operation." In 1964 another commercial printer, Metro Typographers, bought a Mergenthaler machine but dropped it after three months. It said its customers didn't like the quality and complained the price of phototype was too high.[10]

One reason was that new technology, as always, was frightening to adopt. After generations of producing hot-metal type, shops would have to master things like producing tape and building darkrooms. Many master printers were uncertain, if not fearful of the other changes a new production process would include. And failing to master such expensive equipment—much less failing to master it profitably—meant bankruptcy for many firms.

Photon's and Mergenthaler's high-speed typesetters often cost more than $60,000, a huge investment for a small newspaper or even a large printing business. Thus, even by 1965, there were probably only eight photo units operating in commercial shops in New York.[11]

The U.S. government could afford just about anything, however.

It had not stopped funding science since Vannevar Bush had made it start in 1939. Although the government's share of electronics purchases fell after the war, it surged again after the Soviet Union reached into space in 1957. By 1960, the American military was responsible for 70 percent of all computer sales in the United States.[12] A little of that computer budget, if not by design, now went toward Bush's "information technology." In the nick of time, a sliver of that portion fell to struggling Photon.

After years of announcing big sales and predicting profits, Photon, its new president confessed, finally had come "painfully near closing its door" in 1961. It had put itself up for sale but could not find a buyer when it heard General Electric was looking for a junior partner on a government project. GE, developing ways to sell its big mainframe computers, had won a contract to produce the National Library of Medicine's massive monthly index of world medical literature. GE's computer (which it rejiggered and renamed GRACE, for graphic arts composing equipment) would process the listings.[13] But it needed a way to make the listings readable. Until then, the best a computer could do was loudly plot out unburst folds of large, unwieldy sheets of paper. The letters and numbers were tough to read and were all in the same mind-numbing size and font. The big sheets typically ended up between two pliable covers, were put on carts and rolled from the computer "clean room" to be analyzed. GE wanted smaller output, perhaps printable as a book and readable by laymen. Photon offered the big electronics company a solution. It would separate its photo unit from the keyboard and adapt the thing into what amounted to a high-speed film printer for GE's computer. GE liked Photon's bid, and after it won the Library of Medicine job, awarded the little company a contract to hook its photo unit onto a mainframe in 1962. For GE, producing the medical index—called the *Index Medicum*—was a nice addition to its revenues. For Photon, it was a lifesaver. More importantly, the unlikely couple's combination of computer and phototype finally lit the fuse on the revolution Vannevar Bush and William Garth had been predicting since 1949.

The two technologies were cousins anyway. Like a computer the Photon was, as one of its executives put it, built to treat typesetting as a communications problem involving the transmission of codes. Until that moment, a

Photon operator created those codes by typing on a keyboard. A card or a perforated tape, now with the code physically punched into it, inched out of side of the keyboard until the story or ad or statistical table was done. Then he or she brought the tape to a companion machine—the photo unit—which read them, magically turned them into pulses of light that shined through film negatives, and translated them into letters on the film that, after considerable banging, came out of the photo unit. But now GE's GRACE, not the Photon operator, punched code into cards and magnetic tapes. The cards and tapes then drove the photo unit. Out came strips of type produced "at a photocomposing speed not hitherto achieved." It spit out up to five justified lines per second, in alphabetical order. It used to take the government twenty-two days to compile and print the *Index Medicum*; now it took only five. (Later it would fall to one day.) The book's size was half that of its old hot-metal version.[14]

"Type for the pages of a telephone book," a trade journal gasped, "can be set in the matter of a minute and a half." Moreover, typists could readily insert, delete, and correct words without recasting a single letter or resizing the stories on a page. Impressed AT&T, then the monopoly telephone company, asked businesses to help it find cheaper ways to produce its phone books. Photon bid on that project too. New York Telephone, among others, soon bought two of its machines.[15]

Photon began to breathe at last. Thanks mostly to the government contract, its backlog of orders grew from zero in August 1961 to $1.1 million in August 1962. It enjoyed its first profitable quarter. By the end of 1962, its sales backlog was $1.75 million. Sales hit $2 million in 1965, and $8.4 million in 1966. It moved to a new building. All the good fortune, its president said, was due to new computer front ends that produced type too fast for any previous technology, especially hot-metal Linotypes, to process.[16]

The Mergenthaler Company, among others, noticed immediately. Celebrating its seventy-fifth anniversary in 1961, it had become something very much like the economy its first machines had helped build: huge, diverse, and a little diffuse. At its anniversary party, executives cited the firm's storied history in printing, the speed of its latest linecasters, and even the aging promise of its seven-year-old Linofilm phototype system. But, with some 5,000 employees around the world, it mostly emphasized how it had changed. Among other things it now manufactured gauges, batteries, and bowling equipment. It sold helicopters and leased equipment. The year before, it had acquired Hiller Aircraft. The next year it would acquire an electrical equipment manufacturer that was three times its size. Its strategy was to build up government sales, which already had grown from about $13,000 in 1957 to $3.8 million. Soon after Photon and GE hooked up with the federal government, Mergenthaler won its own deal to "develop high-quality printing tied in with computer inputs" for the Rome Air Development Center. Partnering with CBS Labs, it aimed to adapt its slow-selling machine into the same kind computer-driven phototypesetter Photon was making. It put it on the market in 1964 and promptly sold $2.185 million worth of the devices—now called the Linotron—to the Government Printing Office. The air force bought another $4 million worth. Like the Photon system, Mergenthaler's type machine took its cues from coded magnetic tape and spit out high-quality film negatives. The system's proud parent claimed it could set a standard book page of type in three seconds.[17]

More companies rushed into the trade. Harris-Intertype—formed when the old Intertype type machine company had been acquired in the mid-1950s—introduced a smaller computer in 1964 that could drive either a hot-metal linecaster or a photo unit, and then a photo unit that could be driven by its computer. American Type Founders brought out a model called the CS, for "computer slave." Still more: IBM, Singer Graphic Systems, Crosfield, Sun Chemical, MGD, and RCA all announced or started making typesetting products immediately after Photon and GE arranged the marriage of phototype and computers in the early 1960s.[18]

"For years," *Business Week* magazine reported, "Photon Inc has knocked on printing house doors and found them closed to its ideas of photographic typesetting." Now, though, "it has a new ally, the computer." Partnering with one from RCA, Photon sold twenty units to Newhouse publishing, which, after testing some at the *Newark Star-Ledger* and the *Portland Oregonian*, planned to create display ads on them. Perry Publications in Florida ordered $800,000 worth of Photons.[19]

Mergenthaler would soon produce a 36,000-page Department of Defense supply catalog in six weeks, churning out 1,000 characters per second. Champion hot-metal linecasters, by contrast, could do 8,000 characters per hour. The company bragged it could set all the type the entire Government Printing Office normally turned out in a year in just three weeks.[20]

"This isn't Buck Rogers stuff any more," a San Francisco printer owner told the *Wall Street Journal*. "It's here." Western Electric, using a Photon, put the 1,800-page Manhattan phone book into type in ten hours. A Pennsylvania book publisher, using a new computer/photo system, found it could reuse type, thus saving it the cost of recasting whole works for later editions of the same book.[21]

"Phototypesetting is often described as the third major development to change the structure of the printing industry," *Business Week* added. The first two, it said, were Johannes Gutenberg's and Ottmar Mergenthaler's.[22]

To the operations director of the *Los Angeles Times*, it was "the fourth fundamental step in the history of written communication, " following the written alphabet, Gutenberg's invention of movable type, and Mergenthaler's typesetting machine.[23]

Joined to a computer, still another reporter wrote, the phototypesetter had become "a seemingly miraculous device."[24]

Always alert to cost-cutting ideas, newspapers began sniffing around it too. The nonunion *Los Angeles Times* installed an RCA computer to drive a new phototype unit, hoping it could live up to its promise to fill a newspaper column in seventeen seconds. The *Oklahoman* of Oklahoma City tested an IBM computer that promised to do general-purpose accounting as well as typesetting.[25]

But, having looked at phototype before, most newspapers did not have the chance to weigh the new advances before a new round of conflict with the ITU erupted. By the time it was over, however, almost everyone had started to believe that this time they truly might be on the cusp of another dramatic drop in the cost of the printed word. And the great unions that had regulated those costs in effect for the prior seventy years would be mortally wounded.

The nation's newspapers never enjoyed much of a peace even after the Taft-Hartley strikes ended. There were forty-three strikes at newspapers belonging to the American Newspaper Publishers Association (ANPA) between 1951 and 1955. It only got worse during the next four years: 122 ANPA strikes broke out. The ITU had been on the sidelines of most of them, as machinists, bookbinders, press operators, and lithographers fought each other to hold onto jobs that new technology made unnecessary and to control jobs that new technology was creating. Press operators, by adding an attachment to their presses, were doing projects that perforators and folders and slitters used to do. Papermakers got machines that made boxes, envelopes, and business forms, things that press operators used to produce. Lithographers made printing plates that photoengravers and stereotypers used to make. All these specialists had their own unions, and with each contract renewal all tried to force their employers to recognize them as the sole representative of the newly ambiguous production processes.

In this minefield employers, once again, were stuck. Recognizing the papermakers union's sway over box-making jobs enraged the press operators. Or the folders. Still hesitant to interrupt operations any longer than necessary over what they considered ugly "jurisdictional" squabbles between workers, many employers settled wage issues as aggressively as they could, and waffled on everything else. As they did with the ITU in Detroit, they often delayed buying the new tools. If nothing else, it let them put off offending one group of workers or another, and keep their doors open. Those who bought new technology found themselves ensnared in awful civil wars. In Portland, Oregon, in 1959, for example, stereotypers (they made copies of type that could be used instead of the more expensive metal type) wanted to run a new plate-casting machine one of the city's papers had just agreed to buy. Photoengravers felt they should run it. One union walked out and other unions chose sides. Some refused to cross a picket line. A few said they would. Amid the shouting, both dailies in the city were idled for seven months.

Everyone in the business knew things could not stay this way much longer. Science and market conditions finally had conspired to produce a potentially wonderful array of fast, efficient new tools. A powerful momentum to buy them was building too. Nonunion competitors were buying them and, with significantly lower costs, were threatening to steal whole print markets from the unionized master printers. But buying the tools meant costly, unwinnable wars with one or more factions in their employees' parliamentary jumble of splinter labor unions. Labor relations in the newspaper industry, in sum, were "deteriorating rapidly."[26] The analyst understated the case. They had already devolved from their usual state of anger and mutual distrust into a World War I–like landscape of land mines and stalemate. Any movement was risky, maybe fatal.

The most powerful printing union, the compositors, was itself in a tense, fragile peace as the 1960s began. GE's and Photon's new marriage of computer and phototype was only then being consummated. At best it could sire only artless directories. At worst, it was just another of the fantastic and ultimately empty promises that companies like Photon had been floating for years. As for the noncomputer phototypesetters, the ITU already had defeated the smaller lithographers union in most cities for the right to run the few photo machines newspapers had ventured to buy. As for the other union wars over folders, cutters, and other machinery, the ITU often stayed above the fray. (Its neutrality earned it still more resentment from the embattled members of less powerful unions and would come back to haunt it a decade later.) So, as they prepared to bang out new contracts in Cleveland and New York in 1962, the typographers and publishers barely mentioned phototype. They did, however, have other issues.

Newspaper publishers, on one side of the bargaining table, were again in decent economic shape. Despite the wild bloom of network television, the rising popularity of music radio, the labor civil wars and their own escalating costs, newspapers in general had made "remarkable gains" during the postwar era. Ad lineage had more than doubled since 1945, and ad revenues had quadrupled.[27]

On its side, the ITU also had regained its strength. Membership nationwide had reached 92,000, and its members' average wages had increased by 230 percent since 1945, to $4,743 per year. Despite the threatening new tools and daunting new costs (it ran its own consistently unprofitable chain of newspapers), it once again managed to preserve jobs around the nation. In New York, newspaper employment from 1958 through 1962 had boomed. The composing room staff at the rapidly automating *New York Times* rose 21 percent, from 646 to 786 people. At the less prosperous *Daily News*, which was also automating, composing room jobs had increased 13 percent, from 627 to 708. The other five papers in the city had minor increases or decreases of five to ten type jobs each.[28]

The important new tools on the table in 1962, most publishers believed, were teletypesetting and Mergenthaler's eye-popping new hot-metal machine, the Linotype Comet. With teletype, or TTS, an operator fed a coded, perforated tape into a hot-metal linecaster, and the tape—not someone on the keyboard—drove the linecaster's pulleys and levers and circuits. The Comet, which was run by perforated tape, was particularly fast. One person tending three Comets, it was said, could produce as much metal as "seven or eight linotypists." While only three of New York's seven dailies had even one phototype machine, all hungered for teletype and the Comet. With it, they could get perforated tape directly from wire services and outside advertisers, saving hours and probably millions in labor costs otherwise spent tapping stories on a keyboard.[29]

To use it, however, they would have to overcome the ITU's hallowed work rules about "bogus," which prohibited using outside type or outside tape in union shops.[30]

In New York the ITU local union—officially Local No. 6 but almost always called Big Six—had yet another issue as the climactic hour approached. Its new leader, a tall, confrontational strategic thinker named Bertram Powers, was particularly galled by the contracts his predecessors had signed. Since the 1930s, publishers in the city had negotiated with their smaller, weaker unions first. They talked to the ITU only after they had signed agreements with the reporters, press operators, and other craft unions. As a result, even if the ITU struck, their other unions—now legally bound to stay on the job—probably would have to help them continue to put their papers out. Powers fumed. Without his most potent bargaining tool, the threat of a general strike that would shut the papers down, he had won only minor wage increases for his members in his first Big Six contract. In his lone victory, the papers agreed to train ITU compositors on new typesetting equipment as they bought it. For this next contract, Powers aimed for bigger hikes and to become the first, not the last, union to negotiate with the publishers.[31]

Stuck mostly on wage and expiration date issues, Powers thus called his members out on strike on December 8, 1962, without bothering to warn the other printing unions. The publishers, in part to get the other unions to help pressure Powers into giving up, closed down and forced everyone to go without a paycheck for the time being.

NOTES

1. Elizabeth Faulkner Baker, *Printers and Technology: A History of the International Printing Pressmen and Assistants Union* (Westport, Conn.: Greenwood, 1974), 464; Michael Wallace, "Technological Changes in Printing: Union Response in Three Countries," *Monthly Labor Review*, July 1985, 41–43.

2. "Jurisdiction over Unborn Jobs Drags Out Routine Bargaining," *Business Week*, January 28, 1956, 152.

3. "Printing War," *Fortune*, October 1957, 242.

4. "ITU Will Fight for Jurisdiction over Improved Printing Processes," *Business Week*, October 6, 1956, 77.

5. "Labor Boosts Automation," *New York Times*, December 7, 1956, 26; Mitchell Gordon, "Here's a Labor Union That Pushes for More Labor-Saving Devices," *Wall Street Journal*, December 3, 1956, 1. In an eerie echo of the language the ITU had used in the 1890s to urge its members to accept hot metal type, Amalgamated Lithographers Union President Edward Swayduck told his own members that automation meant "lower costs to buyers . . . open vast new markets for lithography, which will insure fair profits to employers and full employment to workers." "Lithographers Get Bid on Automation," *New York Times*, September 24, 1957, 23; "Union Leader Urges Spur to Automation," *New York Times*, September 22, 1957, 1. It eventually applied to join "four employers associations" to promote printing technology. Two years later, the union created a director of technology to "work with manufacturers to find out about new processes and machinery coming out." "New Post

Created by Lithographers," *New York Times*, February 23, 1958, 1; "Lithographers Get Bid on Automation," *New York Times*, September 24, 1957, 23; "Lithographers Plan Organizing Drive Whether AFL-CIO Approves or Not," *New York Times*, September 27, 1957, 20.

6. "Printing War," *Fortune*, 242.

7. Harry Kelber and Carl Schlesinger, *Union Printers and Controlled Automation* (New York: Free Press, 1967), 73–80.

8. "Printing Wakes Up to Modern Technology," *Business Week*, October 11, 1958, 94; George Corben Goble, *The Obituary of a Machine: The Rise and Fall of Ottmar Mergenthaler's Linotype at U.S. Newspapers* (Bloomington: Indiana University Mass Communications Program, 1984), 371.

9. "Another Industry Where Big Changes Lie Ahead," *U.S. News & World Report*, June 13, 1958, 90.

10. The commercial shop that jettisoned its free Mergenthaler Linofilm was called Howard O. Bullard. Kelber & Schlesinger, *Union Printers*, 200.

11. Kelber & Schlesinger, *Union Printers*, 196. At the time, the Photon 200 cost $66,505, Fotosetters $29,000, and the AFT Typesetter $20,000. Lawrence W. Wallis, *Electronic Typesetting: A Quarter Century of Upheaval* (Gatehead, U.K.: Paradigm, 1984), 51.

12. The federal government's share of electronics purchases in the United States had fallen to 25 percent in 1953. Ronald J. Deibert, *Parchment, Printing, and Hypermedia: Communication in World Order Transformation* (New York: Columbia University Press, 1997), 120–21.

13. "MEDLARS System Is Subject of Briefing," *Publishers Weekly*, January 4, 1964, 105.

14. "Bookbuilders Review Use of Photon, Other Devices," *Publishers Weekly*, January 2, 1961, 76. The project formally was managed by the MEDLARS system of the National Library of Medicine. "Photon Makes Fast Printer for Medical Data System," *Publishers Weekly*, October 1, 1962, 98.

15. "MEDLARS," 105; "Photon Earned $15,000 in Period; 1st Profitable Quarter Ever for Firm," *Wall Street Journal*, April 16, 1962, 5; "Photon Says Sales, Net Set Records in 1966," *Wall Street Journal*, February 21, 1967, 12.

16. "Abreast of the Market," *Wall Street Journal*, August 9, 1962, 21; "Photon Sees Record Sales and Earnings This Year," *Wall Street Journal*, October 9, 1962, 17; "Photon Says Sales, Net Set Records in 1966," *Wall Street Journal*, February 21, 1967, 12. Photon called its new machine the ZIP and priced it at $75,000. "Photon Sees Record Sales and Earnings This Year," *Wall Street Journal*, October 9, 1962, 17.

17. "New Products Emphasized in Mergenthaler Anniversary," *Publishers Weekly*, July 10, 1961, 76–79; "Mergenthaler Plans to Make Devices to Set Bowling Pins," *Wall Street Journal*, May 23, 1961, 9; "Mergenthaler Aims at More Military Sales," *Aviation Week*, April 9, 1962, 118; Goble, *Obituary*, 355; "New Lino Contract with GPO: Ultra-fast Phototypesetters," *Publishers Weekly*, June 1, 1964, 92–95; "Mergenthaler Typesetting Systems Sold to Government," *Wall Street Journal*, April 2, 1964,

5; "GE Awarded Contract of $24,410,000 by Army. Eltra Unit Wins Order," *Wall Street Journal*, November 9, 1964, 30.

18. "Debut in the Composing Room," *Business Week,* April 25, 1964, 133; "ATF Announces High-Speed 'Computer-Slave' Phototypesetter," *Publishers Weekly*, June 1, 1964, 86; "ATF's New Desk-top Photo Headline Units," *Publishers Weekly*, September 7, 1964, 87–89; Wallis, *Electronic Typesetting*, 36.

19. "Phototypesetting Picks Up the Pace," *Business Week*, December 14, 1963, 156–58; "Photon Gets $1,250,000 Order From Newhouse," *Wall Street Journal*, October 3, 1963, 12.

20. "Business Bulletin," *Wall Street Journal*, November 16, 1967, 1.

21. William E. Blundell, "Research Push Brings Speedier Typesetting, Other Major Advances," *Wall Street Journal*, December 10, 1964, 1.

22. "Phototypesetting," *Business Week*, 156–58.

23. Kelber and Schlesinger, *Union Printers*, 169.

24. "CBS Labs Demonstrate Composition via Computer," *Publishers Weekly,* January 1, 1962, 86.

25. Blundell, "Research," 1; Kelber and Schlesinger, *Union Printers*, 108–11.

26. "Pressures in the Print Shop," *Fortune,* July 1960, 214. Newhouse, owner of the *Oregonian*, tempted fate again by being one of the few papers to buy a Photon.

27. Goble, *Obituary*, 370.

28. Goble, *Obituary*, 368; Kelber and Schlesinger, *Union Printers*, 102–5.

29. Kelber and Schlesinger, *Union Printers*, 99.

30. Richard Kluger, *The Paper: The Life and Death of the New York Herald Tribune* (New York: Knopf, 1986), 672.

31. Kelber and Schlesinger, *Union Printers*, 85, 87.

19

LIKE A BURLESQUE BLONDE

A nd now the dispute, as labor disputes seemed to do, escalated insanely. This time is was because it unfolded in the nation's media center. This first New York newspaper strike since 1883 assumed immediate national political importance. It was not just New York's news blackout, it was the nation's. Great principles of progress, not just wage and workweek issues, appeared to be at stake. Alarmed, the president of the United States sent his labor secretary to hold hearings. (Powers boycotted the hearings; the labor panel report, without ITU input, ultimately blamed the ITU for the shutdown.) Even the usually pro-labor *New Republic* blamed the ITU for the news blackout, sarcastically calling it an example of the "pride that remains in the American labor movement" and asking "is there anywhere a God who will deliver us from its results?" It called the compositors Luddites.[1]

To many, automation had become the fulcrum of the dispute. The publishers would give the ITU wage hikes but in return wanted to use outside tape on the sleek new Mergenthaler linecaster machines to set time-consuming baseball box scores and stock market tables. The *Herald Tribune*, Whitelaw Reid's old paper, spent thirty-four man-hours setting the stock tables on its aging Lino keyboards each night. The *Wall Street Journal*, using outside teletype tapes, spent only three.[2]

But the publishers' portrayal of the strike as a struggle between the forces of the past (the compositors) and the forces of progress (themselves) was not accurate. Taking a page from its old nineteenth-century strategy, the ITU had in fact embraced automation. It had already invested heavily in retraining its people. The Cincinnati local, for example, spent $20,000 training 280 members on phototype from 1957 through 1961, when the first phototype device was installed in town. The Minneapolis local started its training program in 1957. The Austin (Texas) local sent two members to be trained in Indianapolis in 1956, and then bought its own equipment to train on in 1957. (Before that it had, like all the union's locals, embraced teletype-setting.) And in 1956, the international union invested $80,000 to build a modern training center in Colorado Springs. By the year of the showdown in New York, it had ramped up its annual support of the training center to $607,000. Its officials were repeating, almost word for word, the ITU technology mantra since 1888. "The advent of new technology," an ITU official in Colorado Springs predicted in 1958, "is going to create hundreds of new job opportunities that do not now exist. Instead of throwing up our hands in horror, our members equip themselves to handle the new technology."[3]

New York members, another union official pointed out, were actively supporting the *Daily News*'s automated presses, supplying outside tape to the *Times*'s West Coast and Paris editions, and training on the *Times*'s new phototype machines. Their highest priority, he argued, was keeping their jobs, not stopping their employers from using efficient new tools.[4] Powers, thinking along the same lines, said he aimed not to ban the new machines but to make sure his members got to run them.

Hardly Luddite, the ITU was no longer unalterably opposed to running "bogus" tape through the fast new machines. Compositors had been trading away bogus work rules for other benefits—usually a pension plan of some kind—around the country for at least ten years. Only 2–5 percent of ITU locals still had contracts that banned all outside type, according to one estimate. The union's new national president favored doing away with bogus altogether. ("No man likes to do useless work," he pointed out.) In 1958, Big Six leaders had offered to compromise on bogus, although the members voted down the idea.[5]

To give up bogus this time, Powers wanted something big in return: the papers would have to use whatever money they saved in running the new machines and using outside type to retrain his members and pay for the retirement of those who lost their jobs. "We are concerned that the members presently employed not be thrown on the slag pile," he explained. "We think that these two points should be covered at least: one, job security for present employees; and, two, an opportunity to share in the increased productivity."[6]

There the dispute sank into stalemate. Powers's price was too high. One publisher estimated that "featherbedding" (bogus sometimes was also called "dead horse") cost New York papers $1.5 million a year in unnecessary typesetting expenses.[7] Now Powers, in essence, was asking them to pay that much for his compositors *not* to retype outside materials. By agreeing, the publishers not only would have to buy expensive new equipment but also forgo any savings the equipment might afford.

Worse yet, Big Six and the New York publishers were no longer always talking about the same tools. While the publishers focused on teletype and the ever faster new hot-metal machines, the ITU had started to look westward, toward the places where the new computer/phototype marriage was starting to work. "The *Los Angeles Times*," a union official noted ominously as the New York strike stretched into its second month, "has just finished a month-long test of a system in which a reporter him or herself produces a tape from his typewriter, by-passing not only the printer, but the men with the copy pencils and at the typewriters." He also cited a new IBM product that supposedly could convert stock ticker tape into TTS tape in seven minutes, "eliminating at one blow all typesetters and teletypesetters now working at setting these tables."[8]

Even "girl typists" would be obsolete in such a world. In Los Angeles, *Time* wrote, "*Times* reporters write stories on electric typewriters that simultaneously produce sheets and tapes." It amounted not just to what Photon once promoted as "typeless type," but to what the magazine now called "typesetterless typesetting."[9]

"This," the ITU official added with a note of desperation, "is what automation means, and printers would rightly vote down any contract that agreed to their displacement without some compensatory process."[10] Something had to be done to help them move on.

The impasse took 114 days to resolve. In that span, the papers lost a cumulative $100 million in revenues, and the union spent millions in strike benefits. In the end, ITU members got a raise of $12.63 in weekly wages and benefits. (The publishers' initial offer was $10.20 a week. The union's was $18.) Their work week was reduced to thirty-five hours, and they got the publishers to agree to let the new contract expire at the same time as the other newspaper union contracts. In return, they got to establish a retraining and retirement fund with a share, although not all, of the savings the publishers would realize from using outside tape and installing new composing equipment.[11]

Something bigger and something palpable, however, had changed. Its attention drawn to the seemingly intractable ITU in the nation's media center, the American printed word industry now stopped waffling, almost in unison, about adopting new tools. But what they added was not the teletype and Lino Comets that had stopped the news in New York. Often without consulting its unions, the master printers instead began buying computers to do accounting and, as an attachment, phototypesetters to produce some of their type.

Days after the New York settlement, for example, the *Oklahoma City Times* inaugurated a new computer/phototype system much like the *Los Angeles Times* had tested. Once plugged in, it set its twenty-two-page edition in ten man-hours, six fewer than normal. Other papers made inquiries.

Four months after the settlement, Photon's president reported that the newspaper strikes in New York and Cleveland had stimulated a "tremendous" number of print owners to price out its equipment.[12]

Seven months after the cease-fire in New York, the *South Bend (Ind.) Tribune* installed an IBM 1620 to do typesetting and accounting. It could also print letters to delinquent advertisers and store biographies so the paper could produce quick obituaries. The keyboards sometimes weren't even near compositors. They were instead on the desks of collections and clerical and even editorial people, who typed out their own work on floors far from the ITU or its composing room fiefdom. With type originating in accounting and the newsroom, the *Tribune* took a hard line in its talks with the abruptly less consequential ITU in the composing room. It agreed to keep the Lino operators currently on the payroll, but as they retired, it would replace them with low-paid typists.

The next month, seventy compositors, concerned they would soon suffer the same fate, struck the dailies in West Palm Beach and Pensacola, Florida. They failed to win any rights to run the papers' new computer/phototype systems.

In July 1964, Canadian members walked out when the Toronto *Globe and Mail, Daily Star,* and *Telegram* installed computers without prior ITU agreement. With reporters manning the new computers, the papers not only kept publishing for more than a year but did it more cheaply. The *Telegram* figured it was saving $10,000 a week in composing costs.

And so it went. Two Baltimore papers soon announced they would install similar devices. Much as the *Chicago Inter-Ocean* in 1887 had asked an arbitrator to decide if its new union hand composition contract covered typesetting machines, the Baltimore papers asked an arbitrator to decide if their ITU contract covering hot-metal machines also applied to computers. A few months later, the *New York Post* announced that it too would install computers. In Chicago, the *Sun-Times* and *Daily News* unveiled "long-range plans that include a city desk where the editor can dummy his paper on TV-like screens."

In all, more than one newspaper a month took action. By the end of 1964, twenty-one months after the strike in New York ended, twenty-four dailies either were using or were planning to use computers and phototype for typesetting.[13] Reporters, who belonged to a different union, and white-collar clerks, who often belonged to no union, would operate them.

"It was becoming evident," said two contemporary scholars, "that the computer, with all its other capabilities, offered publishers an opportunity to harden their resistance toward the ITU and, if necessary, produce their newspapers without union printers."[14] They now had computer-fed cameras to do their accounting, dun their clients, do a little library storage work, and, by the way, set their type.

Other printers began buying phototype as quickly as newspaper publishers. The ITU, fed up, went on strike in San Francisco when fourteen commercial printing businesses, all of them unionized, bought or announced they would soon buy phototype equipment. The compositors wanted both wage hikes and the exclusive right to run the phototypesetters. Their bosses, however, managed to stay open without them, operating with strikebreakers for eleven long months into 1964. (They ultimately agreed to raise wages and give the union jurisdiction over phototype in the future.) In Massachusetts, the commercial Colonial Press installed a system in December, 1963. Among book publishers, Little, Brown produced its first computer-typed book in 1964. In England, Pitman Press boasted that its experimental computer center fifty miles south of London let it send coded magnetic tape to whatever printer happened to be cheapest. In New York, the Ad Press, installed Mergenthaler's new Linasec system and became so profitable that it bought other commercial shops in Cleveland, Philadelphia, and Chicago. Pressing his advantage, the firm's president soon switched to yet another computer system that he did not have to staff with ITU members. He thus liberated himself of the need to pay the ITU any savings he realized from "typeless type" and cut his composing room staff by another five people to boot.[15]

For print owners like him it seemed that, after 120 years, nothing less than the ultimate girl typist fantasy was coming true. The computer typesetter, one publisher exulted at the otherwise staid American Institute of Graphic Arts meeting in October, 1964, "is something like a Minsky blonde—it's big, it's stupid and, my God, it's fast!"[16]

To hear Gary Krohm tell it, nobody knew exactly how to behave around this new office bombshell.

In 1966, Krohm was a young dropout from the University of Missouri–Kansas City, and got to meet the sexy new machine essentially under false pretenses. "It was all by accident," he recalls. "I was at the university the first year that they tried to teach computer programming. UMKC had engineers come in, and they could program, but they couldn't teach it. I flunked out and had to get a job. I think because they saw I had taken a computer course, the *Kansas City Star* hired me" to help it try to run its big new computer. "I was just nineteen. They (management) didn't really know what to do with it, and I really didn't know what to do with it."[17]

The *Star*'s ignorance was not unusual. The New York *Daily News* installed an IBM 1620 in 1964, but, leery of further inflaming the just-pacified ITU, never got around to using it to set type. It brought in a still more sophisticated machine eight months later but could not figure out how to use that one, either. The *Times*'s IBM system sat unused too, seemingly because of a lack of understanding of what to do with it.[18]

At the *Star*, Krohm "was cheap labor to operate the machine. I was happy because I could push the big buttons. We'd sit around for hours watching the lights."

At first, "when the accounting was done, there wasn't anything for me to do but just sit there." He did it three days and two nights a week, fiddling and watching after his work was done.

The thing "was essentially brought in as an accounting machine. But when the accounting was done, we had a special switch on the machine that IBM put on there that allowed the typesetting to start." A light went on in the newsroom below, and someone would start using it to create tape coded to produce letters.

He'd seen people like Lou Felicio at work around the office. When one of the Linos in the composing room jammed up, "you had to turn on a light and an engineer would come over and go behind it and hit it with a hammer." When the strange new computer system needed to be fixed, however, the untrained Krohm was what passed for the staff expert. "If it locked up, which it did a lot, I'd essentially reboot it and tell the people downstairs they could start typing again. But after a few weeks of just sitting there, well, I'd do small programs at first . . . And pretty soon, you figure out how to make it work. It was just sort of self-taught."

He liked programming. "I tried to get myself promoted from operator to full-time programmer, but I didn't have a college degree. I got a little upset when they hired a college grad on top of me. The [data processing] manager promised to hire me the next time they needed someone, and then he probably forgot all about it. Right away, he sent the new guy out of town for three weeks to take a programming course, and while he was gone I saw a job at an investment firm [that fit] the other guy's qualifications, at quite a bit more money. When he came back, I told him about it, and he took the job, and I got promoted."

His supposedly hapless stumbling in reality was far from being hapless stumbling. During the next thirty years the self-effacing Krohn became a highly regarded pioneer in making phototype and then desktop publishing work in the real world, installing systems at scores of newspapers and graphic arts firms around the country and, without much exaggeration, bringing the printed word into new technical realms. Immediately after his supposed promotion by default at the *Star*, for example, he had resumed coming up with new ways to use the system. To his surprise, he soon discovered that he and a coworker at the paper were "the only ones in Kansas City who knew typesetting programming." He began fielding calls from other companies who either were interested in moving out of hot-metal type or needed to find ways to make their expensive new computers work. Krohn and his buddy at the *Star* thus found themselves moonlighting, putting together computer-fed photo systems for other companies in their off hours, often flying by the seat of their pants.

Sometimes he'd train people on the systems he and his colleague helped rig. His nonunion customers "were bringing in typists" to run them. "They figured, 'Hey, these people can type, we'll let them type.'" An experienced typographer would figure out type sizes, calculate the spacing and layout, mark up someone's typed-out ad or story with the correct codes to use, and hand it to the nonunion typist to tap the codes into the computer.

Training ITU compositors on the things, however, was different. For them, running phototype "was a step down in morale."

One grizzled veteran called it being "robotized." Others called it becoming button pushers. All that was required, an ITU officer reported, was "a push of a button to produce the page on paper, on film, or on a plate ready for the press." The new devices "do all the typesetting tricks that were possible on Linotype and with hand type before that, but add the flexibility of phototype. A line won't fit? Reset, take out a unit or two from between letters—like setting rubber type."[19]

The thrill was gone. "All the messy, awkward work that used to raise blood pressures in sweltering Linotype rooms is reduced to button pushing: Type faces can be changed, paragraphs switched around, sentences inserted and removed," one magazine marveled.[20]

The changes not only began robbing the nation's compositors of power, they also began nudging them toward a collective funk. They all still had their jobs; nationally, the union's membership continued to grow for seven years after Krohn joined the *Star*. But their professional status was being compromised. Hot-metal machines lost status. Intertype had stopped making them, and Mergenthaler was pumping its money and marketing into promoting its own computing type devices. (It would soon shut down its historic U.S. linecasting factory.) "Psychologically," noted two historians who studied the phenomenon as it unfolded, the hot-metal compositors "felt more comfortable in front of a Linotype machine, where there was more physical movement, and where they could produce hot-metal type, a tangible symbol of their traditional craftsmanship."[21]

There was nothing tangible about the flat, one-dimensional letters that appeared on the slick photo paper that spooled out of the back end of these new systems. They were not even type. Real type—the Chinese and Korean hard block letters, Gutenberg's thin metal letters, and Mergenthaler's leaden slugs of letters—pressed or crashed onto paper to leave imprinted words. It made noise. It smelled. It could be felt. Now compositors created things they could not recognize that literally left no impression. "Letters of the alphabet and all the rest of the symbols of the printed page," as another scholar put it, had become mere "congeries of electronic impulses, bits lacking spatial or material existence."[22] Engineers like Lou Rosenblum and programmers like Gary Krohm already had done the complex math, figured the friction coefficients, fit them into acceptable tolerances, and translated the analog thought into calculations that produced the flat letters and shapes. All that was left for the compositor was to cue the mathematical dominoes experts had hard-wired into the machines, and, all things being equal, the gears and lights would tip in the correct order. When they were done, the pre-drawn pattern of letters would appear.

Compositors no longer needed professional judgment. "Regardless of where the camera is pointed," one observer explained, "the photograph at the instant of its conception is a product of a standardized, non-living, technological piece of equipment." For the compositor, there was no push, tweak, or balancing of heat and content required. There was no need to apply experience or feel when design, time, grammar, and commerce were in conflict. There was not even a piece of type that could be felt or fitted. "Given the same lighting conditions, a given camera can be counted upon to take exactly the same picture of the same object over and over again."[23] In this case, distant engineers and programmers had already fixed the lighting, calibrated the gears, organized the invisible electronic impulses, and made the optical judgments compositors used to make. Even if the Lino operators knew how to do it, fiddling with wiring and gerry-rigging the engineers' judgments to make a big story fit into a small space would be ill-advised.

These were the people, moreover, who had controlled the production and most of the economics of their workplace for hundreds of years. Now they had lost crucial parts of their control to the reporter who typed a story on one end and to the remote engineer, speaking an alien binary language, on the other. In the space of a few months their jobs had come to consist of safely ferrying the work of reporters to be produced by machines that did the work of scientists.

To more than a few of them, it "seemed too much like the work of an office typist." Hot-metal printers in Toledo complained the perforated tape made them feel like they were "cutting paper dolls." Cold type was best suited, as one business magazine later observed admiringly in an East Coast newsroom, to "stylish clerical workers drinking from Styrofoam coffee cups instead of beer cans."[24] The union printers may have been more than capable of doing the less challenging and less important work, but for many it was turning out to be a devastating, unacceptable loss of professional status.

"Here you are operating a big dangerous $10,000 machine, squirting molten lead and telling war stories," Krohm recalled of the compositors who soon began leaving the *Star* one by one. "It took skill. Real skill. Then you've got them punching paper tape. They felt they'd been, I don't know, feminized somewhat."

NOTES

1. "Fixing the Blame," *Time*, January 18, 1963, 68; Murray Kempton, "Return of the Luddites," *New Republic*, December 22, 1962, 6–7.

2. Richard Kluger, *The Paper: The Life and Death of the New York Herald Tribune* (New York: Knopf, 1986), 649.

3. Cincinnati Typographical Union no. 3, *125th Anniversary Commemorating the Founding of Cincinnati Typographical Union no. 3*, International Typographical Union, Special Collections, Norlin Library, University of Colorado–Boulder, First Accession, Box 7; Minneapolis Typographic Union no. 42, *A Century of Service: Minneapolis Typographic Union no. 42, 1873–1973*, Typographical Union, Special Collections, Norlin Library, University of Colorado–Boulder, First Accession, Box 7, 46; Gilmer T. Woods, ed., *100th Anniversary Celebration Souvenir Book*, Austin Typographical Union no. 138, International Typographical Union, Special Collections, Norlin Library, University of Colorado–Boulder, Second Accession, Box 7, 37; International Typographical Union, *Report of the Secretary-Treasurer, 1971–1980*, International Typographical Union, Special Collections, Norlin Library, University of Colorado–Boulder, Second Accession, Box 33, 49; "Printers Prepare for Change," *Business Week*, August 31, 1963, 68–70.

4. Samuel Coleman, letter to the editor, *New Republic*, January 19, 1963, 31.

5. Paul Jacobs, "Dead Horse and the Featherbed," *Harper's*, September 1962, 47–54; "Francis Barrett: His Problem Was 'Bogus,'" *Fortune*, August 1959, 177.

6. Harry Kelber and Carl Schlesinger, *Union Printers and Controlled Automation* (New York: Free Press, 1967), 121; "Signs of the Future?" *Newsweek*, November 9, 1964, 88.

7. Joseph Kingsbury Smith, publisher of the *Journal-American*, made the $1.5 million estimate. Kelber and Schlesinger, *Union Printers*, 258; "Deadlock," *Time*, December 21, 1962, 41–42.

8. Coleman, letter to editor, 31.

9. "Printing a Dream," *Time*, January 18, 1963, 69.

10. Coleman, letter to editor, 31.

11. Kluger, *The Paper*, 648; Kempton, "Return," 7; "After a Three-Month Shutdown, What Striking Printers Got," *U.S. News & World Report*, March 18, 1963, 98.

12. "Photon Sees Record Sales, Its First Profit This Year," *Wall Street Journal*, July 12, 1963.

13. Kelber and Schlesinger, *Union Printers*, 172, 176, 169. "Printers Invited Back in Toronto," *Wall Street Journal*, August 7, 1964, 8; "Signs of the Future?" *Newsweek*, November 9, 1964, 88.

14. Kelber and Schlesinger, *Union Printers*, 176.

15. "ITU Members to Vote on San Francisco Pact," *Wall Street Journal*, August 3, 1964, 4; "ITU Ends Long Strike in San Francisco Against 14 Print Shops," *Wall Street Journal*, August 7, 1964, 8; San Francisco Typographical Union no. 21, news release, August 6, 1964, International Typographical Union, Special Collections, Norlin Library, University of Colorado–Boulder, Second Accession, Box 55; "Clinic Speakers Examine Computer Composition," *Publishers Weekly*, November 9, 1964, 112–13; Kelber and Schlesinger, *Union Printers*, 207.

16. The publisher was Andrew Stewart of Denhard & Stewart Publishers. "Clinic Speakers," 113.

17. Gary Krohm, telephone interview, October 15, 1998.

18. Kelber and Schlesinger, *Union Printers*, 168–69.

19. Harry Lesser, "Vox Pop: Letter to the Editor," *Typographical Journal*, May 1974, 183; A. Sandy Bevis, "Annual Report to the Membership," *Typographical Journal*, July 1975, 39.

20. "Market-wise: Compugraphic Corp.'s Formula: Thinking Small When Others Think Big," *Forbes*, March 1, 1977, 59.

21. Kelber and Schlesinger, *Union Printers*, 90.

22. Walker Rumble, *The Swifts: Printers in the Age of Typesetting Races* (Charlottesville: University of Virginia Press, 2003), xvii.

23. Paul Levinson, *The Soft Edge: A Natural History and Future of the Information Revolution* (London: Routledge, 1997), 40.

24. Kelber and Schlesinger, *Union Printers*, 90; Ward Harkavy, "The Castle on the Hill," *Westword*, May 11, 1994, www.westword.com/issues/1994-05-11/feature2 .html (accessed September 17, 2004); "Market-wise," 59.

20

SPEEDUPS AND SLOWDOWNS

Just about everyone agreed the bulky new machine systems did inferior work, at least at first. The *San Francisco Chronicle*, for instance, "has looked worse ever since we got" an IBM 1620/phototype system, executive editor Scott Newhall complained. Somehow the system kept turning "hangover" into "han-gover" and "Goodyear" into "Goo-dyear." Circuits, relays, and valves were notoriously erratic. One religious book publisher found its new $500,000 system could not meet its "esthetic" needs or, in the problem Lou Rosenblum once pondered at an MIT alum party in the early 1950s, typeset Hebrew characters. "The electronics of the day," as one industry observer put it, "proved to be generally capricious."[1]

But things improved quickly. Gary Krohm kept seeing "mind-boggling" technical changes and, with the profits from their moonlighting in hand, he and his partner decamped for New Jersey. At a firm called Typetron, they began outfitting newspapers and printing plants all around the United States with phototype systems, fed either by big mainframes built in dedicated "clean rooms" or, increasingly, by specialized new "minicomputers."

Their efforts, he allows modestly, were thought to be "pretty innovative." Engineers from Mergenthaler Linotype and Photon, among others, came to New Jersey to see what they were doing. So too did William Garth, the MIT businessman who had cofounded Photon.

Photon's stockholders, weary of Garth's big promises and disappointing sales, had pushed him out in 1959. By then, however, he had decided to try an old idea out again. He would bring phototype to the masses.

Or at least to small newspapers, print shops, and ad agencies. When he started his phototype career with Vannevar Bush, Rene Higonnet, and Louis

Moyroud in the 1940s, he had hoped to sell his machine for an inexpensive $5,000. He had seen how his ex-college mates, then at Polaroid, had made photography simpler and moved it into more hands. They had profited handsomely. Garth hoped to do the same thing with the printed word, but his Photons, years in development, kept getting more expensive. By the time he left the company, low-end Photon models were complex machines selling for $65,000 (equivalent to $219,000 in 2000). Their few customers were large companies.

In 1960, he recruited some Photon colleagues (at least two, Ellis Hansen and Carl Dantas, subsequently joined him; another, Lou Rosenblum, was about to become a father again and opted for a more secure job) to form a printing consulting company and raise money to fulfill his new vision. His venture, which he called Compugraphic, would make low-cost, hybrid computer/phototype machines for small businesses. The old Photons, Dantas later said, "were too expensive and sophisticated for any newspapers other than the country's top 200 or so dailies." There were only 1,700 dailies in the country at the time, but 7,500 weeklies and 35,000 commercial print shops. The entrepreneurs estimated there were a good 40,000 "in-plant" producers of the printed word—businesses, schools, government offices—out there as well. A lot of them, Garth guessed, could afford an $8,000 to $10,000 bare-bones machine. If they couldn't, Garth would lease the devices to them.[2]

Garth got it right this time. He and Hansen floated the company first by selling some technology (a tape feeder) to Mergenthaler, which used it in its own "Linasec" machines for a while. In the meantime, they designed and began to build their own limited-use machines. They would be hardwired to set type, period. There'd be no accounting or storing of text for obituaries. "Frills and fussiness were excised from the machines by sober production planning and by rigorous value engineering," one critic approvingly noted. When he was ready to unveil the machine, Garth exercised Compugraphic's option to buy its feeder back from Mergenthaler. The timing could not have been worse for the older, bigger company; its Linasec was finally about to become profitable. Mergenthaler, Lou Rosenblum recalls, "had its nose out of joint."[3]

But Garth needed the feeder for his own machine, which he introduced with characteristic fanfare at a trade show in Chicago in 1968. "I remember it," one executive stated thirty years later. "You walked through this big convention hall, with row after row of exhibitors, and then there was this big crowd of people jostling and trying to get into the Compugraphic booth."

The appeal was down-market. Alan Haley, who would soon go to work at Compugraphic, recalls that "at all the other booths, people were wearing tuxedos and top hats, but Bill's booth looked like a used car lot . . . People would say to him, 'You can afford a better booth, you know.' And he would say, 'yeah, but my customers don't understand that.' He had a wonderful feel for his market."[4]

It was memorable. As one unnamed executive told the *Wall Street Journal*, "Usually printers come to machinery shows just to look around and then go home to think about it a few months before buying. But at this show we've been writing orders right and left." Phototypesetters in general were a big hit. (They accounted for only 10 percent of all the composition produced in the United States, although their sales were growing by 20 percent a year). Harris-Intertype had a system there for $300,000. Mergenthaler's low-end Linotron was available at $60,000. (Its fastest hot-metal linecaster was priced at $40,000.) Photon introduced a low-end device that fed tape into a linecaster for $55,000. RCA's VideoComp system cost $1 million. In 1967, Mergenthalter had sold four of its high-end Linotrons to the government for more than $1 million each.[5] But Compugraphic's system cost $8,000.

Garth "wrote a million dollars worth of business at that show," Rosenblum adds. "And that was it. From 1968 to 1975, Garth ran the show, and pretty much the whole industry."

His appeals, if not his invention, were traditional. "Typesetting was a male-dominated industry," one of his managers pointed out years later, and the idea was that expensive men could be replaced. "We were trying to get into in-plant (print shops), and we advertised that 'Your secretary can become a typesetter.' Well, the type union didn't like that, and sued, and we had to retract the ad."[6]

Garth's keyboard was in fact beyond the ken of an ordinary office typist, but it was far easier to understand than the other computer input devices of the day. Yet much was going on under its lightweight metallic skin: impulses from the keyboard traveled through sophisticated circuits to shoot stroboscopic beams of light through a rotating drum, exposing them in the shapes of letters and symbols into photographic film. When the operator finished typing a story or an ad, she pushed a button that rolled the film into light-tight canister about the size of shoe box. She then removed the canister, took it to a darkroom, and, after unraveling the film from the canister, developed the film. The result was a long galley of developed photo paper, usually about eight inches wide, with type on it. Finally the operator or another staffer cut the paper into the lengths in which it would ultimately appear on the printed page and pasted it onto makeup sheets or boards. Later the sheets were photographed and their images transferred onto printing press plates.

To people used to hot-metal type's raucous cacophony or computer-fed phototype's intimidating expense and size, Garth's machine—dismissed as mere "mechanical photoflash units" by sellers of more expensive digital alphabet machines—was the soul of simplicity. Far cheaper than any other kind of type machine on the market, it required neither special clean rooms nor industrial-weight type matrices. Even skeptics saw it as representing a "spirit of egalitarianism." It was phototype that was affordable for "the smallest printing offices as well as the biggest" offices.[7]

And offices, big and small, did jump on it. From the moment Garth unveiled it in Chicago, it "destabilized the economics" of the whole organized printed word industry, letting "back-room operations compete with big ones . . . The entire marketplace was turned upside down." Out of nowhere, Compugraphic was at the front of a business that few knew existed. Suddenly aware that type could be cheap, competitors brought out their own low-end machines (although Compugraphic was not caught for another fifteen years). And many began sprouting still newer innovations: editing screens and soon digital type that dropped in price even more quickly than phototype.[8]

New kinds of businesses bought it. Typesetting shops proliferated when low-cost "cold type" appeared. Their numbers grew by almost 56 percent from 1967, the year before Garth introduced his first Compugraphic, to 1977. (Only 265 of the nation's type shops were hot metal in 1977, versus 1,188 of them in 1958.)[9] The new business's payrolls rose 74 percent, sales by 105 percent. The numbers would multiply by another 28 percent in the next five years. These were, in effect, outlets open to people who previously never could have afforded to create formally printed words.

Big businesses adopted the new machines as well. In North Carolina, where it typeset its technical manuals, Western Electric found its keyboarding productivity rose by 30 percent when it started using the new editing screens.[10]

All of American commercial printing and publishing boomed along with them, sales jumping by 129 percent from 1967 to 1977.[11]

It was a wonderful time for Garth and his investors. More than twenty years after the first planting, their harvest had finally come in. They took Compugraphic public in March 1970, selling close to $5 million in stock and making themselves rich. By the end of that year, their company's sales had jumped from $8 million to $16 million. Its earnings per share more than doubled. Its stock price, $13 in 1970, hit $37 in 1977. "Everybody had stock options and the stock was going crazy," a typeface designer who modestly described himself as "just a step or two removed from the worker bees" at Compugraphic at the time. "We couldn't make machines fast enough . . . It wasn't so much we were supplying the world with inexpensive phototype and spreading knowledge. It was just an exploding company, and a lot of fun." He likened it being in the heart of the Silicon Valley during the computing tech boom of the mid-1980s. "It was a magic place."[12]

Annual sales were $95 million by the mid-1970s, and growing by about 20 percent a year. The company claimed that 69 percent of the nation's dailies owned one piece of Compugraphic equipment or another.[13]

It was in 1974 that the spreading spider cracks in the International Typographical Union's control over the production of the printed word in the United States finally broke open.

By then, small systems like Compugraphic's were everywhere. They were birthing entirely new kinds of businesses. There were type shops, "quick printers," in-plant print centers, and "underground newspapers" in which union printers had no role. Unions were not needed to produce the great, uncounted reams of printed sheets generated by office workers, teachers, students, writers, physicians, engineers, attorneys, church secretaries, and publicists off the office copiers then spreading rapidly. And because unions were expensive and none too adaptable, they seemed increasingly out of place at newspapers, many of which (in Miami, Los Angeles, Detroit, Milwaukee, Akron, Philadelphia, and San Francisco, among others) already had sophisticated cold-type composing systems churning out words.[14]

But New York newspapers, by one *Times* executive's accounting, were about ten years behind their peers in 1974. Four had gone out of business since the last big showdown with the ITU in 1962, and many observers directly (and unfairly) blamed Bert Powers, Big Six's president, for killing them. (According to popular legend, he refused to let them automate.) The surviving papers remained desperate to catch up with the rest of the industry. The New York Times Company, for one, owned a chain of automated papers in Florida which, with its computers, enjoyed pretax profits of 26.6 percent during the first half of 1974. Its partially automated flagship paper in New York, by comparison, had pretax profits of 6.2 percent during the same period.[15] Determined to improve, the *Times* and its competitors set up some phototype machines across the river in New Jersey and, as their ITU contract ended in 1973 and they negotiated a new one, trained people to use them.

Bert Powers was now a no-nonsense, conservatively dressed fifty-two-year-old bargainer, accustomed to the ways of power (he was said to speak softly primarily to make his listeners bow slightly in order to hear him). To prod the owners after more than a year of stalled contract talks, he ordered his members to start making the publishers feel some pain. He told members to relax, completing their work at speeds that were "normal, slow, and very slow." The impact was immediate: the compositors' slowdown prevented the *News* from getting some seven hundred ads into print during the first two weeks, costing it some $2 million in lost revenue. The paper's publishers replied with an ultimatum: get back to normal speed by May 6, 1974, or they would use their equipment across the river to produce their May 7 edition.

When midnight struck on May 6, Powers was with his men in the *News* composing room, waiting to see who would blink first. In about an hour, editors and executives came in, brandishing one of the thin metal press plates produced by the new machines. They ordered the compositors to use it to make up a page for the next edition. The compositors refused; the unholy nonunion-made image, of course, was forbidden. Powers, fastidious and reserved and famous for his self-control, angrily grabbed the plate from the editor, crumpled it in his hands, and flung it disgustedly to the floor. In the yelling that erupted, the editors officially fired the compositors for refusing to work and ordered them from the building. Powers was arrested and booked at 3:00 A.M. for destroying company property.

The action, one news magazine contended, "harked back to the nineteenth-century wrecking of machines by Luddites."[16]

Powers was out on bail by daylight, proclaiming as he joined the picket line his lieutenants had thrown around the building that this was a lockout, not a strike. (Legally a lockout would have been the paper's fault; a strike the union's.) But then someone handed him a copy of that morning's *News*, set in type by computer and created despite the ITU's absence the night before. There were only sixty pages, about half the normal number. A mere 687,000 copies, about a third the normal number, had been produced. It looked "sloppy and crude," not unlike the lousy-looking issues the Chicago papers had printed with Veritypers in 1947. Powers looked at it, scanned through the pages, closed it, and considered it for a few silent moments. "They still need the printers' product," he finally said. "This kind of paper doesn't satisfy the standards of the *News*. The computers they're using are on about a 1960 level of technology."[17]

He was right, but it was not to be a good week for Bert Powers and the mighty Big Six. The *News* announced its composing room was now open to anyone who wanted to work there. It not only kept publishing without the ITU workers, but each edition grew bigger than the previous one. Each looked better too, although the date on the Thursday edition was wrong. Worse yet for Powers, members of the other main unions at the *News*—the reporters and the press operators who had never forgiven the ITU for its snubs during the jurisdictional wars of the 1950s—crossed the ITU picket line to help the owners continue to publish. The reporters' betrayal was a special affront: at the time their union, the Newspaper Guild, was preparing to start merger talks with the ITU's national leaders. But even the national leaders crossed Powers, ruling the action in New York technically was not a lockout. It was therefore a strike and Big Six, in effect, thus had struck without the national ITU's approval. The bylaws, the national ITU said, were clear: it could not supply relief funds to workers out on an unauthorized strike.[18]

Broke, abandoned by just about everyone in organized labor, and publicly reviled as antitechnology ignoramuses, Big Six nonetheless managed to keep its picket line up for nineteen days and force *News* managers, who still could not produce full-size or full-revenue newspapers, back to the bargaining table.

Their talks produced a dramatic proposal: the papers, in effect, would pay the union workers to go away or, if they chose to stay, to not interfere with the new tools. Those who took early retirement would get bonus payments of up to $10,000. Those who stayed would get immediate raises of $40 a week, plus guaranteed annual raises of 3 percent and cost-of-living adjustments for as long as they came into the office, even if there was no work for them to do. But those who stayed would give up their antibogus work rules, their jobs on the new machines, and even the prospect that future members of their union would run them. Newspapers would have a free hand to produce type any way they wanted.[19]

Powers held the vote on the buyout proposal in August, but everyone seemed to know which way it would go. As some 1,060 Lino operators took their seats to hear Powers, one compositor spontaneously serenaded the crowd with a mordant and irony-laden version of "After You've Gone." At the podium, Powers once again pulled no punches. He predicted that the agreement would mean that as many as 50 percent of the local's members would leave the union during the next decade. Forty-one of them voted against; 1,019 in favor.[20]

Years later, Powers recalled that he had seen the future earlier in 1974 on a visit to the *Miami Herald*. It was "a nonunion newspaper that had no restriction on the way it operated. And something told me that we better make a settlement with the publishers pretty quickly or else we were going to be in real trouble." The union would soon be "dying by inches. Or by yards." All around him, the bargaining power of hot-metal printers was already slipping away. As Powers pondered Miami and his upcoming contract talks in New York, ITU workers had been locked out of the *Chattanooga News-Free Press* for more than two years and the *Omaha World Herald* for more than a year.[21] It was for those reasons that, using whatever irritating "slowdowns" or dramatic midnight plate crumplings that were necessary, he thus led his historically powerful union to what amounted to a negotiated surrender, complete with reparations. Whether he realized it or not, he had successfully outfoxed his publisher/opponents by applying game theory and achieving the "minimum maximum loss."

Those who chose to keep working instead of taking early retirement soon found themselves without a thing to do. Usually to the scorn of others who still had difficult responsibilities and didn't have guaranteed lifetime employment, they made their way each day to a special room that, at the *New York Times*, became known as "the rubber room."

Bored, they played cards all day.[22]

Vannevar Bush had a stroke that year. Much decorated, often credited and blamed for the creation of a military–industrial complex, a founder of the Raytheon Corporation as well as Photon, a board member at Merck Pharmaceuticals, president of the MIT Corporation, and most recently an indirect sponsor of a thing called ARPANET, Bush caught pneumonia while he was recuperating from his stroke. He died in Belmont, Massachusetts, on June 30, just a few weeks after New York's papers freed themselves of type.

Seven months after that a Harvard student named Bill Gates saw an article in an issue of *Popular Mechanics*. It told of a man in New Mexico who had come up with a computer language called BASIC. Where most computers were hardwired to do specific functions, this was software language that told the hardware what functions to perform. It was, the inventor claimed, pretty easy to learn. Now programming—once the province of institutions that could afford to arrange and rearrange wires and transistor chips in certain hard to fathom intervals—was "like an open kimono."[23] Gates and his buddy Paul Allen impetuously headed out to New Mexico to see what they could see.

Had they gone on to California, they would have found people doing multitasking. In the past, programmers had to install an expensive computer chip for each task they wanted their computer to do: print, calculate, type, save a file. Now they could move those tasks through a central processor, letting chips that weren't busy calculating, for example, help print.[24] Soon it would be cheaper to create even more powerful machines. Soon it might even be possible to make little personal computers for people.

As the hot-metal printers filed into their rubber rooms, an inventive fury was building in New Mexico, California, and Massachusetts. "From January 1975 through the end of 1977," a chronicler of the era later wrote, "saw a burst of energy and creativity in computing that had almost no equal in its history." From it, among other things, came protocols for letting computers talk to each other over long distances and a Bush-like "database as big as the whole world." There was also a dedicated word processing minicomputer that "nearly caused a riot" when it was introduced at a 1976 New York trade show by An Wang, a Chinese immigrant who had pretty much invented core computer memories and the desktop calculator. In 1977 came the first mass-produced personal computer, called Apple II. Suddenly there were functioning computer networks that, according to one of the network architects whose imagination had also originally been stoked by Vannevar Bush's article in 1945, would someday be run by a bunch of machines and ideas linked by a still more obscure mathematical language he called HUMBERS. The name stood for "HUMongous numbers."[25] Already it was making the phototype that was replacing hot metal obsolete.

NOTES

1. "Signs of the Future?" *Newsweek*, November 9, 1964, 88. The religious book publisher was Parthenon Press, owned by the United Methodist Publishing House. "United Methodists Pioneer Electronic Printing Facility," *Publishers Weekly*, September 26, 1977, 72; Lawrence W. Wallis, *Electronic Typesetting: A Quarter Century of Upheaval* (Gatehead, U.K.: Paradigm, 1984), 7. Photo units had long had problems with eccentric hyphenation and letter placement. At Photon, Lou Rosenblum worked on the problem of why certain letters in certain words came out printed higher than the other letters on a line of type. He eventually traced the problem to the way certain combinations of letters intermittently sent mixed optical signals to the system's brain.

2. Lou Rosenblum, telephone interview, November 25, 1998; "Market-wise: Compugraphic Corp.'s Formula: Thinking Small When Others Think Big," *Forbes*, March 1, 1977, 59.

3. Mergenthaler's Linasec, which was marketed to large newspapers, sold for about $27,000 in 1963. "Printing a Dream," *Time*, January 18, 1963, 69; Rosenblum, November 25, 1996. The tape feeder apparently was based in part on the

work of one Walter Peery, whose patents Compugraphic acquired. Wallis, *Electronic Typesetting*, 13–14.

4. Alan Haley, telephone interview, September 23, 1998.

5. John A. Prestro, "Printing Equipment Concerns, Bolstered by Electronic Items," *Wall Street Journal*, June 26, 1968, 8; "Digital Technology Is Slashing Cost of Typesetting Machines," *New York Times*, September 8, 1980, D5.

6. Haley, telephone interview. Haley, a type designer, started at Compugraphic in 1971 and later went on to become an executive at Agfa-Gaevert and a consultant to the type industry.

7. David Henry Goodstein, "Typesetting Moves from a Master Craft to a Computer Application in Today's World," *Graphic Arts Monthly*, June 1981, 40; Wallis, *Electronic Typesetting*, 21.

8. Competitors in the years immediately after 1968 included Fairchild, Star Parts Co., Graphex, Singer, and of course Mergenthaler. Photon tried to merge with Mohawk Data in 1969 in part to challenge its old cofounder with a "low-cost, limited capability phototypesetting device," but the marriage was never consummated. "Mohawk Data, Photon Disclose Plan For Merger," *Wall Street Journal*, April 9, 1969, 4. Louis Moyroud, the machine's original codeveloper, sold about 40 percent of his Photon shares in 1968, before the merger. "Changes in Stockholdings," *Wall Street Journal*, September 12, 1968, 28; "Mohawk Data, Photon End Talks Started Last Month," *Wall Street Journal*, May 27, 1969, 21. Only Mergenthaler ever enjoyed phototype sales close to Compugraphics'. Wallis, *Electronic Typesetting*, 13, 21, 2324.

9. In 1982, just 145 linecasting shops were still open. By 1992, there were twenty-nine. William Lofquist, telephone interview, September 23, 1998; U.S. Department of Commerce, Economic Census, Industry Statistics, Major Groups 20 to 28, SIC Codes 2791 (1967, 1972, 1977, 1982).

10. Jerry A. Carlson, "Video Editing," in Lowell H. Hattery and George P. Bush, eds., *Technological Changes in Printing and Publishing* (Mt. Airy, Md.: Lomond, 1973), 116.

11. U.S. Department of Commerce, Bureau of the Census, *Census of Manufactures*, vol. 2, *Industry Statistics*, pt. 2, SIC Major Groups 27–34, 1947, 1954, 1958,1963, 1967, 1972, 1977.

12. "Compugraphic Stock Marketed," *Wall Street Journal*, March 20, 1970, 20; "Digest of Earnings Reports," *Wall Street Journal*, December 8, 1970, 28; Haley, telephone interview.

13. "Market-wise," 59.

14. John J. Pilcher, "Annual Report of the President to the Membership," *Typographical Journal*, May 1974, 6.

15. "New York Goes Modern," *Time*, August 12, 1974, 58. There were many other, probably more lethal influences driving newspapers out of business in those days, including tax laws that encouraged chain building and mergers, the mass migration of consumers and advertisers into the suburbs, and the expansion of both national and local TV news outlets. The publishers of some of New York's failed

dailies, moreover, were notably unwilling to invest in staff, news, and marketing even as they complained the ITU was keeping them from acquiring new technology. The ITU did not prohibit new technology. Its contracts certainly made the technology more expensive for publishers to buy than it needed to be. But publishers in other cities often faced the same additional expenses—having to pay unions part of the money they saved in operating the new machines—as New York's publishers. Yet they managed not only to automate but also to stay in business.

16. "Powers Play," *Time*, May 20, 1974, 61.

17. "Push-Button Warfare," *Newsweek*, May 20, 1974, 96; Pete Axthelm, "Bert Powers's Last Stand," *Newsweek*, May 20, 1974, 97.

18. "Powers," 62; Axthelm, "Bert Powers," 97; "Push-Button Warfare," 99; A. Sandy Bevis, "Annual Report to the Membership," *Typographical Journal*, July 1975, 36.

19. "New York Goes Modern," 57. "Automation: A Landmark Agreement," *Newsweek*, June 3, 1974, 63–64.

20. "New York Goes Modern," 57; "Automation," 64.

21. David E. Pitt, "His Vision Realized, a Union Leader Retires," *New York Times*, June 15, 1990, B1. Powers had seen the future long before 1974. After viewing an RCA computer demonstrated in July 1963, he said, "Those [ITU] members who doubt the effects of total automation or rely on economic theories of the past to stabilize our industry had better re-examine their thinking. We are headed for many changes in the printing industry." Harry Kelber and Carl Schlesinger, *Union Printers and Controlled Automation* (New York: Free Press, 1967), 167; John J. Pilcher, "Annual Report," *Typographical Journal*, 5s–9s.

22. Elizabeth MacIver Neiva, "Chain Building: The Consolidation of the American Newspaper Industry, 1953–1980," *Business History Review*, Spring 1996, 64.

23. Paul E. Ceruzzi, *A History of Modern Computing* (Cambridge: MIT Press, 1998), 229.

24. Douglas K. Smith and Robert C. Alexander, *Fumbling the Future: How Xerox Invented, Then Ignored, the First Personal Computer* (New York: Morrow, 1988), 151; Ceruzzi, *Modern Computing*, 224.

25. Ceruzzi, *Modern Computing*, 230, 256; Mike Brewster, "An Wang: The Core of the Computer Era," *Business Week Online*, July 14, 2004, http://businessweek .com/bwdaily/dnflash/jul2004/nf20040714_0561_db078.htm (accessed October 14, 2004); Vinton G. Cerf, What Was Your Role in the Founding of the Internet? global.mci.com/us/enterprise/insight/cerfs_up/internet_history/q_and_a.xml#question_1 (accessed October 14, 2004). The "architect" was Theodor Holm Nelson, whose work on text handling programs led to the creation of the HTML language. Christopher Keep and Tim McLaughlin, *The Electronic Labyrinth* (Charlottesville: University of Virginia Press, 1995), www.iath.virginia.edu/elab/hfl0034.html.

21

UNION'S END

To hear the leaders of the powerful union that had controlled the production of printed language for more than a hundred years tell it, things were fine. Lino operators' wages, after all, had jumped 9.1 percent in the prior five years, faster than any other craftspeople in the industry.[1] As for the wildly tilting technological landscape, the labor leaders noted that printers had adapted to earthquakes before. They would do so again.

"There is no disappearance of the composing room threatened here," the ITU's incoming president reassured the annual convention a year after New York's dailies bought out Big Six. Large newspapers may be changing, he conceded, but "the commercial composing room and the smaller newspaper composing room are firmly here to stay."[2]

He was stupendously over-optimistic. Even as he spoke, the small papers he counted on were busily replacing both their linecasting composing rooms and their linecasting unionists. The relatively small *Missoulian* in Montana, for example, had defanged its ITU local in 1973—a year before the New York buyout—by offering its members a rich benefit and pension package to leave. (Lloyd Shermer, who invented the tactic, gave instructional buyout seminars to publishers around the country.) By 1975 the paper's profits were up by 225 percent over the past five years. The Mason City, Iowa, *Globe Gazette* installed eleven video display terminals that dropped its man-hours per page cost from $20 to $10. In 1977, a much quoted industry consultant predicted that every daily in the nation would be doing electronic composition in three years.[3]

Many major national magazines were already doing it even then. *Newsweek, Reader's Digest, National Geographic, Forbes, U.S. News & World Report*, and the *Economist* were all running systems that set type and pictures electronically. So were the Government Printing Office and the Central Intelligence Agency.[4]

The ITU's leader was also wrong about commercial composing rooms. There were more of them popping up but, judging from Lintotype's declining hot-metal sales during the same period, almost all used phototype. Almost all, moreover, were small operations of fewer than twenty people, well beneath the interest levels of most ITU organizers. In other words, they were mostly nonunion shops.

Book publishers were changing as well. A couple of months after the Big Six buyout, three Xerox scientists installed an experimental phototype device at the Boston offices of Ginn & Co., a textbook publisher. The thing didn't have modes or even many command keys like the other computer/phototype systems. To write, you still used a keyboard, but to insert text you used a strange device called a mouse. One of the inventors called the system Gypsy, after a Halloween costume his daughter had worn. Although he was neither a publisher nor a salesperson, he had the same girl typist dream as everyone else: "When it came time to begin instructing people about Gypsy, I went straight for the lady with the Royal typewriter, figuring if I could teach her, it would be clear sailing for the rest," he recalled. She learned it "after a few hours." Ginn soon cut its editing costs by 15–20 percent per title.[5]

And of course large papers, the most visible part of the industry, continued to squeeze the ITU too.

The L.A. *Times* threw out its last Lino in 1974. The *Baltimore Sun* and *Wall Street Journal* followed in 1976, the *New York Times* in 1978, the *New York Daily News* in 1979. Like the *News*, the *Washington Post* surprised itself when it kept publishing during a wildcat strike by press operators. Emboldened, the *Post*'s publisher announced within a month of the New York buyout that she would stop trying to appease the ITU, saying she would no longer sign cowardly, Neville Chamberlain–like "peace at any price" contracts. Later that year, she paid it $2.6 million plus lifetime job guarantees for the freedom to bring in whatever machines she wanted. Other big papers followed, equipping themselves and then taking hard-line stances against their compositors. About two hundred papers had scanners, which could read and convert 500–1,000 words into type per minute without having to use a keyboard, in operation by 1974. (They cost $100,000 each in 1969, $30,000 then. Home versions at the time this book is being written are under $100.) More than 1,000 newspapers were being produced wholly in cold type. Those that were not wholly cold type were racing to get there and cutting costs dramatically in the process. The *Minneapolis Star-Tribune* saved 40 percent of what it had spent to manually set display ads the previous year. The *Boston Globe*, which took three man-hours to set and lay out ninety classified ads on a Lino, tested a system that let it set ninety ads in fifteen minutes. The *Detroit News* had seventy-five video display terminals in place. On them, one union official worriedly noted, "the press of a button sends the copy [from a reporter] into computer storage. An editor sitting at another screen then calls the story up on his VDT, makes all the changes he wants on the screen and with a press of a button transmits the story to the composing room, where it is received as punched tape." Such machines cost $17,000 each in 1970; $5,000 in 1974. "Last year," the retiring ITU president said in his farewell address in 1974, "employers would install a scanner or another piece of equipment. This year they were installing whole systems that blur traditional" job descriptions. Reporters were composing. Engravers were creating pages. In the updraft, he reported that ITU local chapters were tempted to accept whatever pay employers happened to offer.[6]

Some say these ITU leaders had read the handwriting on the wall long before the mid-1970s. An official with the Newspaper Guild, the reporters union that was in merger talks with the compositors at the time, believed the "typos" had already gone through all the stages of grief—including anger, denial, and acceptance—over their loss of production control by 1974. They also knew that trying to recapture it "was not a viable position." So they had fought a "rearguard action to preserve the maximum amount of jobs while obtaining the best possible compensation for printers displaced by the new equipment."[7]

Elmo U. Collins, a union leader in Toledo, had seen hot metal's decline back in the mid-1960s, the first moment he saw primitive versions of the new technology in action. He too had tried, often unsuccessfully, to persuade his colleagues to learn how to produce cold type and had accepted that the folks who resisted were on their way out of the industry. In recalling his union negotiating tactics of that era, he suggested that the union's strategy was to forestall the approach of the machines while trying to arrange the most lucrative possible exit for the printers they would force out of the business.[8] It was exactly what Bertram Powers had done in New York.

In public, however, the leaders at the ITU headquarters in Colorado said no such things. Their official pronouncements and strategies aimed exclusively at getting members happily and lucratively employed on computers forever more.

With or without the leaders, the buyouts continued: in Missoula, New York, Washington, Baltimore, Chicago, and virtually all big newspapers and type businesses across the country. The agreements got money to those who were laid off and preserved jobs for others for a while. The jobs, even Potemkin Village jobs without any real responsibilities, fed some members for more than a decade. Other reparations paid for retraining and retirement. All in all, building a financial floor under its displaced, unneeded members, as the ITU did, may have been one of organized labor's most phenomenal negotiating feats, probably unprecedented in the generations of workers replaced and impoverished by levers, steam, gas, electricity, oil, binary languages, and all the other serial wonders of science and art.

But large pieces of the ITU broke off when the buyouts began in 1974. Employment dried up. In New York, three major papers cut their composing workforce by 31, 34, and 43 percent, respectively, during the next four years. Those who were laid off had trouble finding other jobs in printing. "Computer-based phototypesetting can replace the entire staff of a composing room by one relatively unskilled keyboard operator, assisted by system analysts, computer programmers, and electronic engineers," an ITU report from an European conference on automation said. "It has not proved easy to find employment for all compositors." The unskilled keyboard operators, in turn, were singularly uninterested in joining the union in their stead. As the evangelists of technology had been dreaming for more than a century, many of the new operators were female and saw themselves as white-collar, service workers, positioning them among the two most union-resistant groups of laborers in the United States. Many economists attribute the stark decline in American organized labor since the 1950s to the increasing numbers of union-shy women in low-skilled, white-collar production jobs.[9]

Union morale, in long decline, cratered. Thousands of linecasters seemed to give up entirely. Some stopped trying to learn the new machines; attendance at the union's training center in Colorado Springs fell for the first time in 1975 and continued to fall. It wasn't always for lack of management's cooperation. Charles Mulliken, then head of the Typographers International Association, a trade group that represented type shop owners, says many newspapers and businesses—the *Advertiser* in Huntington, West Virginia, and Western Electric in Winston-Salem, North Carolina, among them—tried to retrain unionists on the slick new systems. But many ITU locals, he recalls, insisted that the unionists with the most seniority get the first chance to learn them. The oldest workers, however, were precisely the least interested in learning something new. "Those guys were probably 64.5 years old," he sighs. "They just didn't have the mentality or the energy."[10]

William B. Printz, for one, had been in and out of printing (although mostly in) since 1926, and was working at the Government Printing Office (GPO) when the computers arrived in the crucible year of 1974. He pounded politicians' speeches into his Monotype for each day's *Congressional Record* and, because politicians were involved, was confident his job was eternally secure. "As long as they talked, we worked. And, boy, they talked." A musician, he also liked the work; its creativity, the fitting of chaos into carefully measured expressions, the tight deadlines, and even the mess. "We had ink all over us," he chuckled many years later. He was also truly impressed by the cold type the GPO was then adopting. "You can work with a tuxedo on." And the GPO gave him a chance to do it. "They wanted me to learn computers. But I said no, I'm too stupid. That's when I retired."[11]

Many of those who took the retraining regretted it. "Here is what I do for a living: I make chads," one compositor with twenty-five years experience wrote of the tiny circles he punched out of pink paper every day. In a guest column in the *New York Times*, he described how the machines into which he fed the tape performed miracles, turning out enormous amounts of material in short order. "It's technologically impressive and it's remarkably efficient. And I hate it." He knew he should appreciate it more, but he missed "the individuality of each typeface, the clarity of Caslon, the grace of Bodoni." His old hot-metal job "was a craft; there was much to learn and learning came slowly. Whether you worked for the printer Aldus Manutius in fifteen-century Venice or sat at a Mergenthaler for William Randolph Hearst, you shared a common skill, a common body of knowledge that was acquired over a period of time." But type was now simple. "I learned the necessary computer codes for typesetting in about eight weeks." He missed the vocabulary of the old ways: ligatures, nonpareils. Now there were "ugly, efficient nouns: chad, input, printout . . . There is no poetry here. The workplace has undergone a similar metamorphosis . . . no more lead fumes from metal pigs, no more ink-stained elbows, no more heavy galleys of type to lift. I miss it. Today's composing room is perilously akin to an office. [The computers] sit behind glass walls and whir and blink and watch over their composing room. On particularly bad days, I glare back . . . The old Luddites would have known how I feel . . . they knew an enemy when they saw one . . . Most of them were hanged or shot, some deported, as perhaps they knew they would be. But, logic be damned. I feel what they felt. THE MACHINE HAS STOLEN MY SKILLS."[12]

With older workers opting to quit and many of the younger ones grieving over their lost master craft skills, many managers gave up on the retraining as well. A shop owner, Mulliken recalled, "couldn't [sustain] it.

There's no way he could afford keeping a metal department next to a phototype department while these guys resisted retraining. So he [the owner] just threw the department out. Into the dumpsters. It literally happened."[13]

The *Times* writer, the paper noted, was leaving the industry; he was back in school "to retool." But many of the people who took buyouts floundered. Two academics who followed forty-four printers after they left a New York publisher of two (unidentified) trade newspapers found that "a man's sense of loss of economic independence and personal dignity appears to be even more overwhelming than his loss of income." The wife of one fifty-eight-year-old printer, for example, "was afraid to go to work and leave my husband alone. He was starting to fall apart." A lone job offer paid a third of what he'd been earning, and the work seemed insultingly clerical. He turned it down. Many months passed before the next nibble; it was as a telephone operator, for pay less than half his old compositor wages. He grabbed it, he said, because his wife had buckled under the strain, was being treated at a mental institution, and was too sick to work herself. Another worker used his severance to go to Colorado for more print training, but it hadn't helped. He was still jobless three years after taking his buyout money. Most employers, he had concluded, were too spooked by his previously high wages and union membership to hire him. The generous retraining offered by the publisher of the trade newspaper hadn't quite worked out, either. Four of the workers who took phototype lessons found that most type houses were already dumping phototype and switching to computer monitors run by writers and reporters themselves. Those who took the publisher's equally generous four-day "business course" of résumé writing and aptitude tests did little better. One counselor, on reviewing the test results, suggested one of the résumé writers see a psychiatrist. Another printer, aged forty-five, was told he should become a dentist. In all, the forty-four people bought out by the trade publisher in 1978 were an average of 55.1 years old, had been printers for twenty-seven years, had two kids in college, and owned their own home. Three years later, twenty of them had new jobs. They were in night security, glass polishing, flower delivery, and house painting. Their average annual earnings were $15,000, versus their printing average of $22,000 plus benefits. "Most" had used their respective $35,000 and $8,000 early retirement money to pay off mortgages and loans, and said they were trying not to spend what remained. Seven of the "buyees" remained retired. Three were disabled.[14]

Thus the union itself quickly lost its footing after 1974. Membership plummeted. Five percent of the members left from mid-1974 to mid-1975, dropping the total from 101,000 to 96,000. Enrollment dove to 81,000 in

1980. By 1985, there were 74,000 members; 30,000 of them were retirees. The ITU budget shriveled accordingly. Annual revenues (almost all from membership dues) fell precipitously, from $38 million in 1975 to $13 million five years later. They never rose above $15 million again. To save itself, the ITU merged with the equally troubled mailers union in 1979. Next it tried to merge with the Newspaper Guild and then the pressmen. "Basically," a Wall Street newspaper analyst later said, "the ITU is presiding over a dying craft, and they're desperately looking for a safe harbor." Yet none of the proposed combinations came about, in part because the typographers—once among the most potent, highly paid ,and arrogant negotiators in the country—by the 1980s could bring little but high dues and weak bargaining positions to their partners in the industry. The then-supposedly corrupt Teamsters Union, perhaps interested in the ITU's fat and potentially plunderable $350 million pension fund, proposed a merger, but the compositors, whose rigorously democratic procedures were much admired, voted it down.[15]

Through these death throes, the organization's leaders bickered endlessly and destructively among themselves over mergers, tactics, budgets, communications, and what to do about automation. One official, refusing to give up after losing an election, had to be rousted from office in 1984 by a federal injunction and a government-monitored election. In the composing rooms, the remaining hot-metal workers were relentlessly losing in contract negotiations. All of these woes, one ITU officer later maintained, were the result of the buyouts that started in 1974, when master printers "decided to purchase the jurisdiction of the Typographical Union . . . and then assigned *our work* to lower-paid employees." Those who accepted the payoffs, he wrote, were shortsighted; mere "buyees." Yes, they had gotten "$5,000 or $10,000," but they had wrecked an important organization.[16]

The International Typographical Union took twelve years to collapse, eventually finding shelter with the Communications Workers of America in 1986. The CWA, a labor economist at George Washington University observed at the time, was "a strong union, a reasonably well-run union, so it seems as good a partner for ITU as any union around." Starting as a telephone operators union in 1947, it had grown into a huge organization of 500,000 telecommunications and public sector employees. At least one ITU national official had approached it about a merger in 1984, but the CWA said it was too busy coping with the breakup of its members' single biggest employer, AT&T. In 1986, fresh from negotiations with the forty-eight different telephone company bargaining units that had replaced AT&T, the CWA finally said yes to merging not only with the ITU but also the similarly endangered United Telegraph Workers Union. In November, 80 percent of the ITU's remaining members approved the merger. "By joining with a union of C.W.A.'s size and sophistication we'll be better equipped to move into the 21st century and beyond," intoned the ITU's last president, who would become head of the CWA's new Printing, Publishing, and Media Workers sector.[17]

Many of his members, despite their long quest for some sort of merger, were appalled. At least eight of the Mailers Union locals—which had joined the ITU in 1979 but had periodically threatened to secede since—began disaffiliating with the compositors even before the CWA merger could be consummated. Some defected to the Teamsters. The ITU, a former U.S. Department of Commerce printing analyst sniffed incredulously, had "sold itself as a department of the *telephone workers'* union."[18]

Even those who didn't hate the idea were pessimistic it would change anything. The merger, a stock analyst noted, "is not really going to change the fact they're going to continue to dwindle in numbers." By 1989, membership dwindled to 62,000. By 1992, it was 35,000.[19]

They had nothing left. The larger CWA proved to be no better at helping them keep their jobs than the old ITU had been. Its solution to metastasizing automation in the telephone industry, in fact, had been the same as the ITU's solution to automation in printing: negotiate buyouts. When 40,000 of its telephone workers—half at the fractured AT&T, half at the new regional phone companies—lost their jobs in 1984, the CWA hammered out an agreement borrowed from the ITU template. It included early retirement packages, mutually agreed-on layoff schedules, six months notice of certain technological changes, and giving the oldest, most senior workers first crack at new jobs operating computers.[20]

And it lost little time crafting similar surrenders for its new compositor members. A long, bitter Chicago strike, begun in 1985, finally ended in 1989 when some unionists got buyouts of $30,000. Others got to choose between taking the buyouts and staying on the job for three more years. When those who stayed on the job retired, the papers would replace them not with CWA members or even compositors, but with low-paid "typographical assistants."[21] It was the same agreement compositors had been getting before the merger.

Even the compositors' storied local in Washington, D.C., which had controlled the flow of the printed word at the capital's newspapers as well as at the Government Printing Office since 1814, was reduced to "collective begging instead of collective bargaining" after the merger. A ten-year agreement with the *Washington Post*, signed in 1991, gave the *Post* the freedom to hire anyone it wanted when an ITU compositor left his or her job.

As the ITU surrendered all its hallowed work rules, control over the composing room officially passed from the workers to the managers.[22]

In Dallas, the *Times Herald* installed computers without notifying the CWA compositors and dared them to strike. They sued instead, and ultimately lost their work rules there too.[23]

The new union's inability to keep its members employed, much less protected, was hardly the union's fault. No group in an unregulated market could protect these masters of type in a world that was, at last, without type.

For now, in the 1970s and 1980s, new kinds of alphabets were in use; flat, instantaneous, ephemeral signals. They were cheap. They became ever easier to use, first by smart college dropouts like Gary Krohm, then by the rest of us. When simple hieratic alphabets appeared in the Egyptian desert in 1800 B.C.E., when type alphabets appeared in Europe in the mid-fifteenth century, and when machine alphabets appeared in the United States in the late nineteenth century, the technicians who had produced the old, progressively more complex ones—the copyists, the block printers, the hand compositors—were no longer needed for us to communicate. Nor were the elites who controlled the technicians: the priests, governors, master printers, publishers, and trade unions. Now the last of the modern agencies—the union—that controlled the output and price of the old printed word fell away. Businesses were freed to use the new alphabets without restraint. Previously inexpert professionals, people like operations managers, accountants, marketers, lawyers, pharmacists, bankers, rushed to adopt them. When the alphabets got still faster and cheaper as the twentieth century ended, they fell into the hands of millions of still more common folk.

The old monopolies over the production of the printed word, in sum, were finally broken with the union's collapse.

And once again, although lost among the cell phones, pocket computers, in-car navigational devices, smart bombs, tech bubbles, on-demand videos, CDs and DVDs, universal timekeeping devices, handheld animations, streaking probes into the distant universe, and the other miracles of human communications that followed, a new boom in printed knowledge was under way.

NOTES

1. Mary Kay Rieg, "Union Pay Rates in the Printing Industry," *Monthly Labor Review*, September 1975, 644.

2. A. Sandy Bevis, "Annual Report to the Membership," *Typographical Journal*, July 1975, 40.

3. Elizabeth MacIver Neiva, "Chain Building: The Consolidation of the American Newspaper Industry, 1953–1980," *Business History Review*, Spring 1996, 52; Nouri Beyrouti, "The History and Development of Newspaper Electronic Pagination Systems in the United States, 1975–1987" (Ph.D. diss., New York University, 1989), 83, 102; "United Methodists Pioneer Electronic Printing Facility," *Publishers Weekly*, September 26, 1977, 72.

4. "Printing by Computer: A USN&WR Gamble Pays Off," *U.S. News & World Report*, September 5, 1977, 57.

5. Douglas K. Smith and Robert C. Alexander, *Fumbling the Future: How Xerox Invented, Then Ignored, the First Personal Computer* (New York: Morrow, 1988), 111–12.

6. George Corben Goble, *The Obituary of a Machine: The Rise and Fall of Ottmar Mergenthaler's Linotype at U.S. Newspapers* (Bloomington: Indiana University Mass Communications Program, 1984), 374; "Push-Button Warfare," *Newsweek*, May 20, 1974, 99; "New York Goes Modern," *Time*, August 12, 1974, 58; Debra Gersh, "The Changing Role of the Typographer: Washington Post Management Is Pleased with Its New 10-year Contract with the Typographical Union but Printers Are More Apprehensive," *Editor & Publisher*, June 8, 1991, 80; Beyrouti, "Pagination," 97; John J. Pilcher, "Annual Report of the President to the Membership," *Typographical Journal*, May 1974, 5s.

7. David J. Eisen, "Union Response to Changes in Printing Technology: Another View," *Monthly Labor Review*, May 1986, 38.

8. Ward Harkavy, "The Castle on the Hill," *Westword*, May 11, 1994, www.westword.com/issues/1994-05-11/feature2.html (accessed September 17, 2004); Elmo Collins, interview, December 11, 1999.

9. Bruce Gilchrist and Ariaana Shenkin, "Disappearing Jobs," *Futurist*, February 1981, 45. Seventy percent of the people displaced in the European Community printing industry from 1975 to 1981 were compositors. "New Technologies in Printing Industry," *Typographical Journal*, October 1981, 26, 32. In 1957, 40.5 percent of the labor force was blue-collar; by 1977, only 34.4 percent. The percentage drop accelerated after that too. By 1983, moreover, 74 percent of the labor force was producing services, not products, versus 59.1 percent in 1950. Henry S. Farber, "The Recent Decline of Unionization in the United States," *Science*, November 13, 1987, 915. Almost half of the production workers in the high-tech industry had a "low" or "very low" opinion of labor unions. Steve Early and Rand Wilson, "Do Unions Have a Future in High Technology?" *Technology Review*, October 1986, 57.

10. Bevis, "Annual Report," 38; "Secretary-Treasurer's Annual Report and Financial Statement," *Typographical Journal*, July 1975, 46, 49; Charles Mulliken, telephone interview, September 23, 1998.

11. William B. Printz, interview, December 11, 1999.

12. Edward P. Hayden, "The Luddites Were Right," *New York Times*, November 14, 1980, A31.

13. Mulliken, interview.

14. Bruce Gilchrist and Ariaana Shenkin, "Disappearing Jobs," *Futurist*, February 1981, 48–49.

15. The analyst was John Morton, then a newspaper analyst for Lynch Jones & Ryan. "A Dying Craft," *New York Times*, November 27, 1986, A26:4; James Cook, "Least-Regulated Money in the Country Today," *Forbes*, June 2, 1986, 74–75.

16. "Union Merger Developments," *Monthly Labor Review*, November 1985, 64; Thomas W. Kopeck, "Annual Report and Financial Statement," *Typographical Journal*, March 1985, 41, 54; Thomas W. Kopeck, "Annual Report and Financial Statement," *Typographical Journal*, March 1985, 40–60; Kopeck, "Membership Decline Pattern Changing," *Typographical Journal*, March 1981, 3.

17. The economist was Sar A. Levitan, "A Dying Craft," A26; "Printers to Join with Communications Union," *New York Times*, November 27, 1986, A26; Thomas W. Kopeck, "Some Things Need to Be Said," *Typographical Journal*, July 1985, 4; "Trade Unions Merge with CWA," *Monthly Labor Review*, February 1987, 39.

18. William Lofquist, telephone interview, September 23, 1998. Among the ITU locals to quit in the months leading up to and following the November 1986 vote on the CWA merger were the Minneapolis St. Paul Mailers Union no. 4, Empire (NY) Media Union no. 15, Cincinnati Mailers Union no. 17, Louisville (KY) Mailers Union no. 99, San Francisco-Oakland Mailers Union No. 18, Des Moines Mailers Union no. 53, Detroit Mailers Union no. 40, and Albuquerque Mailers Union no. 156. Office of the President, *Executive Council Rulings*, International Typographical Union, July 21, 1986, to December 31, 1986, International Typographical Union Special Collections, Norlin Library, University of Colorado–Boulder, Second Accession, Box 11.

19. John Morton of Lynch Jones & Ryan, "A Dying Craft," A26; Lofquist, interview.

20. Early and Wilson, "Unions?" 60.

21. George Ruben, "Two Chicago Newspapers Complete Negotiations," *Monthly Labor Review*, February 1989, 52.

22. When twenty-four D.C. union members took buyouts of $75,000, the local's membership hit 210, down from 800 in 1974. As he announced the new pact, Franklin J. Havlicek, the *Post*'s chief negotiator, recalled that his paper had only won the right to bring in cold type but had to retain expensive hot-metal type union members. The ITU work rules governing who could be hired, how long they could work, and what kinds of equipment they could run had remained in force. All that was changed now, he said in hailing the new agreement. The ITU agreed with the *Post* negotiator's view, although considerably less gleefully. The agreement was "a disappointment," but probably the best the compositors could do in light of "the weakening condition of the role the union plays," local Chairman Robert Mason told a journalism trade magazine before turning reflective, as if at the end of a long war. "I started out in printing in the last part of 1946, and the printing industry has changed at least two times on me. When each of those changes were introduced to

me, I fought them, as well as all of my fellow members fought them but we got through them and we're still here. Ten years from now someone will be sitting here telling someone else the same story, I would imagine." Debra Gersh, "The Changing Role of the Typographer: Washington Post Management Is Pleased with Its New 10-Year Contract with the Typographical Union but Printers Are More Apprehensive," *Editor & Publisher*, June 8, 1991, 80.

23. Dee Hill, "Typesetters Sue Times Herald," *Dallas Business Journal*, October 18, 1991, 4.

22

ARISTOCRATS IN DOTAGE

His not to curb or question
The darts by others hurled
His but to form a link between
The thinker and the world.

—Old-Timer, Union Printers Home, Colorado Springs

From his room on the third floor of the retirement home, Elmo Collins commemorated his forty-ninth wedding anniversary as best as he could. He called his brother and thought about making a toast to his wife, now dead for years.

But these thoughts made his eyes well up a little, which, after a difficult swallow, meant it was time to change the subject. He cleared his throat and pointed toward the corner of his small room. "Look behind there," he tells a visitor.

Behind the dark brown industrial-type door was an old orange-and-black picket sign, announcing the ITU was on strike against the *Toledo Blade*. It was from 1966. "Hey!" his visitor says, "I've read about that strike."

Collins smiles from his wheelchair and taps his chest. "That was me." He had been lead negotiator for the Toledo newspaper local. Unable to reach an accord on wages or on running the *Blade*'s new computer system, Collins led four hundred workers out on strike. They stayed out for 166 long days while he hammered out a deal that would let ITU members learn the new machines.

Now it was thirty-three years later: mid-December of 1999, a few weeks before the millennium and what could be seen as the era of Typographic Man would end. Collins and a handful of surviving hot-metal members of the ITU were spending a mild, brilliantly sunny winter day padding around the magnificent, 107-year-old red sandstone mansion known as the Union Printers Home. The place is dreamlike. Up long, broad, tree-lined driveways, it sits massively on the crest of a hill. From its broad porches, designed long ago for tuberculosis patients to take their sun cures and the easy thin air, there's a heart-pounding view of Pike's Peak and the entire front range of the Rocky Mountains. Formal gardens, fallow at this time, surround the building. Shaded walkways snake through them. A few years ago residents could follow the paths through 175 acres of union-owned land, passing the union's training center, international headquarters, and respiratory hospital. There was a union-owned farm where aging or infirm city boys, long cooped up in rushed and acrid composing rooms, could work outside for a while. In the organization's heyday, it provided both health care and respite to its members for free. Inside the home, finished in dark wood trim and marble, the printers endured lectures in a three-hundred-seat auditorium, ran tournaments in the pool hall, sang in the music room, ate meals together in the dining room, read in the 10,000-volume library and, it was said, debated loudly about the makeup of the fifty-some newspapers delivered each week.

The place, as one observer put it, was more than real estate. It was the cushion on which good compositors ended. In their Darwinian, industrial world, the estate was ultimate and "tangible proof of their power to control their own destiny."[1]

By 1999, of course, the place was as diminished as the craft that built it. All but twenty-seven acres of the union's property were sold off. The hospital was closed in 1989. The training center was long gone, and the headquarters functions were melded into the Communications Workers' Washington offices starting in 1987. The number of retirees in the hundred-bed home dwindled too. Only a few of them were once compositors. The rest were paying customers who may not have been laborers when they were young and spry enough to work.

"You used to have to be a member of the union to get in here," groused Leonard Whitehouse, who was sitting by—but not watching—a blaring TV down the hall from Elmo Collins's room as the century ticked away. "When a printer took sick, he'd come here and they'd cure him and send him home and it didn't cost him a dime. But now any Tom, Dick, and Harry can come here."[2]

The remaining hot-metal printers considered themselves a breed apart from the other residents, just as they always had considered themselves different from other laborers. An admiring outsider thought it might be because of where they worked. "It was a foundry," Charles Mulliken once re-called fondly by phone from Washington, D.C. Mulliken himself was soon retiring as head of an industry trade association whose members negotiated against the ITU, and was feeling nostalgic about the vast composing rooms where Whitehouse and the others toiled. "That was the nicest thing," he adds after a long pause. "It had to be off by itself somewhere. It didn't fit in a nice clean print shop. It didn't fit in an office. They just couldn't handle the dirty metal environment."[3]

Whitehouse, "a union man all my life," thought compositors became a different breed because their work was more important than others'. Born in England in 1904, he emigrated with his family in 1920 to Pittsburgh, where an uncle got him into a printing apprentice program. He was not shy. "I wanted to be better than the next man, and I was. I could set a line, go around a chair, and keep the machine writing. I was that fast." He was so fast, he says, that even later, after he became the kind of elite machinist that Lou Felicio was, he kept performing type miracles. At one Pittsburgh company, the "best operator . . . left one day and never came back. He died at home. I came in that morning, and without being asked, I sat down and finished the job he was working on. It was a book. They thought the world of me because I did it without being asked." But he didn't stay at that shop. He never stayed anywhere for long. "I believe that a man in the printing industry should keep moving. Staying in one plant is no good." You couldn't learn enough about printing in one place, and printing was just too damned important to let go unimproved. "Where would the world be without the printed word?" he asked suddenly over the blare of the television, which was tuned to a soccer game from Dubai, broadcast in Arabic. "It was the most important contribution to the civilization . . . Without printing, there'd be no education. People didn't even know what a vocabulary was before there was printing."

So he worked in Ohio, Pennsylvania, Michigan, and West Virginia, earning a living and, in retrospect, improving the printed word in the process. He put machines together for scores of newspapers and commercial print shops, each with their own ways of doing things. Each machine took about six days to assemble and install. Sometimes he stayed for a while, and was even made composing room foreman on two occasions. The lifestyle was tough, independent, and exciting, something not everyone could pull off. It was pretty hard on marriages, though. As he spoke, his wife was in a nursing home back in Pittsburgh; she'd left him long before. "I drank too much," he growls distractedly. "I could have done better for her."

On the other hand William Printz, a recent arrival at the home, joked that he "never had an argument with my wife because I was never home." He printed by day and played the bass violin in dance bands by night, often three times a week. He was a young man working in the print shop at Campbell Soup in New Jersey and playing nearby clubs at night when he met Elizabeth. "She," he said, placing a long fingernail on a picture of her he pulled from an padded envelope overstuffed with photos, "was a great dancer, great." They were together for sixty years, siring two daughters. "We struggled with everything," he recalled of money and time and parenting issues. They retired in 1974, ending up in Florida where Printz, among other things, played spoons with the retirement community's house band. Elizabeth died in Florida, and Printz "got degeneration of the bones. So I go out, and smile, and be happy" he allowed, wearing a large cowboy hat and pajamas in the TV room at the Union Printers Home. Leonard Whitehouse left the TV on when, perhaps a little hurt by Printz's interruption, he went back to his room.

Printz too had moved around, the Campbell's Soup print shop in the 1930s and then a private printing company in New Jersey that, nearly broken down, got rich doing government printing during World War II. Under a War Department contract, he helped put out phrase books that were printed in English on one side and a foreign language—Italian, French, or German—on the other. "We could tell whatever country the boys were going into. If anyone got ahold of the book, they could tell where we'd be attacking next. Then one night I go to a bar with a buddy and all of a sudden the FBI tapped him on the shoulder. They took him away. I think it was for spying. I haven't seen him since."

Printz too was proud of his work. "I'm not bragging," he says of his next job at the Government Printing Office in New York, "but anything special that needed to be done, the boss would say, 'Printz, get down to the eighth floor and get on the [headline machine].'"[4]

And Elmo Collins, educated at the University of Michigan and the University of Toledo, also was good. He was so good on the Linos that he was chapel chairman at the *Blade*, articulate and strong enough to face down management in 1966, farsighted enough to force his reluctant compositors to at least try to adapt to the new machines when they arrived. "A lot of people didn't want to do it. They were apprehensive about [computers]. It looked like it was just typing. I ran it by myself at first, and then I took one of the best [Lino] operators I ever saw and trained her on it. She was fast and accurate. She sat down at it, and she got it, but she hated it."

Collins himself kept at the technology, learning how to make it behave and training people on it. His hope was that, as had happened when hot-metal type replaced hand type in the late nineteenth century, his colleagues would simply insist on running the cold type that was replacing hot metal in the late twentieth century. He had eighty people trained by 1972 when he heard from the *Toledo City Journal*. Its editor wanted to know if he could set the paper for him. "I got a call at 6:00 P.M. from him saying 'how'd you like to go into business for yourself?'" Collins thus left the *Blade* to start his own type shop; it was phototype, run by union members.

But there was trouble with his partner—"he ripped me off for $100,000"—and his business went bankrupt. Worse yet, his wife got sick. Diagnosed with cancer, she fell into a coma that lasted twenty months before she died. Then he got sick too. Doctors diagnosed the early signs of Parkinson's disease and told him he did not have long to live.

Collins believed it was the nature of the work that had made typesetters special. "A printer had to be knowledgeable in a number of things," Collins had once maintained, before Parkinson's robbed him of the ability to speak clearly and at length. "He had to be up-to-date. It was the kind of work you were doing. And you learned by osmosis, if nothing else. Printers had to read. Printers were the guys who were caught in the middle between the people with ideas and the people they dispersed the information to."

Printers thus "were six jumps ahead of the rest of the people." And they acted like it. "There is an arrogance. They did feel they were the aristocrats of labor. The mind-set was that you had a trade, so you felt egotistical and better than other people. We were trained, and we knew what we were supposed to do."

Collins had started to write a history of the compositors, whom he called "aristocrats of labor," but his Parkinson's finally made his research impossible. In a 1994 interview, he said he hoped someone else would come along either to help him or to take it over from him before it was too late.[5] Five years later, unaware of Collins's previous interview or his unpublished history, another visitor showed up to plumb his memories about the ITU, about type, about the great march into a century in which every Tom, Dick, and Harry could not only get into the Union Printers Home but print anything they wanted, whenever they wanted. No trained laborers—no middlemen "between the people with ideas and the people they dispersed the information to," no links between the thinker and the world—would be necessary.

Elmo Collins was clearly stimulated by the attention and, perhaps, the thought of the costs of printing and the monopolies of information collapsing to nothing before our eyes. But excitement stirred up his disease, which made his parts do unplanned things and thickened his voice to almost unintelligible levels as he rushed to spill out his hope of cowriting a history about the aristocrats of labor, or at least sharing his formidable knowledge about them. Gesturing emphatically in ever shorter sentence fragments, this once articulate self-made man slipped to an improbable, uncomfortable angle in his wheelchair. Desperate to make himself understood, he pointed mysteriously at his computer. It was many years later that his visitor stumbled across the 1994 interview Collins had given and finally realized what the union leader had been trying to say.

With a great effort, Collins fitfully regained enough mastery over his traitorous body to tell brief stories of his life and the wife he missed so much. He could, he boasted, name the cities in which the ITU had held its conventions in each year since 1873. He outlined the 1966 dispute in Toledo, the underlying—and achingly frustrating to someone as distrustful of authority as Collins—conservatism of the ITU's trade unionism, and the history of the Union Printers Home itself. He did not want the day to end. When it was time to finish, he started to object but, beset by an illness that made him more emotional than he wanted to be, his eyes filled up again. Which, after another difficult swallow, meant it was time to gather himself, shake hands as best as he could, and, hoarsely and softly, say good-bye.

NOTES

1. Ward Harkavy, "The Castle on the Hill," *Westword*, May 11, 1994, www .westword.com/issues/1994-05-11/feature2.html (accessed September 17, 2004).

2. Leonard Whitehouse, interview, December 11, 1999.

3. Charles Mulliken, telephone interview, September 23, 1998. Mulliken's Washington-based group was called the Typographers International Association.

4. William Printz, interview, December 11, 1999.

5. Harkavy, "Castle"; Elmo Collins, interview, December 11, 1999.

IV

LIFE AFTER TYPE

23

WORDS OUT OF DOTS, ROLLED OUT OF FACTORIES

The age of movable type was over. Much had been transformed amid its mixed blessings of common information and wildly ricocheting provocations. By its sunset, people in the West had dramatically lengthened human life, learned to live comfortably in previously hostile environments, reduced the injurious and all-consuming struggles for food and shelter to quick errands, transferred spiritual insight and moral authority from the pulpit to the congregant, learned to move on the ground at unprecedented speeds, fly in the air, remain submerged underwater for months at a time, and fitfully began to share political power among huge throngs of people. Merchants often stood where clerics, kings, and even nation-states stood at the era's start. (By the start of the millennium, Microsoft was worth as much as Spain, American Express as much as New Zealand, Citigroup as much as Egypt.)[1] We had been an oral culture. Now we were a visual culture. We could kill from great distances, sometimes with invisible poisons and sometimes without intent. Our cruelties, it's true, were as horrifying as they had been when the age began. By its end, however, the devils who caused them had assumed new names, many of them just a few decades old, out of psychology, sociology, and economics.

No one, needless to say, knows much about what's taking its place yet. Life after type began only a few decades ago and in the broad sweep of history remains a mewling infant. Even its birth date is unclear. A historian could reasonably call it the day Rene Higonnet landed in New York in 1946, looking for funding. Or the day a purchasing director at Western Electronic signed off on buying a Photon in 1960. Or in 1962, when the *Los Angeles Times* started wringing text out of a mainframe computer. It could have been at the press conferences and hotel open houses held to announce the arrival of the transistor in 1947, core computer memory in

1952, or the integrated circuit in the mid-1960s. It could have been more than a century earlier, with the invention of the binary alphabet and the punch card. All those developments and more gradually reduced our reliance on type and let us communicate in unprecedented ways.

We do know that, in the past, other things changed when type—the way we wrote and printed—changed. We have always assigned outsize meaning to the alphabets of Egypt, of Aldus, of Ottmar Mergenthaler and Reginald Orcutt, and now George Boole, to name a few. Arid journal reports about unplugged machines came alive when it came to type. "Ink and paper are the tools," one number-filled story about a 1981 tech show exhibit abruptly noted when it came to type machines, "but type is the essence of thought itself."[2]

So when type changed, thought changed. Marshall McLuhan, perhaps the twentieth century's best-known thinker about such things, believed it too. As type itself became an image, made up of patterns of tiny dots, it occurred to him that our thoughts also had become mere images, products not of facts logically ordered to reveal some conclusion, but of tiny impressions briefly arranged as an idea. Much as impressions randomly occur next to each other to form a new thought, so the pieces of our world—our values as well as our objects—might land in new relationships to each other, creating new views and meanings. Not everyone believed this was good. Warren Chappell, a historian of both artful type and artful thought, feared our thinking was becoming as flat, textureless, imitative, and impermanent as our flimsy new alphabets. Our sense of right and wrong, according to some, also had come unfixed, relative to whatever situation we happened to find ourselves in. Our social memory was shrinking too. "The inherently ephemeral nature of electronic files," added another writer pondering the future of scholarly publishing, "means that everything we thought we knew and believed we could rely on . . . now applies only to those [thoughts] that have been fixed in print. A whole new class of such artifacts, digital texts, has come into being, and while we are exploring the new possibilities they offer . . . we also have a great deal to rethink and relearn: our ideas about textual authority, accessibility, stability, and preservation; even our ideas about what it means to read and how to use information."[3] Evidence might be relative, subject to one's point of view, a shaky thing on which to build a moral code.

Something important, in any case, always seemed to follow such changes in the past and something important, we suspected, was unfolding again.

To many, it arrived in small, unremarkable events and accretions:

For example, when the *Kansas City Star* plunked him down in front of a bunch of lighted computer buttons in 1966, college dropout Gary Krohm saw a machine that was meant to help get rid of the messy, troublesome compositors who made printing the paper so expensive. "Girl" typists and low-wage nineteen-year-olds like Krohm would replace them.

As he learned the machine and watched the effect it had on people, however, he too suspected the device had some broader, deeper meaning. After going on to engineer complex editorial systems for publishers and printers in New Jersey, Arizona, Arkansas, Texas, California, Indiana, Illinois, Oregon, New York, and points between, Krohm came to see technology as a gatekeeper. When it was expensive and hard to run, it denied people certain knowledge, kept them out of certain jobs, and prevented them from earning certain incomes. Then another tool would come along—cheaper, easier to operate—and open the gate, letting new people practice knowledge-based professions.[4] Commerce. Teaching. Law. Warfare. That's what happened when the press let more people create and read written communications in the 1400s. That's what happened in the late nineteenth century, when new technology dropped the price of the printed word again. And that, to Krohm and many others, appeared to be what was happening as the computer was making it still cheaper to manufacture and get one's hands on written knowledge.

To others, it looked like something more than a gate was opening. A fence that had separated those who could communicate in print from those who could not had fallen down.

Master printers were not sure what to make of the death of movable type. On one hand, they abruptly had bold new powers. Two years after he learned to work the *Star*'s big IBM mainframe, for instance, Gary Krohm encountered Compugraphic machines and then minicomputers that made it even easier and cheaper to manufacture printed information. "People started thinking, hmm, we can actually put out a newspaper now . . . That essentially allowed smaller papers to compete with bigger papers," like Krohm's own *Star*. Experts like him next rewired the big computers to "paginate" (arrange elements on a screen to appear just the way they'd look when printed on paper). And then came relatively inexpensive software packages that replaced much of Krohm's hardwiring work. They could paginate and print on computers that fit on a desktop. As a result, one of Krohm's clients went from owning one newspaper in 1983 to twenty-four in 1987, the year the telephone workers officially gave shelter to the under-employed compositors of the International Typographical Union.[5]

In practice, press owners had been freed of many of the historic limits on their businesses. The union that had kept their labor costs high and, in effect, regulated how quickly they could adopt new tools was falling away. Their production costs had dropped again. A print shop owner spent an average of $1.70 to print a full-color eight-and-a-half-by-eleven page for a customer in 1932. The average cost to produce it in 2000, as the new era was gaining traction, was about forty cents.[6]

And the industry boomed. The nation was in a down economic patch during the five years after the ITU disappeared into the communications workers' union. Personal computers and laser printers, which were supposed to take business away from commercial printers, were proliferating. But commercial printers' sales (meaning marketing, packaging, personal and business materials) grew by 18 percent. Total employment, despite wholesale closures of hot-metal type shops as computer type spread, grew by 2 percent. Laborers' pay increased by almost 25 percent. Sales of *all* kinds of manufactured printing and publishing (including books ·and newspapers) jumped by 20 percent. After twelve years of worrisome declines, even the number of newspapers—led by a large increase in the number of weekly papers—abruptly shot up (by more than 25 percent) in the United States. In western Europe, newsprint consumption grew from about 7 million tons per year in 1985—just after the personal computer hit the market—to more than 10 million in 2000. They also produced unprecedented numbers of new books. Virtually all nations were publishing more—usually substantially more—new book titles each year at the end of the 1990s than they were at the beginning. Argentina (167 percent), Brazil (188 percent), France (29 percent), Germany (32 percent), Japan (61 percent), South Korea (734 percent), Netherlands (26 percent), Portugal (49 percent), and Russia (61 percent), to name a few, were pumping out more titles. Even England and the United States, already the world's most avid book producers, were publishing more (the annual number of new titles in the United Kingdom was 73 percent higher in 2000 than in 1990; the U.S. output was 38 percent higher). Worldwide newspaper production, by one measure, was still increasing at better than a 3.5 percent rate. The number of terabytes of printed information in newspapers rose by 11 percent from 1999 to 2002.[7]

The boom would continue. Through the 1990s, sales in this now mature (meaning slow-growing) industry would jump by another 40 percent in the United States. Even after what was supposed to be the onset of a "paperless society," more than a million people worked in the printing industry at the turn of the century, almost 10 percent more than had worked in it in 1994, the year of the Linotype-Hell open house. Sales had grown faster than the gross domestic product. By the year 2000, print manufacturers collectively were the sixth largest industry in the globe's biggest economy.[8]

They were big companies too. The raw number of printing plants had peaked in the United States in 1993, at 54,462, and then, thanks to a wave or mergers and retirements, declined by 18 percent during the next ten years. (Most of the companies that closed had been small, acquired by more successful firms or liquidated by a retiring generation of phototype printers unwilling to take on the expense and reorganization necessary to adapt to computer type.)[9] The remaining companies, still 44,000-strong, employed more people and sold more printing than the 54,000 smaller firms that preceded them.

And they had come to manufacture different kinds of printed knowledge. Sales of hot-metal era products like business forms, catalogs, legal and medical and technical manuals were dead or dying. Increasingly, press owners sold packaging, periodicals, books, direct mail, freestanding ads, sales materials, and low volumes of the countless kinds of random printed communications we like to make. They also had begun to manage databases, store information for clients, distribute print through the mails and Internet, and, among other new services, provide creative and marketing expertise to their clients.[10]

But those first years after type were troubling too. As in past centuries when the organizations and governments that controlled their trade lost power, master printers in the 1980s and 1990s again found that life without regulation—this time the ITU de facto regulation—was often very uncomfortable.

Competition, for one thing, became white hot. The costs of entering the business had fallen to historic lows. Small offset presses were cheap. Labor was now cheap. Type, as it now existed, was nearly free. Good news on the one hand, the bargains also meant literally thousands of newcomers could compete for low-end printing jobs. Prices for most kinds of manufactured printing, even high quantities of sophisticated multicolor and oversize printing, fell.[11] Produced on standardized and easily operated machines, many varieties of the printed word become a commodity; something one company could do as well as the next. Prices for the press owners' most important remaining raw material, paper, were maddeningly volatile. The forces—foreign and local—that drove the prices fluctuated wildly outside the ability of governments, guilds, industry associations, or unions to control or even influence. They sometimes drove the costs of *staying* in business higher. Soon enough, distracted by competition and looking gray among the glamorous new media popping up around them in the unregulated chaos, even prospering press owners and publishers seemed to lose their confidence. They were, in many ways, confused.

They had reined in their bully, early-twentieth-century American news "empires" decades before. They no longer aimed to serve countless millions of readers. Periodical and news publishers, in fact, were aggressively *eliminating* customers. Hoping to save postage and printing costs, in 1970 *Look* magazine fired—refused to renew subscriptions for—certain readers their advertisers did not care to reach. The trend caught on. Endangered *Life* magazine tried to fire 2 million rural readers before shutting down as a weekly photo book. Gannett newspapers, the *Atlanta Journal and Constitution*, *Minneapolis Star*, *Chicago Tribune*, *Rocky Mountain News*, and *Los Angeles Times*, among many others, also purposely shed readers in the 1980s and early 1990s. In 1991, the American Newspaper Publishers Association's marketing plan recommended that newspapers—the world's first mass medium—no longer seek mass audiences. As a rule of thumb, it suggested they drop a third of their readers by the turn of the twenty-first century.[12]

By then, Reginald Orcutt's messianic spread of Linotypes—and, as he maintained, the printed word and democracy with them—to the Middle East, North Africa, and the darker corners of Europe was long gone. Only crazy publishers still aspired to print prodigious amounts of information and distribute it as broadly as possible. The nation's press barons instead focused exclusively on serving their most profitable customers. The best ones aggressively managed their balance sheets to bulk up financially, consolidate, and often share risk by taking on partners. Both news and printing companies launched big merger waves during the 1990s. Their next steps included mandating operational efficiencies, calming critical stockholders, lobbying to make the tax burdens of passing businesses on to their children less onerous and recalculating the tilting management ratios of running mature, substantial businesses. They did not tend to dart headlong into risk.

In 1994, by contrast, America's ascendant cable, broadcast, broadband, satellite, telephone, and wireless communications companies were on an Orcutt-like mission of world conquest. Their lobbyists were roughly bumping Congress into writing a deregulation bill to help them create a world profitably "wrapped in continuous high-speed transmissions of voices, texts, pictures and moving images." Meanwhile print manufacturers were on the sidelines, struggling mostly with what to call themselves. Like teenagers trying to strike just the right pose in the mirror, they incessantly changed their names in their own trade journals and associations. They tried out the "graphic arts industry," the "document publishing" industry, and the "printing and imaging" industry, among others. "Print and distribute" companies became "distribute and print" companies. "Quick printers" became "on-demand" printers. "Printers . . . are no longer in the printing business," one trade journal editor added at the time, "but in the information services business."[13]

About 25 percent of the nation's "graphic arts firms," one poll found at the end of the century, were "openly wondering what direction their companies will take a year from now."[14]

"The industry I grew up in is having an identity crisis," one of the industry's more learned observers joked to a 1994 "desktop publishers" conference in San Francisco. (Desktop publishers did digitally what compositors used to do with metal.) "Remember when we switched from hot metal to phototypesetting? Then to computer typesetting? And then to video editing and multi-terminal systems? Then to CRT typesetting and then to laser imaging? Then sometime in the Eighties it became publishing. Now I hear of new markets. 'Multimedia' is said to be a half-trillion-dollar market. No one can define 'multimedia', which is why the market is so big. *Business Week* described a $93 billion document publishing market, which is greater than the total value of shipments of the entire commercial printing industry, at just under $60 billion. The difference must be postage and handling."[15]

By the new millennium's early years, printing companies advertising in the industry's trade journals no longer dared to present themselves as anything as romantic or presumptuous as being merchants of knowledge, progress, or democracy. By that point the best the industry could do was try to borrow status from its more glamorous competitors. In 2002, one of the country's most important remaining trade associations—the Graphic Arts Information Network, which had itself been born of a recent merger and adopted a new name—recommended that printers include the phrase "Print: The Original Information Technology" on their cartons, stationery, and business cards. The association advised that the phrase would persuade the public to perceive them not as printers, but "as part of the information technology, or 'IT' sector of the U.S. economy."[16]

In the turmoil, some tried to become IT companies themselves. Prompted by glowing trade journal reports (many placed by equipment manufacturers) of how a printing company had conquered the new world by buying a certain kind of technology, still others frequently shifted strategic directions. Some determined that instability itself might be good management.

In 1989 the head of R. R. Donnelley & Sons looked at his unprecedented arsenal of powerful printing capabilities and announced that the times demanded that his profitable institution, then the nation's biggest printing company, change. John Walter, CEO of the onetime ITU nemesis, said that by 2000 the company should get 50 percent of its sales from products and services it did not produce yet. He proceeded to buy other companies that offered new kinds of products and services, weave them into his existing operations, and realign his own divisions and departments to try to make them all fit together. The bold makeovers, another Donnelley executive proudly proclaimed, sprang from an enlightened, innovative policy of "if it ain't broke, break it!" Ultimately managers had to break even the new products and services. By 1996, it became clear that Donnelley had overpaid for some of its acquisitions. Sales of some of the new services were disappointing, and several of the company's long-profitable management and production practices were troublingly disrupted. A dramatically less profitable Donnelly thus began retrenching, selling off divisions and downsizing.[17]

The industry's prosperity and regulatory freedom, in short, did little to lift its collective mood. To many, the future looked short. Bad news was everywhere.

Two leading analysts, for example, greeted the turn of the century with a warning that the industry was about to suffer yet another "revolution," probably during the next twelve months. (The free radical, they said, was a new kind of computer file—the portable document format [PDF]—that was going to lower demand for manufactured printed communications.) "This is a remarkable time to be in the industry," one of them deadpanned. "It's analogous to the beginning of the industrial revolution when technological change was creating new markets, new groups of customers, and certainly new types of businesses. We're just beginning to understand the scope of change and we see that the effects will be far-reaching for print businesses of all sizes."[18]

Their predictions did not immediately come true, but by then much—perhaps most—printed information did not come out of the companies that used to manufacture it anyway. While good consultants worried about the imminent decline of the printed word industry, the printed word itself had never been more ubiquitous.

The next life of the printed word, it turned out, was not springing from printing organizations at all.

In the early 1930s, an idealistic twenty-one-year-old British graduate student named Ronald Coase toured the United States gathering material for a paper on the structure of certain storied American manufacturing corporations. Visiting Ford and General Motors, however, the young socialist soon found himself pondering an even more fundamental question: Why are we driven to organize ourselves into these vast, smoke-belching, labor-crunching companies in the first place?

After six years of calculations and interviews, he found a reason. It costs us something, he discovered, each time we exchange goods or services with each other. Substantial time, material, labor, and even space costs are required just to get to the point of making a transaction. The knowledge that went into designing a product represented years of tuition, experience, and effort. Bolts, trips to the library, telegrams to potential suppliers, rent; all were expenses both owners and workers had in creating, selling, and delivering their products and services. Coase figured we'd all just act on our own if we could, but such "transaction costs" usually were beyond an individual's ability to bear. Needing to share those costs meant we needed to act in concert with others. In a 1937 paper that helped bring him a Nobel Prize in 1991, he pointed out that we organize ourselves into companies. "In the absence of transaction costs," he wrote, "there is no economic [reason] for the existence of the firm."

The transaction costs of creating many kinds of printed words, it seems, had all but vanished after movable type died. The machinery a person needed to produce a printed black-and-white letter-size sheet of paper had gone cheap. In 1968, Compugraphics had sold its breakthrough phototypesetting models to businesses for about $10,000, about 2.5 times the average American's income in 1970. But by 1982, amateurs could set type with the Commodore 64 (the decade's best-selling personal computer) for $595, less than 6 percent of the average per capita personal income in the United States in 1980. And by 2000, a low-end Dell model—suitable for many business and government purposes—could be had for $599, or about 2 percent of an average American's annual personal income.[19] As the printed word's transaction costs fell, in sum, great hordes of amateurs no longer needed press owners and their puzzlements of pricey, heavy machines to help them communicate in print.

The evolution of the printed word into a personal medium was mostly unplanned. Print tinkerers, entrepreneurs, and regulators had little to do with it. It was instead the spawn of mathematicians and, more eccentrically still, thinkers concerned about memory—the very thing Socrates (at least according to Plato) thought we were in danger of losing and that Vannevar Bush worried we had overloaded. Printing probably was the farthest thing from their minds.

Good minds, needless to say, have been struggling to extend our memories since at least 3000 B.C.E., when the dust abacus, probably the first calculating device, was invented in Babylonia to shorten the work of memorizing formulas. Between the invention of printing by lever and the nineteenth century came quadrants (to calculate astronomical distances), watches (to calculate time), Napier's bones (which numbered things), slide rules, logarithms, Pascal's arithmetic machine, Leibnitz's calculator and punch cards. The inventive storm of the 1800s yielded more dozens of advances: Thomas de Colmar started selling the first commercially useful calculating machine in 1820. Charles Babbage fashioned first a "difference engine" and then, after a falling out with his partner, an "analytical engine" to solve equations with the use of punch cards. George Boole invented an alphabet—binary code—to speed calculating in 1850. In 1875, a Japanese company, the forerunner of Toshiba, brought out a variable-toothed gear that in the 1880s enabled inventors to create still faster math machines. Some computed the results as the numbers themselves were entered in a calculator and then printed them. By century's end, the United States was using punch cards to tabulate data for its census. (Its census contractor, Herman Hollerith, soon founded the company that would become IBM.) The twentieth century started with Nikola Tesla, one of Edison's employees, patenting electrical logic circuits. From there, advances in computing accelerated: Bush's differential analyzer in 1925, C. E. Wynn Williams's binary counter in 1932, Konrad Zuse's mechanical memory (with pins that moved from side to side to suggest a binary code of zero or one) in 1936, the same year Alan Turing published a paper that outlined how more advanced computers might work. The machines arrived immediately. In the short period before World War II began, Claude Shannon figured out a way to tap out binary pin codes with electricity, Zuse created a machine he could control with memory tape, Bell Labs got a machine to do math with Boolean logic, and two Iowa State scientists built a prototype of an automatic digital computer. During World War II came a "complex number calculator" from George Stibitz and an automatically controlled calculating machine from Konrad Zuse. J. Presper Eckert and John W. Mauchly created ENIAC (which stood for electronic numerical integrator and computer and was the first electronic digital calculator), and Harvard's Howard Aiken fashioned the first digital computer. Its 750,000 component parts weighed in at almost five tons. Britain installed three of the big computers, each called Colossus, for war work in 1944. In 1945, the same year Bush's "As We May Think" came out in the *Atlantic Monthly,* John von Neumann—whose research idea Bush once had deemed too impractical to fund—figured out a way to store programs inside the memory of a machine.

Until then programming, like typing, had been a low-paid task usually assigned to women. Charles Babbage may have started the tradition, hiring Ada Tennyson, wife of Lord Tennyson, to program punch cards for his analytical engine in the early nineteenth century. By the middle of the twentieth century, programming remained a ponderous process of "setting dials and plugging a bewildering mass of black cables into the face of the computer, a different configuration for each problem." During the three years spent developing ENIAC in Philadelphia, "dozens of women, many with mathematical backgrounds, had patiently calculated the ballistic tables, as they tediously solved differential equations by using pencil, paper and hand calculation in a long-drawn-out process." To the male engineers, it looked like uncreative work; mere math and vaguely clerical. They demeaned the women, dismissing them as "computers."

Six of the women plotted out and set the maze of plugs to send electrical impulses in the correct order to solve the trajectory problem the men had posed for ENIAC's unveiling in February 1946. The demonstration, all agreed, was a hit. But after the triumph, as one chronicler of the event put it, "the engineers went out for a celebratory dinner. The programmers went home." Two years before, a woman named Grace Hopper had programmed Aiken's historic Harvard Mark I calculating machine (parts of which are now displayed at the Smithsonian Institution in Washington). While straightening up during the work on the Mark II, the machine's next version, she discovered a dead moth in the tangle of parts and wires, and figured out that it had been the reason a delicate relay had been mysteriously failing. She famously taped the moth into the project log with the note, "First actual case of bug being found."[20]

But once taken out of human hands and wired directly into a computer, the limits on programming were pretty much the same as the limits of mechanical memory. And mechanical memory itself expanded almost unimaginably during the last half of the twentieth century. First the transistor in 1947, then the core memory in 1952 and the integrated circuit in 1958 increased memory's power and decreased the space it needed to occupy. In effect, the vast tonnage and maze of wires gradually shrank to fit on boards and panels that could be put into and removed from slots in the machines. The circuits themselves—which conducted electrical impulses to switches to be turned from zero to one, as needed—kept getting smaller too. So did the boards and panels. They promised to shrink more. In 1965, one Gordon Moore predicted the numbers of circuits that could fit on one of the integrated circuits would double each year through 1972, and double every eighteen months thereafter. His prediction came true. After cofounding Intel in 1964, Moore started laying circuits in even tinier strands made of silicon on panels so small they were called chips. By 1971, they could fit in a handheld calculator that was as powerful as ENIAC had been in 1946. They were also cheap. They cost $1,000 each in the early 1960s, $20–$30 by the decade's end.[21]

The lumbering calculating giants of World War II shrank too, but only after a painfully slow commercial start. Few people in the beginning were sure who might buy the things or how they might use them. The War Department, in announcing the fifty-ton ENIAC in 1946, thought companies that made "electron tubes, jet engines, gas turbines and other types of engines" might be interested, proclaiming the big machine was "expected to revolutionize the mathematics of engineering and change many of our industrial design methods." The sale price was $400,000, which translates into a little more than $2 million in early twenty-first century money. In 1947 Harvard's Aiken, whose Mark II became IBM's first marketed mainframe, estimated that the American demand for the behemoths might be a total of six machines. He underestimated the initial demand, but not by much. In 1951 and 1952, a few nonmilitary federal agencies like the U.S. Census Bureau, a few big corporations like Northrup Aircraft, and a handful of universities like Georgia Tech and Manchester University bought mainframes. In 1953, a risk-friendly British catering company bought one to do its data processing. A handful of other companies—DuPont, U.S. Steel, Franklin Life Insurance, Westinghouse, Sylvania, and Consolidated Edison—acquired mainframes during the next few years, using them to process data and replace the labor that used to do their calculating by hand and desk machine. But business in general adopted them only grudgingly during the early 1950s. Size, price, and even language barriers between scientists and executives kept the pace slow. To ENIAC coinventor J. Presper Eckert corporate buyers seemed frustratingly ignorant. "When we first tried to sell businessmen on the idea of using magnetic tape to store their information," he told an interviewer many years later, "one of them . . . said, 'Well, suppose my competitor gets a big magnet and puts it in a truck and drives by and destroys all my records?'" Eckert replied with a precise, probably mindboggling description of how magnetic fields work, concluding that "the size magnet you would have to put on the large truck . . . is beyond getting down most of our streets to do that. It's impossible to do that." (It's not known if he got the sale.) When General Electric bought a UNIVAC (as Remington Rand had renamed the machine when it acquired Eckert and Mauchley's company) in 1954, GE executives were not sure how the company would use it. "While scientists and engineers have been wide-awake in making progress with these remarkable tools, business, like Rip Van Winkle, has been asleep," a company officer explained to dubious stockholders. "GE's installation of a UNIVAC may be Rip Van Business's first 'blink.'"[22]

The U.S. government remained the world's biggest buyer of computers until they got a little smaller in the late 1950s and early 1960s. In 1958 a Harvard-based company called Digital Electronics Corporation introduced a "minicomputer." Although it was still huge by twenty-first-century standards, it was cheaper than mainframes. Markets broadened and sales began to improve. In 1960, the U.S. military still bought half the world's computers. During the next thirteen years, however, large and midsize businesses like, say, newspapers and communications companies bought 94 percent of the machines. They often were hooked into phototype machines. In 1964 the Harris-Intertype company predicted there might be "several thousand" potential buyers for its new, smaller computer designed specifically for creating printed words. Priced at $40,000 (about a third of the price of the cheapest general-purpose computers newspapers were then buying), Harris thought it might revolutionize not only printing but also the computer industry. It was partly correct. While Harris, Compugraphic, Mergenthaler, and others created more affordable computers to connect to photo machines, other companies began fashioning them for more modest business uses. Almost one hundred companies—including Texas Instruments, Varian Associates, California Data Processors, Prime Computer, Lockheed Electronics, and Hewlett Packard—began selling minicomputers from 1968 to 1972. Engineering firms were their biggest customers.

But sometimes companies just sold time on the devices to businesses that could not afford to lease or buy them. One Seattle startup, the Computer Center Corporation, bought a minicomputer and set out to sell time on it to smaller firms. Before it folded in 1970, it brought in a Krohm-like teenager named Bill Gates to help debug the machine. It paid him by giving him time to learn how it worked and play on it.[23]

And as memory chips became smaller, cheaper, and more powerful, the minicomputer owners—not investors or suppliers or even engineers—often were the ones who prodded and pushed for smaller, simpler, downmarket machines that did only a few specialized tasks.

The president of publisher McGraw-Hill, for example, maintained that it had been people like him—"the customer, the publisher"—who had demanded new computers from an unwilling industry during the 1960s. Of the nine printers McGraw-Hill used in the 1960s, "not one saw the potential" in cold type, David Jansen told a printing convention workshop in 1980. Upon hiring someone to adapt computers to his magazines' needs, Jensen "took composition from the printer and gave it to a composition house in New York City. Our printers are no longer our compositors, and they never will be again." He reported he was also working with a supplier to help him add "electronic preparation and scanning abilities" to his company's modified computers. Separately, the publisher of *U.S. News & World Report* recalled it was he, not a computer firm, who decided how his people could best use computer type. When he went looking for an electronic editorial system in 1972, he recalled, he could not find one on the shelf or an "established manufacturer ready to build one." Working with a consultant, he finally unearthed three more Krohm-like wizards, this time in Lexington, Massachusetts. They, according to the by-then standard plot for romantic business legends, had "no money, no customers, and no finished product. They did have a prototype video display terminal, encased in a cardboard whisky carton." Needless to say, backed by $50,000 from the magazine, they engineered a working system and went on to form Atex, one of the era's most successful word processing companies.[24] It might have become another Mergenthaler Linotype Company, had scientists, customers, and innovators—in a rough copy of how inventors in the fifteenth, early nineteenth, and late nineteenth centuries had been separately working on startlingly similar printing ideas—not been moving at warp speed around it.

NOTES

1. Five days before the start of the new millennium, Microsoft had a market value of $593 billion (the same as Spain's gross domestic product), American Express, $66 billion, Citicorp, $184 billion. Similarly IBM and Colombia shared a value of $201 billion; Oracle and Chile a value of $121 billion, and Home Depot and Bangladesh a value of $155 billion. Gretchen Morgenson, "A Company Worth More Than Spain?" *New York Times*, December 26, 1999, 3.

2. David Henry Goodstein, "Typesetting Moves from a Master Craft to a Computer Application in Today's World," *Graphic Arts Monthly*, June 1981, 36.

3. Peter Givler, "University Press Publishing in the United States," in Richard E. Abel and Lyman W. Newman, eds., *Scholarly Publishing: Books, Journals, Publishers, and Libraries in the Twentieth Century* (Hoboken, N.J.: Wiley, 2002), aaupnet.org/resources/upusa.html (accessed November 26, 2004).

4. Gary Krohm, telephone interview, October 15, 1998.

5. Krohm, interview.

6. Frank J. Romano, *Print Media Distribution in a Digital Age* (Rochester: Print Industry Center of the Rochester Institute of Technology, 2002), 11.

7. The number of jobs at type shops shrank by 30.6 percent during the five years after the ITU vanished. The number of composing businesses fell by 25 percent. U.S. Department of Commerce, *Economic Census, 1992*, SIC Code 27; Jaakko Poyry Consulting, "Increase in Newsprint Consumption Despite the Spread of E-media," *Financial Times*, May 18, 2000; Peter Lyman and Hal R. Varian, How Much Information? October 2003, table 1.3, www.sims.berkeley.edu/how-much-info-2003 (accessed December 26, 2004); International Publishers Association, Annual Book Title Production, April 10, 2001, www.ipa.uie.org/statistics/annual_book_prod .html (accessed December 29, 2004).

8. The total number of nonnewspaper weekly periodicals declined precipitously, although monthly, bimonthly, and quarterly periodicals multiplied by more than 50 percent. George Thomas Kurian, *Datapedia of the United States, 1790–2000* (Lanham, Md: Bernan, 1994), 311. Employment in 2000 was 1.2 million people. Printing Industries of America, *Printing Marketing Atlas, 2004* (Alexandria, Va.: Graphic Arts Information Network, 2004); Joe Webb and Jim Whittington, "Forecast 2000," *Trendwatch Reports*, November 15, 1999.

9. One of the industry's leading economists at the turn of the century reported that what was "happening to America's printing plant population is analogous to general population trends. We had a 'baby boom' of printing plants started in the '50s and '60s as the population, economy and industry grew strongly. This 'baby boom' generation of plants naturally evolved and . . . grew from very small, to small, to medium, to large." When small and medium-size plant owners approached retirement age as the century ended, they were confronting an industry that was "changing dramatically, with slower growth of traditional ink-on-paper printing and increased sales of digital printing and ancillary services." Rather than invest in new technology and learn to organize their businesses around it, many boomers did exactly what their predecessors did when, as young adopters of cheap new tools, they brought new kinds of small printing organizations to market: they liquidated. Ronnie H. Davis, "The Changing Landscape of Printing Plants," *Economic and Print Market Report* (Alexandria, Va.: Printing Industries of America, 2004).

10. Printing Industries of America, *Vision 21: The Printing Industry Redefined for the 21st Century* (Alexandria, Va.: Printing Industries of America, 2000), 5, 67.

11. Frank J. Romano, *Print Media Distribution in a Digital Age* (Rochester: Print Industry Center of the Rochester Institute of Technology, 2002), 11.

12. Thomas C. Leonard, *News for All: America's Coming-of-Age with the Press* (New York: Oxford University Press, 1995), 171, 173–75.

13. Reed Hundt, *You Say You Want a Revolution* (New Haven: Yale University Press, 2000), 57, 77, 82–83; Hadley Sharples, "Chief Printers Plot Strategies," *Graphic Arts Monthly*, August 1995.

14. Joe Webb, "Business Vision Seen As Challenge for 1 in 4," *Graphic Arts Monthly*, July 1999.

15. Frank J. Romano, "The Market with No Name," *Seybold Report on Desktop Publishing*, www.isc.rit.edu/~spmswww/frank/frtalk.htm (accessed November 12, 1999).

16. Graphic Arts Information Network, Print: The Original Information Technology, www.gain.net/printIT/main.html (accessed August 22, 2004).

17. Printing Industries of America, *Bridging to a Digital Future* (Alexandria, Va.: Printing Industries of America, 1994), 2: 1. In Walter's years, Donnelley doubled its sales—$6.5 billion by 1996—by acquiring companies that imprinted diskettes and CDs for software companies, did "digital dissemination" of print, merged variable data, supplied online ordering, did computer network design, and even produced and mailed printed materials. Profits never followed. In 1996, the same year the company began retrenching, Walter was named head of the much larger AT&T, where he began pushing the firm to acquire its way into new markets and services. (His tenure at AT&T was short.) Jeff Borden, "Merger Puts Donnelley in Software Big League," *Crain's Chicago Business*, March 27, 1995, 10; Kris Hunter, "Donnelley Goes Digital with New Plant in Memphis," *Memphis Business Journal*, August 14, 1995, 35; Lisa Cross, "CD-ROM Intrigues Printers," *Graphic Arts Monthly*, November 1995; "On-Demand Show Hits a Home Run," *Graphic Arts Monthly*, August 1995; Tom Andreoli, "Lagging R.R. Donnelley Replates Its Future After Growth Spurt: Spinoffs and Focus on Returns," *Crain's Chicago Business*, October 14, 1996, 3; David E. Kalish, "AT&T Choice of Outside Leader Irks Wall Street," Associated Press, October 1996; Mike McKenzie, "Donnelley Offers Web Option for Catalogers," *Seybold Reports*, June 1998. Donnelley was not the only storied printing company interested in radical change. While Donnelley may have been different because it nearly bet the company in hurtling into the unknown, many other corporations had aggressive campaigns to invent and sell products different from the ones that had made them successful. In 1971, for example, the head of Xerox's research center in Palo Alto pledged to invent "information systems we do not yet know how to build, that will include technologies we have yet to discover." His scientists proceeded to develop a stunning series of computer breakthroughs, including the "graphical interface" that later made personal computer so easy and intuitive to use. But, thanks to management judgments about which of the company's inventions it should fund, Xerox (like Donnelley) never got to profit from the fruits of its policy. Douglas K. Smith and Robert C. Alexander, *Fumbling the Future: How Xerox Invented, Then Ignored, the First Personal Computer* (New York: Morrow, 1988), 146. Executives in all industries, uncertain about competing in the future, have funneled money into finding a new tool or product that will give them a competitive edge or have opted to consolidate. Merging with another company, of course, often accomplishes the same thing as innovation: provides different products to sell and, if it works, better access to capital, fresh talent and, not least, a comforting sense that they're not in this alone.

18. Joe Webb and James Whittington, "Forecast 2000," *Trendwatch Reports*, November 15, 1999. The portable document format was a late-1990s innovation by Adobe Systems.

19. Per capita personal income in 1970 was $4,095; in 1980, $10,163; and in 2000, $29,770. U.S. Census Bureau, *Statistical Abstract of the United States 2003*, no. HS-35, 66–67. The 2000 price was for a Dell Dimension Desktop PC. On turn of the millennium, an elderly Coase pointed out that the cost of organizing had dropped as well, sometimes as fast as the cost of transacting business. We may, he suggested, be on the way to becoming a nation of individual entrepreneurs. Thomas Petzinger Jr., "Talking about Tomorrow: Ronald Coase," *Wall Street Journal*, January 1, 2000; Robert L. Formaini and Thomas F. Siems, "Ronald Coase: The Nature of Firms and Their Costs," *Economic Insights* 8, no. 3 (2003).

20. Thomas P. Hughes, *Rescuing Prometheus* (New York: Pantheon, 1998), 55. Many women and many bugs followed. Until mechanical memory replaced them, programming, as DEC founder Gordon Bell put it, remained a function of "a whole floor full of little ladies wiring computers." The quote is from Paul E. Ceruzzi, *A History of Modern Computing* (Cambridge, Mass.: MIT Press, 1998), 180.

21. Ceruzzi, *Modern Computing*, 189, 21718, 354.

22. War Department, Bureau of Public Relations, "New Machine," February 15, 1946, 1; J. Lyons & Co was the British catering company. Frederick G. Kilgour, *The Evolution of the Book* (New York: Oxford University Press, 1998), 152; Ceruzzi, *Modern Computing*, 27–30, 32; Peter Vogt and David Allison, "Transcript of an Interview with J. Presper Eckert, Chief Engineer, ENIAC Computer," in *Development of the ENIAC*, Unit 9537 (Washington, D.C.: Smithsonian Video History Collection Record, 1988). The executive was Roddy F. Osborn. Commercial computer sales began to accelerate in the late 1950s. Bernard L. Peuto, "Mainframe History Provides Lessons," *Microprocessor Report*, March 31, 1997, 21.

23. Ronald J. Deibert, *Parchment, Printing, and Hypermedia: Communication in World Order Transformation* (New York: Columbia University Press, 1997), 122; "Special Computer for Printers," *Business Week*, March 7, 1964, 102; Ceruzzi, *Modern Computing*, 192, 208, 211, 213.

24. Robert S. McMichen, "Materials Preparation to Be Another 'In-House' Problem," *Typographical Journal*, April 1981, 14. Atex was founded by Douglas Drance, Charles Ying, and Richard Ying. "Printing by Computer: A USN&WR Gamble Pays Off," *U.S. News & World Report*, September 5, 1977, 56.

24

. . . AND OFFICES AND . . .

But the pace never slowed. Faster and cheaper communications tools appeared without pause. By 1980, four years after Atex's triumph, less expensive word processors were all the rage in offices. There were chips, cables, bigger monitors, trackballs, optical mice, eight-inch movable storage disks that shrank into three-inch disks and hundreds of new sets of programs along with them. And there were laser typesetters and dot matrix printers that, paired with cheap word processors, collectively gave private businesses nothing less than a "compatible, electronically interfaced, cooperative electronic production system."[1] They could now print things on their own. Unskilled typists, once again, would do the work.

Any company with money for a down payment and a line of credit could buy these things. Once dependent on expensive specialists, it could readily create printed information for itself. Businesses no longer needed a commercial printer to produce their forms, invoices, presentations, and analyses. "A significant amount of printing was moving in-house on to inkjet and laser printers," a printing industry association fretted in a study of what was happening. "In reality, it was this substitute for the print shop, combined with electronic alternatives, that led to the printing industry's loss of ground."

It promised to get worse. More office wonders were coming all the time now. "Intelligent copiers may one day become output printers," another observer warned.[2]

Lab closets, it seemed, overflowed with new office machines spilling out of them. Needless to say, it was a little more complicated than that, but the period was full of fantastic technical progress. Digital computing was then something like thirty-five years old. Software was perhaps twenty-five; microprocessors barely fifteen. Scientifically, a sort of sweet spot had been reached where discoveries of previous decades were combining into large, useful understandings, and where excited minds flocked to work the puzzles. Commercial minds saw possibilities, and money, thanks to Congress, began to flow to them. With anti-Vietnam war sentiment high and turmoil in the streets in 1970, Congress had forbidden using federal research money for "a specific military function or operation." Protesters were mostly concerned with limiting scarifying weapons, but the measure almost invisibly shifted resources away from the weapons- and systems-making products they'd funded since Vannevar Bush's day. They'd produced ever larger differential analyzers, ENIACs, and vast blinking control systems that, by the day of the shift, could remotely steer missiles and satellites and spaceships. But now money—and the computer talent trained on federal funds—went to quick-payback business products and applications that would have to fit within "the parameters of cost and marketing."[3]

Hewing to the new market discipline, the stalwarts in the business of hooking big computers up to big purposes—companies like Mergenthaler, Photon, Harris, Xerox, MITRE, RCA, Remington Rand, Fairchild, Alphanumeric, Bobst, DEC, and IBM, among others—began turning their attention to producing simple and easy-to-use office machines. Upstarts like Texas Instruments, Tandy, Casio, and Apple joined them. Aiming to win quick returns on their investment from cost-conscious (as opposed to federal) buyers, they collectively began to roll out waves of simple, small, relatively inexpensive computer products in the early 1970s. Most aimed to meet narrower needs than the ones helping governments track their enemies' movements moment by moment.

Some of the modest new business and office tools only did math: fantastically capable calculators came out for $3,500 in the late 1960s and $400 in 1971. Later that same year Intel brought out a new microprocessor that "executed at approximately the same speed as ENIAC," and sold it first to a Japanese company that used it in its desk calculators.[4] In 1972, HP offered a small $300 calculator that did most of the logarithms and trigonometry engineers recently could do only on room-size minicomputers. By 1976 Sharp, Casio, and Texas Instruments were selling lightweight math computers for under $50. They fit in a hand.

Some did special business tasks. In France, a $2,000 computer called MICRAL did a set number of industrial tasks for which companies previously had to buy time on general-purpose minicomputers. Intel briefly sold a chip that would let minicomputer users burn their own small programs into it. (Programs could not be changed after the first burn, however.) For $200, or for free in some cases, it distributed a printed circuit board with timing and control chips on it to engineers in certain small companies. In 1974, it marketed a $10,000 development system to let technically savvy business people create and save their own code to manage operations.[5]

And some printed. Getting computers to physically create a printed word had been in the works at least since the early 1960s, when MIT students programmed a $120,000 minicomputer to work like an "expensive typewriter." They did it, in part, to prove it could be done. In 1964, IBM unveiled a typewriter that, with a magnetic tape, could recall keystrokes and thus type out the same document time and again. In 1968, a Brown University professor hooked a small, unthinking monitor into a distant minicomputer and wired a way for a typist to insert copy, retrieve information from a file, delete it, or even move it around a screen lighted by a cathode ray tube. With another signal, it could reproduce the copy on a big, scratchy printer. He figured, however, that it would cost about $8 million ($23 million today) in minicomputer timesharing to let a dozen people in an office use it. In 1970, a Palo Alto firm unveiled a new computerized electrostatic printer that could splash 5,000 lines a minute onto a specially coated paper. But at $15,300, it cost considerably more than a typewriter and even many copiers.[6]

There were doubts it was ever going to get much better. An American University professor, for one, figured using computers to compose and print in offices probably was always going to be too expensive. He calculated that the variable costs of using a video monitor to talk to a computer to in turn talk to a printer were higher even than hot-metal typesetting in the late 1960s.

The print consultant who published the professor's calculations, moreover, thought his estimate was "unduly optimistic."[7]

By then, in fact, the industry's many skeptics routinely expected computers to disappoint them. In 1964 they had held their first computer type conference, excited and bullish. "We all got together and congratulated ourselves about how much money we were going to make and how . . . we'd all laugh our way with the truckloads of money to the bank," one attendee recalled. It hadn't worked out that way. By the second computer type conference, held in 1970, the attendee reported how the past six years had been filled with little more than technological failure and a lot of debt. "To say our industry is in financial difficulty, I think, is an understatement at best." Conference host John Seybold added, "There was too much leading down the garden path." The pre-Compugraphic print computers connected to phototypesetters were unreliable and so expensive that commercial compositors had to borrow heavily to buy them. Worse yet, their customers often didn't like the results.

"We all know that if software doesn't work," Seybold added years later, "[the system] won't operate at any characters per second, and that if the equipment is down it doesn't operate at any characters per second. But, more important, if the business isn't there, it operates at zero dollars a second."[8]

None of the naysayers, though, knew how quickly the innards—memory chips—of these machines would change, or that they could be wedged into office machines as well as print production machines like Compugraphics. But as they became more powerful and cheaper, the devices they drove went a long way in a very short time. By 1973, just three years after Seybold's depressed computer type conference, American businesses had bought more than 10,000 word processing computers, costing anywhere from $4,000 to $13,000 each. While they created documents with them, some also found novel applications. In 1970, for example, a Dallas apartment complex tried to rent apartments to engineers working at two nearby tech companies by installing a central printout facility and linking it by phone to a downtown computer. Tenants thus could do personal calculating at home.[9]

More ideas appeared. While government agencies and insurance companies bought its mainframes, IBM (perhaps with an eye on France's MITRAL; perhaps in the knowledge that Congress had cut off weapons applications) assigned a handful of its engineers to try to build a relatively small single-user machine. They produced a prototype in 1973. Two years later, it became IBM's new portable computer. Priced as low as $8,975, it was marketed to "engineers, analysts, statisticians, and other problem-solvers." It weighed fifty pounds.[10]

Xerox, also in the mainframe computer business in those days, was thinking along similar lines. At about the same time IBM was trying to figure out how to build a portable computer, Xerox engineer Chuck Thacker was at his company's California lab finishing an even smaller, software-driven desktop word processor that could also calculate. Unlike all previous computers, large or small, it had a unique graphical user interface, a mouse, and a screen that featured an image approximating the finished printed document. Called the Alto, it operated much like the desktop computers people throughout the Western world would soon begin using by the millions. But at the time Xerox famously thought it too futuristic and put its money into selling more practical products.[11]

The Alto did not die, however. Word of it passed from lab to engineer to programmer through a unique community of technical gossips and computer hobbyists who had formed around Xerox's research center south of San Francisco, and then beyond. Like a giant game of telephone, news of breakthroughs and hirings often became more intriguing with each retelling among the gossips working for the computer companies, government agencies, and university labs concentrated in Massachusetts, southern New Jersey, southern California, northern California, and Washington State. Many of the gossips had met each other during their often short college careers or in research centers that, hungry for specialists, kept stealing them away to new opportunities. They were, according both to their chroniclers and themselves, very smart. While Vannevar Bush's generation of scientists spent remarkably similar childhoods disassembling radios, these gossips often spent remarkably similar youths disassembling televisions, telephones, electrical circuits, and, when given the chance, computers. They communicated often with each other, cross-pollinating their own work with rumors and critiques from other parts of their communities. They were fickle. At their center for a while was a California man—immortalized in a 1971 magazine article under the nom de guerre Al Gilbertson—who could use a "blue box" to create electronic beeps and, by holding it up to a receiver, fool the phone company into connecting him for free to any phone in the world.[12]

Gilbertson (not his real name, the article said) inspired many of the more antic hobbyists. Not least was Steve Wozniak. Soon after dropping out of Cal-Berkeley and getting an engineering job at Hewlett-Packard, he teamed up with some friends to start making and selling their own blue boxes. They were, of course, illegal. "Woz's first call was to the pope," Wozniak's initial partner later recalled. "He wanted to make a confession."[13]

Wozniak and his partner trumped Gilbertson's toy, powering their box with a novel circuit board. Wozniak, his "phone phreak" pals, low-level engineers from other companies like Xerox and Intel, and soon a former Atari game programmer named Steven Jobs, gradually began meeting as an informal group they called the Homebrew Computer Club. Jobs was yet another college dropout (from Reed College), just back from a "spiritual quest" to India. But the twenty-year-old looked at the twenty-one-year-old Wozniak's hobbyist advances and, with a vision probably more of the material world than the spiritual, saw a product: an easy-to-use computer for small businesses. Unlike ready-to-assemble machines like the popular Heath and Intel "development" kits sold in hobby shops, this would come assembled and ready to use. Unlike the one well-known "personal computer" on the market (the Altair, which ran on a program sold by recent Harvard dropouts Bill Gates and Paul Allen), this would be easy for amateurs to use.

There are, it is said, two types of innovation: disruptive change that profoundly alters the course of a life, an industry, or a whole society, and sustaining technologies that improve or expand on an earlier change.[14] To scholars, Gutenberg's press and movable type were shining examples of a disruptive tool: they displaced copyists and made a new profession possible. Telephones, autos, steam engines wiped out whole categories of jobs and created whole new fields of endeavor and ultimately human possibility. All, moreover, were the work of tinkerers and artisans who had happened on their civilization-shaking discoveries by improving and recombining old notions and products (like the wine presses and wood blocks of Gutenberg's time) to fill narrow, usually spectacularly banal purposes. Sustaining technologies might be the wires, the tires, and hardened exhaust pipes that broadened the use of phones, cars, and steam power, made them better, and usually increased their price. They, in turn, were usually the work of mechanical engineers.

Unlike Gutenberg, Koenig, Mergenthaler, Higonnet, or Moyroud working in investor-funded workshops before them, Wozniak and Jobs designed their machine in a bedroom and built it in Jobs's garage. Jobs then took it to a local electronics retailer, who, perhaps mindful that a novel retail store devoted eccentrically to computers had opened only months before in Santa Monica, agreed to buy twenty-five machines. The retailer would sell them for $666 each, probably to hobbyists. Jobs rushed to tell Wozniak and beg him to quit his day job at Hewlett-Packard to help build the machines. To buy parts, Jobs would sell his VW microbus. The reluctant Wozniak would have to sell his expensive HP scientific calculator. But with a fine title of vice president of research and development, he did quit Hewlett-Packard and threw himself into the new company, which he and Jobs dubbed "Apple." Together they built and sold six hundred of the machines and netted a total of $744,000. Excited, they prepared an improved version, called Apple II.[15] They'd unveil it at a computer show in San Francisco in 1976.

Attendees loved it. Unlike other small computers on the market, which were hardwired to perform specific tasks or solve specific kinds of problems, the Apple was wired to do whatever a software program they inserted in it told it to do. Wozniak, moreover, had hardwired the program that translated keyboard strokes into machine language directly on the circuit board inside the machine. (Owners of the Altair, Apple's main competitor at the time, had to load the program—called BASIC, but then marketed by Gates and Allen as Micro Soft and the Micro-Soft 235—using a paper tape.) Other than that, the thing depended on whatever prepackaged instructions its owners could get and plug into the machine's convenient slots. To demonstrate, the irreverent Wozniak created a program that, depending on the name a visitor to his booth typed into the keyboard, told Polish, Italian, Jewish, or other ethnic jokes. There was also a game called Breakout. (Wozniak later maintained that gamers, not businesses, bought most of the initial Apples.) Jobs challenged engineers and hobbyists to write still more programs—the coded instructions for calculating, creating, or showing things—for buyers to plug into their Apple IIs. (The most significant programs that followed were a word processor and VisiCalc, which created accounting spreadsheets.) Even as they left the 1976 computer show and loaded their wares back into their car at San Francisco's Civic Auditorium, one of the dropouts' new colleagues excitedly predicted, "it's really going to happen." He told Wozniak "he'd seen the signs at this show to know that we were on the track that would make us worth $500 million in five years."[16] He was not far off. When Wozniak left Apple in 1985 as one of millions of stockholders, his stake was worth an estimated $45 million.

By then, of course, everything had changed. The new office automation machines—small single-purpose computers—were ubiquitous. The most common were $30,000 Wang word processors that "nearly caused a riot" when introduced at yet another open house (at yet another hotel) in 1976. IBM—the industry's biggest player—soon brought out a $7,900 word processor, although it went to $26,000 when a printer and "paper handler" were added. Using similar technology for lower-end markets, Tandy introduced a $400 microcomputer in 1977. Commodore offered one called PET. In 1978 IBM unveiled its own personal computer. Made specifically for small and midsize businesses, it had programs that could analyze sales, schedule operations, and track inventory costs. A company called Punxsutawney Electric Repair Company bought the first one. "If you can type and use a hand-held calculator," the company's president gushed, "you have all the skills necessary to operate a 5110."[17]

But, much to IBM's disappointment, the personal computer did not attract the scores of independent tech-heads who wrote programs for the Altair and the Apple II. While its even newer Datamaster computer seemed perfect for the world's large and midsize businesses, IBM remained determined, as Microsoft's Bill Gates recalled years later, "to do a home and very low-end business machine." The company, he added, expected "it wouldn't be a high-volume product." Unlike most of the products it developed before, IBM decided it would have outsiders do the bulk of the work while it devoted its in-house talent to more sophisticated, profitable projects.[18]

And so in August 1980, IBM sent some people—now derided in industry histories as "suits"—to Seattle to talk to the twenty-five-year-old Gates about helping it build the small device. They wanted it to run on a bigger processor than other "hobbyist" machines used, which meant it needed a beefier operating system. Gates, they knew, was good. He and his partner had been writing programs for the Altair and other small computers for almost five years.

"IBM," Gates recalled many years later, "came to us because we were the common element of all PCs. If you took Apple, the [Tandy] TRS-80, the Atari, the North Star, the IMSAI, there was only one thing in common with all those PCs. That was, Microsoft had done the BASIC-language software on all those things."[19]

Gates also seemed to speak IBM's language, something not all technical people could do. Four years earlier, he had horrified the far-flung computer tech communities by complaining that people were copying the paper tape on which his company had encoded its software. To Gates, it was piracy. To historians, it would appear to be the same kind of unauthorized copying and selling that had ravaged entrepreneurs and authors of the printed word in the late fifteenth and early sixteenth centuries, before printers and monarchies learned how to regulate their new industry. But to much of the computer community, it was heresy. The pirates themselves, having earned their technical stripes fooling phone companies and outwitting suits, were ideologically and ostentatiously hostile to other people's property rights. Gates, by asserting that programmers should be paid for their work on an ongoing basis, looked like the greedy merchant among them.[20] To IBM, however, Gates and Allen seemed eminently capable of understanding what a corporation might be trying to accomplish.

But Gates turned IBM away. He said he was unsure he could help and suggested that a friend of his down in California might have a better handle on the operating system IBM would need. Gary Kildall, Gates explained, already had written a cutting-edge operating system (called CP/M) that might work on the new memory chip IBM wanted to use.

The executives' visit to Kildall in Pacific Grove, California, would become one of personal computing's great founding myths. Various apostles have described the visit in contradictory ways. According to some, it was a tale of evil merchants in the garden, this time with Adam refusing on principle to eat the forbidden commercial fruit. One version, probably apocryphal, had Kildall arrogantly leaving his visitors to go fly his airplane instead of meeting that afternoon. Another has Kildall's wife, his company's business manager, refusing to sign IBM's nondisclosure statement, thus keeping the executives from even describing the secret project they wanted to discuss. Others swear Kildall was there and reached a handshake deal with the big company. Others swear he was there but did not make a deal. Whatever happened, IBM soon concluded it was not going to get to use CP/M. Unsure where to turn next, one of the executives had heard of yet another programmer, Tim Paterson, who might be able to help.

The executive asked Gates about Paterson, and Gates agreed he probably could write a workable operating system. But the IBM executive, perhaps wary of another confusing reception in this alien anticorporate corner of the universe, had Gates approach Paterson for him.

Gates returned with a deal in hand, although not one between IBM and Paterson. It instead was between Gates and Paterson; the young executive would pay Paterson $50,000 to develop the new operating system. Microsoft then renamed it DOS (for disk operating system) and licensed it to IBM (as well as to other manufacturers). When IBM included it in its new low-end machine (finally called the IBM PC) in 1981, Microsoft began earning money on every personal computer IBM and its competitors sold. Consequently Microsoft became one of the globe's most profitable companies during the next decades and Gates, according to the business magazines that tracked such things, became the richest man in the world.[21]

The IBM PC was easy to use. It really did fit on a desk and, unlike its predecessors, was compatible with most other kinds of low-end machines (now also called microcomputers). Selling mostly to businesses and tiny businesses, IBM found the market for the hobbyist machines immeasurably bigger than it had dreamed. Competitors like Osborne, Commodore, Compaq, Tandy, and NBI (whose name stood for Nothing But Initials) jumped into it. In all, fifty different small computer makers licensed MS-DOS in the first sixteen months after Microsoft put it on the market in 1982. In 1983, Compaq sold $111 million worth of equipment, the best first year sales of any company in American business history. By then, 10 million computers were at work in the United States, up from a million three years earlier.[22]

Then they got what amounted to a new alphabet, and it turned the office communications machines into something more—personal communications machines.

To get one of these early-1980s computers to do something, the person at the keyboard typed in text commands. With some judiciously placed forward slashes, dollar signs, or upper-case plusses, a typist told the computer where to insert a word, make a number in a spreadsheet relative to another number, use a certain kind of punctuation mark, or save or copy or delete text. The codes were simpler but no more related to spoken language than the "quad" and other commands that Lino and phototype compositors used to break lines or start new paragraphs.

Jobs, Wozniak, and just about everyone else in the Silicon Valley tech community, however, still remembered Xerox and Chuck Thacker's unexploited Alto from the early 1970s. Instead of typing symbols, users told it what to do by using a mouse to click on simple signs, or icons. To find out more, Jobs bought some Xerox stock and, using it as a ticket for a show, in 1979 visited researchers at Xerox's Palo Alto Research Center (PARC), where the Alto's graphical user interface had been developed. He left the center inspired. Some $150 million, two model failures, and five years later, Apple introduced its Macintosh computer. It had the Alto's graphical user interface, plus a drop-down menu bar and a hierarchal file system. Instead of scrolling down one infinite screen of words and symbols, users moved from screen to screen, or "window," to see different documents or programs. They could also use more than one program at a time. When writing or calculating, they could copy and paste and place files in easy-to-find electronic folders. A year later Microsoft came out with its version, which it called Windows. (Apple sued almost immediately, claiming Microsoft had stolen the Macintosh's "look and feel." In court, Gates replied, "Hey, we both got it from Xerox.")[23]

In effect, their programs amounted to a simple sign language that children could (and did) use to operate powerful communications machines. The six-year apprenticeship programs needed to learn hot-metal type communications were completely unnecessary. So were the six-month retraining programs Lino operators had endured to "learn computers."

Even the inexpensive office workers who worked the office machines were being replaced. When *Harvard* magazine, for example, adopted the new devices in 1990, it decided to make its editors do the work. Its publisher sent them away for three days of training, and they returned to find their "lives changed most profoundly." Until then, one of them recalled, "ladies" had cut and pasted "computer-generated type produced by a Cambridge firm called DNH. (The proprietor's name was David Flanagan. He was often out of the office, and the company's name was an abbreviation of what the receptionist frequently had to say: "Dave's not here.") Now the ladies were gone. Editors themselves physically created the magazine. "Editors found themselves spending huge hunks of their time in the production business. They knew they were intended to edit, perhaps to write a bit, and to have long lunches at somebody else's expense with interesting people. Instead, they were fused to their computers, positioning picture credits exactly two points away from the lower right-hand corners of pictures." (Happily, the magazine soon hired an art director. "The magazine looked better at once," the editor reported, "and the editors, at last, could have a decent lunch.")[24]

Professionals like writers and editors had, like the compositors and clerical workers they were supplanting, a long history of resisting efficiency. In 1887, the inventor of the Monotype designed his keyboard for writers to operate, and had to change his advertising to appeal to compositors when writers showed no interest. When newfangled teletypes arrived in the 1930s, they refused to operate them too. Efforts to make reporters type their stories into perforated tape (which would then be fed to phototype machines) in the 1960s were similarly unsuccessful. Their reasons for hating it, one Iowa State University study found, all had to do with the horrible sloppiness of the creative process: the machines made it hard to correct typing errors, start paragraphs over a second or third time, make late additions to a sentence, or delete part of a sentence to replace it with something better. At the *Los Angeles Times,* an effort by editors to get reporters to use perforating typewriters was "a disaster." Before the easy new desktop alphabet, "even commission-hungry video display salesmen doubted that writers would write on the display tube," one publisher recalled. "Printers laughed at the notion, although nervously."

But now the new alphabets not only dropped the costs of producing printed words in business again, but, installed in newly inexpensive, easy-to-use computers, also helped solve the sticky problem of personal printing.[25]

When they printed at all, most computers since World War II had sent their numbers and signals to be reproduced on large, loud electrostatic machines. In the beginning they drove long, spindly fingers that moved from one side of a wide piece of paper to the other. The fingers spit minute, momentarily electrified dots of ink in patterns that—thanks to the static electricity—stuck to the paper. In the 1960s computers learned to send letters and numbers to photo units that, in turn, created images on film. And marginally quieter and still better "line printers" arrived, operating on the same principles as the electrostatic plotters. Both kinds of "electronic" printing, however, generally remained as manufacturing tasks. Both required a heavy investment in equipment, training, and materials.

They were ugly too. The "data processing alphabet" itself, an academic mourned at the time about computer type, "is a restricted one. It generally includes only capital letters of poor character design." The spacing was poor. The paper it was printed on was "large and bulky."[26]

And they were finicky. Even in business offices, every computer and every printer had to be individually introduced to each other with special formal cues and rituals. Reminiscent of arranged marriages or mating dances in some cultures, only certain specialists were qualified to perform these ceremonies. "If you had a IBM 1130 and you were driving a Photon," specialist Gary Krohm recalled, "and you wanted to drive a Merg, you needed more software to drive the other machine." Even then, they "couldn't handle graphics . . . That was a major thing too. The old machines were limited to numbers of point sizes and different range type."[27]

IBM hired a company called Alphanumeric as far back as 1967 to work out a marriage contract between the video monitors it was putting on its newest editorial computers and its printers. But even the muscular new processors corporations bought in the late 1960s and early 1970s were not always strong enough to power the complex, instantaneous internal signaling that produced a letter, a sentence, a paragraph, a page full of images. By 1973 reporters at both the *Detroit News* and the *Los Angeles Times* could write stories at monitors and, after handing off disks or tapes, have them electronically inserted into a page. But they were working on massive mainframe computers well beyond the budgets of most companies. The editor of the smaller *Farm Journal*, for example, could not find a system in 1970 that would let his writers signal his more modest magazine's phototypesetter to print stories. The best his budget would allow was a "minicomputer [that] may call for help from a big time-sharing mamma computer" to muster the energy to print out a page or a swath of film.[28]

In those days small businesses were likely to be using line printers, which tended to turn out ragged, low-quality letters. Unknown to most people using them, their computers were sending the printers a code (called "page description language" in computer circles, "printer controls" or "computer controls" in marginally less technical places) that told the machine when to double space, when to go to the top of the next page, when to start one line immediately after another without a break and when to overprint a line.

By 1970, technical journals reported on new "printer controls" that moved letters from video screen to printer in more readable form. They showed promise. "It is possible that [the type they produced] will be letterforms with a whole new dimension, a dimension added by the application of the laser beam to graphic communications," a researcher forecast. But, she warned, "these letterforms . . . could no longer be called type. They would be part of a new system which would require a new name, new terminology and new rules of design."[29]

Companies like Autologic, Harris, Hell, and Mergenthaler subsequently called the results "digital fonts" and put them in contraptions that, at base prices of $80,000, were sold to newspapers. Commercial type shops disdained them at first, claiming they produced low-quality type. Small businesses could not afford them. Xerox's first commercial laser printer, a "monster" that could churn out 120 pages per minute, cost nearly $350,000 (about $530,000 in early twenty-first-century currency).[30]

Gary Starkweather, yet another of Xerox's collection of inventive minds, had been fussing with a laser to paint information in digital form onto the drum or belt of a copying machine. Once transferred to California in 1972, he hooked up with a colleague to create the prototype of what probably was the world's first small laser printer. Hooked to an Alto through Ethernet cables (also just invented at Palo Alto), it could print a wide variety of images. The Lawrence Livermore National Laboratory, sniffing the wind, offered to buy five laser printers and asked for bids. Xerox, worried about the costs of maintaining them, ultimately decided not to bid or to try to build them. Perhaps responding to the same proposal, Photon used a laser instead of a lamp to "eke out" an image in its newest photosetter at the same time. Two years later, the company that finally took over Photon used one to create wholly synthetic characters and lines of text. But that project bled money and was abandoned in 1977. In the meantime, yet another handful of Xerox engineers broke away to start selling Dovers to college campuses and to Xerox itself. The Dovers were junked copiers, restored and fitted with lasers. (They built only twenty-four, some of which were still being used twenty years later). In the late 1970s, Monotype created a Lasercomp that was able to create a whole page of type at a time. But it produced images that could not be seen or corrected until they had been laboriously and expensively printed out. Writers then would have to start the whole process again. Oce, a European firm, introduced a model that printed text directly on a special paper. By 1979, Mergenthaler had one that did the same thing. Although it "set minds racing again," it too was complicated, messy, and affordable only to print manufacturing companies, not small businesses or individuals. Sales were disappointing. Two years later the company produced a "practically portable" 143-pound machine, available for $17,000.[31]

In the meantime, IBM adapted its strike-on typewriters to create Daisywriters, small printers that tapped letters onto a sheet of paper. IBM, Apple, and the other hobbyist machines spoke to dot matrix printers that were smaller, marginally quieter versions of the behemoth electrostatic plotters the old mainframes drove before phototype. All were slow, intermittently reliable, and, except in their most expensive incarnations, unable to produce the printed word as readably or graphically as the print shop down the block.

The reason, one reporter explained, was that laser printers were trying to create a whole page at a time, not just letters or even lines of type. The electronic controls to instruct them to paint and print pages full of words, images, and pictures, in all their varying sizes and styles, all at once proved to be complex. They also needed a lot of power and memory to work. Packing that much muscle into a computer kept the devices well beyond the budgets and patience of most nonprofessional producers of printed word for years.[32]

But another generation of computer chips powerful, small, and cheap enough to be put in the printers themselves arrived in the late 1970s. They could provide the power to process and translate complex images. All at once companies like Xerox, IBM, Wang, Canon, Ricoh, and Hewlett-Packard were in an accelerated race to create writing software (usually called electronic page makeup, pagination, or desktop publishing software) and laser printers to reproduce the results.[33]

According to some, a printing equipment company called Hastech won the race. Working for Gannett newspapers, it installed a system in 1982 that showed both text and graphics on computer monitors at the *Star-News* in Pasadena, California.[34] Other communications companies—newspaper chains and some book publishers—adopted similar systems.

It was another three years and two faster generations of computer chips later until Wozniak and Jobs brought printed computer type to civilization's cheaper, lower reaches. In a memorable ad they ran during the Super Bowl, they dramatically cast their new Macintosh in 1984 as something that would liberate the masses from expensive (read: IBM) communications. The next year Jobs, concerned about his freedom-fighting machine's weak sales, wanted something new. He put $2.5 million into a small company called Adobe, then a three-year-old firm that sold electronic type fonts. But its owners—also wonderfully talented refugees from Xerox's Palo Alto skunkworks—had developed printer controls that were an innovative *patois* of programming, page description, and programming language its inventors called Postscript.[35] "Hackers," one website author sighed admiringly, "consider it among the most elegant hacks of all time." It could let just about any computer talk to just about any kind of laser printer. It was capable of describing just about any kind of page a typist could imagine. And it was stored in the printer, not the computer. Jobs licensed it and linked his new Mac to an inexpensive, Postscript-reading little printer called a Laserwriter. Rounded, solid black letters replaced jagged bit-mapped images.

Then there were more: a New York company announced an industrial-size plain-paper laser printer the same year. It was ten times faster than a photosetter and less expensive, too. Individual plain paper sheets cost less than 1 percent of the cost of the sheets of film coming out of a phototype machine.[36] IBM, Compaq, Commmodore, and others followed with their own versions, and suddenly there were all-in-one print communications tools priced for small businesses, type shops, and private citizens. Soon they were a staple for writers and graphic artists.

One was also a programmer named Paul Brainard, who hoped to write an editing and graphics program for small businesses and individual artists like himself. He grandly called his company Aldus, after Erasmus's favorite printer of the fifteenth century. After tying it into Postscript, in July 1985 he released one of the first workable desktop publishing programs, Page-maker. It allowed people to manipulate words and images on a computer screen and print them out just as they had arranged them. A fantastic flood of innovations—word processing programs called Word or WordPerfect, desktop publishers (Ventura and Quark), drawing tools (Illustrator, Cricket Draw, Digital Darkroom), accounting tools (Lotus 1-2-3, Excel, and Quicken), games, dictionaries, encyclopedia—followed, all launched at classes of businesses and individuals who, until that moment in human history, had to hire professionals to write, draw, do bookkeeping, or print.[37] If they could not hire such help, they simply had shied away from pursuits that required it. All the innovations, of course, were powered by small computers and written to little printers, each the equivalent of squads of compositors and pressmen, made of plastic and metal.

Where the old human models were driven by money, pride, foremen, and, as Lou Felicio once pointed out, fights with their spouses, these were driven by code and math. Many an engineer would dismiss these printers as mere slaves to the impulses computers sent to them. Although something vital and warm was lost in their ascent, a new age appeared to be taking shape in the deceptively complex images they produced first in black and then in color and then, even more miraculously, distributed around the world without using a train, plane, or even a piece of paper.

NOTES

1. Thomas Dunn, "Lasers in Graphics, the Continuing Evolution," *Graphic Arts Monthly*, October 1981, 50.

2. Printing Industries of America, *Vision 21: The Printing Industry Redefined for the 21st Century* (Alexandria, Va.: Printing Industries of America, 2000), 18. The second observer was Wayne Dowdle of the National Composition Association, "PIA Briefs Trade Publications on Steady Growth and Future Plans," *Graphic Arts Monthly*, May 1981, 102.

3. Paul E. Ceruzzi, *A History of Modern Computing* (Cambridge, Mass.: MIT Press, 1998), 261.

4. The Japanese company was called Busicom. Bernard L. Peuto, "Mainframe History Provides Lessons," *Microprocessor Report*, March 31, 1997, 19.

5. Ceruzzi, *Modern Computing*, 222–24.

6. Ceruzzi, *Modern Computing*, 255. The program, FRESS (File Retrieval and Editing System), was invented by Andries Van Dam. Jerry A. Carlson, "Video Editing at the Farm Journal," in Lowell H. Hattery and George P. Bush, eds., *Technological Change in Printing and Publishing* (Mt. Airy, Md.: Lomond, 1972), 117; "Varian Associates New Printer," *Wall Street Journal*, September 9, 1970, 14.

7. E. R. Lannon, "A Review of the Costs of Electronic Composition," in John W. Seybold, ed., *Computers in Typesetting* (Washington, D.C.: Government Printing Office, 1970), 15.

8. John Seybold interview, by telephone (November 5, 1998). The speaker at both conferences was Henry D. Sedgwick, a consultant.

9. The complex was called Creekside North Apartments. "Business Bulletin," *Wall Street Journal*, December 24, 1970, 1.

10. Before the Beginning: Ancestors of the IBM Personal Computer, www-1.ibm.com/ibm/history/exhibits/pc/pc_1.html (accessed November 2, 2004).

11. Douglas K. Smith and Robert C. Alexander, *Fumbling the Future: How Xerox Invented, Then Ignored, the First Personal Computer* (New York: Morrow, 1988). Frustrated by the company's unwillingness to market their work, a number of the inventors at Xerox's Palo Alto Research Center took it elsewhere. Bob Metcalf, who fashioned an ethernet connection between computers, left to start 3Com. John Warnock, who invented the postscript language that tells a printer what a page is supposed to look like, left to start Adobe Systems.

12. Ron Rosenbaum, "Secrets of the Little Blue Box: A Story So Incredible It May Even Make You Feel Sorry for the Phone Company," *Esquire*, October 1971, 116.

13. Manish Srivastava, Steven Wozniak, ei.cs.vt.edu/~history/WOZNIAK.HTM (accessed November 1, 2004).

14. Clayton Christianson, *The Innovator's Dilemma* (New York: HarperCollins, 2000).

15. A Chronology of Computer History, www.cyberstreet.com/hcs/museum/chron.htm (accessed November 2, 2004); Srivastava, Wozniak.

16. Steve Wozniak, Speaking of Pranks . . . A Reader Asks, www.woz.org (accessed November 1, 2004). Another Apple II innovation was expandable memory. If their new programs needed it, buyers could expand the memory to a heady maximum of 48K. It was less than 1/1000th of the memory available on standard Apple computers at the beginning of the twenty-first century.

17. Ceruzzi, *Modern Computing*, 256; Before the Beginning.

18. Ceruzzi, *Modern Computing*, 248. "Remembering the Beginning: Interview with Bill Gates," *PC Magazine*, March 25, 1997, www.pcmag.com/article2/0,1759,1204,00.asp (accessed November 2, 2004).

19. BASIC, initially developed at Dartmouth and improved at Microsoft, translated keyboard commands into language the machine could understand before

sparking the minute impulses that help it perform a task. "Gates Talks," *U.S. News & World Report*, August 20, 2001, USNews.com, www.usnews.com/usnews/biztech/gatesivu.htm (accessed November 2, 2004).

20. Ceruzzi, *Modern Computing*, 236.

21. Kildall and Paterson's futures were less spectacular. When the IBM PC came out in 1981, Kildall objected that Microsoft, Paterson, and IBM had in effect plagiarized his CP/M operating software. Software copyright laws, then in their infancy, provided no clear legal recourse for the injured Kildall. He eventually settled for licensing his software to IBM, which gave buyers the choice of buying CP/M at $240 per machine or DOS at $40 per machine. Not surprisingly, they typically chose DOS. In 1991, Kildall sold his company to Novell for $120 million but died the next year at age fifty-two. Paterson later sued Microsoft, claiming the company had not told him of its relationship to IBM and had unfairly shut him out the millions in royalties that resulted from its deal with the computer giant. Steve Hamm and Jay Greene, "The Man Who Could Have Been Bill Gates," *Business Week*, October 25, 2004, www.businessweek.com/magazine/content/04_43/b3905109_mz063.htm (accessed November 2, 2004); William Henry Gates III, www.fact-index.com/b/bi/bill_gates.html (accessed November 2, 2004).

22. Chronology.

23. Microsoft agreed not to use Macintosh technology in Windows 1.0 but was free to use similar technology in its future Windows versions. Mary Bellis, The History of the Graphical User Interface, or GUI, inventors.about.com/library/weekly/aa043099.htm (accessed November 1, 2004).

24. Christopher Reed, "The Cost of a Comma," Harvard Magazine November-December 1998, harvard-magazine.com 128.103.142.209/issues/nd98/nd98issue.ssi (accessed November 7, 1999).

25. Carlson, "Video Editing," 118; Nouri Beyrouti, "The History and Development of Newspaper Electronic Pagination Systems in the United States, 1975–1987" (Ph.D. diss., New York University, 1989), 11. Correcting documents and stories had always been expensive. In 1970, the *New York Times* figured 65 percent of its composition costs came from having to alter a story to fit into a certain space in the paper. A few years later, another publisher estimated that while the newspaper industry saved "millions of dollars" when it switched from hot-metal type to phototype, it could save $2 billion if it could ever get writers and editors to write directly to plate. In its first year of using its industrial brand of desktop publishing, the *U.S. News & World Report*'s production costs rose only 1.9 percent, despite huge 20–40 percent hikes in the costs of paper and ink, respectively. "Printing by Computer: A USN&WR Gamble Pays Off," *U.S. News & World Report*, September 5, 1977, 56–58.

26. Kathleen Spangler, "New Technologies Challenge Classical Typography," in Hattery and Bush, *Technological Changes*, 41.

27. Gary Krohm, telephone interview, October 15, 1998.

28. "IBM Will Be Given Photocomposition Data by Alphanumeric Inc.," *Wall Street Journal,* February 21, 1967, 16; George Corben Goble, *The Obituary of a Machine: The Rise and Fall of Ottmar Mergenthaler's Linotype at U.S. Newspapers* (Bloomington: Indiana University Mass Communications Program, 1984), 374; Carlson, "Video Editing," 124.

29. The controls, eventually incorporated in a PDL called WYSIWYG, stood for "what you see (on a screen) is what you get (on a piece of paper)." Kathleen Spangler, "New Technologies," in Hattery and Bush, *Technological Change,* 44, 47.

30. David Henry Goodstein, "Typesetting Moves from a Master Craft to a Computer Application in Today's World," *Graphic Arts Monthly,* June 1981, 42; Early Laser Printer Development, www.printerworks.com/Catalogs/CX-Catalog/CX-HP_LaserJet-History.html, 1994 (accessed November 27, 2004).

31. Starkweather and colleague Ron Rider's prototype, called EARS, had technical problems, particularly in printing certain complex images. The company's Electro-Optical Systems division worried that maintenance costs would eventually make the Lawrence Livermore laser printers unprofitable and consequently declined to bid on the project. "Inside the PARC: the 'information architects' insiders who became outsiders describe the trials and successes of the Xerox Palo Alto Research Center as it sought to create the electronic 'office of the future,'" www.stanford.edu/group/mmdd/SiliconValley/Perry/xerox1.html, June 17, 1996 (accessed November 27, 2004); "Printing by Computer," *U.S. News & World Report,* 58. Dymo Graphics acquired Photon in 1972. To use Mergenthalter's 1979 laser printer, the operator had to treat the paper with a zinc oxide concoction to make the image appear; the software to arrange the text on the page was both rare and expensive. Lawrence W. Wallis, *Electronic Typesetting: A Quarter Century of Upheaval* (Gatehead, U.K.: Paradigm, 1984), 4749, 33; Goodstein, "Typesetting," 42.

32. Goodstein, "Typesetting," 42; "PIA Briefs Trade Publications on Steady Growth and Future Plans," *Graphic Arts Monthly,* May 1981, 102.

33. Goodstein, "Typesetting, "42; Wallis, *Electronic Typesetting,* 120.

34. Beyrouti, "Pagination," 10.

35. John Warnock developed Postscript at PARC before setting out in 1982 with a partner, Charles Geschke, to form a company to sell computer type fonts. The company, called Adobe, then played off another programmer's 1976 improvements on Warnock's work to create Postscript. Released in 1984, it told a printer how to produce a monitor's image on a printer, and it quickly became most computer makers' standard. Postcript Introduction, www.mefco.com/psc/intro.html (accessed November 5, 2004). The other programmer of 1976 was John Gaffney. History of Postscript, mm.iit,uni-miskolc.hu/Data/texts/hackers_jargon/postscript.HTML (accessed November 10, 1999).

36. The New York company was Data Recording Systems. Another plain-paper machine, the Genesis from Tegra, produced even bolder, sharper images. "Electronic Publishing Systems Come of Age at Massive Print 85 Exhibition," *Publishers Weekly,* June 7, 1985, 52.

37. Peter C. S. Adams, PageMaker Past, Present, and Future: A Brief History of Publishing, www.makingpages.org/pagemaker/history (accessed October 14, 2004). Big business–size systems that allowed typists to paginate and produce their work on laser printers came out too. American Printing Technologies, Compugraphic, Computer Composition, Interleaf, Penta Systems, Royce Data Systems, Scitex, Texet, Xerox, and Xyvision, among others, introduced them. Xerox's went for $137,000. "Electronic Publishing Systems," 52, 55, 56. On the lower end of the spectrum, Apple's Newroom was released at the same time as its new Laserwriter, but sales were disappointing. In the next years came PFS: First Publisher from Software Publishing Group, Newsmaster II from Kyocera Unison, Publish-It Lite from Timeworks, and Ventura 2.0 in 1988, from Xerox, desktoppub.about.com/gi/dynamic/offsite.htm?site=http%3A%2F%2Fhome.pmt.org%2F%7Edrose%2Faw.html (accessed on November 30, 2004).

25

ONE LAST TRANSACTION COST

With its mighty rocket, the Soviet Union in 1957 lifted the species' first man-made object into orbit around the planet. The United States reacted with a kind of research panic and threw money at everything scientific. Soon 18,000 people were working on the Atlas intercontinental ballistic system, some of them developing computers. As it always had, the Pentagon looked at computers as a way to calculate the enormous trajectories of sending tons of weaponry and rockets across changing weather systems and air currents, and landing them reasonably near unseen, mobile targets hundreds and then thousands of miles away. Submarine depths, troop placements, supply routes, weight displacements; all were determined in large part by mathematically estimating equipment tolerances, enemy capabilities, the age of perishable supplies, and so on, against continuously updated records of how heavily equipment was being used, the enemy's defenses, and the likely demands on supplies. Calculating these variables was not easy. In those days smart people outlined the problem, broke it down into numbers, punched coded numbers into cards, and fed the cards into computers. They then waited for the machines to do the appropriate functions—division, multiplication, addition, and so on—one at a time, in sequence, to deliver the answer. If one of the variables changed, they'd start the whole time-consuming process again. As *Sputnik* orbited above it, the government figured it had to find a better way.

To do it, it would hire university labs. To award grants and track what the professors and their grad students were doing with the money it was giving them during the science panic, the Department of Defense formed a Bush-like science group that, with its historic penchant for unwieldy names, it dubbed the Advanced Research Projects Agency (or ARPA).

By August 1958, in the initial scramble to duplicate the USSR's feat and assure the public the country was not too far behind, ARPA-funded engineers used a mainframe in Kingston, New York, to guide a missile launched from Florida to intercept a simulated Soviet bomber somewhere in the skies just below heaven. (Congress was duly impressed and bought twenty-two more mainframes for the bomber-intercept program. By the time the machines were ordered, built, installed, fine-tuned, and tested, however, the bombers against which they protected us had been replaced by fast, evasive Soviet missiles.)[1]

As its projects unfolded, ARPA, like Bush's group in World War II, drew all sorts of wonderful minds to its payroll. Perhaps chief among them was J. C. R. Licklider, who would be remembered as computing's Johnny Appleseed, spreading ideas that others would take to unimagined places. He had long been doing government work, first solving the communications problems inside noisy bombers and later working on the Pentagon's real-time computer-based air defense system. He was fully smitten with computers by 1960. At their best they could, he wrote in a now famous paper published in an obscure technical journal, be great, immediate decision-making partners for us. The rest of the world might believe humans were good at "intuition and understanding" while computers "worked mechanically in tables and hierarchies," but Licklider thought we could work together more closely than that. He saw computers becoming a whole new medium, much more than the calculation engines they were at the time. Like the printing press, telegraph, radio, and television before it, it could be, as one Licklider admirer put it, a "means of enhancing human thought and communication."[2] Though Licklider had not yet read Vannevar Bush's article, his description of a computer sounded like Bush's memex machine.

But first, he said, we had to train computers how to calculate differently, more like people. Observing how he himself approached a problem, Licklider noticed that he spent most of his time just "getting into position" to think. Getting into position, he said, consisted of "essentially clerical or mechanical" tasks: defining terms, collecting facts, testing assumptions, and plotting out their relation to each other in charts and graphs. Once that was done, calculating and actually solving the problem (at least to him) was relatively easy. The hard part was the rigorous preparation. It took British physicist D. R. Hartree, for example, fifteen years to get into position to calculate the structure of the atom. Licklider found getting into position so difficult and time-consuming that it kept him from tackling certain projects. Embarrassed to admit it, he often chose which projects to undertake based on their "clerical feasibility, not intellectual capability." It was the same problem Bush had posed: the more information we had in our vast storehouses of knowledge, the harder it was to find and arrange to create new knowledge. Even people like Joseph Licklider were shying away from using it.

In 1945 Bush had hoped that a "computational device" could help people "free their brains for something more than repetitive detailed transformations." In 1960, Licklider and the scores of ARPA acolytes who followed him set out to get these machines to help do the clerical prep work of human thought. Licklider foresaw hundreds and maybe thousands of people working together on a computer, offering the routine preparations they needed in order to solve knotty problems. It would be nothing less than a "man-computer symbiosis."[3]

Time sharing was still impossible in Licklider's day. But thanks to ARPA money, scientists, entrepreneurs, and graduate students like Richard Bold, Leo Branek, Robert Newman, Leonard Kleinrock, Ivan Sutherland, and Lawrence Roberts were soon experimenting with ways to let more than one person use a computer at a time. Qualified users would get to rummage around the machine's great pantries of data through a phone or telegraph line. Needless to say, the imaginary computer would have to be huge, able to accommodate scores and hundreds and maybe thousands of users digging through, borrowing from, or adding to its vast libraries of numbers at the same time. In 1963, Licklider headed an ARPA time-sharing project for a while. His group managed to connect thirty researchers to an IBM mainframe by phone, but when they tried to use the centrally stored data, they kept losing some of it.[4]

As they struggled to save it, though, they were being questioned from afar. The Pentagon hoped to share these big central data libraries and the massive accumulations of calculating power to help guide its missiles and coolly assess battlefield data in the angriest of times. But in Los Angeles, it occurred to a Polish émigré named Paul Baran that the Defense Department, Licklider, and all the others at ARPA might be flirting with catastrophe. With a relatively new (1959) master's degree in electrical engineering in hand, Baran was working at the Rand Corporation, one of the Pentagon's favorite think tanks of the time. Although he also thought computers were going to change the future, he warned that relying on just one of them would leave the country vulnerable. An enemy could wipe out the Pentagon's entire command-and-control system, for instance, with just one blast.

"Both the US and USSR were building hair-trigger nuclear ballistic missile systems," he pointed out. Knowing it could rob the United States of all its battlefield calculations and subsequently blind any artillery, missiles, and airplanes that might survive a nuclear volley, Baran figured the Soviet

Union might be tempted to launch a preemptive first strike.[5] He advised the Pentagon that to make sure its communications survived a first strike, it should be using and keeping its records in more than one command computer at a time.

But that too was unrealistic at the time. Using one machine was hard enough; coordinating two or more was mind-boggling. How could you update more than one at a time? How could an IBM computer understand a Remington Rand? What if one got overloaded or had to be shut down for repair? "Many of the things I thought possible," Baran later reflected, "would tend to sound like utter nonsense, or impractical, depending on the generosity of spirit in those brought up in an earlier world." (The Pentagon was not the only doubter. A few years later AT&T flatly—and none too politely—rejected Baran's ideas for replacing its "seamlessly organized and coordinated" network of copper wiring with the interesting but relatively untidy jumble of cross-communications of a digital network.)[6]

Baran believed he could solve the problem with digital computers— then something of a backwater technology—and a process that, like Licklider's model, worked more like the human brain. Consulting with an MIT psychiatrist, he found out how neural impulses sometimes simply bypassed a brain's dysfunctional sections. Baran wondered if he couldn't design a similar system for military communications.[7]

In a series of technical papers he hammered out a model of how such "distributed networks," as opposed to time-sharing arrangements, might work. Others began exploring along the same lines. In 1966, for example, two recent grads asked Stanford to let them try hooking two computers together. Although a Yale consultant agreed it was a good idea, the university turned them down, opting to buy an equally unproven time-sharing system instead. (One of the grads, who later went on to be a high-ranking engineer at Apple, maintained Stanford thus "missed the opportunity to invent local networking.") The same year, an MIT faculty member named Tom Marill also thought linking mainframes together might work and made the suggestion to his colleague Licklider. Licklider, in turn, had both access to funding and a mind open enough to probe beyond his own pet time-sharing project. He bit.[8]

And so ARPA, with added Pentagon funding, forged into still newer communications territory. It solved the problem of overloading one of the machines by letting a computer with unused time do some of the work of the busy one. It parceled out the work for different computers to process by breaking it up into small pieces. (The process was called "packet switching." It involved fracturing the electronic language signals sent from one computer to another into small "packets" of ones and zeroes, the only two "letters" in the binary alphabet. While traveling from one point to another, they were incomprehensible, nonsensical. It was only when they reached the destination computer that they were reassembled into something meaningful.)[9] None too slowly, from about 1959 through 1969, the notions of Bush, Licklider, Baran, and scores of similarly odd thinkers began to coalesce into something like a digital communications network.

Most people, of course, did not fully understand what these eggheads were doing. Senator Ted Kennedy, on hearing that a company in his state had won an ARPA contract to build an "interface message processor" for the project, sent a note congratulating it on its new "interfaith message processor."[10]

But seers did. "By the year 2000," the *Wall Street Journal* reported in a 1967 survey of futurists, "you will be able to do just about everything but shake hands or kiss your wife via electronic communications." It predicted being able to have "a face-to-face chat with a business associate on the other side of the globe. While you're talking, you can instantaneously transmit a facsimile of a blueprint or contract for his inspection." Cables would "flash spoken, visual or computer-coded information . . . over great distances."

The experts interviewed in the article also warned there were obstacles. Someone would have to invent a way to give cables then-incomprehensible amounts of bandwidth to carry all those signals. And, at least according to the people charging tolls to use print's remaining paid channels, none of it seemed very compatible with the printed word. The deputy postmaster general pointed out that private citizens would never embrace e-mail; it was just too public and too easy to hijack. Newspaper executives pointed out no one would ever be able to deliver electronic newspapers for as little as the $1 a week it cost to deliver paper newspapers in those days. It would cost more than that, one engineer pointed out, just "to have men periodically visit the home to service the machine and replenish the paper."[11]

The worries were premature. It was another two years before a UCLA grad student named Charley Kline, in a moment much like Ottmar Mergenthaler trying out his new composing machine for Whitelaw Reid at the *New York Herald* in 1886, prepared to send the first packet of information over a wobbly new ARPA digital network. Upon getting a signal to try connecting to computers at UC–Santa Barbara, Stanford, and the University of Utah, he began by typing "LOGIN!" into the machine. The system crashed when he got to the *g*.[12]

ARPA's collection of scientists and grad students got the four remote computers talking to each other, if sometimes haltingly, by the end of 1969. In the tradition of Johann Fust and Whitelaw Reid, it was enough for some to try using it to make money. Two ARPA researchers promptly spun away to create a private network, thinking they'd rent out terminals linked to a mainframe for $40 a month. They'd print customers' work on "an ingenious, Rube Goldberg-inspired 'printing robot' which one placed over a standard IBM Selectric typewriter." The thing tapped out twelve characters per second. But that too proved premature, and the operation folded in 1971.[13]

Those who stayed continued fortifying and expanding their experimental government network. By 1971, they had fifteen computer centers hooked in, with twenty-three host computers working. Still frustrated by how slowly and erratically the computers spoke to each other, two of the project leaders—Robert Kahn and Lawrence Roberts—decided to open the floodgates: they'd publish papers and, like Friedrich Koenig, Ottmar Mergenthaler, William Garth before them, hold an open house. From their gathering, though, they did not intend to attract investors but to get fresh ideas to make the network work better.

They staged the International Conference on Computer Communication at the Hilton Hotel in Washington, D.C., in October 1972. They set up computers from different manufacturers—machines that ordinarily could not talk to each other—in a ballroom and urged visitors to use them to communicate with others in the room. About 1,000 people showed up. "It was a major event," Kahn later recalled. "It was a happening." It made ARPANET and packet switching "real to others . . . It was almost like the train industry disbelieving that airplanes could really fly until they actually saw one in flight."[14]

Just as Kahn and Roberts had hoped, the new believers sped home from Washington cooking with ideas. They hooked their own lab computers into ARPANET too. The network reached thirty nodes within a couple of months, by the end of 1972.

Back home, the attendees—corporate engineers, college professors, and grad students—mostly used this network, designed to let military command centers share massive amounts of data and computing power, to type to each other. With "requests for comments" and shared discoveries, they made up rules. "We were just rank amateurs," recalled Vinton Cerf, one of the researchers who was then based at UCLA, "and we were expecting that some authority would finally come along and say, 'Here's how we are going to do it.' And nobody ever came along."[15]

Perhaps it was because no one else could speak their language. As one of them mused in 1973, there was an Alice in Wonderland quality to their exchanges:

Twas brillig, and the Protocols
Did USER-SERVER in the wabe.
All mimsey was the FTP,
And the RJE outgrabe,

Beware the ARPANET, my son;
The bits that byte, the heads that scratch;
Beware the NCP, and shun
the frumious system patch,

He took his coding pad in hand;
Long time the Echo-plex he sought.
When his HOST-to-IMP began to limp
he stood a while in thought,

And while he stood, in uffish thought,
The ARPANET, with IMPish bent,
Sent packets through conditioned lines,
And checked them as they went,

One-two, one-two, and through and through
The IMP-to-IMP went ACK and NACK,
When the RFNM came, he said "I'm game",
And sent the answer back,

Then hast thou joined the ARPANET?
Oh come to me, my bankrupt boy!
Quick, call the NIC! Send RFCs!
He chortled in his joy.

Twas brillig, and the Protocols
Did USER-SERVER in the wabe.
All mimsey was the FTP,
And the RJE outgrabe. (ARPAWOCKY, by D. L. Covill, May 1973)[16]

In fact, they were communally designing unprecedented kinds of communications paths. When Cerf, then in his late twenties, and his colleague Robert Kahn came up with protocols that outlined how different kinds of computers along the paths could exchange their customized and purposefully broken-up packets of information more readily, the community adopted them more or less because it liked them. (ARPA began requiring all computers connected to its network to use the protocols in 1983.) Calling themselves the National and then the International Working Group, they had increased the time their network was up and running from 2 to 98 or 99 percent within a year of the Washington open house.[17]

In 1974 and 1975 they produced a series of papers, including Cerf's and Kahn's, defining the network's terms and describing its design. They also began to use a word, "internet," that Cerf and Kahn had coined in their paper to describe the vague new thing then abuilding.[18]

As they finished—at the same time the anarchic hacker community was building blue boxes to defraud the phone company—the Defense Communications Agency said it was not particularly interested in the message processing system its network was becoming. Two-thirds of its traffic was made up not of huge data exchanges or rushed recalculations of missile trajectories, but of personal messages—e-mail. When it had gotten into the network business fifteen years before, it had aimed to improve its "command, control, and communications" abilities. The foundation obviously was now in place, and it officially took control of ARPANET in 1975.[19]

Work on it continued inside the government and outside, among a few excited businesses and in a few dorm rooms. In November 1977, the government-funded researchers successfully linked not just computers but three other *networks* of computers stretching from Menlo Park to London and back to Marina Del Rey. Other networks sprung up, some accessible not just to big mainframes and minicomputers but to relatively underpowered hobbyist machines. Some came from corporations looking for opportunity: Bell Labs developed UUCP (which stood for Unix to Unix CoPy) in 1976; IBM created BITNET (which stood, more understandably, for Because It's Time Network) in 1979. Others came from students following their noses: a University of North Carolina grad student and two programmers created USENET (which apparently stood for nothing) the same year. The National Science Foundation hooked together another network, called CSNET, in 1981. Out of Ohio State came a private commercial network called Compuserve. Others called The Source, America Online, LexisNexis, Dialog, and Prodigy would follow. In 1983, the Department of Defense divided its own burgeoning network in two: MILNET for military users and ARPANET for computer researchers, as more businesses joined the hunt too. By the end of the decade Novell, then a relatively new Utah company dreaming of becoming its generation's Bell Telephone, was marketing its own computer network, with its own special protocols and e-mail capabilities.[20]

Less visibly, in 1980 an Oxford grad named Tim Berners-Lee, new to a job at a Swiss lab that coordinated physics research projects around the world, cobbled together a filing system to help him track the complex relationships between the lab's people, projects, and subcontractor scientists around the world. "One of the things computers have not done for an organization," he noted, "is to be able to store random associations between disparate things, although this is something the brain has always done relatively well." Called Enquire, it would be his first stab at training computers to find little bits of code inside electronic files. His more famous stab at it in 1990 would be a code to label files so different computers around the world could read them. It became the source code of the World Wide Web.[21]

It was Berners-Lee's fortuitously free web that caught on, first including and then outstripping all the other new public and private computer communications networks. From 1991 to 1994, traffic on the first web server (at CERN, the Swiss physics lab where Berners-Lee worked) increased by a factor of ten each year.

Berners-Lee, once described as the smartest man never to make a fortune from the information age, was modest about it. "In 1992 academia, and in 1993 industry, was taking notice," he understated.[22]

Berners-Lee's employer, CERN, held a seminar about how to use the World Wide Web in mid-June 1991. Within twelve months, there were a million web addresses. Within twenty-four, there were 2 million. By 1994, the Internet use was growing at a 341,634 percent annual rate. There were 9 million addresses in January 1996, 16 million a year later. At the start of the twenty-first century, less than a decade after CERN's seminar, 304 million people around the world had access to the Internet.

They would contribute many wonders, irrelevancies, and horrors to it. But in the mix they found that the last important transaction cost in the life of the printed word—distributing it—had sunk almost down to zero. With little or no costs or labor left to bear, they longer needed an outside organization, a firm, to share the burden for many of the stages—composing, reproducing, or delivering—of many common kinds of communications. Thus schools, governments, churches, and companies, enterprises otherwise devoted to trade or photo frames, farming or finance, found themselves able to print enormous numbers of documents on and from their cheap new personal computers, copiers, laser printers, and now intranets and websites. Once customers of businesses that had special expertise, they became producers of printed information in the last years of the twentieth century.

Their clients were breaking away to print and spread information on their own, but a few of Gutenberg's heirs were confident they'd soon be back. They surely would be chastened by the pain and suffering of producing the printed word. And the amateurs' work, after all, often didn't look very good. Formats were inconsistent, produced in what press owners sneeringly portrayed as low-rent "acceptable color." Untrained desktop publishers, they argued, would drive up their total printing costs by not getting it right the first couple of times and ignoring the time-tested rules of esthetic appeal. Unmindful of Gresham's Law—an economics theory that says that bad money chases good money away, and that low-quality goods usually drive high-quality goods from the market—some printers waited for their wayward customers' calls.

But most scrambled to adapt. First, they'd need to learn how to sell to different kinds of print buyers. "The creative function," the Printing Industries of America warned as the alarming spread of cheap communications tools accelerated again in 1990, "is likely to involve more people." For press owners, that meant print customers were no longer professional art directors or even pasteup artists but marketing strategists.[23] There would be secretaries producing business presentations, station attendants producing vendor directories, graduate assistants producing invitations, bookkeepers producing business cards.

Many big press owners, however, simply let the amateurs' work go and focused on corporate customers. Corporate clients and their ad agencies, they reasoned, still needed master printers to create the massive quantities of high-quality complex images that laser and other computer printers could not do. They added conveniences for their big clients: companies could send them their artwork via e-mail or peek into production schedules to track their projects.[24] Print itself was now composed of data, and huge amounts of print required huge amounts of data management. For smaller quantities of documents, they offered digital printing. With pricey new digital presses, they would print relatively small quantities of sophisticated multicolor magazines, brochures, reports, packages, and marketing materials—things that, on a per-piece basis, had been prohibitively expensive on a traditional press. To reclaim short-run, time-critical printing their customers had taken over, some master printers offered their own paradigm change: the information technology industry had distributed computing and distributed networks. The graphics communications industry would have distributed printing.

We could, some entrepreneurs decided, now print the way we think.[25] Just as we produced a thought only when we needed it, we'd create the printed word only at the moment we needed it. Press owners would keep all those corporate characters, words, and pictures stored in electronic form until and unless they were needed. When needed, the files would be sent to a digital press in a distant place—for a mailing or a convention in, say, Atlanta or Beijing—and printed there. The shop that sent the file would share the sale with the shop that printed it. Customers, in turn, would save money by not having to print and store thousands of sheets of yellowing paper (and information) in inventory in the warehouse back home and not having to ship heavy pallets of paper and books to the faraway locales where they now did business.

To the beleaguered master printers, one skeptical British editor who covered the industry for years explained, "this holds that buyers will only want the precise number of magazines, brochures etc, they need at any one time and second, that they will want these near the point of use. There is no point in transporting paper for thousands of miles if you can transport data at almost zero cost over the same distance and print where the job is needed."[26]

Its promoters foresaw not only savings for customers but prosperity for the press owners who, linked into these global networks, soon would be harvesting print orders and art files from colleagues around the world. They'd print just enough copies and then take them to the local hotel or office where the buyer, in from out of town, was going to be meeting. Or they'd create e-books and micronewspapers, customized to each reader's peculiar needs and tastes. The Swiss daily *Neue Zürcher Zeitung*, Germany's *Börsen-Zeitung*, Australia's *Sydney Morning Herald*, and Canada's *Globe and Mail* joined a network to consolidate and distribute their printing, depending on the current demand for their stories, in various parts of the world. In a survey of fifty European papers, almost half predicted they'd be doing similarly short, customized, digital news presentations early in the twenty-first century. Microsoft predicted 90 percent of all books would appear in electronic, as opposed to paper, form by the year 2020.[27] Some would be molded to fit an individual reader's needs, fantasies, and interests.

But the first generation of such businesses struggled. By the end of their first decade, traffic in e-books remained light, far less robust than old-fashioned tangible books. Panelists at one industry seminar attributed the disappointment to readers having to squint at words on the screen. Sales, they counseled, surely would improve as screens improved.[28]

Corporate demand for "distributed" services also began weakly. Companies often found their carefully designed materials looked different in foreign places. Paper size and quality varied among countries and even regions. Pricing was inconsistent. The projects they did order, moreover, typically were small. Even the press owners shrugged at them. "Orders of a few hundred dollars didn't generate much enthusiasm among printing company owners or their salespeople," one consultant noted even as the phenomenon unfolded. During the 1990s, U.S. venture capitalists bankrolled thirty-seven different variations on the distributed commercial printing theme, and most of them tanked. One company, Impresse, hoped to collect and flash orders to press owners around the world but had first-year sales of only $4,000. Another, Noosh, had no sales during its first six months. Two others had combined sales of $15 million in 1999, but most of it came from traditional offline printing work. More prosperous Mimeo, Inc., took orders online at its factory next to the Federal Express hub in Memphis and shipped out orders overnight.[29] But it was not really an example of "distributed printing." Like print shops of old, it printed something first and then distributed it.

While press owners struggled to make the idea work, however, distributed printing caught on among their former customers.

Like Reginald Orcutt selling Linos and literacy in emerging nations in the 1920s, for example, one executive selling souped-up copiers and laser printers in Europe in the 1990s reported once unreachable prospects suddenly were returning his calls. Bureaucrats in the nations then emerging from the Soviet bloc, he reported in a trade journal, were telling him that printing on their own, in all its banal incarnations, had become a critical step in joining the free markets of the West. "An example of this," he wrote, "is a recent customer visit I made to a key government ministry in an Eastern European country. This ministry would like to move from a process of printing driver's licenses at a centralized location (one national center printing over six million drivers licenses a year) to distributed printing at local drivers licensing bureaus." It would be more efficient, more economical, get more drivers on the road, "greatly reduce the waiting time to receive a new driver's license, and, at the same time, greatly reduce the chance of the driver's license being intercepted and stolen." He had already sold similar systems to "several" state and county governments in the United States, he added.[30] And big organizations already used to such concerns (National Australia Bank, Indiana University, Subway Sandwiches, Jeppeson Sanderson Aviation, MedWeb, Cargill, and ADP, among them) announced during the same year that they bought similar systems from manufacturers like Lexmark, Xerox, Novell, Ikon, IBM, Kodak, and, among many others, Oce. None of the buyers were in the business of printing. All, though, were now reproducing and distributing their own knowledge and forms on paper, sometimes thousands of miles from the minds and fingers of their creators.

Coworkers often willingly assumed the minor costs of rendering a couple of copies of the document in toner. The senders effectively spent nothing.

But most important, individuals were now doing it too. As the cost of information kept falling in the 1990s, the medium was no longer just decentralizing. It was multiplying as if some atom had been split and great gusts of energy had been released.

NOTES

1. Thomas P. Hughes, *Rescuing Prometheus* (New York: Pantheon, 1998), 5, 65.

2. M. Waldrop, "Computing's Johnny Appleseed," *Technology Review*, January-February 2000, www.techreview.com/articles/jan00/waldrop.htm (accessed November 15, 2004); Tim Berners-Lee, The World Wide Web: A Very Short Personal History, www.w3.org/People/Berners-Lee/ShortHistory.html (accessed November 10, 1999). Berners-Lee, who would write the source code for the World Wide Web in 1990, was the son of academics who taught him "to understand this distinction in the 50s and 60s." Hughes, *Prometheus*, 260–61.

3. Vannever Bush, "As We May Think," *Atlantic Monthly*, July 1945, www.theatlantic.com/unbound/flasshbks/computer/hushf.htm (accessed June 17, 2004); L. C. R. Licklider, "Man-Computer Symbiosis," *IRE Transactions on Human Factors in Electronics*, 1960, 4–11, http://memex.org/licklider.html (accessed November 15, 2004).

4. Licklider's group was called the Information Processing Techniques Office. Hughes, *Prometheus*, 263–66.

5. J. Abbate, *Inventing the Internet* (Cambridge, Mass.: MIT Press, 1999), 10.

6. Hughes, *Prometheus*, 273.

7. The psychiatrist was Warren McCullock of MIT's Research Laboratory of Electronics. K. Hafner and M. Lyon, *Where Wizards Stay Up Late: The Origins of the Internet* (New York: Simon & Schuster, 1996), 55; Paul Baran, www.ibiblio.org/pioneers/baran.html (accessed on November 15, 2004).

8. The Stanford grad who later joined Apple was Larry Tesler, whose proposal was eventually supported by Yale's Alan Perlis. "Inside the PARC: The 'information architects': Insiders who became outsiders describe the trials and successes of the Xerox Palo Alto Research Center as it sought to create the electronic 'office of the future,'" www.stanford.edu/group/mmdd/SiliconValley/Perry/xerox1.html (accessed November 27, 2004); Hughes, *Prometheus*, 268, 272–74.

9. A British researcher, Donald Davies of the National Physical Laboratory in Teddington, U.K., hatched the notion of packet switching as a way of improving the use of telephone lines and delivered a seminar on the subject in 1966. As a grad student, Kleinrock had done a paper on "time slicing," a theoretically similar process. Hughes, *Prometheus*, 275.

10. The company was BBN of Cambridge. Walt Howe, A Brief History of the Internet: An Anecdotal History of the People and Communities That Brought About the Internet and the Web (updated September 17, 2004), www.walthowe.com/navnet/history.html (accessed December 3, 2004).

11. Jerry E. Bishop, "Shape of the Future: Satellites Will Make Global 'Picture Phones' and Facsimile Possible," *Wall Street Journal*, January 16, 1967, 1.

12. Kline's first message was sent on October 12, 1969. Howe, Brief History.

13. MIT scientists Joseph Spiegel and Edward Bennett led the spin-off, called Viatron. Paul E. Ceruzzi, *A History of Modern Computing* (Cambridge, Mass.: MIT Press, 1998), 253–54.

14. Hughes, *Prometheus*, 292. Vinton Cerf, Cerf's Up: Frequently Asked Questions, global.mci.com/us/enterprise/insight/cerfs_up (accessed October 14, 2004).

15. Abbate, *Inventing*, 73.

16. Cited at www.cis.ohio-state.ed/htbin/rfc/rfc/rfc527.html (accessed November 15, 1999).

17. Hughes, *Prometheus*, 292–93; Cerf, Cerf's Up.

18. Hafner and Lyon, *Wizards*, 235; Dave Kristula, The History of the Internet, www.davesite.com/webstation/net-history.shtml (accessed December 3, 2004).

19. Hughes, *Prometheus*, 293; Ceruzzi, *Modern Computing*, 194.

20. The three networks were SatNet, PRNET, and ARPANET. Cerf, Cerf's Up; Kristula, History of the Internet; Hughes, *Prometheus*, 294. Internetwork Packet Exchange, en.wikipedia.org/wiki/IPX (accessed November 28, 2004); Eric A. Hall, "Towards an Internet NOS," *net.Opinion*, January 24, 1998, www.ehsco.com/opinion/19980124.html (accessed November 25, 2004).

21. Berners-Lee, World Wide Web; R. Wright, "The Man Who Invented the Web: Tim Berners-Lee Started a Revolution, But It Didn't Go Exactly as Planned," *Time*, May 19, 1997, 64.

22. Berners-Lee, World Wide Web.

23. Printing Industries of America, *Printing 2000* (Alexandria, Va.: Printing Industries of America, 1990), 2:11.

24. Joe Webb and Jim Whittington, "How Printers Are Using the Internet," *Trendwatch*, December 2, 1999.

25. The promoters were mostly business people out of Xerox, Oce, and other office product manufacturing companies.

26. Gareth Ward, "The History of Digital Printing and Future Prospects," *British Printer*, August 1998, www.printcollege.co.uk/Dbase/docs/Digital_Printing_Inkjet/digital_printing.htm (accessed November 25, 2004).

27. Tony Stewart, "Distributed Printing Shifting Impact of Newspapers," *Newspapers and Technology*, February 2004; reprinted from *The International Journal of Newspaper Technology*, October 2004; Wendy Butler, Microsoft Predicts the Death of Paper Publishing, about.com (accessed December 30, 1999).

28. The seminar was the 1999 Seybold Conference on Desktop Publishing. Butler, Microsoft Predicts.

29. William C. Lamparter, "Distributed Printing, The Second Time Around," *American Printer*, July 1, 1998, americanprinter.com/mag/printing_distributed_printing_second_2 (accessed December 4, 2004). The two companies with $15 million in sales were called Iprint.com and ImageX.com. Venture investment in print-related Internet companies during the 1990s was as much as $75 million, according to James Harvey of the Graphic Communications Association. Lee Gomes, "Once Hot Business-to-Business Dot-coms Are Next Area of Web Worry," *Wall Street Journal*, April 7, 2000, B1.

30. Ed Crowley, "Super Short Run Printing: Distributing the Print Center," *On-Demand Journal.com*, www.ondemandjournal.com/specialfeatures/crowley9.cfm (accessed November 26, 2004).

26

THE DESCENT INTO FREE

We were by then good at proclaiming eras. Books, magazines, and especially newspapers reported the beginnings or ends of eras throughout the millennium's last decades. The comings and goings were alternately marked by the election of a fresh-faced politician, the ascension of a distant cleric, the adoption of a new economic policy, the fall of a communist wall, the improved yield of an Indian harvest, or the outbreak of a war. There were considered articles and books variously announcing the "age of Prozac," the "dot-org era," the "age of rising inequality" and, among others, a "fourth turning" (in which the "millennial saeculum" was to pitch into its final crisis). Other books outlined how we were venturing "beyond the age of innocence," ending "the American era," and starting "the Chinese century."

The "information age" was supposed to be dawning at the same time too. Hundreds of writers were describing what it meant even before the last transaction costs of written communications had fully disappeared. In their new journals (*Infoworld* was founded in 1980, *PC* magazine in 1982, *Wired* in 1993), they celebrated how we would broadcast, retrieve, and store all manner of electronic information on our computers, in our refrigerators and appliances, and beside our hospital beds. Few of their excited speculations even considered that some portion of the information would appear on paper. But we were sure that transformations were afoot. Computers would "deliver the services of a full-time maid, butler, gardener, chauffeur and so on without the invasions of privacy" the irritating old human servants had imposed on us. "The computer will be doing reading and highlighting what you like for you," the founder of MIT's media lab predicted. There'd be "electronic shopping, trading securities, political polling and voting, home entertainment, corporate TV networks, electronic house calls by

physicians, psychotherapy practiced via closed circuit TV, electronic publishing and even religious services conducted via computer conferencing
systems," another pundit predicted just as the World Wide Web began to
spread. He added, "most of today's social functions performed in person
could be replaced by their electronic equivalents." Social intercourse might
actually narrow. Two professors wondered if we would not become *too*
communicative, plugged into so many devices that we'd lose the ability to
interact with any one thing or person for very long. "It's magnetic," one said
of the constant flow of information. "It's like a tar baby; the more you touch
it the more you have to." He thought it amounted to data addiction and
worried that people would grow too busy feeding their addictions to get
out much. Commerce would be different too. Electronic stores could in-
stantly supply you with exactly the goods you wanted, when you wanted
them. Shopping centers, where linear-era brick stores then sat, would become ghost towns. And politics: there would be electronic town halls, direct
conversations with the White House, and easy access to government data.
"Computer networks," another futurist counseled, "can be powerful friends
for anybody who wants an electronic democracy."

Movable type "in the fifteenth century helped to produce the Renaissance and Reformation. Telegraph, railroads, and high-speed presses in the
nineteenth century led to the overthrow of oligarchies and launched mass
politics," a historian added. "Inventions that increase the speed and imme-
diacy of information have always changed the nature of their world."[1]
Surely something like that was brewing in the latest new information technology too.

We entered the twenty-first century, in sum, much as we entered the
twentieth: impressed by our own inventions. Telephones, trains, blast furnaces, and electricity wowed our forebears. Air travel, television, and, literally, sliced bread fired the imagination of observers at the next great parting
of history, when World War II ended. And now even our best thinkers predicted in printed books, magazines, periodicals, and white papers that all the
new information we now could create, store, retrieve, and distribute surely
would change entire civilizations.

Civilization itself "*is* information," wrote a persuasive mathematician
who contended the computer was sparking nothing less than a new Renaissance. Limit information, he said, and things change. Expand it, and
things change again.[2]

The printed word did more than expand in the closing decades of the twentieth century. Creating it, of course, had been an expensive, difficult task at

least since the first cave paintings some 37,000 years ago. We came up with new tools to speed the effort in the past five hundred of those years. Most, in fact, arrived only in the last two hundred. The best of them gave new groups of once silent people the chance to compose and react ever more cheaply and ever more easily. Each widening of access to the printed word and each bump it caused did seem to jar old truths loose.

It was only when a few more tools arrived in the 1960s, 1970s, and 1980s that offices and finally *individuals*, for the very first time during that vast 37,000-year arc, could produce and reproduce printed information on their own. Just a few years later, with the appearance of the World Wide Web, their written personal communicating reached literally ethereal speeds. People needed no type. They needed to use someone else's presses or folders or slitters less often. Even the organizations that these lone citizens once needed to distribute much of their work had become largely unnecessary.

By the mid-1990s millions of people, most of them new to the sport, were creating, reproducing, and distributing the printed word on their own (or their employers') computers, copiers, label makers, fax machines, printers, and networks. Without so much as a product announcement or a corporate open house, they spontaneously and accidentally generated what amounted to a new print medium. It was different from the one that printing companies ran. Noncommercial and decentralized, it was used and operated by the amateurs themselves. They had no real rules for using it, aside from a few voluntary and often ignored codes of behavior. They had only fleeting relationships with each other and, for that matter, with the words they produced. They, not the print industry, owned the means of its production, and they plugged them into the medium only at the moment they needed them. Usually these unpaid media barons manufactured the printed word only incidentally, in pursuit of other purposes as important as world peace and as critical as soccer uniforms for their kids.

These everyday real estate agents, doctors, writers, and clerks were rarely aware of the miracles going on under the hoods of their personal machines. Their computers, printers, and connections were, like Vannevar Bush's memex machine, "primarily the piece of furniture" where they worked.[3] But at them accountants now dryly manufactured and delivered their own invoices in the spaces where seal makers, wood block artisans, copyists, lever pullers, inkers, apprentices, press operators and press feeders, type founders, paper cutters, engravers, copy editors, machinists, compositors, teamsters, freight pilots, and mail carriers had once tread. In offices, dens, basements, and dorm rooms, students were publishing their own reports. Salespeople created their own ads and fashioned their own manuals.

Consultants imprinted their own stationery. Lawyers copied their own case histories. Then they sent them out globally or next door, immediately and almost without cost. They had no guilds or employees to please or pay. Their transactions usually did not include an exchange of money. Governments did not tax or recognize them. They did not identify themselves as part of a communications group. They did not look, sound, or act like an organized industry.

But, cumulatively, they created prodigious blizzards of the stuff. No one really knows how much printed information they were spewing out by century's end in their statements, mortgage refinancing come-ons, newsletters, white papers, ceaseless daily memos, market analyses, operations bulletins, customer alerts, and presentations. Even Gordon Moore had trouble counting that high. Cofounder of Intel, Moore once managed to calculate and accurately forecast the complex, timed changes in computing power and price from 1965 through 2000. But "trying to estimate the number of characters printed is far more challenging than estimating the number of transistors produced," he conceded in 1995. "Taking into account newspapers, books, the Xerox copies that clutter up your desks, all such printed matter, I estimate that it is an order of magnitude greater than the number of transistors being produced."[4]

Some hearty souls did try to estimate it. In a multiyear study at the University of California–Berkeley School of Information Management and Systems, researchers concluded that the production of new information—whether initially appearing on paper or stored electronically—increased by 30 percent a year from 1999 to 2002 alone. Put another way, *every* man, woman, and child on Earth would have to clear shelf space for thirty feet of new books to accommodate the information being generated each year. Worldwide, we produced about 1,200 terabytes of new information just on paper in 1999. (A terabyte is 1024 gigabytes, or about the amount of information you could fit on the paper from 50,000 trees. The Library of Congress, the biggest in the country, probably contains about 10 terabytes.) Three years later, we were producing 36 percent more per year. Similarly measuring letters as information units, University of Colorado mathematician Douglas Robertson calculated that an average personal computer in the year 2000 could store and spit out twice the amount of information once contained in the library at Alexandria, repository of much of ancient Greece's great literary output. In an hour.[5]

And then, the Berkeley researchers found, we created another 5 million terabytes of new information that we first stored on hard drives. But it did not always stay that way. From his perch in high corporate circles Peter

Drucker, one of the day's best-known management consultants, pointed out in 1999 that "we did have a real 'information revolution' these last 50 years, from 1950 on. But . . . the real boom—and it has been veritable—has been in the old 'no-tech' medium, PRINT. And now printed media are taking off of the electronic channels. The new distribution channels always do change what they distribute, but however delivered or stored, [the information] will remain a printed product. And will still provide information."[6]

Paper was everywhere. In the new era's first years, "paper was being consumed at a tremendous rate, flaunting the 'paperless society' predicted by many a turn-of-the-decade soothsayer." Uses of all kinds of "communications papers" rose by 32 percent worldwide during the Internet's first decade as a popular medium. Asia's use grew by almost 66 percent and Latin America's by 57 percent. It expanded dramatically even in the globe's most mature literary cultures (in Europe by 23 percent, in North America by 19 percent), where paper was already in broad use. Print and stationery papers—the kind used in offices and homes by the amateurs who created the new, incidental printed word medium—grew even faster. Sales rose fastest in North America, where the use of these office papers increased by almost a third from 1990 through 1999. By then, the world's personal computers alone accounted for more than 115 billion pieces of paper per year.[7]

Great megabyte mountains of it, including the information produced by professional master printers (whose sales continued to grow along with their anxieties), were erupting, spreading, surrounding, and folding over humanity.[8]

They were apt to be about anything. Commercial, legal, and regulatory papers and forms were multiplying. But so were other materials. By the mid-1990s, for example, newspeople noticed they had new competition. Newspaper, TV, and radio "journalists have not been the only ones who circulated news in print," a journalism professor pointed out. "The public itself has passed along these publications, across great distances and time periods. Editors have not been the only ones who have edited news." Out of nowhere, everyone had become an editor, he said. News was moving *from* readers as well as to readers. They often changed it before passing it on. Everyone was a writer. "Everyone," a copier industry executive added, was "his own publisher." It was easy. "You don't even have to have a press to be a publisher," the now-wizened Gary Krohm agreed. "You don't have to have an editorial system." Matthew Carter, cofounder of Bitstream, a company that made electronic fonts, added that "today, for the cost of a personal computer, laser printer and software, anybody can have access to [digital] type." As a result, even "producing books and publications [was] no longer a specialized business." We had put "the necessary tools into the hands of people who once were merely the customers of printers and typesetters." Weird author–reader inversions were taking place, one academic maintained.[9] In the new century's first years came still odder creatures, Weblogs or "blogs," individuals' musings and reportings available globally on the Internet. Readers had become authors, and vice versa. Typographic Man apparently had evolved into some strange creature that was half reader–half author.

The beast produced political information too. In 1999, the distinguished leaders of the five-year-old World Trade Organization got off their planes in Seattle only to find themselves confronted by thousands of protesters and motley seekers. All had collected in response to discussions, exchanges, clarion calls to actions, and dire warnings circulated on the Internet. Along with a smaller disruption of the signers of the obscure Multilateral Agreement on Investment in 1998, pundits saw their siege of the WTO meeting as the dawning of a new age of dissent. "Word of Web was the driving force here," boasted one of the Seattle protest organizers, a Berkeley group called the Ruckus Society that, unlike the Lutherans or the Bolsheviks or the African National Congress before it, had a web designer on staff to irritate authority. "Businesses have realized the low cost of e-mail," he added, "and now so have activists." Among them were Roquefort cheese manufacturers, the conservative pundit Pat Buchanan, Free Tibet, the Sierra Club, the Teamsters Union, opponents of hormone-fed beef, and the Sisters of Perpetual Indulgence.[10] By the 2004 elections, activists were readily cutting new paths to power even within the established political parties, using the new medium to push (nearly successfully) outsider candidates like a former governor of Vermont to the presidency. Political information, in sum, had moved in new directions, *from* as well as *to* citizens. Political money, raised electronically, would soon follow it.

Bumps and disorder have always followed drops in the production costs of information, and then in the resulting spread of information. Well before we could accurately describe what this new age might be, hints again began to appear. Observers found new communications tools at the scenes of civilization's most sublime, as well as its most ridiculous, events. In recounting the final hours of the Soviet Union, which had tightly controlled the flow of information for almost seventy years, one political observer thought the most significant scene was the revolutionists' leader, Boris Yeltsin, standing on a tank outside the Russian parliament and freely communicating with the rest of the nation on Compuserve and GlasNet.[11]

The arrival of suddenly empowered communicators like Yeltsin has never been good news for elites who keep order in our clans, villages, and states. For thousands of years, our rulers enforced order through the limited numbers of people who created and copied knowledge. They subjected ideas to mighty tests before they would agree to spend the time and money to produce and distribute them. They could do it because they, "minuscule cadres . . . keepers of the faith and protectors of monopolies of knowledge," were the only ones who could afford to create even single letters. "Carving a character into a stone tablet with a chisel probably cost quite a bit, maybe the equivalent of a few dollars today," Moore guessed many thousands of years later.[12] Not many princes would invest in manufacturing an unneeded, unproven, or (especially) a threatening string of letters. When a rare someone outside their circle managed to pull together the resources to produce one, rulers could spot and silence the lone publishers pretty easily. These were societies that, as one scientist calculated it, readily "destroyed more information than [they] produced." They often did it not because they broke a lot of tablets or tore up a lot of scrolls, but because they never produced many of the expensive tablets or scrolls in the first place.

Information got harder to track as, in one blow after another, the cost of producing it was chopped down and still more groups of people could afford to communicate in writing. For one thing, there were more people communicating and thus more to watch; it was physically difficult and expensive to do it. For another, there was more information to monitor. And the printing press made maintaining order much harder. "The rate at which information was produced" during the age of movable type "nearly always exceeded that rate at which it was destroyed," Robertson figured. The new technology, he estimated, put about a million times more information at the disposal of the average European than he had in the age of script. Regulating that many impressions, we know, was a tall order. When the hard-won controls on them slipped from time to time, authorities had to scramble to get the lid back on the output. But costs fell yet again when antipiracy and copyright laws took hold in the sixteenth and eighteenth centuries; when guild and printer monopolies failed; when taxes on knowledge were cut; when telegraph companies lost control over the movement of signals to and from newspapers; when the International Typographers Union failed in the United States and the National Graphics Union failed in England; and—as we've spent the past three hundred pages documenting—when new tools appeared that created and then obliterated type.[13] Each time, more established and unfamiliar groups abruptly could afford to publish. So the "minuscule cadres" who could afford carvers were compromised first by arrivistes using easy new alphabets, inexpensive writing tools, and papers. Then came copyists and finally the multiplying hordes of hired specialists who fed and ran telegraph, telephone, radio, television, and ever faster, more inexpensive printing machines. With each change, still newer kinds of publishers—religious dissidents, universities, newspapers, professional associations, and neighborhood watch groups—got to communicate.

And then costs plummeted again at the end of the twentieth century. Existing information got cheaper. Home computers suddenly could store, search through, and transport whole libraries full of civilization's prior works. Then costs fell again. Thanks to slow transmission speeds and the expense of long-distance calls, for example, it cost $187 to transmit the contents of the *Encyclopedia Britannica* from a big computer on one American coast to a big computer on the other in 1970. By 2000, you could transmit all the information in the Library of Congress for $40. You would not need to, however, since you could now inexpensively pick and choose whatever you needed from it without having to visit or electronically lift the whole building. Britannica, threatened by Microsoft's Encarta electronic encyclopedia, had also put its contents online by then. Slices of what had been a thirty-two-volume, $1,600 body of knowledge could now be had for pennies. The competition from amateurs—plus the ease with which they could copy and redistribute the work of artists, scholars, reporters, and directors—was driving down the prices of intellectual property. Businesses found it harder to charge their old premium prices not only for books, dissertations, articles, music, shows, and directories, but also meteorological data, health care outcomes, pornography, movie listings, insurance pricings, sports scores, job postings, and corporate stock analyses. Computers, in sum, had sparked a "rapid acceleration in the rate at which information is produced."[14] As the supply expanded, the prices tended to drop.

On one hand, all that loose information might make it easier for states to collect data and keep an eye on their citizens. On the other, there were perhaps way too many writers and editors and publishers for any one government to herd or, certainly, jail.

Whatever the reason, the world had in one sense become decidedly more democratic as the legions of writers, editors, and publishers multiplied. By one count, there were fifty-five sovereign nations in 1900, and not one was fully democratic. (Britain and the United States were republics but denied voting rights to blocs of people, including women and African Americans, who collectively made up a majority of their adult populations at the time.) Almost a quarter of the states were repressive centralized empires that held colonies. By century's end all of the 1900 empires—the Belgian, British, Chinese, Dutch, French, German, Italian, Japanese, Ottoman, Portuguese,

Russian, and Spanish—were dead, replaced by 192 sovereign nations. Eighty-five of them were choosing their leaders by competitive multiparty and multicandidate processes. About 38 percent of the world's population lived in nations with universal suffrage. The breakup of repressive states, moreover, accelerated at the millennium's end. Albania, Andorra, Bangladesh, Bolivia, Costa Rica, Monaco, and, among many others, Paraguay became "fully democratic" during the last decades of the twentieth century, meaning they had at least limited their leaders' power to act without their citizens' consent.[15] People in the dozen or so independent states born in the collapse of the Soviet empire were among the emerging "free" nations.

But the same capricious, cockeyed rains of information that helped soak and rot authoritarian states vexed the new democratic leaders too. Stability was tough to maintain. In the Philippines, one commentator complained the "pervasive" American news, information, and entertainment inundating his country "has saddled us with two legacies: American-style elections, which require the commitment of massive financial resources, which have to be recouped and rolled over many times, [and] which [are] the main source of corruption in government; and American-style free press in which media feel free to attack and criticize everything that the government does or says, which adds to disunity and loss of confidence in government." Communication, added Phillip Bobbitt, a former National Security Council official and now a University of Texas law professor, "has become so rapid that our leaders don't have the luxury of thinking before they act. That has a de-legitimizing effect."[16] Terrorist groups moving money and information through the new information channels during the first years of the twenty-first century could command sophisticated military operations farther and farther afield from the locales of their grievances in, say, the Middle East and Chechnya. They readily disrupted, embarrassed, bled, and weakened state authority which, with its missiles, tanks, physics, and aircraft, only recently had had all the military power it needed to be secure and enforce order.

Some wondered if the sovereign nation-states forged in the Gutenberg and hot-metal type eras ultimately would survive the breakup of their control over the lines of communication. Bobbitt wondered if the nation-state itself hadn't ended 1990. Some saw power flowing to regional supergovernments that regulated only select activities, like trade. Others saw it falling to overlapping "interpretative communities"—trade activists, New Yorkers, oil executives, gun traders, astrologers, convention planners, anti-abortionists, sports stadium opponents, eBay users—that looked a lot like chatty interest groups. People entered and left them at whim. Beyond a government's control, they might briefly coalesce into a larger and more effective community, as they did physically in Moscow and Seattle or as they frequently do virtually in bombarding legislators and celebrities with information around an event or a cause.[17] Before dissipating back into the cloud chamber, they might well force a change in policy or behavior. Each might look a lot like how our communication is organized. Power might course among them much like Paul Baran's network of nodes, with information bypassing dysfunctional or disinterested parts.

The new age, others contended, may not tolerate communities any bigger than that. As we retreat to our little one-person communication cells, they pointed out, we share fewer experiences with each other. One writer pondering computer data's unintended consequences wondered if, alone in our customized information universes and fed products that fit our previously established tastes, we'd miss the common "small talk, gossip, news, jokes and commercials" we gleaned from our old mass media TV channels, large-circulation magazines, and national radio syndicates. All the material "can be irritating, distasteful and worse, but they account for the sense we all have that 'America' is a nationwide phenomenon."[18]

Thanks to the instant, customized responses we were turning, Texas's Bobbitt agreed more than a decade later, "from a representative system and toward direct democracy" that is "a step away from the nation-state and toward a market state." Even maps—the things that defined our nationwide spatial bias—of nation-states were heading for the attic, still others figured. For we were, they said, entering a borderless, virtual world, where we had more in common with the dispersed members of our chat groups than with someone who happened to be born in the same state or country. Fixed, linear demarcations of political space were less necessary, less descriptive of who we were and maybe, when it came to buying pharmaceuticals or trading data, as obstructive as those tollbooths at each medieval fiefdom's border along the Seine.[19]

Religious authorities, as in the Middle Ages, weren't faring well amid the new onslaught of information either. The old elites had lost influence. As Martin Luther had done in Europe, new voices had seized the new lines of communications in the United States to talk directly to parishioners, mostly through radio, television, and direct marketing. (Some, like Luther's Catholic opponents had done, sold indulgences; this time by direct mail.) None too gradually, they built big new congregations, often devoted like the original Protestants to correcting what they saw as doctrinal or worldly error that had distracted them from the fundamental faith. Traditional Protestant churches shrank. The number of Americans who called themselves mainline Protestants, long a majority, fell to 52 percent from 1993 to 2002. Demographers predicted they might no longer be a majority by early in the twenty-first century.[20]

But the new leaders' positions were as unstable as the old leaders'. The number of American adults who identified themselves more broadly as Christian fell by 9.7 percent during the last ten years of the second Christian millennium. The numbers who said they did not belong to any organized religion grew from 8 percent of the population in 1990 to 14 percent in 2001. Even the new denominations that attracted the most converts (almost all Baptist) had the highest numbers of apostates—people who left the fold—and, in the end, shrank in total numbers of adherents.[21] There were many theories why organized religion contracted in the 1990s. Religious leaders, like their political peers, pointed at the communication tools found near the scene of the crime. They often blamed the shrinkage on "media"—information conduits—for exposing us to, glorifying, and seducing us into the least biblical of human behaviors.

The challenges to scriptural authority continued anyway. Occasionally they came from newer religious shepherds, updating the age-old varieties of received knowledge in more "fundamental" interpretations and sometimes in more "modern" interpretations of morality. Other times they came from the holdover industrial era practitioners of conceived knowledge, with their notions that truth and morality might be discovered like a page of type was built, with the rigorous application of human intelligence, the candid empirical examination of evidence, and ceaseless erasure and improvement limited only by what we could imagine. And perhaps with increasing frequency it came from our new hybrid reader/author creature, practicing what might be called perceived knowledge.

Few liked it. Even the culture's kindest critics maintained that the fantastic, contradictory tidal eruptions and eddies of information and impressions were not up to many classical Greek, biblical, or Enlightenment standards. If civilization was indeed information, a building chorus of critics around the dawn of the twenty-first century suspected the often rude free information mushrooming around them was creating nothing less than a chaotic, coarse, and frightening civilization. It was a postmodern, post-Linotype hell.

Concerned and then shell-shocked observers always warned that disaster was surely coming amid the drastic collapses in grammar, language, politics, and taste that followed each quickening of information through the ages. The present was horrible, and the future didn't look much better. "This machine will make many impressions," a Leipzig lever printer predicted upon seeing Koenig and Bauer's new steam press in 1814, "but nothing beautiful." In 1900, when Mergenthaler's new composing machines sparked the historic boom in Western publishing, they argued that quality had sunk even lower. "The general quality of books was low," a historian judged many years later. It was low "for substantially the same reason as today—that is, the decline of [its] cultural level as the mass market broadened. The more the markets increased, and the more printing technology made it easier to supply them, the wider the gap grew between quality writing and mass writing." As phototype took hold in American commercial shops in the late 1960s, one observer added it was "difficult to perceive any great literary sensitivity coming as the result of the flood of print that has turned reading into a process of gulping rather than savoring."[22]

By the start of the twenty-first century, when hundreds of millions of individuals were both gulping and publishing, virtually all of the culture's professional observers were appalled by the riotous sounds, sights, and words crashing around them.

"Great literature contributes to the moral life through its broadening and deepening of experience," author, critic, and University of California–Santa Cruz Professor John M. Ellis pointed out. But much modern output, he argued, was falling far short. To many, our banging, brute, and conflicting expressions—fiction, ads, nonfiction, pop TV, weblogs, music assembled from other people's work, news, glommed-together sculptures, graffiti-strewn canvases, pandering political speeches, and so on—were plotless, obscure, manipulative, and so focused on the false and the freakish that most of our life experiences were never discussed, much less broadened or deepened. Their fruits, a sympathetic editorialist added, were "impoverishing and intrusive government in Washington, political correctness on campus, vicious lyrics and mind-shattering rhythms in music as well as [the visual arts]." Even "popular culture is getting more juvenile," added a more centrist *New York Times* critic just after the century turned, "and the serious arts, or what used to be the serious arts, often emulate popular culture." A *Christian Science Monitor* critic noted, "If it took two millenniums for *Plato's Republic* to reach North America, the latest hit from [then popular boy-band singer] Justin Timberlake can be found in Greek (and Japanese) stores within days. Sometimes, US ideals get transmitted—such as individual rights, freedom of speech, and respect for women—and local cultures are enriched. At other times, materialism or worse becomes the message and local traditions get crushed."

The big problem, added Joost Smiers of the Utrecht School of the Arts in the Netherlands, is that "culture is no longer a protected species." The elites who used to control it have fallen away and become just another voice in the chaos. Now just about anyone with the tools can create a thing he or she might call "art," "literature," "music," "science," or a "true" story. There is no one around to vet or improve his or her work. The academic critics who once might have demanded that it be supported by data before being unleashed on the public, the erudite Ellis added, are too paralyzed by campus politics and relativism to evaluate work objectively anymore. They don't believe that being "objective" is possible anyway. "The respect for the essential underpinnings of academic life—knowledge, argument, evidence, logic—is at an astonishingly low level," he mourned.[23] The hundreds of thousands of amateur communicators causing words to be printed around the world at any one moment no longer even consult the editors who, in an earlier age, might ensure that a story, paragraph, or commentary is balanced and has journalistic rigor and clarity before it is distributed. The professionals as well the amateurs who created the civilization's heaving impressions, books, observations, guesses, poems, and analyses are now not only too numerous to be counted but almost completely unregulated. A lot of junk, the critics argued, gets loose. It is, once again, a contagion.

And once again, our place in the cosmos shifted when the way we retrieved and used information changed. In ancient times, when all knowledge was received from on high, we were firmly at the center of the universe—God's (or the gods') direct descendants. We were his—or their—main concern. Things changed when the press came along, and we began to create and uncover knowledge on our own. Knowledge and even wisdom arose from our own imagination, from whatever we might conceive of and ultimately be able to prove. We revealed them in the same way we read, line by line, always in the same direction (left to right in the West, right to left in the Middle East, top to bottom in the East). We organized them for the first time in indexes and chronologies. Our universe became a "place of order and symmetry ... within man's power to understand and even to control." Using the new methods of learning, Copernicus moved us to its side. Our world, he found, was merely one world among many in a big, mechanical sky. As a result, our philosophers figured we might not always be on the mind of a creator, who was, after all, tending to a bigger, extended family.

And now, in the first decades after tangible type turned into electronic signals, knowledge came not only from reading and reciting or from the heavens, but also from intangible words. They were created by millions of us, each stationed at one moving dot on one morphing network tied to a vast, ever growing network of communications networks. Sure enough, our place in the universe began to look a lot like our place on the gigantic new networks. Astronomers came to see us on one small planet in one galaxy among unimaginably huge networks of galaxies. Philosophers, in turn, had to rejigger our existential seating arrangement. We were more than just off from the center. We didn't even know where the center was.

Much as we communicated in multiple directions at once, we now lived in multiple universes and, closer to home, plural realities. Our signals to each other were invisible, beyond our sense of touch, and apt to be broken into tiny ticks that had no meaning until someone received them. And then the recipient who reassembled them might retouch them or combine them with signals arriving from another correspondent, from the recipient's past or the TV he had on in the background. Like the impressions we sent out, we also became "an assemblage of [our] environment, a multiple self that changes in response to different social situations."[24] We too were made up of thousands of discrete parental, natural, physical, emotional, and even cultural parts that made little sense on their own until we compiled some of them to form an impression, make a point, or perceive the spouses, ideas, meals, objects, movies, pets, and feelings glancing their way through our networks of unmappable networks. None of it was either true or false. In our writhing, breathing worlds of received, conceived, and now perceived knowledge there was no absolute truth; no irreducible way to measure the value of an idea or a person apart from how we perceived it.

Our universe began to look like anything but Copernicus's orderly place. In these first years of the new age, alas, we sometimes appeared to have become as ephemeral as the type we used.

"What has produced the cacophony of change we see all around us?" a University of Minnesota professor asked in 1990, just as he and twenty-eight other intellectuals from around the world were finishing a high-minded, four-year assessment of what the heck was going on. "More than anything else, I think, it is precisely the spread of knowledge." He was optimistic. Democracy was expanding. Famine, at least everywhere outside Africa, could soon be conquered. With sworn enemies increasingly becoming trade partners, we were improving our chances for avoiding general, global wars. The Soviet Union had just collapsed. Vietnam was out of Cambodia. "Information leakage" was undermining the "narrow priesthoods of policy makers" and soulless merchants who had kept so many in poverty for so long.[25]

"Presumably," Vannevar Bush wrote when he envisioned these things in 1945, "man's spirit should be elevated if he can better review his shady past and analyze more completely and objectively his present problems. He has built a civilization so complex that he needs to mechanize his records more fully if he is to experiment to its logical conclusion and not merely become bogged down part way there by overtaxing his limited memory."[26]

The enlightened Bush probably would have trouble finding the studious, ever experimenting memex user he had conjured up in his considered *Atlantic Monthly* article. He had portrayed a patent attorney, a physician, a chemist, and a scholar interested in the history of the short bow using his memex, remotely scrolling through libraries, checking data, and keeping an eye on variables to reach a "logical conclusion." But by the start of the twenty-first century some 400 million of us, many unschooled and unsupervised, were bounding through and adding to an exponentially expanding pantry of knowledge. We fielded, dodged, and manipulated riots of flashing visual signals, broadcast words, thumping sounds, stored hypertext, and suggestive lighting. We moved information—regardless of its veracity—not only from the sources we consulted, but also sideways and upward at our whim. As always, when any of it—cogent or disassembled, researched or fabricated, enriched or divorced from its context—reached someone else, it elicited the same small responses, alterations in human perception and unimaginable pingings of change as communication always had when it bounced, dribbled, ricocheted, or echoed through a community.

This time, it raced through the environment faster than ever. The community it moved through, finally, was global.

As good as we may be at proclaiming new epochs, we are not always good at envisioning them accurately. We've been wrong about eras before. It's not unlikely our best minds could be wrong about what this one will be like too.

After all, are in just the first years of an era that exists so far mostly in magazine articles, technology manufacturers' boastful extrapolations, books like this one, and confused observations about how easily strangers can push aside authority in business, education, and politics these days. Much of the new age is indicated, as opposed to being seen. Smart critics, chattering like creatures instinctually sensing approaching storms, issue warnings. Clerics, relatives, and especially financial planners raise fears that we are losing what we most hate to lose: family, security, intimacy, wealth, and identity.

But we speak little about the wonderful, pensive, ennobling, sensitive, and insightful information amid the great outpourings of literature, charity, popular culture, science, and even political and commercial thought. Many of our resources, natural and man-made, are expanding. Many millions have access to them.

To overlook it all is to be nearsighted, ill informed, or dishonest. Maybe we are a little blinded by the glare of our descent into free information. Few in Typographic Man's infancy in the 1500s and 1600s saw beyond the bloody, absurd chaos of the Reformation, the unfathomably cruel enslavement of Indians and Africans, the mournful unwillingness to investigate and temper plagues and the sundry horrors of their time to the unceasing flowerings of science, personal freedom, and enterprise that were evolving in their midst. The notion of living in a relatively peaceful community free of famine was idealistic at best. In some circles, it was heresy. Seeing through the first stirrings of cheaper information in our own time isn't any easier. All we know for sure is that each abrupt increase of knowledge in the past profoundly changed the world. Something like that seems to be coming in the printed word's new life.

NOTES

1. Herb Brody, "Machine Dreams: An Interview with Nicholas Negroponte," *Technology Review*, January 1992, 36; William E. Halal, "The Information Technology Revolution," *Futurist*, July–August 1992, 12; Matt Richtel, "The Lure of Data: Is It Addictive?" *New York Times*, July 6, 2003, 3:1; Andre Bacard, "Electronic Democracy: Can We Retake Our Government?" *Humanist*, July–August, 1993, 42–43; Ben H. Bagdikian, *The Information Machines: The Impact on Men and the Media* (New York: Harper & Row, 1971), xii.

2. Douglas S. Robertson, *The New Renaissance: Computers and the Next Level of Civilization* (New York: Oxford University Press, 2000), 9.

3. Vannevar Bush, "As We May Think," *Atlantic Monthly*, July 1945, 9, www.theatlantic.com/unbound/flasshbks/computer/hushf.htm (accessed June 17, 2004).

4. G. E. Moore, "To the 1995 Meeting of the Society of Photo-Optical Instrumentation Engineers," in Richard Rhodes, ed., *Visions of Technology* (New York: Simon & Schuster, 1999), 145.

5. Peter Lyman and Hal R. Varian, How Much Information, 2003, www.sims.berkeley.edu/how-much-info-2003 (accessed December 26, 2004), 24. Robertson, *New Renaissance*, 30, 23.

6. Lyman and Varian, How Much Information; Peter Drucker, *Management Challenges for the 21st Century* (New York: HarperCollins, 1999).

7. PaperCom Alliance, *PaperCom Index Report* (Arlington, Va: PaperCom Alliance, 2000), 7–8; Printing Industries of America, *Vision 21: The Printing Industry Redefined for the 21st Century* (Alexandria: Printing Industries of America, 2000), 18; *Operating Statistics: United States Postal Service 1998 Annual Report*, 74; World Resources Institute, Production and Consumption: No End to Paperwork, www.wri.org/wr-98-99/paperwk.htm#use (accessed July 29, 2004).

8. Most of the formal American print industry's vital signs, considered against the tribulations of the economy as a whole, remained healthy. For example, books, perhaps the ultimate symbol of formal, commercial print culture, also continued to grow. Numbers of book publishers and book titles both soared. In 1990, after the arrival of the personal computer but before the arrival of the Internet, 4,000 new or first-time publishers applied for international standard book numbers (ISBNs), which indicate that something is about to be printed. In 1995, after the arrival of the Web, 10,000 new publishers applied for ISBNs. Book titles published each year soared around the world from the beginning to the end of the 1990s: they doubled or almost doubled in Brazil, Colombia, and Argentina; rose by 75 percent in the United Kingdom and South Korea; increased by more than 60 percent in Japan and Russia. Poland, Italy, the United States, and Germany were each churning a third more book titles each year. France published 28 percent more. Total employment grew. Industry-wide sales grew by almost 40 percent. Mail boomed too. In the United States, total mail volume rose almost 11 percent from 1994 to 1998. First-class mail, the type of mail most likely to be supplanted by e-mail, simply kept growing. During the same period it thickened by 6.3 percent to over 100 million pieces for the first time ever. And there was still money to be made the old-fashioned way. In all, Standard & Poor's index of paper and publishing stock prices rose faster than its overall stock index in the twenty-first century's first four years. Frederick Kilgour, *The Evolution of the Book* (New York: Oxford University Press, 1998), 147; International Publishers Association, Annual Book Title Production, www.ipa-uie.org/statistics/annual_book_prod.html (accessed on December 28, 2004).

9. Thomas C. Leonard, *News for All: America's Coming-of-Age with the Press* (New York: Oxford University Press, 1995), 117; Paul G. Zurkowski, "Microform Publishing," in Lowell Hattery and George P. Bush, eds., *Technological Change in Printing and Publishing* (Mt. Airy, Md.: Lomond, 1973), 135. When he wrote in 1970, Zurkowski was with the Information Industry Association; Gary Krohm, telephone interview, October 15, 1998; Matthew Carter, "The Type Revolution," *Publishers Weekly*, November 18, 1988, 46; Paul Levinson, *The Soft Edge: A Natural History and Future of the Information Revolution* (London: Routledge, 1997), 136. "Today," added yet another observer, "almost anyone with a computer, a modem, and an Internet connection can have virtually instantaneous access to information, graphics, and multimedia through links with computers all over the world." Alain Smith, "The Way of the Web," *Public Health Reports*, September–October 1996, 111.

10. Kenneth Klee, "The Siege of Seattle," *Newsweek*, December 13, 1999, 34; Michael Elliott, "The New Radicals," *Newsweek*, December 13, 1999, 37.

11. Ronald J. Deibert, *Parchment, Printing, and Hypermedia: Communication in World Order Transformation* (New York: Columbia University Press, 1997), 169.

12. Levinson, *Soft Edge*, 117; G. E. Moore, "To the 1995 Meeting of the Society of Photo-Optical Instrumentation Engineers," in Richard Rhodes, ed., *Visions of Technology* (New York: Simon & Schuster, 1999), 145.

13. Robertson, *New Renaissance*, 23. Robertson figured each written letter had

five bits of information in it. He estimated that each printed book would thus contain five million bits of information. Assuming it stayed on people's shelves for an average of twenty years, an individual book made about 100 million bits of information available to them. S. H. Steinberg, *Five Hundred Years of Printing* (New York: Criterion, 1959), 212.

14. Pam Woodall, "Untangling E-conomics," *Economist*, September 21, 2000, www.economist.com/surveys/PrinterFriendly.cfm?Story_ID=375486 (accessed August 12, 2004); James Harding, "New Chapter As Internet Kicks In," *Financial Times*, May 18, 2000, special section, 6. Robertson, *New Renaissance*, 23.

15. A total of 120 governments—representing 63 percent of the species—had electoral democracies by the turn of the century, but ruling parties pulled the levers of power in thirty-five of them. Freedom House, *Democracy's Century: A Survey of Global Political Change in the 20th Century* (Washington, D.C: 1999), www.freedom house.org/reports/century.html (accessed December 20, 2004).

16. The analyst was Antonio C. Abaya. Mark Rice-Oxley, "In 2,000 Years, Will the World Remember Disney or Plato?" *Christian Science Monitor*, January 15, 2004, www.csmonitor.com/2004/0115/p16s02-usfp.html (accessed February 14, 2005); Paul O'Donnell, "Technology Is Killing Democracy," *Wired*, June 2004, 44. In *The Shield of Achilles* (New York: Knopf, 2002) Bobbitt argues that information technology rapidly destabilized all formerly dominant geopolitical powers.

17. Deibert, *Parchment*, 195.

18. Cullen Murphy, "Force of Numbers: Demographics and Destiny," *Atlantic*, July 1992, 22.

19. O'Donnell, "Killing Democracy," 44; Deibert, *Parchment*, 187.

20. The number of U.S. Catholics held steady during the same period, at 23 percent of the population, as did the numbers of Jews and Muslims, at 4 percent each. The biggest jump was among agnostics, who said they don't belong to an organized religion. The poll was by the National Opinion Research Center. David van Biema, "Roll Over, Martin Luther," *Time*, August 16, 2004, 53.

21. Graduate Center of the City University of New York, American Religious Identification Survey, 2001, www.gc.cuny.edu/studies (accessed December 29, 2004). The ARIS study notes that if the trend continues, non-Christians will outnumber Christians in the United States by the year 2042.

22. Steinberg, *Five Hundred Years*, 201; John Tebbel, *Between Covers: The Rise and Transformation of Book Publishing in America* (New York: Oxford University Press, 1987), 82; Warren Chappell, *A Short History of the Printed Word* (New York: Knopf, 1970), 242.

23. Michael Kimmelman, "What's This about Cultural Pollution?" *New York Times*, November 5, 2000; as well as Ellis cited in Roger Conway, "Decline Demands Philosophers, Not Censors," *Navigator*, January 2001, www.objectivistcenter .org/text/rdonway_decline-demands-philosophers.asp? (accessed February 14, 2004); Rice-Oxley, "Disney or Plato?" *Christian Science Monitor*, January 15, 2004.

24. David Hackett Fischer, *The Great Wave: Price Revolutions and the Rhythm of*

History (New York: Oxford University Press, 1996), 113; Robertson, *New Renaissance*, 38; Diebert, *Parchment*, 187, 181.

25. Harlan Cleveland, "The Age of Spreading Knowledge," *Futurist*, March–April 1990, 37.

26. Vannever Bush, "As We May Think," *Atlantic Monthly*, July 1945, www .theatlantic.com/unbound/flasshbks/computer/hushf.htm (accessed June 17, 2004), 12.

BIBLIOGRAPHY

MAGAZINE, NEWSPAPER, ELECTRONIC, AND SCHOLARLY ARTICLES

"$990,000 in Grants by Carnegie Fund." *New York Times*, July 24, 1953, 16.

"A Dying Craft." *New York Times*, November 27, 1986, A26.

"Abreast of the Market." *Wall Street Journal*, January 17, 1955, 19.

"Abreast of the Market." *Wall Street Journal*, April 26, 1957, 21.

"Abreast of the Market." *Wall Street Journal*, August 9, 1962, 21.

"Abreast of the Market." *Wall Street Journal*, September 20, 1967, 33.

"Acquisition of Photon Considered." *Wall Street Journal*, November 8, 1960, 7.

"Adjustments in Printing." *Survey*, May 14, 1921, 197–98.

"After a Three-Month Shutdown, What Striking Printers Got." *U.S. News & World Report*, March 18, 1963, 98.

"Air Material Command Discloses $106 Million New Contract Awards." *Wall Street Journal*, July 11, 1956, 14.

"Another Industry Where Big Changes Lie Ahead." *U.S. News & World Report*, June 13, 1958, 90.

"Approach to Peace in Printing Dispute." *U.S. News & World Report*, April 9, 1948, 45–46.

"ATF Announces High-Speed 'Computer-Salve' Phototypesetter." *Publishers Weekly*, June 1, 1964, 86.

"ATF's New Desk-top Photo Headline Units." *Publishers Weekly*, September 7, 1964, 87–89.

"Attack on Proxy Data for Autolite Merger into Mergenthaler Wins Top Court Review." *Wall Street Journal*, April 22, 1969, 4.

"Automatic Paper-Feeders for Printing Machinery." *Scientific American*, August 29, 1903, 149.

"Automation: A Landmark Agreement." *Newsweek*, June 3, 1974, 63–64.

"Being a Retrospective of the Printers and Printing Offices of Chicago to the Year 1857." *Inland Printer*, May 1886, 499–500.

"Big Printing Show in Chicago Today." *New York Times*, September 11, 1950, 37.

"Bogus Man." *Time*, May 11, 1959, 60.

"Bomb among Publishers." *New Republic*, July 23, 1951, 7.

"Bookbuilders Review Use of Photon, Other Devices." *Publishers Weekly*, January 2, 1961, 76.

"Brief History of Early Printing." *Scientific American Supplement*, July 7, 1900, 20501.

Brief on Behalf of the Unions: In the Matter of R.R. Donnelley & Sons Company (Lakeside Press) and Organization Committee of Chicago Printing Trades Unions. Meeting of the National War Labor Board, January 5, 1943.

"Bush Elected Director." *New York Times*, November 11, 1949, 52.

"Business Bulletin." *Wall Street Journal*, November 16, 1967, 1.

"Business Bulletin." *Wall Street Journal*, December 24, 1970, 1.

"Buyers Are Active at Printing Exhibit." *New York Times*, September 13, 1950, 40.

"Canny Lithographers." *New York Times*, March 8, 1958, 16.

"CBS Labs Demonstrate Composition via Computer." *Publishers Weekly*, January 1, 1962, 86.

"Changes in Stockholdings." *Wall Street Journal*, April 14, 1958, 17.

"Changes in Stockholdings." *Wall Street Journal*, May 18, 1962, 62.

"Changes in Stockholdings." *Wall Street Journal*, September 12, 1968, 28.

"Changes in Stockholdings." *Wall Street Journal*, August 20, 1970, 21.

"Chicago Notes." *Inland Printer*, July 1896.

"Chicago Notes." *Inland Printer*, September 1896, 665.

"Chicago Printers Give In." *Business Week*, September 25, 1949, 110.

"Clevite Computer Printer." *Wall Street Journal*, April 7, 1969, 13.

"Clinic Speakers Examine Computer Composition." *Publishers Weekly*, November 9, 1964, 112–13.

"Competition." *Newsweek*, July 10, 1950, 54.

"Compugraphic Stock Marketed." *Wall Street Journal*, March 20, 1970, 20.

"Convention of the International Typographical Union." *Inland Printer*, July 1893, 325–27.

"Correspondence from Chicago." *Typographical Journal*, February 15, 1890, 2.

"Dayton Newspapers Hit by Printers Strike." *Wall Street Journal*, August 25, 1969, 12.

"Deadlock." *Time*, December 21, 1962, 41–42.

"Debut in the Composing Room." *Business Week*, April 25, 1964, 133.

"Demoralizing Influences." *Inland Printer*, August 1895, 483.

"Detroit Newspapers Resume Publication As Strike Is Settled." *Wall Street Journal*, August 26, 1957, 5.

"Dick Buys Lithomat." *Business Week*, October 2, 1950, 20.

"Digest of Earnings Reports." *Wall Street Journal*, April 29, 1958, 18.

"Digest of Earnings Reports." *Wall Street Journal*, May 6, 1960, 18.

"Digest of Earnings Reports." *Wall Street Journal*, May 15, 1961, 14.

"Digest of Earnings Reports." *Wall Street Journal*, March 15, 1963, 22.

"Digest of Earnings Reports." *Wall Street Journal*, March 16, 1964, 14.

"Digest of Earnings Reports." *Wall Street Journal*, March 11, 1970, 16.

"Digest of Earnings Reports." *Wall Street Journal*, December 8, 1970, 28.

"Digital Technology Is Slashing Cost of Typesetting Machines." *New York Times*, September 8, 1980, D5.

"Douglas C. Engelbart." www.daimi.aau.dk/~jms/Engelbart.html. Accessed November 25, 1999.

"Dow Jones News Service to Change Over to High-Speed Printers Produced by GE." *Wall Street Journal*, June 2, 1969, 6.

"Duplicator Business Sold." *New York Times*, October 23, 1950, 34.

"Earnings Reports." *Wall Street Journal*, December 5, 1968, 26.

"Educational Qualification for Typesetting." *Inland Printer*, August 1895, 485.

"Effects of the Printers' Strike." *Literary Digest*, October 25, 1919, 14–15.

"Electronic Publishing Systems Come of Age at Massive Print 85 Exhibition." *Publishers Weekly*, June 7, 1985, 52.

"Eltra First Period Net Expected to Be Hurt by Industry Strikes." *Wall Street Journal*, October 12, 1967, 18.

"Eltra Corp. Violated Two Photon Patents for Years, Judge Rules." *Wall Street Journal*, August 28, 1969, 7.

"Eltra Division to Cease U.S. Linotype Production." *Wall Street Journal*, November 16, 1970, 17.

"Eltra Says It Acquired on Market 25 Percent Share in Ludlow Typograph." *Wall Street Journal*, February 6, 1969, 5.

"Eltra Sells Its Holdings in Ludlow Typograph." *Wall Street Journal*, March 12, 1969, 14.

"Eltra to Unveil Line of Phototypesetters." *Wall Street Journal*, December 6, 1967, 2.

"Executive Changes." *New York Times*, July 25, 1951, 35.

"Fairchild Camera to Buy Mergenthaler Unit for Cash." *Wall Street Journal*, September 4, 1962, 9.

"Fantastic Photon." *Newsweek*, September 20, 1954, 60.

"Fixing the Blame." *Time*, January 18, 1963, 68.

"For Printing: A Step Beyond the Linotype." *Business Week*, May 15, 1954, 66–69.

"Fotosetter from Intertype Corp." *Business Week*, July 19, 1947, 21.

"Four Unions Move toward Single Union for Newspaper Industry, Pact Possible." *Wall Street Journal*, April 22, 1960, 2.

"Francis Barrett: His Problem Was 'Bogus.'" *Fortune*, August 1959, 177.

"Gates Talks." *U.S. News & World Report*, August 20, 2001, www.usnews.com/usnews/biztech/gatesivu.htm. Accessed November 2, 2004.

"GE Awarded Contract of $24,410,000 by Army. Eltra Unit Wins Order." *Wall Street Journal*, November 9, 1964, 30.

"Goodrich Uses Cold Type." *Business Week*, June 26, 1948, 23.

"Graphic Arts Show Beings in Chicago." *New York Times*, September 12, 1950, 35.

"Gutenberg Typesetter." *Inland Printer*, June 1886, 545.

"Hard Times." *Time*, March 1, 1963, 13–17.

"Harris-Intertype Computers Made Especially for Type Composition." *Publishers Weekly*, April 4, 1964, 62–65.

"Harris-Intertype Unveils Electronic Typesetter Using Cathode Ray Tube." *Wall Street Journal*, January 24, 1967, 32.

"Have We Passed the Zenith of Our Industrial Efficiency?" *American Monthly Review of Reviews*, July 1907, 89–90.

"Heard on the Street." *Wall Street Journal*, December 12, 1959, 27.

"Heard on the Street." *Wall Street Journal*, May 25, 1960, 29.

"IBM Will Be Given Photocomposition Data by Alphanumeric Inc." *Wall Street Journal*, February 21, 1967, 16.

"Industry and Employment." *Scientific American*, October 1936, 241.

"Intertype's Fotosetter." *Publishers Weekly*, February 7, 1948, 858.

"Invention of the Modern Press." *Scientific American*, November 14, 1903, 343.

"It's Equal Pay for Women Newspaper Linotype Operators." *National Business Woman*, September 1960, 13.

"ITU Ends Long Strike in San Francisco Against 14 Print Shops." *Wall Street Journal*, August 7, 1964, 8.

"I.T.U. Head Calls for Ballot Drive." *New York Times*, August 20, 1950, 50.

"ITU Members Give Pilcher Record Vote for President." *Wall Street Journal*, June 4, 1968, 17.

"ITU Members to Vote on San Francisco Pact." *Wall Street Journal*, August 3, 1964, 4.

"I.T.U. to Oppose Merger." *Wall Street Journal*, August 15, 1955, 3.

"ITU Will Fight for Jurisdiction over Improved Printing Processes." *Business Week*, October 6, 1956, 77.

"ITU: We Defy." *Newsweek*, August 30, 1948, 50.

"ITU's Weapon." *Newsweek*, August 31, 1953, 58.

"Jurisdiction over Unborn Jobs Drags Out Routine Bargaining." *Business Week*, January 28, 1956, 152.

"King of Printers." *Literary Digest*, October 9, 1920, 30–31.

"Kingsport Loses Challenge to Union Representation." *Publishers Weekly*, July 13, 1964, 151–51.

"Kingsport Strike Goes On and On." *Publishers Weekly*, June 1, 1964, 37.

"Kingsport Strike Nears End." *New York Times*, April 28, 1967, 55.

"Kingsport Unions Back by AFL-CIO, Firm States Views." *Publishers Weekly*, December 2, 1963, 28–29.

"Koreans Were Ahead of Gutenberg." *Natural History*, October 1950, 376–78.

"Labor Boosts Automation." *New York Times*, December 7, 1956, 26.

"Labor Chieftain's View." *Wall Street Journal*, December 19, 1956, 10.

"Labor Letter." *Wall Street Journal*, August 27, 1968, 1.

"Labor Letter." *Wall Street Journal*, January 28, 1969, 5.

"Labor Letter." *Wall Street Journal*, August 18, 1970, 1.

"Lady Compositor." *Inland Printer*, May 1886, 505.

"Lanston Monotype." *Inland Printer*, August, 1893, 408–9.

"Letter from Oil City." *Typographical Journal*, April 1, 1892, 1.

"Letters to the editor." *Business Week*, June 12, 1954, 8.

"Linotype at 50." *Time*, July 13, 1936, 51–58.

"Linotype Metal." *Scientific American*, supplement 62, November 10, 1906, 257–97.

"Lithographers Get Bid on Automation." *New York Times*, September 24, 1957, 23.

"Lithographers Plan Organizing Drive Whether AFL-CIO Approves or Not." *New York Times*, September 27, 1957, 20.

"Lithomat's Composing Machine: New Advances in Production." *Publishers Weekly*, September 24, 1949, 1503.

"Machine Work in New Orleans." *Typographical Journal*, November 2, 1891, 1.

"Machinery and Its Benefits." *Inland Printer*, July 1897, 405.

"Manhattan Project." *Time*, April 3, 1948, 65.

"Market-wise: Compugraphic Corp.'s Formula: Thinking Small When Others Think Big." *Forbes*, March 1, 1977, 59–60.

"Mayor Called Foe at Labor Meeting." *New York Times*, October 29, 1966, 59.

"MEDLARS System Is Subject of Briefing." *Publishers Weekly*, January 4, 1964, 105.

"Mergenthaler Aims at More Military Sales." *Aviation Week*, April 9, 1962, 117–18.

"Mergenthaler Buys Interest in Davidson." *New York Times*, June 7, 1950, 45.

"Mergenthaler Buys Stock in Auto-Lite and Electronics Firm." *Wall Street Journal*, April 29, 1957, 11.

"Mergenthaler Company and Schools." *Typographical Journal*, January 15, 1896, 1.

"Mergenthaler Discloses Terms of Acquisition." *Wall Street Journal*, March 2, 1962, 24.

"Mergenthaler Holders Vote Proposed Merger with Electric Autolite." *Wall Street Journal*, June 27, 1963, 2.

"Mergenthaler Linotype Declares 4-for-1 Split, Increases Dividend." *Wall Street Journal*, March 2, 1961, 16.

"Mergenthaler Linotype." *Wall Street Journal*, December 10, 1962, 23.

"Mergenthaler Lintotype Will Raise Matrix Prices April 15." *Wall Street Journal*, April 11, 1957, 2.

"Mergenthaler Plans to Make Devices to Set Bowling Pins." *Wall Street Journal*, May 23, 1961, 9.

"Mergenthaler Produces 3-Shift Chemical Formula Typewriter." *Publishers Weekly*, January 6, 1964, 100.

"Mergenthaler to Keep Plant on Long Island; Labor Pact Extended." *Wall Street Journal*, December 23, 1957, 15.

"Mergenthaler to Move Brooklyn Plant; New Site to be Chosen Soon." *Wall Street Journal*, November 29, 1957, 10.

"Mergenthaler Typesetting Systems Sold to Government." *Wall Street Journal*, April 2, 1964, 5.

"Mergenthalter Seeking to Acquire Control of Electric AutoLite." *Wall Street Journal*, February 1, 1962, 4.

"M.I.T. to Get Book 'Set' without Type." *New York Times*, February 1, 1953, 74.

"Modern Typesetting Turns Fifty!" *Seybold Report on Publishing Systems* 23, 1994, 20.

"Mohawk Data, Photon Disclose Plan for Merger." *Wall Street Journal*, April 9, 1969, 4.

"Mohawk Data, Photon End Talks Started Last Month." *Wall Street Journal*, May 27, 1969, 21.

"Monotype Composing Machine." *Scientific American*, Supplement 52, August 31, 1901, 214–67.

"Morning with Theodore L. De Vinne." *Scientific American*, November 14, 1903, 339–40.

"Mr. Reid's Question Answered." *Inland Printer*, June 1896, 322.

"Music Typesetting Machine Built." *New York Times*, October 16, 1949, 4.

"N.A.B.P. Backs Employing Printers in Wage Cut Demand." *Publishers Weekly*, February 20, 1931, 859.

"National Labor Daily to Die April 30 Unless Unions Raise $50,000." *Wall Street Journal*, March 4, 1958, 17.

"New Composing Technique Speeds Production of the New Bowker 'Books in Print' Index." *Publishers Weekly*, September 11, 1948, 1038–43.

"New Lino Contract with GPO: Ultra-fast Phototypesetters." *Publishers Weekly*, June 1, 1964, 92–95.

"New Machines Shown Printers." *New York Times*, September 28, 1958, 67.

"New Post Created by Lithographers." *New York Times*, February 23, 1958, 62.

"New Printing Device." *New York Times*, September 16, 1954, 48.

"New Products Emphasized in Mergenthaler Anniversary." *Publishers Weekly*, July 10, 1961, 76–79.

"New Technologies in Printing Industry." *Typographical Journal*, October 1981, 26.

"New Typesetting Machine." *Scientific American*, July 20, 1901, 37–38.

"New York Goes Modern." *Time*, August 12, 1974, 58.

"New York's Publishing Crisis." *Literary Digest*, October 4, 1919, 13.

"Newspaper Finds Film Is Faster Than Type." *Business Week*, February 5, 1955, 88–90.

"NLRB Authorizes Union Election at Kingsport." *Publishers Weekly*, March 23, 1964, 32.

"NLRB Dismissed Unfair Labor Charges against Kingsport." *Publishers Weekly*, August 9, 1965, 32–33.

"No Contract, No ITU." *Newsweek*, August 23, 1948, 53.

"No Settlement in Sight for Kingsport Press Strike." *Publishers Weekly*, November 4, 1963, 26.

"No Wage Cut for Compositors." *Publishers Weekly*, April 2, 1932, 1568.

"North American Philips' New Printer." *Wall Street Journal*, July 9, 1969, 30.

"Notes on Typesetting Machines." *Inland Printer*, July 1894, 64.

"Of Interest to the Craft." *Inland Printer*, June 1896, 324.

"Of Making Many Books." *Arena*, December 1901, 645–55.

"Officers of the International Typographical Union." *Inland Printer*, September 1891.

"Offset Printing Wins Increasing Favor among Daily Newspapers." *Wall Street Journal*, September 28, 1967, 1.

"Oldest Type-Printed Book in Existence." *Nation*, October 24, 1901, 324.

"One for the Unions." *Business Week*, March 1964, 154.

"One-Step Camera." *Business Week*, March 1, 1947, 40–41.

"Our Commercial Supremacy: The Alarm over American Invasion of Foreign Markets." *Current Literature*, November 1901, 540–43.

"Outline of the Report of the Delegates Sent East." *Typographical Journal*, March 2, 1891, 1.

"Out-of-Work Printers." *Inland Printer*, August 1895, 484.

"Perforator for Printing Presses." *Scientific American*, August 4, 1900, 69.

"Peril to Printers Denied." *New York Times*, October 28, 1951, 60.

"Photo Typesetting without Metal Displayed in Offset Catalog." *Publishers Weekly*, June 7, 1947, 28–25.

"Photon Acquisition Accord." *Wall Street Journal*, November 16, 1970, 20.

"Photon Composing Machine." *Popular Photography*, April 1956, 14.

"Photon Earned $15,000 in Period; 1st Profitable Quarter Ever for Firm." *Wall Street Journal*, April 16, 1962, 5.

"Photon Gets $1,250,000 Order from Newhouse." *Wall Street Journal*, October 3, 1963, 12.

"Photon Gets Stock in Tender Bid for International Photon." *Wall Street Journal*, January 29, 1968, 6.

"Photon Makes Fast Printer for Medical Data System." *Publishers Weekly*, October 1, 1962, 98.

"Photon Outlook Brightens." *Wall Street Journal*, January 24, 1957, 19.

"Photon Picks Representative." *Wall Street Journal*, June 30, 1970, 29.

"Photon Says Financial Difficulties Seem to Be on Way to Solution." *Wall Street Journal*, May 29, 1961, 15.

"Photon Says It Will Get $2.5 Million From Eltra in Patent Settlement." *Wall Street Journal*, February 17, 1970, 14.

"Photon Says Its Sales Rate Is at One Machine a Week." *Wall Street Journal*, May 20, 1957, 10.

"Photon Says Sales, Net Set Highs." *Wall Street Journal*, March 5, 1968, 31.

"Photon Says Sales, Net Set Records in 1966." *Wall Street Journal*, February 21, 1967, 12.

"Photon Sees Big Sales Rise and a Profit for 1st Half." *Wall Street Journal*, March 26, 1964.

"Photon Sees Earnings at Record Level in 1968." *Wall Street Journal*, April 10, 1968, 26.

"Photon Sees Record Sales and Earnings This Year." *Wall Street Journal*, October 9, 1962, 17.

"Photon Sees Record Sales, Its First Profit This Year." *Wall Street Journal*, July 12, 1963, 20.

"Photon Sells Common Stock." *Wall Street Journal*, April 27, 1955, 16.

"Photon Ships First 'ZIP' Model for High-Speed Computer Setting." *Publishers Weekly*, June 1, 1964, 88.

"Photon Votes a 4-for-1 split; Holders Will Meet July 24." *Wall Street Journal*, May 28, 1968, 33.

"Photon ZIP." *Publishers Weekly*, November 4, 1963, 82.

"Photon, Inc. Tender Offer Draws 94% of Shares of International Photon." *Wall Street Journal*, January 4, 1968, 2.

"Photon, Inc. Negotiates Loan of $4 Million with Prudential." *Wall Street Journal*, July 31, 1967, 17.

"Photon, Inc. Predicts Loss from Operations in 1955 but Profit in 1956." *Wall Street Journal*, May 23, 1955, 11.

"Photon's Holders Approve 4-for-1 Split, Stock Boost." *Wall Street Journal*, July 25, 1968, 16.

"Phototypesetting Picks Up the Pace." *Business Week*, December 14, 1963, 156–58.

"PIA Briefs Trade Publications on Steady Growth and Future Plans." *Graphic Arts Monthly*, May 1981, 102.

"PIA: The Challenge of Changing Markets in a Changing World." *Publishers Weekly*, November 5, 1962, 70.

"Pittsburgh's Press Run." *Newsweek*, November 27, 1950, 54.

"Plan Parlay on Type." *New York Times*, June 9, 1949, 47.

"Powers Play." *Time*, May 20, 1974, 61–62.

"Premium Wage Situation in the Closed-shop Branch of the Printing Industry." *Monthly Labor Review*, November 1922, 1038–43.

"Present State of the Typographical Industry." *Inland Printer*, March 1896, 627.

"President Kennedy on the Position of Unionists toward Type-setting Machines." *Typographical Journal*, August 1, 1891, 1.

"Pressmen versus Compositors." *Inland Printer*, June 1897, 289.

"Pressures in the Print Shop." *Fortune*, July 1960, 214.

"Printers Battle over Closed Shop." *U.S. News & World Report*, December 5, 1947, 35–37.

"Printers Invited Back in Toronto." *Wall Street Journal*, August 7, 1964, 8.

"Printers May Seek 4-Day Week." *Wall Street Journal*, August 21, 1957, 8.

"Printers Prepare for Change." *Business Week*, August 31, 1963, 68–70.

"Printers' Strike." *Outlook*, January 13, 1906, 54–55.

"Printers Widening 'Closed Shop' Fight." *U.S. News & World Report*, September 2, 1949, 44.

"Printers' Work Stoppage Cuts Congressional Record." *Wall Street Journal*, May 27, 1970, 30.

"Printing a Dream." *Time*, January 18, 1963, 69.

"Printing by Computer: A USN&WR Gamble Pays Off." *U.S. News & World Report*, September 5, 1977, 56–58.

"Printing by Electricity." *Current Literature*, June 1901, 742.

"Printing by Photo Is Shown to Public." *New York Times*, September 16, 1949, 29.

"Printing Faces a New Era." *Business Week*, March 13, 1948, 22.

"Printing Unions Talk Merger with Increasing Fervor." *Wall Street Journal*, October 3, 1967, 1.

"Printing Wage Controversy Becomes Acute." *Publishers Weekly*, October 8, 1932, 1435.

"Printing Wakes Up to Modern Technology." *Business Week*, October 11, 1958, 94–96.

"Printing War." *Fortune*, October 1957, 242.

"Printing without Type in New York City." *Review of Reviews*, December 1919, 650.

"Printing without Type." *Business Week*, October 1, 1949, 57.

"Printing: Ancient Craft Is Stirring with New Inventions." *Fortune*, October, 1949, 100–9.

"Progress Report." *Time*, November 29, 1943, 40.

"Push-Button Warfare." *Newsweek*, May 20, 1974, 99.

"R.R. Donnelley Partners with Microsoft in E-book Deal." *Printshare History of Postscript*. mm.iit,uni-miskolc.hu/Data/texts/hackers_jargon/postscript.HTML. Accessed November 5, 1999.

"R.R. Donnelley to Close Its Digital Printing Division." *Graphic Arts Monthly*, January 28, 1997.

"RCA Typesetting Unite Is Able to Produce 6,000 Characters a Second." *Wall Street Journal*, February 20, 1968, 5.

"Remembering the Beginning with Bill Gates." *PC*, March 25, 1997. www.pcmag.com/article2/0,1759,1204,00.asp. Accessed November 2, 2004.

"Renewal of the Second Class Mail Matter." *Scientific American*, February 24, 1900, 114.

"Scientific Cyclone." *Newsweek*, January 10, 1944, 50.

"Scientific High Command." *Time* 44, July 3, 1944, 54.

"Secretary-Treasurer's Annual Report and Financial Statement." *Typographical Journal*, July 1975, 46.

"Setting Type by Photograph." *Literary Digest*, April 11, 1931, 22.

"Signs of the Future?" *Newsweek*, November 9, 1964, 88.

"Some Magazine Circulations." *Inland Printer*, June 1897, 290.

"Special Computer for Printers." *Business Week*, March 7, 1964, 102.

"St. Louis Notes." *Inland Printer*, August 1891, 17.

"St. Louis Printers Walkout Continues to Block 2 Papers." *New York Times*, October 14, 1966, 86.

"State of the Trade." *Typographical Journal*, August 15, 1889, 5.

"Strange Chain." *Time*, March 3, 1958, 59.

"Strike's End." *Time*, October 18, 1954, 47.

"Strikes and Lockouts." *Typographical Journal*, August 15, 1889, 1–2.

"Surplus Plant Resold." *New York Times*, July 21, 1948, 37.

"Tacoma's Long Strike." *Newsweek*, July 14, 1952, 81.

"Taft-Hartley Strike Enters Second Year." *Business Week*, December 11, 1948, 96–99.

"Tennessee Strike Raises Issue Here." *New York Times*, February 13, 1966, 65.

"Textbook Boycott by Schools Voided." *New York Times*, October 14, 1966, 86.

"Three Unions Certified in Kingsport Strike." *Publishers Weekly*, March 1, 1965, 48.

"Three-year Wage Pact Ends 7-Day Mergenthaler Strike." *Wall Street Journal*, October 11, 1955, 4.

"Top Court Backs Minority Holders, Fails to Settle Issue of Auto-Lite Merger." *Wall Street Journal*, January 21, 1970, 4.

"Trade Unions Merge with CWA." *Monthly Labor Review*, February 1987, 39.

"Two Composing Machines Make Their Bow." *Publishers Weekly*, May 1, 1948, 1948–50.

"Two Convictions Upheld in Mergenthaler Case." *New York Times*, April 20, 1948, 18.

"Two Eltra Holders to Receive Judgment Favoring Their '63 Suit." *Wall Street Journal*, September 26, 1967, 3.

"Two Manufacturers Boost Prices of Type Matrices." *Wall Street Journal*, September 27, 1956, 4.

"Two Unions in Accord." *New York Times*, November 14, 1958, 19.

"Type-Composing Machine upon Which Mark Twain Lost His Fortune." *Inland Printer*, April 1896.

"Typeless Typesetting: The Last Step." *Business Week*, January 17, 1953, 58.

"Typesetting by Machinery." *Inland Printer*, September 1886, 754.

"Typesetting Competition." *Inland Printer*, June 1897, 290.

"Typesetting Device Slated for Market." *New York Times*, October 8, 1958, 57.

"Typesetting Machine Inventor." *Inland Printer*, July 1897, 404–5.

"Typesetting Machines." *Inland Printer*, February 1891, 415.

"Typesetting Machines." *Inland Printer*, September 1891, 1060.

"Type-setting Machines: An Arbitrator Decides That the Chicago Agreement Does Not Apply." *Typographical Journal*, September 1, 1891, 1.

"Typewriter Composition." *Publishers Weekly*, November 1, 1953, 1899.

"Typewriter with a Memory Sets Type On Photo Fil." *Popular Science*, August 1950, 93–97.

"Typographical Union Defeat." *Inland Printer*, August 1897, 534–35.

"Typographical Union May Sell Newspaper to Nevada Publisher." *Wall Street Journal*, February 13, 1970, 2.

"Typographical Union Votes a Relaxation on Reproduction Rules." *Wall Street Journal*, August 8, 1969, 26.

"Typothetae and the Union." *Inland Printer*, September 1895, 594.

"Union Leader Urges Spur to Automation." *New York Times*, September 22, 1957, 1.

"Union Merger Developments." *Monthly Labor Review*, November 1985, 64.

"Union Shop in Pittsburgh." *Nation*, November 18, 1950, 453–55.

"Unions Explain Their Side of Kingsport Strike." *Publishers Weekly*, September 2, 1963, 43–44.

"United Methodists Pioneer Electronic Printing Facility." *Publishers Weekly*, September 26, 1977, 72.

"United to Support, Not Combined to Injure." *Inland Printer*, August 1895, 484–85.

"Up from the Stone Age." *Time*, March 16, 1962, 43.

"Upsetting the Typesetter; A Note on Anticipation." *Library Journal*, February 15, 1945, 177.

"Varian Associates New Printer." *Wall Street Journal*, September 9, 1970, 14.

"Wage Regulations of Typesetting Machine Operators." *Inland Printer*, September 1895, 595.

"Wage Scales in the Printing Industry." *Monthly Labor Review*, May 1960, 486–90.

"What Comes Naturally." *Time*, September 1, 1947, 38.

"Who's News." *Wall Street Journal*, June 4, 1956, 15.

"Who's News." *Wall Street Journal*, March 2, 1960, 9.

"Why the Ancients Did Not Invent Printing." *Literary Digest*, February 3, 1912, 208.

"Wireless Telegraph Typewriter." *Current Literature*, August 1903, 150.

"Wrong Approach." *Publishers Weekly*, March 22, 1965, 54.

"Yankee Scientist." *Time*, April 3, 1944, 52.

Adams, Peter C.S. "Pagemaker Past, Present, and Future: A Brief History of Publishing." www.makingpages.org/pagemaker/history. Accessed October 14, 2004.

Adler, Waldo. "Printers Trade School in New York." *Review of Reviews*, April 1918, 414–15.

Alex. "The Type-Setting Machine." *Typographical Journal*, February 2, 1891, 4.

Alexander, George. "Technology's Role as a Disruptive Force." *Seybold Report on Publishing Systems*, May 17, 1999.

Andreoli, Tom. "Lagging R.R. Donnelley Replates Its Future. After Growth Spurt: Spinoffs and Focus on Returns." *Crains Chicago Business*, October 14, 1996, 19.

Axthelm, Pete. "Bert Powers's Last Stand." *Newsweek*, May 20, 1974, 97.

Bacard, Andre. "Electronic Democracy: Can We Retake Our Government?" *Humanist* 53 July-August 1993, 42.

Baker, Elizabeth F. "Technological Change and Organized Labor in Commercial Printing." *American Economic Review*, December 1932, 669–90.

———. "Unemployment and Technical Progress in Commercial Printing." *American Economic Review*, September 1930, 442–66.

Barnett, G. E. "The Introduction of the Linotype: The Displacement Of Labor." *Yale Review*, November 1904, 251–73.

Bellis, Mary. The History of the Graphical User Interface, or GUI. inventors.about.com/library/weekly/aa043099.htm. Accessed November 1, 2004.

Berners-Lee, Tim. "The World Wide Web: A Very Very Short Personal History." www.w3.org/Peple/Berners-Lee/ShortHistory.html. Accessed November 10, 1999.

Bevis, A. Sandy. "Annual Report to the Membership." *Typographical Journal*, July 1975, 40.

Beyrouti, Nouri. "The History and Development of Newspaper Electronic Pagination Systems in the United States, 1975–1987." Ph.D. diss., New York University, 1989.

Bishop, Jerry E. "Shape of the Future: Satellites Will Make Global 'Picture Phones' and Facsimile Possible." *Wall Street Journal*, January 16, 1967, 1.

Blundell, William E. "Research Push Brings Speedier Typesetting, Other Major Advances." *Wall Street Journal*, December 10, 1964, 1.

Bolas, Thomas. "Origination of Printing Types by Photographic Methods." *Scientific American*, supplement, March 10, 1900, 202–31.

Borden, Jeff. "Merger Puts Donnelley in Software Big League." *Crain's Chicago Business*, March 27, 1995, 10.

Brody, Herb. "Machine Dreams: An Interview with Nicholas Negroponte." *Technology Review*, January 1992, 34.

Brown, Emily Clark. "Price Competition In Chicago Printing." *Journal of Political Economy*, December 1930, 194–212.

Brutus, Marcus. "Elmira Progressing." *Typographical Journal*, January 1, 1896, 28.

Bush, Vannever. Letter to the editor. *New York Times*, November 28, 1949, 28.

———. "As We May Think." *Atlantic Monthly*, July 1945. www.theatlantic.com/unbound/flasshbks/computer/hushf.htm. Accessed June 17, 2004.

Butler, Wendy. Microsoft Predicts the Death of Paper Publishing. www.About.com. Accessed December 30, 1999.

Byers, Don. "Smaller Shops Disappearing." printowners@printweb.org. Accessed September 28, 2000.

Campsie, John W. "The Cost and Value of Composition." *Inland Printer*, August 1897, 580.

Carter, Matthew. "The Type Revolution." *Publishers Weekly*, November 18, 1988, 46.

Caughey, Bernard. "Four Generations of Low Family Ownership Ends." *Quincy Patriot Ledger*, February 4, 1998, 1.

Champney, Freeman. "Taft-Hartley and the Printers." *Antioch Review*, Spring 1948. International Typographical Union Collection, Norlin Library, University of Colorado–Boulder. Accession 1, Box 60, Notebook 2.

Cheney, William L. "Peace in Printing." *Survey*, December 25, 1920, 451.

Cleveland, Harlan. "The Age of Spreading Knowledge." *Futurist*, March–April 1990, 36.

Cody, David. The Victorian Web: John Locke. http://65.107.211.206/victorian/religion/locke1.html. Accessed February 11, 2002.

Coleman, Samuel. Letter to the editor. *New Republic*, January 19, 1963, 31.

Conrad, Edith. "A Chat with the Printer Girls," *Inland Printer*, June 1893, 230.

Cook, James. "Least-regulated Money in the Country Today," *Forbes*, June 2, 1986, 74–75.

Corcoran, Phil. "Provisional Membership." *Typographical Journal*, December 16, 1889, 2.

Cross, Lisa. "On-demand Enigma: Undefinable Success: While Everyone Agrees to Disagree, All Concede That Print-On-Demand Is a Catalyst for Progress." *Graphic Arts Monthly*, April 1998.

Crowley, Ed. "Super Short Run Printing: Distributing the Print Center." OnDemand Journal.com. www.ondemandjournal.com/specialfeatures/crowley9cfm. Accessed November 26, 2004.

Crown, Judith. "Ink-stained Stretch." *Crain's Chicago Business*, August 11, 1997, 1.

D.F.Y. "From New Orleans." *Inland Printer*, July–August 1891, 805, 993.

David, Paul A., and Gavin Wright. *Early Twentieth-Century Productivity Growth Dynamics: An Inquiry into the Economic History of "Our Ignorance."* Stanford, Calif.: Stanford Institute for Economic Policy Research Institute for Economic Policy Research, 1999.

Davies, David R. "An Industry in Transition: Major Trends in American Daily Newspapers, 1945–1955." Ph.D. diss., University of Alabama, 1997.

Davis, Ronnie H. "The Changing Landscape of Printing Plants." *Economic & Print Market Report*, 2004.

De la Mare, Pierre. "An Industry Born." *Printing World*, April 21, 1997.

——— ."Printing in the Victorian Era." *Printing World*. www.dotprint.com. Accessed May 19, 1997.

——— ."The Literary Era." *Printing World*. www.dotprint.com. Accessed April 25, 1997.

Dumar, Charles F. "Women as Typesetters." *Inland Printer*, August, 1891, 1001–2.

Dunn, Alan. "Utopia–1955." *Saturday Evening Post*, December 30, 1944, 36–37.

Dunn, Thomas. "Lasers in Graphics: The Continuing Evolution." *Graphic Arts Monthly*, October 1981, 50.

E.C. "Report Upon the American Printing Trade by French Experts." *Inland Printer*, October 1895, 57.

Early, Steve, and Rand Wilson. "Do Unions Have a Future in High Technology?" *Technology Review*, October 1986, 56.

Eisen, David J. "Union Response to Changes in Printing Technology: Another View." *Monthly Labor Review*, May 1986, 38.

Elliott, Michael. "The New Radicals." *Newsweek*, December 13, 1999, 36.

Em Dash. Letter from Washington, D.C. *Inland Printer*, August 1891, 995.

Farber, Henry S. "The Recent Decline of Unionization in the United States." *Science*, November 13, 1987, 915–20.

Fidelities. "Letter from Baltimore." *Inland Printer*, August 1891, 7.

Field, Alexander. "The Telegraphic Transmission of Financial Asset Prices and Orders to Trade: Implications for Economic Growth, Trading Volume, and Securities Market Regulation." Paper presented at the All-UC Economic History Group Conference, University of Santa Clara, March 1998.

Formaini, Robert L., and Thomas F. Siems. "Ronald Coase: The Nature of Firms and Their Costs." *Dallas Economic Insights* 8 (2003).

Freedom House. Democracy's Century. www.freedomhouse.org. Accessed December 29, 2004.

G. H. "A Higher and Nobler Unionism." *Inland Printer*, September 1893, 483–84.

Gersh, Debra. "The Changing Role of the Typographer: Washington Post Management Is Pleased with New 10-Year Contract with the Typographical Union but Printers Are More Apprehensive." *Editor & Publisher*, June 8, 1991, 3.

Gilchrist, Bruce, and Ariana Shenking. "Disappearing Jobs." *Futurist*, February 1981, 44–49.

Gilman, C. H. "Modern Mechanism: Will Type-Setting Machines Have a Good or Demoralizing Influence?" *Typographical Journal*, December 1, 1891, 1.

Gomes, Lee. "Once Hot Business-to-Business Dot-coms Are Next Area of Web Worry." *Wall Street Journal*, April 7, 2000, B1.

Goodstein, David Henry. "Typesetting Moves from a Master Craft to a Computer Application in Today's World." *Graphic Arts Monthly*, June 1981, 42.

Gordon, Mitchell. "Here's a Labor Union That Pushes for More Labor-Saving Devices." *Wall Street Journal*, December 3, 1956, 1, 3.

Graphic Arts Information Network. Print: The Original Information Technology. www.gain.net/printIT/main.html. Accessed August 22, 2004.

H.L.F. "Linotype Machines and the Typographical Union." *Typographical Journal*, February 1, 1896.

H.S. "From Milwaukee." *Inland Printer*, August 1891, 805.

Halal, William E. "The Information Technology Revolution." *Futurist*, July–August 1992, 12.

Hamm, Steve, and Jay Greene. "The Man Who Could Have Been Bill Gates." *Business Week*, October 25, 2004. www.businessweek.com/magazine/content/04_43/b3905109_mz063.htm. Accessed November 2, 2004.

Harkavy, Ward. "The Castle on the Hill." *Westword*, May 11, 1994. www.westword.com/issues/1994-05-11/feature2.html. Accessed September 17, 2004.

Hill, Dee. "Typesetters Sue Times Herald." *Dallas Business Journal*, October 18, 1991, 4.

Hoffman, Frederick L. "Dust Phthisis in the Printing Industry." *Monthly Labor Review*, September 1922, 659–71.

Hoke, Donald. "The Woman and the Typewriter: A Case Study in Technological Innovation and Social Change." *Business and Economic History*, 8 (1979): 76–88.

Holland, Caryl. "Is Bigger Better?" *Printing World*, May 1, 1998.

Howard, C. H. "Publishers and the Postal Department." *Arena*, December 1901, 570–77.

Hunter, Kris. "Donnelley Goes Digital with New Plant in Memphis." *Memphis Business Journal*, August 14, 1995, 35.

Iacone, Audrey Abbott. "Early Printing in Pittsburgh, 1786–1856." *Pittsburgh History*, Summer 1990. clpgh.org/exhibit/neighborhoods/downtown/down_n43.html. Accessed January 10, 2004.

IBM Archives. "Before the Beginning: Ancestors of the IBM Personal Computer." www-1.im.com/ibm/history/exhibits/pc/pc_1.html. November 2, 2004.

International Publishers Association. Annual Book Title Production. www.ipa-uie.org/statistics/annual_book_prod.html. Accessed December 29, 2004.

Jacobs, Paul. "Dead Horse and the Featherbed." *Harper's*, September 1962, 47–54.

———."Union Democracy and the Public Good." *Commentary*, January 1958, 68–74.

Johnson, Eric A. "We're Not Washed Up." *Readers Digest*, November 1943, 11–16.

Johnston, Louis. "The Growth of the Service Sector in Historical Perspective: Explaining Trends in U.S. Sectoral Output and Employment, 1840–1990." Paper presented at Cliometrics Conference, University of Toronto, May 1997.

Joner, Urban. "Heidelberg Sees Linotype as Key to Digital Future." *Seybold Report on Publishing Systems*, April 4, 1997, 25.

Keep, Christopher, and Tim McLaughlin. The Electronic Labyrinth.www.iath.virginia.edu/elab/hfl0034.html. (Accessed June 5, 1999).

Kempton, Murray. "Return of the Luddites." *New Republic*, December 22, 1962, 6–7.

Kielbowicz, Richard Burket. *Origins of the Second-Class Mail Category and the Business of Policymaking, 1863–1879.* Journalism Monographs, no. 96, Association for Education in Journalism and Mass Communications, 1986.

Kinnear, Samuel. "Reception of the Linotype in Edinburgh." *Inland Printer*, May 1896.

Klee, Kenneth. "The Siege of Seattle." *Newsweek*, December 13, 1999, 30–35.

Knights, Peter R. "The Press Association War of 1866–1867." *Journalism Monographs* December 1967, 6.

Kopeck, Thomas W. "Annual Report and Financial Statement." *Typographical Journal*, March 1985, 40–60.

———."Membership Decline Pattern Changing." *Typographical Journal*, March 1981, 3.

———."Mixed Blessing in Chicago." *Typographical Journal*, December 1985, 4–5.

———."Some Things Need to Be Said." *Typographical Journal*, July 1985, 4.

Lamparter, William C. "Distributed Printing, the Second Time Around." *American Printer*, July 1, 1998. americanprinter.com/mag/printing_distributed_second_2. Accessed December 4, 2004.

Laugero, Gregory V. "Infrastructures of Enlightenment." Ph.D. dissertation, State University of New York at Stony Brook, 1994.

Leonidas. "From New York." *Inland Printer*, August 1891, 995.

Lesser, Harry. "Vox Pop: Letter to the Editor." *Typographical Journal*, May 1974, 183.

Lewis, Regina. "Relation between Newspaper Subscription Price and Circulation, 1971–1992." *Journal of Media Economics* 8 (1995).

Licklider, L. C. R. "Man-Computer Symbiosis." *IRE Transactions on Human Factors in Electronics*, 1960, 4–11.

Lyman, Peter, and Hal R. Varian. How Much Information? 2003. www.sims.berkeley.edu/how-much-info-2003. Accessed December 26, 2004.

MacIver Neiva, Elizabeth. "Chain Building: The Consolidation of the American Newspaper Industry, 1953–1980." *Business History Review*, Spring 1996, 1–42.

Marsh, Peter. "Pressing On with High Technology." *Financial Times*, May 18, 2000, 1.

McAlister, J. "Printers and Telegraphic Ownership." *Inland Printer*, June 1894, 238–39.

McDonald, George. "A Contrast: The Interests of the Membership vs. the Interests of the Few." *Typographical Journal*, December 1, 1890, 2.

McFarland, H. C. "The Pressmen, from an I.T.U. Standpoint." *Inland Printer*, September 1893, 484–85.

McLean, Ian, and Kris James Mitchener. "U.S. Regional Growth and Convergence, 1880–1980." Presented at the Cliometric Society–sponsored ASSA session Growth and Institutions, January 3, 1998.

Melcher, Daniel. "Can Important Economies Be Expected from New Developments in Typesetting?" *Publishers Weekly*, September 6, 1947, 70.

Merryman, R. ARPAWOCKY. Network Working Group. June 22, 1973. http://www.cis.ohio-state.ed/htbin/rfc/rfc/rfc527.html. Accessed June 4, 2000.

Merton, Robert K., and H. Zuckerman. "Patterns of Evolution in Science." *Minerva* 68, 1971.

Morgenson, Gretchen. "A Company Worth More Than Spain?" *New York Times*, December 26, 1999, sec. 3, p. 1.

Murphy, Colleen. "Force of Numbers: Demographics and Destiny." *Atlantic*, July 1992, 22.

Nichols, W. M. "Increase Our Members." *Typographical Journal*, September 15, 1889.

O'Donnell, Paul. "Technology Is Killing Democracy." *Wired*, June 2004, 44.

Olbrich, Bill. "A&E Gutenberg." Society for the History of Authorship, Reading, and Publishing Archives. www.sharpweb.org/sharp-l.html. Accessed October 13, 1999.

Old-Time Printer. "We Want More Labor-Saving Devices and Materials." *Inland Printer*, September 1891, 1043.

PaperCom Allliance. "PaperCom Index Shows Worldwide Paper Consumption Increasing." PaperCom Index Report, November 27, 2000. www.papercom.org. Accessed December 30, 2004.

Paschell, William. "The International Typographical Union." *Monthly Labor Review*, May 1952, 493–98.

Peavy, Asa. "A&E Gutenberg." Society for the History of Authorship, Reading, and Publishing Archives. www.sharpweb.org/sharp-l.html. Accessed October 12, 1999.

Petzinger, Thomas Jr. "Talking about Tomorrow." *Wall Street Journal*, January 1, 2000.

Peuto, Bernard L. "Mainframe History Provides Lessons." *Microprocessor Report*, March 31, 1997, 19.

Pilcher, John J. "Annual Report of the President to the Membership." *Typographical Journal*, May 1974, 5s–9s.

Pitt, David E. "His Vision Realized, a Union Leader Retires." *New York Times*, June 15, 1990, B1.

Portenar, A. J. "'Vacations in the Printing Industry in New York City." *Monthly Labor Review*, January 1920, 270–79.

Powell, Leona M. "Typothetae and the Eight-Hour Day." *Journal of Political Economy*, December 1925, 660–83.

Prescott, W. B. "Trade Teaching under the Auspices of the Typographical Union." *Annals of the American Academy of Political and Social Sciences*, January 1910, 178–84.

Prestro, John A. "Printing Equipment Concerns, Bolstered by Electronic Items." *Wall Street Journal*, June 26, 1968, 8.

Quinones, Eric R. "Sorry, Wrong Number for Walter: AT&T Fires Onetime Future Leader." *Crains Chicago Business*, July 17, 1997, 1.

Reed, Christopher. "The Cost of a Comma." Harvard Magazine, November-December 1998. www.harvard-magazine.com/128.103.142.209/issues/nd98/nd98issue.ssi. Accessed November 7, 1999.

Reeves, J. G. "The Rogers Typograph." *Typographical Journal*, November 1, 1890, 1.

Rice-Oxley, Mark. "In 2,000 Years, Will the World Remember Disney or Plato?" *Christian Science Monitor*, January 15, 2004. www.csmonitor.com/2004/0115/p16s02-usfp.html. Accessed February 14, 2005.

Richtel, Matt. "The Lure of Data: Is It Addictive?" *New York Times*, July 6, 2003, 3.

Rieg, Mary Kay. "Union Pay Rates in the Printing Industry." *Monthly Labor Review*, September 1975, 644.

Roberts, W. C. "The Paige Typesetting Machine." *Inland Printer*, June 1893, 248–49.

Romano, Frank J. "The Market with No Name." *Seybold Report on Desktop Publishing 1994*. www.isc.rit.edu/-spmswww/frank/frtalk.htm. Accessed August 22, 2004.

———. *Media Distribution in a Digital Age*. Rochester: Print Industry Center of the Rochester Institute of Technology, 2002.

Rosenbaum, Ron. "Secrets of the Little Blue Bo: A Story So Incredible It May Even Make You Feel Sorry for the Phone Company." *Esquire*, October 1971, 116.

Rossiter, W. S. "Printing and Publishing: The Barometer Industry." *American Monthly Review of Reviews*, September 1906, 388–42.

Ruben, George. "Two Chicago Newspapers Complete Negotiations." *Monthly Labor Review*, February 1989, 52.

Russo, David J. "The Origins of Local News in the U.S. Country Press, 1840s–1870." *Journalism Monographs*, February 1980, 65.

Rutledge, J. Howard. "New Machines Promise to Outdate Newspaper Methods, Simplify Jobs." *Wall Street Journal*, January 13, 1948, 1.

Seitz, Don C. "The Price of Paper: A Tax on Knowledge." *World's Work*, January 1908, 9765–68.

Sharples, Hadley. "Chief Printers Plot Strategies." *Graphic Arts Monthly*, August 1995.

———."Digital Presses Eye the Market of One." *Graphic Arts Monthly*, April 1996.

———."Innovators See Promise in Digital Asset Management." *Graphic Arts Monthly*, October 1997.

———."Prepress Alert: Amid Worrisome Shifts, Managers See Opportunity." *Graphic Arts Monthly*, July 1999.

Shelton, Willard. "Labor: First Fruits." *New Republic*, December 8, 1947, 33.

Shields, W. E. "Letter from Washington." *Typographical Journal*, December 15, 1890.

Slider, James R. "Atlanta and the Printing Interest." *Inland Printer*, September 1893, 482.

Smith, Alain. "The Way of the Web." *Public Health Reports*, September-October 1996, 459–63.

Spencer, A. "Type-Setting Machines." *Typographical Journal*, September 15, 1889, 2.

Squire, J. C. "The Revival of Printing." *Publishers Weekly*, April 4, 1931, 1817.

Srivastava, Manish. Steven Wozniak. ei.cs.vt.edu/~history/WOZNIAK.HTM. Accessed November 1, 2004.

Stewart, Tony. "Distributed Printing Shifting Impact of Newspapers." *Newspapers and Technology*, February 2004.

Symons, Lenore. "Michael Faraday (1791–1867)." *Institution of Electrical Engineers.* www.iee.org.uk. Accessed November 22, 1999.

Taylor, Conrad. "What Has WYSIWYG Done to Us?" *Seybold Report on Publishing Systems*, September 30, 1996, 26.

T.M.R. "Observations of a Country Printer." *Inland Printer*, May 1897, 181.

Toth, Debora. "Chief Printers Plot Strategies." *Graphic Arts Monthly*, September 1996.

Tribute, Andrew. "The Future of Print: From a Craft to a Manufacturing Business." *Seybold Report on Publishing Systems*, September 14, 1998.

Tuttle, R. M. "Out of Work Printers." *Inland Printer*, October 1895, 55.

Typo. "Invention–Evolution." *Inland Printer*, September 1893, 472.

U.S. Census Bureau. *Computer Use in the United States: 1989.* Current Population Reports: Special Studies, Series P-23, no. 171.

———. *Current Population Survey, September 2001: Presence of a Computer and the Internet for Households.* Table 1A. Internet Release Date November 19, 2004.

U.S. Postal Service. "Operating Statistics." *1998 Annual Report*, 74.

U.S. War Department. "New Machine." Press release. February 15, 1946.

Valkin, Vanessa. "In Good Shape Despite Slowdown." *Financial Times*, May 18, 2000, 4.

Vogt, Peter, and David Allison. "Transcript of an Interview with J. Presper Eckert Chief Engineer, ENIAC Computer." *Development of the ENIAC*, Smithsonian Video History Collection Record Unit 9537, February 2, 1988.

W.W.D. "Machine Operators Should Be Admitted." *Typographical Journal*, February 15, 1891.

Waites, Meyrick. "The Typograph vs. Hand Composition." *Typographical Journal*, December 1, 1890, 1.

Waldrop, M. "Computing's Johnny Appleseed." *Technology Review*, January-February 2000. www.techreview.com/articles/jan00/waldrop.htm. Accessed November 10, 1999.

Walker, Charles R. "A National Council for the Printing Trades." *Monthly Labor Review*, January 1921, 23–44.

Wallace, Hugh. "Linotype Operators." *Inland Printer*, April 1897, 45.

———. "Typesetting Machines and Union Legislation." *Inland Printer*, September 1895, 603–4.

Wallace, Michael. "Technological Changes in Printing: Union Response in Three Countries." *Monthly Labor Review*, July 1985, 41–43.

Wallis, Lawrence. "Hungarian Rhapsody." *Printing World*, March 14, 1994, 24.

Ward, Gareth. "The End of Dupont's Digital Dream Will Pose Many Questions." *Printing World*, June 2, 1997.

———. "The History of Digital Printing." *British Printer*, August 1998. www.print college.co.uk/Dbase/docs/Digital_Printing_Inkjet/digital_printing.htm. Accessed November 25, 2004.

———. "The World of Scitex." *Printing World*, October 14, 1996.

Webb, Joe. "Business Vision Seen As Challenge for 1 in 4." *Graphic Arts Monthly*, July 1999.

———. "Trendwatch Reports." *Graphic Arts Monthly*, January 1999.

Webb, Joe, and James Whittington. "Believe It Now or Later: We Will Call 1998 'The Good Ol' Days!'" *Trendwatch*, November 9, 1999, 1.

———. "Forecast 2000." *Trendwatch*, November 15, 1999, 1.

———. "How Printers Are Using and Plan to Use the Internet." *Trendwatch*, December 2, 1999.

Webb, Joe, Jim Whittington, and Craig Kevghas. "Major Changes and Challenges for Commercial Printers in Next 12 Months." *Trendwatch*, November 4, 1999, 1.

Wilford, John Noble. "Egypt Carvings Set Earlier Date for Alphabet." *New York Times*, November 14, 1999, 1.

———. "Study Uncovers Prewriting in Asia." *New York Times*, May 13, 2001, 1.

Wilken, Earl. "Printers Adopt New Business Models." *Graphic Arts Monthly*, February 1996.

Williams, E. B. "The Linotype." *Inland Printer*, June 1891, 790–91.

Winn, Will H. "A Cheerfully Optimistic View: Everything Has Rounded for the Best." *Typographical Journal*, February 1, 1896, 3.

Woodall, Pam. "Un-tangling Economics." *Economist*, September 21, 2000. www .economist.com/surveys'/PrinterFriendly.cfm?Story_ID=375486. Accessed August 12, 2004.

Woodbury, David O. "Your Life Tomorrow." *Colliers*, May 8, 1943, 40.

World Resources Institute. Production and Consumption: No End to Paperwork. www.wri.org/wr-98-99/paperwk.htm#use. Accessed July 29, 2004.

Wozniak, Steve. Speaking of Pranks. A Reader Asks. www.woz.org. Accessed November 1, 2004.

Wren, W. B. "Electric Printing." *Scientific American*, November 24, 1900, 324.

Wright, Carroll D. "Great Industrial Changes since 1893." *World's Work*, August 1901, 1107–11.

Wright, R. "The Man Who Invented the Internet." *Time*, May 19, 1997, 64.

X.Y.Z. "Machine Gossip in the West." *Typographical Journal*, January 1, 1896, 59.

BOOKS AND ARCHIVAL SOURCES

Abbate, Janet. *Inventing the Internet*. Cambridge: MIT Press, 1999.

Bagdikian, Ben H. *The Information Machines: Their Impact on Men and the Media*. New York: Harper & Row, 1971.

Baker, Elizabeth Faulkner. *Printers and Technology: A History of the International Printing Pressmen and Assistants' Union*. Westport, Conn.: Greenwood, 1974.

Barry, John M. *Rising Tide. The Great Mississippi Flood of 1927 and How It Changed America*. New York: Touchstone, 1997.

Barzun, Jacques. *From Dawn to Decadence: 500 Years of Western Cultural Life*. New York: HarperCollins, 2000.

Blumenthal, Joseph. *The Printed Book in America*. Boston: Godine, 1977.

Bouchet, Henri. *The Book: Its Printers, Illustrators, and Binders from Gutenberg to the Present Time*. Edited by H. Grevel. New York: Scribner & Welford, 1890.

Braudel, Fernand. *The Wheels of Commerce*. Translated by Sian Reynold. New York: Harper & Row, 1982.

Brown, R. J. *An Overview of the History of the Linotype Machine*. Newspaper Collectors Society of America, 1984.

Cantor, Norman F. *Medieval History: The Life and Death of a Civilization*. London: Macmillan, 1969.

Carlson, Jerry. "Video Editing at Farm Journal." In *Technological Changes in Printing and Publishing*, edited by George P. Hattery, Lowell H. Bush, and George Pollock Bush, 111–43. Mt. Airy, Md.: Lomond, 1973.

Ceruzzi, Paul E. *A History of Modern Computing*. Cambridge, Mass.: MIT Press, 1998.

Cetron, Marvin J. "A Microtechnology Assessment of the Printing and Publishing Industry." In *Technological Changes in Printing and Publishing*, edited by George P. Hattery, Lowell H. Bush, George Pollock Bush. Mt. Airy, Md.: Lomond, 1973.

Chappell, Warren. *A Short History of the Printed Word*. New York: Knopf, 1970.

Christianson, Clayton. *The Innovator's Dilemma*. New York: HarperCollins, 2000.

Colin Clair. *A History of European Printing*. London: Academic, 1976.

Dahl, Svend. *History of the Book*. Metuchen, N.J.: Scarecrow, 1968.

Darnton, Robert, and Daniel Roche, eds. *Revolution in Print: The Press in France, 1775–1800*. Berkeley: University of California Press, 1989.

Darnton, Robert. *The Great Cat Massacre and Other Episodes in French Cultural History*. New York: Basic, 1984.

Davies, Glyn. *A History of Money*. Cardiff: University of Wales Press, 1996.

Deibert, Ronald J. *Parchment, Printing, and Hypermedia: Communication in World Order*. New York: Columbia University Press, 1997.

Diamond, Jared. *Guns, Germs, and Steel*. New York: Norton, 1997.

Drucker, Peter. *Management Challenges for the 21st Century*. New York: Harper-Collins, 1999.

Edwards, Mark U., Jr. *Printing, Propaganda, and Martin Luther*. Berkeley: University of California Press, 1994.

Eisenstein, Elizabeth. *The Printing Press as an Agent of Change*. 2 vols. Cambridge: Cambridge University Press, 1979.

Executive Council of the International Typographical Union. *A Study of the History of the International Typographical Union, 1852–1963*. Colorado Springs: International Typographical Union, 1964.

Faludy, George. *Erasmus*. New York: Stein & Day, 1970.

Fischer, David Hackett. *The Great Wave: Price Revolutions and the Rhythm of History*. New York: Oxford University Press, 1996.

Givler, Peter. "University Press Publishing in the United States." In Richard E. Abel and Lyman W. Newman, eds., *Scholarly Publishing: Books Journals, Publishers, and Libraries in the Twentieth Century*. Hoboken, N.J.: Wiley, 2002.

Goble, George Corben. *The Obituary of a Machine: The Rise and Fall of Ottmar Mergenthaler's Linotype at U.S. Newspapers*. Bloomington: Indiana University Mass Communications Program, 1984.

Gordon, George N. *The Communications Revolution: A History of Mass Media in the United States*. New York: Hastings House, 1977.

Gould, Stephen Jay. *Leonardo's Mountain of Clams and the Diet of Worms: Essays on Natural History*. New York: Harmony, 1998.

Hafner, Katie, and Matthew Lyon. *Where Wizards Stay Up Late: The Origins of the Internet*. New York: Simon & Schuster, 1996.

Hale, J. R. *Renaissance Europe, 1480–1520*. 2nd ed. Malden, Mass.: Blackwell.

Hamilton, Frederick W. *A Brief History of Printing in America*. Chicago: United Typothetae of America, 1918.

Handover, P.M. *Printing in London: From Caxton to Modern Times*. Cambridge: Harvard University Press, 1960.

Harris, Bob. *Politics and the Rise of the Press*. London: Routledge, 1996.

Herrick, Jim. *Against the Faith*. London: Glover & Blair, 1985.

Hodges, Henry. *Technology in the Ancient World*. New York: Barnes & Noble Books, 1992.

Hughes, Thomas P. *Rescuing Prometheus*. New York: Pantheon, 1998.

Hundt, Reed. *You Say You Want a Revolution*. New Haven: Yale University Press, 2000.

Ing, Janet. *Johann Gutenberg and His Bible: A Historical Study.* New York: Typophiles, 1988.

John, Richard R. *Spreading the News: The American Postal System from Franklin to Morse.* Cambridge: Harvard University Press, 1995.

Johns, Adrian. *The Nature of the Book: Print and Knowledge in the Making.* Chicago: University of Chicago Press, 1998.

Johnson, H. L. *Gutenberg and the Book of Books.* New York: Rudge, 1932.

Kahan, Basil. *Ottmar Mergenthaler: The Man and His Machine.* New Castle, Del.: Oak Knoll, 2000.

Kelber, Harry, and Carl Schlesinger. *Union Printers and Controlled Automation.* New York: Free Press, 1967.

Kennedy, Paul. *The Rise and Fall of the Great Powers: Economic Change and Military Conflict from 1500 to 2000.* New York: Random House, 1987.

Kilgour, Frederick G. *The Evolution of the Book.* New York: Oxford University Press, 1998.

Kluger, Richard. *The Paper: The Life and Death of the New York Herald Tribune.* New York: Knopf, 1986.

Kobre, Sidney. *Development of American Journalism.* Dubuque: Brown, 1969.

Kurian, George Thomas. Datapedia of the United States, 1790–2000. Lanham, Md.: Bernan, 1994.

Leonard, Thomas C. *News for All: America's Coming-of-Age with the Press.* New York: Oxford University Press, 1995.

Levenson, Roger. *Women in Printing: Northern California, 1857–1890.* Santa Barbara, Calif.: Capra, 1994.

Levinson, Paul. *The Soft Edge: A Natural History and Future of the Information Revolution.* London: Routledge, 1997.

Lewis, Bernard. *What Went Wrong: The Clash between Islam and Modernity in the Middle East.* New York: HarperCollins, 2002.

Lewis, Michael. *Next: The Future Just Happened.* New York: Norton, 2001.

Lipset, Seymour Martin, Martin A. Trow, and James S. Coleman. *Union Democracy: The Internal Politics of the International Typographical Union.* Glencoe, Ill.: Free Press, 1972.

Manguel, Alberto. *A History of Reading.* New York: Viking, 1996.

Marshall, Alan "Les origines de la photocomposition moderne." In *La Lumitype-Photon. Rene Higonnet, Louis Moyroud et l'invention de la photocompoition moderne,* edited by Alan Marshall, 59–72. Lyon: Musee de l'imprimerie et de la banque. 1994.

McMurtrie, Douglas C. *A History of Printing in the United States.* Vol. 2, *Middle and South Atlantic States.* 2nd ed. New York: Burt Franklin, 1969.

Mee, Charles L. Erasmus. *The Eye of the Hurricane.* New York: Coward, McCann & Geoghegan, 1974.

Mengel, Willi. *Ottmar Mergenthaler and the Printing Revolution.* Brooklyn: Mergenthaler Linotype Company, 1954.

Mergenthaler, Ottmar. *Biography of Ottmar Mergenthaler and History of the Linotype.* Baltimore: Self-published, 1898.

Mitchell, B. R. *International Historical Statistics: The Americas, 1750–2000.* 5th ed. New York: Palgrave Macmillan, 2003.

Mosley, James. "The Enigma of Early Lyonnaise Printing Types," in *La Lumitype-Photon. Rene Higonnet, Louis Moyroud et l'invention de la photocompoition moderne,* edited by Alan Marshall, 13–28. Lyon: Musee de l'imprimerie et de la banque, 1994.

Mott, Frank Luther. *American Journalism: A History, 1690–1960.* 3rd ed. New York: Macmillan, 1962.

Orcutt, Reginald. *Merchant of Alphabets.* Garden City, N.Y.: Doubleday, Doran, 1945.

Patterson, James T. *Mr. Republican: A Biography of Robert A. Taft.* Boston: Houghton Mifflin, 1972.

Perlman, Selig, and Philip Taft. *History of Labor in the United States.* New York: Macmillan, 1935.

Petro, Sylvester. *The Kingsport Strike.* New Rochelle, N.Y.: Arlington House, 1967.

Polanyi, Karl. *The Great Transformation: The Political and Economic Origins Of Our Time.* Boston: Beacon, 1944.

Printing Industries of America. *Bridging to a Digital Future.* Alexandria, Va.: Printing Industries of America, 1994.

———. *Printing 2000.* Alexandria, Va.: Printing Industries of America, 1990.

———. *Printing Marketing Atlas, 2004.* Alexandria, Va.: Graphic Arts Information Network, 2004.

———. *Vision 21: The Printing Industry Redefined for the 21st Century.* Alexandria, Va.: Printing Industries of America, 2000.

Putnam, George Haven. *The Censorship of the Church of Rome.* Vol. 1. New York: Putnam's, 1906.

Remer, Rosalind. *Printers and Men of Capital: Philadelphia Book Publishers in the New Republic.* Philadelphia: University of Pennsylvania Press, 1996.

Rhodes, Richard. *Visions of Technology.* New York: Simon & Schuster, 1999.

Romano, Frank J. *Machine Writing and Typesetting.* Salem, N.H.: Gama, 1986.

Rosenberg, Nathan, and L. E. Birdzell Jr. *How the West Grew Rich: The Economic Transformation of the Industrial World.* New York: Basic, 1986.

Rumble, Walker. *The Swifts: Printers in the Age of Typesetting Races.* Charlottesville: University of Virginia Press, 2003.

Seybold, John W. *The Philadelphia Printing Industry: A Case Study.* Philadelphia: University of Pennsylvania Press, 1949.

Seybold, John W., ed. *Computers in Typesetting.* Washington, D.C.: U.S. Government Printing Office, 1970.

Smith, Douglas K., and Robert C. Alexander. *Fumbling the Future: How Xerox Invented, Then Ignored, the First Personal Computer.* New York: Morrow, 1988.

Southern, R. W. *The Making of the Middle Ages.* New Haven: Yale University Press, 1953.

Spangler, Kathleen. "New Technologies Challenge Classical Typography." In *Technological Changes in Printing and Publishing*, edited by George P. Hattery, Lowell H. Bush, and George Pollock Bush. Mt. Airy, Md.: Lomond, 1973.

Stanford, Peter. *The Devil: A Biography*. New York: Holt, 1996.

Steinberg, S. H. *Five Hundred Years of Printing*. New York: Criterion, 1959.

Strauss, Victor. "Pressroom Technology." In *Technological Changes in Printing and Publishing*, edited by George P. Hattery, Lowell H. Bush, and George Pollock Bush. Mt. Airy, Md.: Lomond, 1973.

Tebbel, John. *Between Covers: The Rise and Transformation of Book Publishing in America*. New York: Oxford University Press, 1987.

Thomas, Isaiah. *The History of Printing in America*. Edited by Marcus A. McCorison. 1810. New York: Weathervane, 1970.

Thompson, Lawrence S. *Printing in Colonial Spanish America*. Hamden, Conn.: Archon, 1962.

U.S. Census Bureau. *Census of Manufactures*. Vol. 11, *Industry Statistics*, pt. 2, SIC Major Groups 2734, 1947, 1954, 1958, 1963, 1967, 1972, 1977.

Van Loon, Willam Hendrick. *Observations on the Mystery of Print*. New York: Book Manufacturers Institute, 1937.

Vatter, Harold G. *The Drive to Industrial Maturity: The U.S. Economy, 1860–1914*. Westport, Conn.: Greenwood, 1975.

Wallis, Lawrence W. *Electronic Typesetting: A Quarter Century of Upheaval*. Gatehead, U.K.: Paradigm, 1984.

Waltz, George H. Jr. *The House That Quality Built*. Chicago: Lakeside, 1957.

Wecter, Dixon. *Sam Clemens of Hannibal*. Boston: Houghton Mifflin, 1952.

Whitley, Peggy, ed. "American Cultural History, 1900–1909." Kingwood College Library, May 2002.

Zachary, G. Pascal. *Endless Frontier: Vannevar Bush, Engineer of the American Century*. New York: Free Press, 1997.

Zurkowski, Paul G. "Microform Publishing." In *Technological Changes in Printing and Publishing*, edited by George P. Hattery, Lowell H. Bush, and George Pollock Bush. Mt. Airy, Md.: Lomond, 1973.

ARCHIVAL SOURCES

"Arbitration Proceedings and the Findings and Award of Frank Morrison, Arbitrator." *In re Typographical Union no. 6, versus the Publishers Association of New York, 1919*. International Typographical Union Collection, Norlin Library, University of Colorado–Boulder. Accession 1, Box 63, Book 1.

"Arbitration Proceedings and the Findings and Award of George W. Kirchwey, Arbitrator." *In re Typographical Union no. 6 versus Employing Printers Association of New*

York, 1920. International Typographical Union Collection, Norlin Library, University of Colorado–Boulder. Accession 1, Box 63, Book 2.

Cincinnati Typographical Union no. 3. *125th Anniversary Commemorating the Founding of Cincinnati Typographical Union no. 3.* International Typographical Union Collection, Norlin Library, University of Colorado–Boulder. Accession 1, Box 7.

Henry Laughlin, letter to Alfred Knopf, December 1, 1948. Alfred A. Knopf Collection, Harry Ransom Humanities Research Center, University of Texas–Austin, Box 5, Folder 13.

Lithomat Corporation. "Proposal for Research in Graphic Arts through Photocomposition," January 16, 1949. Alfred A. Knopf Collection, Harry Ransom Humanities Research Center, University of Texas–Austin, Box 5, Folder 13.

Minneapolis Typographical Union no. 42. *A Century of Service: Minneapolis Typographical Union no. 4, 1873–1973.* International Typographical Union Collection, Norlin Library, University of Colorado–Boulder. Accession 1, Box 7.

National War Labor Board, Mediation Section. *Brief on Behalf of the Unions, March 6, 1943, in the Matter of R.R. Donnelley & Sons Company (Lakeside Press) and Organization Committee of Chicago Printing Trades Unions.* International Typographical Union Collection, Norlin Library, University of Colorado–Boulder. Accession 1, Box 63, Book 2.

National War Labor Board, Mediation Section. *Brief on Behalf of the Unions, February 24, 1943, in the Matter of R.R. Donnelley & Sons Company (Lakeside Press) and Organization Committee of Chicago Printing Trades Unions.* International Typographical Union Collection, Norlin Library, University of Colorado–Boulder. Accession 1, Box 63, Book 2.

Office of the President. *Executive Council Rulings: July 21, 1986 to December 31, 1986.* International Typographical Union Collection, Norlin Library, University of Colorado–Boulder. Accession 2, Box 11.

San Francisco Typographical Union No. 21. News release. International Typographical Union Collection, Norlin Library, University of Colorado–Boulder. Accession 2, Box 55.

Woods, Gilmer T., ed. *100th Anniversary Celebration Souvenir Book.* Austin Typographical Union no. 138. International Typographical Union Collection, Norlin Library, University of Colorado–Boulder. Accession 1, Box 7.

INTERVIEWS

Bigalk, Gerald L. Telephone interview by author, October 9, 1997.

Collins, Elmo U. Interview by author, December 12, 1999.

Haley, Alan. Telephone interview by author, September 23, 1997.

Krohm, Gary. Telephone interview by author, October 15, 1997.

Lofquist, William. Telephone interview by author, 1997.
Mulliken, Charles. Telephone interview by author, 1997.
Printz, William B. Interview by author, December 12, 1999.
Rosenblum, Louis. Telephone interview by author, November 25, 1997.
Seybold, John. Telephone interview by author, 1998.
Whitehouse, Leonard. Interview by author, December 12, 1999.

INDEX

ABOUT THE AUTHOR

Bill Sonn is an independent historian and a longtime professional writer. He has served as editor or managing editor, at one time or another, of College Press Service, the *Straight Creek Journal*, *Financial Advertising Review*, *Healthcare Advertising Review*, *TWINS* magazine, *Profiles in Healthcare Marketing*, and *Print Daily*. Over the years his writing has appeared in *Outside* magazine, *Chicago* magazine, *Columbia Journalism Review*, *Crawdaddy*, *Bild am Sontag*, *Boston Globe*, *Rocky Mountain News*, *Denver Magazine*, *Colorado Business Magazine*, *Westword*, *California Business*, and a clutch of trade magazines and journals. He has also served as a communications, publishing, and writing consultant with a number of companies in health care and the graphic arts, as well as a senior executive with several publishing and marketing communications companies. He now lives in Colorado, where he is a principal with Business Development Communications and is editor and publisher of *Health Care Market Bulletins*. He holds a degree in history and English from Michigan State University, and did graduate work in history at the University of Denver.